Family Life in the Time of COVID

Family Life in the Time of COVID

International perspectives

Edited by

Katherine Twamley, Humera Iqbal
and Charlotte Faircloth

First published in 2023 by
UCL Press
University College London
Gower Street
London WC1E 6BT

Available to download free: www.uclpress.co.uk

Collection © Editors, 2023
Text © Contributors, 2023
Images © Contributors and copyright holders named in captions, 2023

The authors have asserted their rights under the Copyright, Designs and Patents Act 1988 to be identified as the authors of this work.

A CIP catalogue record for this book is available from The British Library.

Any third-party material in this book is not covered by the book's Creative Commons licence. Details of the copyright ownership and permitted use of third-party material is given in the image (or extract) credit lines. If you would like to reuse any third-party material not covered by the book's Creative Commons licence, you will need to obtain permission directly from the copyright owner.

This book is published under a Creative Commons Attribution-Non-Commercial 4.0 International licence (CC BY-NC 4.0), https://creativecommons.org/licenses/by-nc/4.0/. This licence allows you to share and adapt the work for non-commercial use providing attribution is made to the author and publisher (but not in any way that suggests that they endorse you or your use of the work) and any changes are indicated. Attribution should include the following information:

Twamley, K., Iqbal, H. and Faircloth, C. (eds). 2023. *Family Life in the Time of COVID: International perspectives*. London: UCL Press. https://doi.org/10.14324/111.9781800081727

Further details about Creative Commons licences are available at https://creativecommons.org/licenses/

ISBN: 978-1-80008-174-1 (Hbk)
ISBN: 978-1-80008-173-4 (Pbk)
ISBN: 978-1-80008-172-7 (PDF)
ISBN: 978-1-80008-175-8 (epub)
DOI: https://doi.org/10.14324/111.9781800081727

This book is dedicated to all the families who shared their stories with us.

Contents

List of figures and tables	ix
Key terms, abbreviations and acronyms	xi
List of contributors	xv
Artist's note on the cover image	xxiii
Acknowledgements	xxv

1 Families and COVID-19: the beginning of our story   1
   Humera Iqbal, Charlotte Faircloth, Katherine Twamley and Rachel Benchekroun

2 Argentina: gendered effects of the COVID-19 lockdown and the transformations in well-being   25
   Mariana de Santibañes and Gabriela Marzonetto

3 Chile: pandemic, neoliberal precarity and social outbreak   49
   Ana Vergara del Solar, Mauricio Sepúlveda, Juan Pablo Pinilla, Daniela Leyton, Cristián Ortega and Claudia Calquín

4 Pakistan: families in Karachi recalibrating care during COVID-19   71
   Safina Azeem, Shama Dossa, Asiya Jawed, Ayesha Khan, Mahnoor Mahar and Faiza Mushtaq

5 Russia: life, learning and family agency under COVID-19   97
   Maria Dobryakova, Elizaveta Sivak and Olesya Yurchenko

6 Singapore: families living in and through the pandemic   123
   Vineeta Sinha, Pooja Nair, Narayanan Ganapathy and Daniel Goh

7 South Africa: COVID-19 and family well-being   147
   Sadiyya Haffejee, Anita Mwanda and Thandi Simelane

8 Sweden: everyday family life during COVID-19 173
   Disa Bergnehr, Laura Darcy and Annelie J. Sundler

9 Taiwan: a unique trajectory of the pandemic as both
   blessing and curse 199
   Ching-Yu Huang, Fen-Ling Chen and An-Ti Shih

10 United Kingdom: inclusions and exclusions in personal life
   during the COVID-19 pandemic 223
   *Katherine Twamley, Humera Iqbal, Charlotte Faircloth and
   Nicola Carroll*

11 United States of America: polarization, politicization and
   positionality in COVID-19 policies and family practices 249
   Marjorie Faulstich Orellana, Sophia L. Ángeles and Lu Liu

12 Family life in a time of crisis: trust, risk, labour and love 277
   Charlotte Faircloth, Katherine Twamley and Humera Iqbal

Index 299

List of figures and tables

Figures

1.1	Timeline of COVID-19 pandemic.	3
2.1	Timeline of COVID-19 in Argentina.	26
3.1	Timeline of COVID-19 in Chile.	52
4.1	Timeline of COVID-19 in Pakistan.	74
4.2	Prompt 5 sent to participants in Pakistan, 16 November 2020.	78
4.3	Prompt 8 sent to participants in Pakistan, 9 February 2021.	79
5.1	Timeline of COVID-19 in Russia.	99
6.1	Timeline of COVID-19 in Singapore.	125
6.2	During the pandemic, Archana and family, masked, and on an outing to Pulau Ubin, a small island off Singapore.	133
6.3	Kamala family celebrating daughter Neha's sixth birthday, with cake cutting via Zoom, while keeping to restricted numbers for social gatherings.	143
7.1	Timeline of COVID-19 in South Africa.	152
8.1	Timeline of COVID-19 in Sweden.	176
9.1	Timeline of COVID-19 in Taiwan.	201
9.2	Daily new confirmed COVID-19 cases in Taiwan, 28 January 2020 to 6 October 2021.	203
10.1	Timeline of COVID-19 in the UK.	224
10.2	UK government public health poster, April 2020.	225
11.1	Timeline of COVID-19 in the United States.	250

Tables

4.1	Number of research participants by gender and age in Pakistan study.	76
9.1	Summary of participating families in Taiwan and the levels of economic impact the pandemic had on them.	206

Key terms, abbreviations and acronyms

AMBA	Metropolitan Area of Buenos Aires (Argentina)
ASPO	Preventive and Mandatory Social Isolation, in Spanish, Aislamiento Social, Preventivo y Obligatorio (Argentina).
ATP	Emergency Assistance Programme for Work and Production, in Spanish, Asistencia al Trabajo y Producción (Argentina)
'Bubble' Legislation	A term used in the United Kingdom to refer to the legal combining of two households for the purpose of mutual support (typically to assist with care for elderly or junior members), when otherwise prohibited under lockdown rules.
Circuit Breaker	Term used by the Singapore Government to refer to the preventative measures implemented to reduce the spread of COVID-19.
COVID-19	Coronavirus disease
DISPO	Preventive and Mandatory Social Distancing, in Spanish, Distanciamiento Social Preventivo y Obligatorio (Argentina)
GDP	Gross Domestic Product
HBL	HBL stands for home-based learning, which refers to students studying from home during the peak of the pandemic.
HDB	HDB stands for the Housing and Development Board, which is essentially a statutory board under Singapore's Ministry of National Development and is responsible for public housing.
Homeland	Any of 10 partially self-governing areas in South Africa designated for specific indigenous African

	peoples under the former policy of apartheid (Oxford Languages).
Household/Family	Authors in this volume often use the terms family and household interchangeably. See further discussion in Chapters 1 and 12.
ICo-FACT COVID-19	International Consortium of Families and Communities in the Time of COVID-19
IFE	Emergency Family Income Subsidy, in Spanish, Ingreso Familiar de Emergencia (Argentina)
INDEC	National Institute of Statistics and Census data (Argentina)
Indeemo	A digital ethnographic app used for data collection in four of the case studies. For more information, see www.indeemo.com.
Influx Control	The rigid limitation and control imposed upon the movement of black people into urban areas (in South Africa during the apartheid era) (Oxford Languages).
Informal Housing	Term used in South Africa to refer to makeshift structures that have not been erected according to approved plans and planning regulations, typically on land that has been unlawfully occupied (StatsSA).
KI	Key Informant
Loadshedding	Action to reduce the load on something, especially the interruption of an electricity supply to avoid excessive load on the generating plant (Oxford Languages).
Lockdown	A term used in the United Kingdom to refer to the closure of various institutions during the height of the pandemic, and a stay-at-home order from the UK government which restricted movement in public spaces.
Migrant Labour Systems	The laws and structures under which black contract labourers from rural areas, the homelands, or neighbouring states were recruited to work in the cities and mines (Oxford Languages).
Pass Laws	A body of laws in operation in South Africa under apartheid, controlling the rights of black people to

	residence and travel and implemented by means of identity documents compulsorily carried. (Walsh 2021 – see Chapter 7 for full reference).
SARS	Severe Acute Respiratory Syndrome, caused by a strain of coronavirus (SARS-Cov), is an epidemic outbreak in Southeast Asia between 2002 to 2004.
SOPs	Standard Operating Procedures (term used in Pakistan to refer to institutional and/or governmental guidelines during the pandemic).
WFH	WFH stands for 'work-from-home', in this context applyting to where individuals whose work could be done from home were told to work from home during the pandemic.

List of contributors

Katherine Twamley is Associate Professor of Sociology and Programme Director for the BSc Sociology programme at the Social Research Institute, UCL. Her research has been funded by the ESRC, the British Academy and the Leverhulme Trust, amongst other funding bodies, and focuses on love and intimacy, gender and family, with a geographical focus on the UK and India. Katherine is particularly interested in longitudinal and comparative research, to understand how time and context shape experience and meaning. She currently leads a consortium of studies across 10 countries exploring family life during COVID-19.

Humera Iqbal is Associate Professor of Social and Cultural Psychology based at the Social Research Institute, UCL. Her work looks at young people and families particularly from migrant and minority groups, social representations and identity. Another strand of her research interrogates the influence of culture, nature and the arts on well-being and belonging. Humera uses mixed methods, arts and film-based methods in her research.

Charlotte Faircloth is Associate Professor in the Social Research Institute at UCL. From sociological and anthropological perspectives, her work has focused on parenting, gender and reproduction using qualitative and cross-cultural methodologies. This research has explored infant feeding, couple relationships, intergenerational relations and, recently, the impact of coronavirus on family life.

Sophia L. Ángeles is Assistant Professor of Multilingual Education in the College of Education at the Pennsylvania State University. She graduated from the School of Education and Information Studies with a PhD in Education with an emphasis on Urban Schooling. Prior to that, she worked as a professional K-12 school counsellor in North Carolina and California. Her research examines how immigration and language policies shape the educational trajectories of high school immigrant youth.

Safina Azeem is Research Associate at the NGO Aahung, in Karachi. She graduated with a Bachelor's degree in Social Sciences and Liberal Arts from the Institute of Business Administration, Karachi. Her interest lies in anthropological research on gender, care and health practices.

Rachel Benchekroun is a sociologist and ethnographer, and is an ESRC Research Fellow at the UCL Social Research Institute. Her research interests focus on migration and mobilities, and on mothering, family and friendship practices, and how these are shaped by context and structural factors.

Disa Bergnehr is Professor of Education at the Department of Pedagogy and Learning, Linnæus University. She conducts interdisciplinary research that focuses on families in contemporary Sweden, and her main current interests are family life during COVID-19, media representations of single parents, resettlement strategies of migrant parents and youth, care practices in families, schooling and parenting in disadvantaged areas, children and parents' well-being, and children's socialization.

Claudia Calquín is Associate Professor at the School of Psychology, Faculty of Humanities, Universidad de Santiago, Chile.

Nicola Carroll was awarded her PhD for comparative research exploring experiences of single parents in the context of welfare reform, austerity and media stigmatization. She worked as Associate on UCL's 'Families and Community Transitions under COVID-19' project following postdoctoral researcher roles on projects covering domestic abuse, mental health support in the community and local government policymaking. Her interests centre upon family diversity, class and gender inequalities and research–policy engagement.

Fen-Ling Chen is Professor at the Department of Social Work at National Taipei University. Her areas of research specialization include: social policy analysis, gender studies, and work and health.

Laura Darcy is a paediatric nurse, Master of Public Health and Associate Professor in Caring Science. Her research aims to give young children a voice in healthcare and her field of research includes nursing with focus on children's rights, needs and participation in their care. She is also interested in everyday life and functioning of young children living with illness, child abuse and mental ill health. She works as Senior Lecturer in Nursing at the University of Borås.

Maria Dobryakova graduated from the Moscow School of Social and Economic Sciences and Manchester University (MA in Sociology) and defended her PhD in social stratification at the Institute of Sociology of the Russian Academy of Sciences. Between 2006 and 2022 she worked at the National Research University Higher School of Economics, where she headed and coordinated large-scale projects in education, social sciences, and web-development, as well as publications and translation projects. Prior to that, she had worked at the Independent Institute for Social Policy (as Head of Publications) and the Ford Foundation (Higher Education and Scholarship programme). Her professional interests include curriculum studies, teacher and learner's agency, transversal competences and new literacies, digital inequality and home-schooling, as well as educational web representations.

Shama Dossa is Associate Professor in Social Development and Policy at Habib University, Karachi, Pakistan and also heads Learning and Evaluation at Fenomenal Funds, a Global Feminist Funding Collaborative. She is a community development practitioner, researcher and academic with a specific focus in feminist participatory action research and arts-based research. Her recent publication on New Feminisms in Pakistan can be found in the *Routledge Handbook of Gender in South Asia*. Shama holds a PhD in Adult Education and Community Development from the Ontario Institute for Studies in Education (OISE) at University of Toronto.

Narayanan Ganapathy is Associate Professor in the Department of Sociology and Anthropology, at the National University of Singapore. He is concurrently an Associate Dean at the Faculty of Arts and Social Sciences. His research and teaching interests are criminology and criminal-justice-related issues. He is a member of the Editorial Boards of the *European Journal of Criminology*, the *Asian Journal of Criminology*, and the *International Journal of Comparative and Applied Criminal Justice*.

Daniel Goh is Associate Professor in the Department of Sociology and Anthropology, at the National University of Singapore. His research interests are in the areas of culture and state formation, race and multiculturalism, Asian urbanisms, and religion. His current research focuses on the growth of Christian megachurches and the production of urban futurities, both in Southeast Asia including Singapore. His work can be found at www.danielpsgoh.com.

Sadiyya Haffejee is a practising psychologist and Senior Researcher at the Centre for Social Development in Africa, University of Johannesburg. She enjoys working at the interface of research, practice and policy and her research interests include children and youth exposed to adversity, resilience, gender and mental health. She is particularly interested in participatory visual methods that reposition participants as experts of their lives and which may be used as a vehicle for change.

Ching-Yu Huang is Lecturer in Psychology at Keele University. Her research specializations include investigative interviews with vulnerable populations, working with families in challenging circumstances, as well as cognitive factors influencing investigative decision-making. She is passionate about using knowledge to help solve real-world issues and challenges.

Asiya Jawed is an Erasmus Mundus scholar for Masters in Urban Studies in the 4CITIES programme based in Brussels, Vienna, Copenhagen and Madrid. She completed her BA in International Relations and Psychology from Mount Holyoke College, USA in 2019 and worked as a researcher at the Collective for Social Science Research until 2021 where she focused on civic space, protest politics, power relations and gender. She is currently utilizing a post-colonial and feminist lens to explore narrative cartography in urban spaces.

Ayesha Khan is Senior Research Fellow at the global think tank ODI in London. Her research expertise lies in qualitative research methodologies which she uses to study gender issues such as reproductive health, political participation and feminist mobilizations. She is author of *The Women's Movement in Pakistan: Activism, Islam and democracy* and holds a doctoral degree from the Institute of Development Studies in the UK.

Daniela Leyton is Assistant Professor of Anthropology at the Faculty of Social Sciences, Universidad de Concepción, Chile. Her research is carried out in the field of medical anthropology, on issues of healthcare, body and medicalization of everyday life. She has developed ethnographic methods in several ethnic and urban contexts in Chile. She is the coordinator, for Bio-Bío, of the project COVID 0341-ANID.

Lu Liu is a postdoctoral fellow in the School of Education and Information Studies at UCLA. Her research focuses on language policy and planning, language socialization, and the ethnographic study of education, with a geographical focus on the United States and China.

Mahnoor Mahar is a researcher and filmmaker who has been involved in various creative feminist projects. She graduated from Habib University with a degree in Communication & Design and recently completed her Master's degree at Goldsmiths University of London in Gender, Media and Culture where her research focused on home-making and belonging.

Gabriela Marzonetto is a postdoctoral fellow at CONICET – Universidad Nacional de Cuyo, Argentina. Since 2019 she has collaborated as researcher at the Interdisciplinary Center for Policy Research (CIEPP) where she was doctoral fellow, and since 2020 she has been a researcher at the state, public administration and policy area at the Universidad Nacional de San Martín, and member of the steering committee at the Carework Network. Her research interests lie in the area of comparative social policies, specifically in the study of early childhood care and education, families and gender policies in Latin America.

Faiza Mushtaq is Dean and Executive Director at the Indus Valley School of Art and Architecture in Karachi. She holds a PhD in Sociology from Northwestern University, and her areas of interest are gender, social movements and collective action, culture and religion.

Anita Mwanda is an MA Industrial Student at the University of Johannesburg and a Research Assistant at the Centre for Social Development in Africa. Anita's research interests include race, gender and identity. In addition to her work on the ICo-FACT study, Anita's current research project focuses on homeless women and sexual and reproductive rights and resources.

Pooja Nair is currently pursuing a Master's degree at the Department of International Relations at the University of Sydney. She was a Research Assistant on the COVID-19 research project. Prior to this, she completed her Bachelor of Arts with Honours (Distinction) in Global Studies with a Minor in Sociology at the National University of Singapore. Her research interests include gender, marriage and social policies.

Marjorie Faulstich Orellana is Professor of Urban Schooling in the School of Education and Information Studies at UCLA. Her research focuses on the experiences of immigrant families and children in and out of school.

Cristian Ortega is Professor at the Faculty of Human Sciences, Universidad Arturo Prat, teaching in the Sociology degree and in the Master's degree 'Intangible Heritage, Society and Territorial Development'. His research has been carried out in the field of epistemology of social sciences and social studies of science. He is the coordinator, for Tarapacá, of the project COVID 0341-ANID.

Juan Pablo Pinilla is Associate Professor of Public Policy in the Department of Sociology at the Universidad de Valparaíso, Chile. He has been a Fulbright Grantee and has conducted research on public policies, transparency and accountability in Chile and Latin America. He has used mixed-method research designs in his work, involving case studies and large-N comparative analysis. He is the coordinator, for Valparaíso, of the project COVID 0341-ANID.

Mariana de Santibañes is a PhD candidate in Public Administration at New York University's Robert F. Wagner Graduate School of Public Service. She holds a BA in Philosophy from the University of Buenos Aires, and a Master's in Public Administration from NYU. Coming from a feminist critical policy tradition, her research focuses on explaining changes, outcomes and future directions of care policies in Latin America. She has worked with Latina immigrants in the United States and indigenous women leaders in Colombia to advance women's health and social justice agendas.

Mauricio Sepúlveda is Professor and a researcher at the Faculty of Psychology of the Universidad Diego Portales (Santiago, Chile). His interests lie in Governmentality and Biopolitics Studies applied to social problems related to identity, body and subjectivity. He was also a researcher associated with the Millennium Nucleus 'Authority and Asymmetries of Power' (NUMAAP-ANID) and the alternate director of the project COVID 0341-ANID.

An-Ti Shih is Assistant Professor at the Department of Social Work at National Taipei University. Her areas of research specialization include: couple and family therapy using a postmodernist approach, family relationships and child protective services.

Thandi Simelane is a research assistant at the Centre for Social Development in Africa (CSDA) and a sociology tutor at the University of Johannesburg. Broadly, she is interested in research that helps to reduce inequality – in education, gender, race and economic and social positions. Outside of the ICo-FACT study, she previously conducted a quantitative study that touches on gender inequality in Pentecostal churches and is currently researching the challenges of online education in the context of the Covid pandemic, which consequently, exposes the inequalities in educational opportunities.

Vineeta Sinha is Professor at the Department of Sociology and Anthropology, National University of Singapore (NUS). She is trained in the disciplines of Anthropology and Sociology. She uses ethnographic and historical methods in her work and has conducted fieldwork in Singapore, Malaysia, and Tamil Nadu. Her research interests include Hindu religiosity in the Diaspora, intersections of religion, commodification and consumption processes, interface of religion and materiality, religion–state encounters in colonial and post-colonial moments, formation of concepts and categories in the social sciences, Eurocentric and Androcentric critique of classical sociological theory, pedagogy and innovating alternative teaching practices.

Elizaveta Sivak is Director of the Center for Modern Childhood Research at the National Research University Higher School of Economics, Moscow, Russia. She uses qualitative, quantitative, and computational methods to study childhood and parenting. Her main research interests are concerned with modern parenting cultures, children's behaviour and social networks, factors influencing children's psychological well-being, and how we can study behaviour, attitudes and well-being using digital traces.

Annelie J. Sundler is Professor of Caring Science at the Faculty of Caring Science, Work Life and Social Welfare, University of Borås. Annelie has a clinical nursing background and her areas of research include nursing, with focus on patient experiences and individual's exposure in relation to health problems and illnesses. She has conducted research on child and school health services, child abuse, mental health and well-being of children and adults, person-centred care and healthcare communication.

Ana Vergara del Solar is Associate Professor at the School of Psychology, Universidad de Santiago de Chile. She has developed research, with funding from the Chilean State (Conicyt, ANID), in the field of Childhood and Parenting Studies, and on topics such as children's perspectives on childhood and adulthood, and the reciprocal care between parents and children. She is the researcher in charge of a project on families and COVID-19, funded by the Chilean State, COVID 0341-ANID, and included as part of ICo-FACT.

Olesya Yurchenko, PhD (De Montfort University, Leicester, UK) is a social researcher working at the Institute of Sociology of the Russian Academy of Sciences and at the National Research University Higher School of Economics. Her research focuses on sociology of professions (especially of doctors and teachers) and sociology of education (teachers' beliefs, attitudes and agency, family strategies in literacy and reading). She is an accomplished qualitative researcher.

Artist's note on the cover image

Sabika Qaisar

The cover image was designed by Sabika Qaisar, who is an artist based in Pakistan. You can follow her artwork at https://www.instagram.com/sabika_zaman/

The pandemic forced us all into isolation and yet two years later I feel more connected than ever; to people, my surroundings, and myself. I have found love in places forgotten; in evening walks, in cycling and in the calmness and stillness only yoga brings. The pandemic was hard on a lot of us and although there were desolate times it amazes me how humanity persevered and rose higher. How we in our individual little worlds found things to do and ways to connect. How we helped ourselves and helped each other.

I realized that love transcends all boundaries of distance and time and reigns stronger than any tragedy we go through. My work depicts the rediscovery of the simple mundane joys we had forgotten in our fast-paced lives. It is this realization of how love is actually in the little things that led me to the encapsulation of these moments. It is a study of love in a contemporary style through an in-depth concept exploration reflecting love from different perspectives.

From the series: *The love we found when the world closed down*.

Acknowledgements

A huge thank you to all our contributors who responded so enthusiastically and energetically to our proposal for the International FACT-COVID study. It has been an honour to collaborate with you all. Thanks also to our editor at UCL Press, Pat Gordon-Smith, for encouraging us with this volume, and to the anonymous reviewers for their valuable feedback.

A special thank you to Eugene Murphy from Indeemo.com who was incredibly generous in his support for our project. Your enthusiasm was infectious and your support invaluable. We hope that the project lives up to those initial conversations back in April 2020!

1
Families and COVID-19: the beginning of our story

Humera Iqbal, Charlotte Faircloth, Katherine Twamley and Rachel Benchekroun

On a wall adjacent to the river Thames in London, you would be hard pressed to miss the great stretch of red and pink hearts in different shapes and sizes covered with messages of love, names of lost ones and photographs of smiling people who were once with us. This is the 'National Covid Memorial Wall', set up by volunteers and those who have lost family members though COVID-19. Walking past it, one can't help but be reminded of the sheer scale of the pandemic and how it turned our lives upside down. Yet this is just one wall of hearts, in one city. In Buenos Aires, Argentina small black rocks etched with the names of loved ones in stark white letters formed a monument outside the government building. In Johannesburg, South Africa blue and white ribbons tied to the railings of churches were used as a sign of remembrance. Twenty acres of white flags in Washington, DC symbolized the death of hundreds of thousands in the United States. With an estimated loss of over 6.64 million lives across the world, no place was left untouched.

Our global inter-connectivity has never been more apparent than during the COVID-19 pandemic, from the first identification of the new strain of SARS-Cov2 in China at the end of 2019, to its rapid spread across the world. Families everywhere found themselves thrown into a new reality. This book tells the everyday accounts of some of these families, in 10 different countries across the world. The authors are an international team of researchers who were keen to capture these accounts: as the pandemic took hold, for the first time in the post-industrial era the main institutions of social life, including education, care and work, were largely pushed into the home. Governments around the world mandated protective measures, often closing all but 'essential' services and requiring individuals to 'stay in place'. Everyday life was transformed, in particular for those with caring responsibilities across generations. How did families cope during this stressful period?

Using in-depth qualitative methods, this book explores how families experienced and responded to the pandemic and the factors which contributed to their experiences, across 10 countries: Argentina, Chile, Pakistan, Russia, Singapore, South Africa, Sweden, Taiwan, the United Kingdom and the United States. These countries represent geographic, cultural and socio-political diversity, as well as a range of different approaches to the management of COVID-19 by state governments. Certainly, as events played out they shone a spotlight not only on global inequalities but also on inequalities of gender and generation around which family life revolves, as well as illuminating just how embedded families are in everyday institutions. As authors we were aware that we needed to be careful about making assumptions about what a 'family' was − a topic we return to shortly, and in our concluding chapter.

As we conducted our research, and later our writing, the pandemic spread, halted and then emerged anew through various 'waves' and new variants. In the timeline in Figure 1.1 we attempt to capture some of the key global events of the COVID-19 pandemic, from the first identification of the virus and the World Health Organization (WHO) pandemic declaration to the later emergence of vaccines. The scale and pace at which the virus wreaked havoc globally, was clear from these major events, many of which informed how we conducted our studies, the questions we asked and of course the everyday lives of our participants.

From the onset of the pandemic, globalized commodity chains were put to the test, with an international demand for personal protective equipment, masks, oxygen supplies, ventilators and all the many other material requirements associated with managing the effects of the virus. International scientific collaboration between countries saw the development of a series of vaccines in record time. At the same time, the global distribution of these vaccines highlighted the economic divide across countries, with initial stockpiling by wealthier nations. Meanwhile, differing levels of access within countries to safety equipment and, later, differing rates of take-up of vaccines, often mirrored previous social inequalities. So, for example, in Sweden, the UK and USA, there was a lower take-up of vaccines amongst those in lower socio-economic groups (Dolby et al. 2022). In fact, the COVID-19 pandemic has exacerbated inequalities within nations. While those from lower socio-economic groups tended to experience a decline in their social

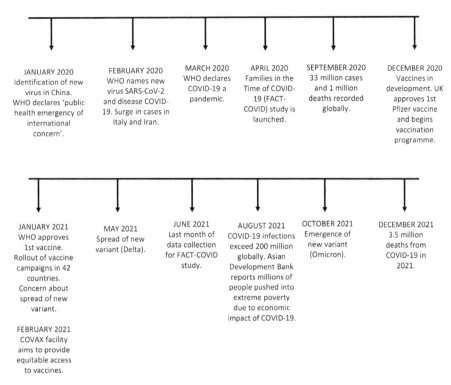

Figure 1.1 Timeline of COVID-19 pandemic. Source: editors.

well-being through loss of income and employment, those from higher socio-economic groups saw an improvement in personal wealth, with an ability to work remotely and save daily costs in different ways (for example by forgoing the commute to work) (Berkhout et al. 2021; Ferreira at al. 2021).

Much attention has also been paid to generational differences in experiences of the pandemic. Older people are generally more vulnerable to the COVID-19 virus; in some countries this resulted in them having very long periods of 'shielding' (see for example evidence from Sweden – Eldén et al. 2022). Children were forced to experience their education in vastly different ways. Where this moved to online classes, access to resources and internet connection mediated learning experiences, which we see now has had a marked impact on different aspects of children's well-being (Lee 2020). How the 'pandemic generation' of children are affected in the long term remains to be seen.

Our aim in this book is to capture some of these complex experiences through exploring how the everyday lives of families with children were affected by government responses to the pandemic. These governmental responses were realized very differently across the 10 countries in our study and this, in turn, had varied repercussions for families. As social scientists researching family practices, capturing family-related concerns, uncertainties and transformations associated with the pandemic has been critical.

Research during a crisis: bringing together families in the time of COVID

By March 2020 it was apparent that we were in the midst of a global pandemic. We, the editors of this book, recognized it was vital to capture this important historical juncture, not only in the UK, where we are based, but internationally. We were keenly aware that this was a global phenomenon and deserved a global research response. We knew that the COVID-19 pandemic was likely to be framed differently in each context (Bacchi and Goodwin 2016) and that societal responses would vary, having very different impacts on the everyday lives of families with children.

Thus, in addition to the UK, we reached out to fellow social scientists across nine other countries with varied geographical regions and diverse social systems. Our selection of countries was both strategic and serendipitous: we aimed to include countries from the Global South and North; countries with a recent history of responding to a pandemic (such as Taiwan and Singapore); and those with recognizably differing government responses in those early days of the pandemic (such as South Africa's military-imposed lockdowns versus Sweden's public health 'recommendations'). There was a degree of immediacy to the project since events were unfolding in real time. We predicted then that the pandemic would last only a few months at most and we were concerned to start gathering data before it 'ended'; little did we realize how pernicious and extended the impact of the virus would be. We were fortunate to be able to build on a network of scholars with shared interests who could start fieldwork rapidly. Ultimately, we gathered a formidable group of researchers from a range of disciplinary backgrounds for the consortium we named International Consortium of Families and Community in the Time of COVID (ICo-FACT COVID).

Across all 10 country case studies, ICo-FACT members investigated the challenges experienced by families with children during the COVID-19 pandemic and how they attempted to overcome them. Of particular interest were the varied ways families responded to contrasting governmental approaches to the management of COVID-19. The focus on families with children allowed us to explore how position in the household (such as that determined by gender and generation) could influence the interpretation of public health measures. We were interested in how children and their caregivers adapted to life under the COVID-19 pandemic and how it affected their relationships with one another. We each addressed the following research questions and aims within our respective case studies:

1. How did participants understand and respond to government guidelines around COVID?

    The aim here was to describe how people reacted to and implemented (or did not implement) the various public health restrictions that were put in place in the country settings. We were interested in capturing change over time and/or differences in behaviours within the sample (for example via gender, generation or socio-economic class).

2. What impact has this had on family life?

    This aim involved describing whether and how participants' responses to government guidelines transformed and/or consolidated family practices and everyday life.

The sampling strategies and data collection techniques varied somewhat amongst the 10 country case studies, but all followed a qualitative approach and included families with children. Within the shock and sadness we were all experiencing as our lives transformed, the experience of working together as an international team was immensely rewarding. In our online monthly meetings, we exchanged updates about the situations in our respective countries and reflected together on issues such as each country's protocols for ethical research and the varied terminologies used for discussions around COVID-19 guidelines. For many of us, the chance to meet monthly over a period of almost 18 months offered us opportunities to check in on each other's well-being, exchange life updates and forge deep connections. Our meetings were a safe space to laugh, feel concerned together and share life moments. We became a family of scholars, based across the world, digitally connecting regularly for over two years. The international nature of the group meant that at every meeting, to make the time-zones work, someone was forced to contend with waking up very early and someone else had to stay up late. Yet we made it work. As an interdisciplinary consortium, at times we spoke very different research languages, and we didn't automatically draw from similar scholarship. We took this as an opportunity to learn from one another, an aspect discussed in more depth in the final chapter of this book.

In the following sections of this chapter we outline some of the pre-existing work as well as theoretical approaches that influenced the main research questions in the project.

Living through a pandemic: scholarship to date

Research on the impact of the pandemic on family life suggests that changes to the running of institutions during the pandemic, such as provision of education, have made increased demands on parents to 'flexibly develop new routines, rules, and limits' (Prime et al. 2020, 635). Nguyen (2020) highlighted how the pandemic exacerbated tensions and lack of privacy in families and households, while others have identified shifts in family dynamics as family members adapted to changes caused by living in heightened proximity within households.

One area which has received much focus is the additional care work resulting from the closure of childcare institutions. For some, there was the potential for a radical shift in gendered care practices (ONS 2020). However, the literature has on the whole *not* observed such transformations. Mooi-Reci and Risman (2021) in a special issue of the journal *Gender and Society* call attention to the gendered inequalities that were *heightened* during this period in a range of contexts, with a focus particularly on household chores such as laundry and cleaning. These studies consistently show women taking up more unpaid care work than men. Such disparities in caregiving were particularly challenging in contexts of precarity. In a digital ethnographic study conducted in households located in the favelas of Rio de Janeiro, Brazil, Parreiras (2021) reported mothers feeling overwhelmed and experiencing a mental toll due to the extra care responsibilities linked to the pandemic in the domestic realm. Similarly, in this book, we are interested in how traditional roles associated with motherhood and domestic labour have changed or been impacted, and how different members of the family discuss this. We build on existing research by attempting to understand a more global comparative story of family experiences.

For many, the family unit was an integral part in meaning-making, intimacy, care and support during this uncertain period. Dawson and Dennis (2020) have argued that the pandemic has transformed existing intimacies at different levels, among them couple relationships, families, citizen–state relationships and relations between nations. Yet, they also note it has created new forms of intimacy which are 'in and of themselves transforming society more broadly' (Dawson and Dennis 2020, 7). In the UK, McNeilly and Reece (2020) reflect on how families with children had to find new ways to manage 'space, time, selves and relationships' (p. 18) as mothers attempted to create a safe space in the home far from the 'contaminated outside world' (p. 19). Similarly, Benchekroun (2022) in her study of the impact of the pandemic on family and friendship in the UK considers everyday practices of care. The study reveals the efforts made by people to connect with others beyond the household through things like video calling and more frequent messaging. Yet participants also recognized the limitations of video and messaging in enabling those small acts of care which need physical proximity such as giving a hug, or making a friend a cup of tea. In Sweden, Eldén and colleagues (2022) have argued that the pandemic has disrupted intergenerational care practices through distance and isolation, and has made them more visible.

In terms of mental health, being on a low income was found to be a risk factor for anxiety and depression at the start of the first lockdown (Fancourt et al. 2020; Santomauro 2021). Moreover, parents with young children and women reported particularly high levels of stress (Pierce et al. 2020; Shum et al. 2020). Reviewing a range of data sources on the impact of COVID-19, Cowie and Myers (2021, 64) highlight that the pandemic has created additional stress for children and young people. They argue that school closures and reduced access to friend groups can result in acute anxiety. Increased exposure to media coverage of the crises can also exacerbate mental distress in young people. Prime et al. (2020, 634–5) highlight the threats to the well-being of children and caregivers posed by the pandemic and lockdowns, including the need to negotiate previously non-existent or unproblematic issues, and the disruptive effects of isolation and home confinement on often taken-for-granted family routines and rituals. Some parents, especially single parents, reported feeling stressed due to loneliness, social isolation and/or additional caring responsibilities (Evans et al. 2020; Vaterlaus et al. 2021; Brown et al. 2020). Stress was intensified for parents by overcrowded accommodation, no outdoor space and the pressures of home-schooling (Evans et al. 2020; Vaterlaus et al. 2021; Prime et al. 2020).

A range of international studies found that mental health started to improve at an early stage of the first lockdown. This implies that the negative effects were experienced before the imposition of lockdown measures, rather than being caused by lockdown. Betterments in mental health at early stages could be associated with adaptation over time through the development of coping strategies, leading to the stabilization of depression levels, as well as with the reduction of stressors, such as fears of catching COVID-19 or becoming very ill with it (Banks and Xu 2020). Other studies on mental health during the pandemic argue that increases in stress and reduction in well-being amongst families are likely to be affected by uncertainty (Kneale et al. 2020); financial difficulties due to job losses (Howes et al. 2020); difficulties of dealing with a lack of personal space, and increased stress levels due to the collapse of the typical boundaries between professional and private spheres (Risi et al. 2021). Discrimination against minoritized groups during the pandemic has also been shown to impact on well-being (Kneale and Bécares 2021; Ma and Zhan 2022). Research from previous pandemics has shown how blame and stigma may arise as individuals attempt to find a 'cause' for the pandemic (Lee and Park 2005) and there was certainly evidence of increased hate crimes against people of Chinese origin (for example, Gray and Hansen 2021).

Blundell et al. (2021) and others have highlighted how the experiences and consequences of lockdown have been stratified across socio-economic groups. Most urgently, studies around infection rates, deaths and illness have shown that deprivation is strongly associated with rates of COVID-19. Globally, racially minoritized groups and people from migrant backgrounds are often disproportionally affected, particularly as many of them are in frontline worker roles (for example see OECD 2022; Marc et al. 2020). The links between income, ethnicity and health are well established (Benzeval et al. 2014; Marmot et al. 2020; Nazroo 2003). Disparities arise from a combination of differences in access to, and use of, health services, as well as material and structural inequalities (poverty, housing, pollution and working conditions) and racism. While these studies go some way to helping us understand disparities in health outcomes and experiences of living under COVID, they do little to unpack how daily life is accomplished, nor the processes through which inequalities arise. Moreover, early publications indicated the danger of responses which did not attend to socio-economic inequalities in the context of underfunded social care and healthcare (for example, Douglas et al. 2020).

At the societal level, state policies on education, social mobility, the economy and social policy all influence how social capital is generated and mobilized within a society. For example, research suggests that places with higher levels of social capital are more likely to have higher rates of COVID-19 testing, greater compliance with social distancing, fewer cases and slower increases in infection rates (Wu 2021; Barrios et al. 2020; Bartscher et al. 2020; Fraser and Aldrich 2020). This reminds us of the heterogeneity and social stratification within countries in terms of Covid responses and the varying levels of access to support by individuals and families. In relation to this, Wu states: 'social capital, in forms of political trust and collective efficacy, can increase people's compliance with control measures, thereby slowing the spread of COVID19' (Wu 2021, 30). Differences in other forms of capital (economic and cultural) relate to differential access to online technology and educational resources across countries, which is particularly important due to the movement of work and education online in many places. (see Benzeval et al. 2020; Cattan et al. 2021; Blainey and Hannay 2021; Blundell et al. 2021). Public health policies and communication at national and global levels have thus had a significant effect on social capital and health inequalities. Integral factors include how states chose to manage competing policy needs, in particular the national economy and public health, the differential impact on different communities and social groups, and access to healthcare. We saw this at the global level when certain countries in the Global North were seen to be stockpiling vaccines, preventing others in the Global South from acquiring them.

Theoretical approaches in the ICo-FACT study

Taking this literature as a background, we now move to the theoretical framing of our project. The study was originally conceived and designed by the editors, in London, and draws on two main theoretical areas: Families, relationality, and personal life (Smart 2011); and the sociology of everyday life, particularly in relation to family practices (Neal and Murji 2015; Morgan 2011). Cutting across these approaches was a recognition that there would be a range of experiences of the pandemic within families, influenced by social and health inequalities (Nazroo 2003; Marmot 2020).

The theoretical approaches reflect our geographical and, in part, disciplinary backgrounds. In drawing on these theories in the development of the project, we did not intend for studies conducted across multiple international contexts to be seen as 'test sites' for theories developed largely in the UK and Western Europe. Instead, we saw our approaches as a starting block for further discussion, elaboration, and contestation with our collaborators. As you move through the book, you will see that while these approaches remain influential and the research questions remain the same, different countries draw upon different theories that were the most relevant to their discipline or country as an aid to interpreting people's stories. We briefly reflect on this again in the final chapter.

Families, relationality and personal life

The choice of families as our unit of analysis was carefully thought through. While family formations are diverse, we chose to focus on families with children; we were particularly interested in the specific intergenerational dynamics and potential shifts in paid and unpaid work that these families experienced during closures of schools and other childcare institutions. Variation exists within this category: for example, families with two primary caregivers, single parent families, blended families and extended families, amongst other configurations. By considering families with children living in the same *households* (including extended families in the same household), we have been able to show how family members of different ages and generations navigated this challenging time. We define 'family' to include those that identified as being part of a family, regardless of whether they lived in the same household. All of those living under the same roof were treated as a 'household', regardless of whether they considered themselves as 'family'. Although the distinction between household and family was important to us, in this book we use the terms 'family' and 'household' almost interchangeably. In doing so we aim to address the dominant and often inaccurate discourse of families as being nuclear and intact (Smart 2007). Today more than ever, families come in different shapes and sizes and are not always intact and genetically connected (Golombok 2020). Moreover, the idea of a nuclear family is culturally relativistic and not in line with families in much of the 'majority world' (Kagitcibasi 1996).

Furthermore, Carol Smart (2007) has argued for the importance of intimacy in relationships beyond conventional concepts of 'the family', including friendships, fictive kin, chosen families and relatives who have passed away. Central to Smart's ideas is the importance of exploring bonds between people and the significance of shared experiences, possessions, emotions, family secrets, memories and histories of social relationships. Such an approach considers how people make meaning of and within their relationships, how they construct 'families', and how such relationships provide a sense of identity and belonging. Others such as Gabb (2008) and Finch and Mason (1993) have drawn on ideas of intimacy and highlighted the importance of wider kin group relationships in people's lives. Finch and Mason (1993) observe that responsibility and obligation within families are negotiated rather than being automatically given. This is important for our study in that we have tried to capture people's reflections on how the pandemic shaped this personal life and, in some cases, forced people to reflect on relationships with those most significant to them, who were sometimes beyond the 'family' or household. Across a number of chapters, including those from Chile, Singapore, the United States and the UK, authors have written extensively about this and drawn from work on intimacy and personal life. Relationality is widely recognized as decisive in shaping family practices and is mediated by the different positions held by family members – such as gender and generation (Twamley et al. 2021). Our study recognizes that decisions and practices are negotiated across and between connected individuals. This is particularly pertinent in the case of an infectious disease, where all members of the family or household need to maintain public health measures to keep everyone safe.

Family practices in everyday life, when everyday life plays out during a pandemic

Sociologist David Morgan (1996, 2011) emphasized the need to move away from structural understandings of the family unit towards a focus on family practices. Morgan argued that family life should be viewed as a set of activities at a given point in time (Morgan, 2011, 6). If we consider that these family practices are made up of day-to-day routines, rituals and practices which can be both ordinary and mundane, then we bridge the gap between another body of literature on 'everyday life'. As Neal and Murji (2015) recognize, the everyday is far from being straightforward. They argue that 'everyday life is dynamic, surprising and even enchanting; characterized by ambivalences, perils, puzzles, contradictions, accommodations and transformative possibilities' (p. 812). Everyday family life is marked by routines and daily decisions, be it from deciding what is for dinner to, in the context of a global pandemic, wearing masks and negotiating physical distancing from others. An important and shared assumption of this approach and our work is that families create their own cultures and have their own processes, and that the creation of these processes is shaped by wider social forces as well as by the input of individual members.

We use this body of work to inform our thinking around how everyday family practices interact within the context of a global pandemic. For example, how families made and negotiated rules during the pandemic and how they deciphered new public health measures. We also seek to examine what everyday practices of care looked like (Tronto 1998; Gabb and Fink 2015) and how the pandemic caused these to change. One example of this was the greater uptake of technology as a means of communication with friends and loved ones. The approach of considering everyday life within the family, is one which a number of chapters draw on, including those from Chile, Singapore, Taiwan and the UK. A body of work that we had not foreseen being so important is the work of scholars around risk (Beck 1992; Beck and Beck-Gernsheim 2002; Lupton 2013, 2022). This area is developed in the UK contribution, in particular, and discussed in more detail in the final chapter of the book.

A note on social and health inequalities

Differences in life expectancy and illness prevalence, both within and across countries, have deepened over the last 10 years, shaped by broader economic trends such as recession and austerity. These disparities can arise from a combination of differences in access to, and use of, health services, but are mainly due to material and structural inequalities (poverty, income, housing, pollution and working conditions) and health-related behaviours (diet, exercise, alcohol consumption and smoking), which in turn are related (Marmot 2020). Ethnicity tends to overlap with socio-economic inequalities. Nazroo (2003) found that differentials in income, housing and employment play a strong independent role in accounting for health outcome differences across ethnic groups. However, he also notes that racial harassment and discrimination are critical in understanding the inequalities. Analyses from across a range of locations have shown that people from minoritized groups were more likely to die of COVID-19 than those from majority ethnic groups (Agyemang et al. 2021). As project leaders, our reading around inequalities was shaped largely by events in, and literature of, the UK but we recognized that such disparities are not a uniquely British problem. In our discussions with the wider international consortium, we considered different ways of being attentive to inequalities in family life across the 10 countries, which are more prevalent or significant in different locations, as we will discuss further.

Approaching research during the pandemic

ICo-FACT is a multi-method, qualitative, longitudinal and multimodal study. Each country recruited approximately 30 families from diverse socio-economic backgrounds and living arrangements. Because we were interested in capturing different family perspectives, and given our relational approach as outlined before, multiple members of the same households were invited to participate in each study. As such, grandparents, parents and children from 12 years of age upwards from each family were invited to take part. Children under 12 did not participate directly in the research, but their experiences have been captured through accounts from other family members.

Recruitment in each country was led by each team using appropriate methods which addressed pertinent 'diversity' factors for that country. For example, in the United States the authors were concerned to recruit participants from across the political divide, as survey studies had identified this as a major factor in determining reactions to social distancing measures. In Singapore, migration status was particularly important. Some teams were more successful in recruitment than others, dependent on the research time available to the authors in some cases and research incentives in others. Argentina, notably, only managed to recruit women (mothers) to their study, while Sweden boosted their family recruitment with the participation of 95 individual teenagers via school-based data collection.

Our study started in April 2020, with our first online ICo-FACT meeting on 6 May 2020. Our initial and urgent task was to agree on our overall methodological approach and to apply for ethics approval for each country study. Ethics approval procedures varied greatly across countries. New protocols had been developed for research during a pandemic and we were asked to consider carefully the demands placed on study participants. In working with young people, we took care to develop clear explanations about our studies and obtain parental permission prior to commencing. Each research team agreed clear protocols to manage data securely. This was particularly important given the sheer amount of data collected, but also due to the personal and sensitive information that was shared with us (not only names, addresses and email addresses but also private accounts of personal struggle). In many countries data included photographs and video messages. Due to the diversity in research regulations there were staggered start dates for each study, while different levels of research funding meant variations in research periods. Fieldwork had begun in all country studies by June 2020, however, with the shortest study lasting six months (Taiwan, June–December 2020) and the longest lasting 14 months (UK, May 2020–June 2021).

Given the qualitative nature of the research, our aim was not to identify national trends and patterns around COVID-19, but rather to closely follow relatively small numbers of families in enough depth to elicit fine detail about experiences of changing family practices and everyday interactions during a global pandemic. We drew from digital ethnographic methods as a means of gathering data remotely and asynchronously, enabling us to learn about individuals' behaviour in context (Pink et al. 2015). In four of the countries we used Indeemo, a diary-based app designed for qualitative ethnographic research. Use of Indeemo facilitated the collection of multimodal forms of data from family members – that is, photos, text and videos. Other studies relied on email, WhatsApp (the encrypted social media app) and telephone. These 'mobile methods' enable data collection *in situ* and increase the temporal closeness of self-reporting, as participants receive a 'text' each time a new diary probe or question is uploaded (Boase and Humphries 2018).

Qualitative research requires building rapport and trust with participants, and this is particularly the case when working with young people (Bucknall 2014). Such rapport building can be difficult to achieve online (Hewson 2020). Through our 'in situ' digital methods we tried hard to overcome this. Decisions to use diary or other apps, or to rely more on repeat interviews, were based on practical considerations, detailed in the individual chapters that follow. Often digital inequalities were a key factor, since not all families have access to electronic devices or stable internet connections, or to digital knowledge. Nor do all families have access to private and confidential spaces at home to be interviewed online. Extra efforts were thus made in each country to recruit so-called 'hard to reach populations', for example through engagement with charities, third-sector organisations and schools. Extra efforts were also made to facilitate different families' needs where they did participate (for example through offering phone vouchers in some countries). This helped in widening participation in our study and allowed for a more stratified data sample within countries.

Other technical considerations were also prompted by our online approach. These included sourcing the most suitable technology and methods for digital research, thinking through data privacy, and data management. Across the 10 countries, teams carefully identified the best software for gathering evidence for their sample. The platforms selected needed to be user-friendly and data-secure. Most countries used a combination of methods, including phone or online interviews and diary prompts via apps like WhatsApp or Indeemo. A big challenge in our research was keeping people motivated to take part and so preventing attrition. One way we did this was by asking a range of questions and setting tasks which were relevant to what was happening in real time (for example questions around face masks, new guidelines and vaccine roll-out). Some research teams used incentives such as gift vouchers to help recruit and retain participants. Across all studies, the value of the study was made clear to participants, and updates on findings were provided to ensure families recognized that their contributions were important.

National contexts

The 10 countries in this study are spread across five continents and represent geographic and socio-political diversity, as well as a spectrum of approaches to the management of COVID-19 by state governments. At one end of the spectrum lies Argentina, which imposed one of the longest continuous lockdowns in the world (234 days) but still experienced relatively high COVID-19 mortality and morbidity rates. At the other lies Sweden, which had no explicit lockdown and introduced strategies based on recommendations rather than law-enforced restrictions. The majority of countries in our studies had intermittent national lockdowns, lasting weeks or months. In almost all settings schools and early childhood settings were closed, along with 'non-essential' retail outlets and businesses. However, variation existed in the length of these closures and the strictness with which they were enforced.

In Asia, Taiwan quickly focused on the early closing of borders and ultimately experienced very few COVID-19-related deaths, later managing to continue life in ways similar to the pre-pandemic context. It did experience a surge in cases towards the second half of 2021, but the overall number of deaths was low. Similarly, Singapore managed to control its case rates relatively quickly and re-opened its economy; however, surges were recorded amongst migrant workers who lived in crowded conditions. Pakistan, our third Asian country case study, was successful in avoiding the high death toll of neighbouring countries in the region but suffered severe economic effects. South Africa imposed a series of extended lockdowns with strict rules in place. Russia introduced relatively mild and lightly enforced restrictions: its only lockdown was comparatively brief (two months in 2020) and applied mainly to major cities. The UK initially delayed a lockdown response, but ultimately instigated three lockdowns and suffered one of the highest COVID-19-related mortality rates in the world. Similarly, the United States, which has suffered from one of the highest mortality rates globally (WHO 2022), has taken a varied approach to COVID-19 management, largely due to the make-up of the political system, with varied federal and state legislation. In Chile, the pandemic coincided with an economic crisis and social turbulence, which led the government to also initiate a curfew that was in effect for more than one and a half years. Further details on country context and management of COVID-19 are detailed in the country-specific chapters.

How the book is organized

Following this introductory chapter, authors from each country present findings speaking to our shared research questions (Chapters 2–11). The country chapters have been organized alphabetically, given the multiple overlapping themes across chapters and to avoid any unintended hierarchy. Each chapter focuses on how the pandemic has affected family life within the country context, specifically for families with dependent children. After a description of the local policy and cultural context, sampling and methods, the authors address the two main study research questions: How did participants understand and respond to government guidelines around COVID-19? And what impact did this have on family life?

Chapter 2 discusses the Argentinian context. Argentina endured one of the longest continuous nationwide lockdowns due to COVID-19. Circulation without authorization was punishable by law and could lead to arrest by the police or armed forces. This resulted in an abrupt reduction of formal and informal care arrangements, increasing families' care responsibilities. Drawing on in-depth interviews with 35 women with children, and using a care lens, this study explores how the COVID-19 measures adopted by the national and local governments affected women's well-being, social interactions and time-use dynamics in relation to family life. The shrinkage of care networks, home schooling, remote work or unemployment, and new COVID safety routines all introduced challenges to women's time allocation. However, while some participants found their subjective well-being negatively impacted, others felt more enriched in relation to their discretionary time prior to the pandemic. The authors argue that this has led to reflections or existential crises around occupations, careers, education and self-worth, and a desire to act on and be consistent with these epiphanies, ultimately revealing the transformative potential of the pandemic.

Chile is the focus of Chapter 3 and findings are based on research with 38 families of middle, lower-middle and lower socio-economic strata in four regions in the country. The pandemic occurred in Chile within a context of political instability due to a perceived crisis of neoliberalism, massive protests and the beginning of a major constitutional reform process. Government responses to the COVID-19 crisis were erratic, with intermittent lockdowns instigated. Families described their acceptance of lockdowns and other public health measures, yet few workers in families managed to stay at home. This was due to pressure from employers to attend workplaces and the needs of the self-employed and unemployed to generate income. The authors discuss how the pandemic resulted in a reconfiguration of everyday life in many households, in terms of the division of labour, care activities, time and spatial organization and survival strategies.

In Chapter 4, Pakistan's response to COVID-19 is discussed. With a specific lens on the issues of gender and generation, this chapter reflects on changes to family practices and well-being in 27 households from diverse socio-economic and ethnic backgrounds, living in Karachi, Pakistan's largest city (and one of the 'hotspots' of the coronavirus pandemic). Pakistan managed to avoid the high death toll of neighbouring countries in the region. However, the pandemic provoked serious economic impacts in terms of lost incomes and jobs, rising poverty and additional strain on the fragile healthcare system. Coupled with a series of natural disasters in the country in 2020, it was a challenging year for the country. Using a framework of care and emotional work, the authors suggest how the government's response has been inconsistent, with short periods of national lockdown combined with targeted 'smart lockdowns' of urban neighbourhoods. Families responded to this inconsistency by recalibrating their care practices, without lasting changes in gendered roles.

Russia is the focus of Chapter 5. Russia offers a story of the pandemic in a country with a short lockdown overall – only two months in 2020 – mostly applied in major cities. The authors conducted ethnographic observations and online interviews with 38 families from across Russia. They found that despite an overall lack of willingness to cooperate with restrictions, people obeyed the rules mostly because they feared fines. A major challenge faced by families was the abrupt and extended switch to home-based schooling – universal for all regions of Russia. Given this, the authors particularly focus on parental management of education, thinking about different responses by parents, the influence of occupation on these responses, and the role of agency in decision-making around home-based schooling.

Chapter 6 shines a spotlight on Singapore. Here the government responded to the outbreak of COVID-19 through implementing a circuit breaker (CB) period of nearly two months, along with the COVID-19 Temporary Measures Bill in which a range of support packages were introduced for households and businesses. The chapter focuses on the experiences of 28 individuals from diverse family formations (nuclear families with children, extended, intergenerational families, single parent families with children and elderly living alone/with a care-giver) during the CB period and after, and how it impacted their work, family and psychological well-being. Drawing on scholarship from the sociology of everyday life, the authors particularly explore the reproduction of traditionally masculine or feminine identities during a global pandemic within the wider socio-cultural context of Singapore. They argue that many women in households they studied took on larger shares of household and childcare commitments and rationalized their behaviour by addressing their partner's lack of expertise or competency in carrying out these tasks, thus magnifying prevailing gendered divisions within families.

Chapter 7 explores the impact of the pandemic on 21 families living in Gauteng, South Africa. South Africa's response to the pandemic was prompt and decisive; a national lockdown was instituted in March 2020 which resulted in schools, businesses, places of worship and recreational activities shutting down, as well as a ban on movement between provinces. In a context with high levels of households headed by a single adult, where women tend to be the primary breadwinner and caregiver, they found the pandemic resulted in both additional financial strain as well as increased responsibilities. The authors also discuss the challenges of social distancing for families living in the closed, confined spaces of informal housing. Many of the experiences described in this chapter centre on issues of food insecurity, job losses and limited access to educational resources during the lockdown period. These challenges were however mediated by family togetherness, community support through sharing resources and structural supports, such as the COVID-19-specific social distress grant and the top-up of existing social relief grants.

In Chapter 8, Sweden's response to COVID-19 is discussed. Sweden is unique in that it had no formal lockdown, with the overall strategy based on recommendations rather than legal restrictions. Upper secondary school students experienced periods of online teaching, while schools for younger children remained open. Those aged 70 years or older were asked to self-isolate and limit their number of contacts. Findings are based on interviews and written replies to open questions that were collected over a year with 95 adolescents, 17 parents and 5 grandparents from different socio-economic and national backgrounds across the country. The authors discuss how fears and concerns raised by the pandemic generally pertained to how social distancing and isolation affected psychological well-being; many also criticized the government for lax policies with recommendations that leave it up to the individual to decide how to act. Close relationships, physical contacts, being cared for and caring for others were found to be vital in how risk was calculated and how the policies were interpreted and acted upon by individuals.

Chapter 9 focuses on Taiwan. In Taiwan the pandemic (at the time the data were collected) was relatively successfully contained, thanks to the Taiwanese government's early and strict precautionary actions, which were informed by its previous experiences of the SARS outbreak in 2002. The experiences of 22 families across different employment sectors in Taiwan are explored and the authors argue that while on the surface the daily lives of families appeared to be only minimally impacted by the pandemic, in reality certain groups were unevenly affected such as those in travel, hospitality and medical professions. Such groups were either financially impacted or else exposed more to the virus. Therefore, the risks associated with the pandemic were not equally experienced.

The United Kingdom is the focus of Chapter 10. This chapter draws on data from 38 families with children across the UK, from a range of geographic, socio-economic and ethnic backgrounds. The authors explore how participants responded to the shifting national guidelines around social distancing, and the impact of these on everyday family and intimate life. Widely recognized as having had one of the worst responses internationally to the pandemic early on (in terms of mortality rates), but later on having a successful vaccination programme, the UK experienced three national lockdowns. Two of these entailed the closure of schools. Largely speaking, participants reported following social distancing guidelines, but confusion and circumspection around the rules increased after the second lockdown. Variance in interpreting social distance guidance and/or the risk of COVID-19 created fissures between households (rarely within them). For many the home became a 'safe' space where rules around social distancing were agreed and maintained. Those from outside of the home, in particular strangers 'in society', were viewed with more suspicion. The authors connect these findings to ideas around risk and individualization and consider what they tell us about the transformation of family and intimate life during the pandemic.

In Chapter 11, the final country chapter, the authors focus on the United States, using a sociocultural perspective on policy as practice. This chapter reports on a diary-based study asking how 35 families from diverse social, cultural, racial, ethnic, linguistic, social class, and geographical backgrounds and locations across the United States experienced the pandemic within the larger social, cultural and political context. The COVID-19 pandemic played out in the United States in the context of tremendous political polarization, growing inequality, and the deepening of historically rooted racial tensions. The official policy response in the USA varied widely across local, state and federal levels, leading to confusion and uncertainty on the part of participants. Further confusion resulted from the ways in which news and information were distributed. The disruption to daily life and household processes was uneven, resulting in the magnification of previous inequities both within and across households and a 're-traditionalization' of gender relations within many families. Race/ethnicity also mattered in terms of how families experienced the pandemic in relation to growing racism and xenophobia. Sense-making about (and compliance with) pandemic policies was closely bound up with families' views of larger, unfolding socio-political processes: their political affiliations, the media outlets they accessed, and their connections to people in other geopolitical locations.

Chapter 12 is a concluding chapter written by the editors which brings together the differences and similarities that can be identified across different country contexts. In this reflective chapter, we consider what we have learned about family life, intimacy and care as well as the role of families in the management of a pandemic. We focus on the interplay between COVID-19-response policies, which emerged within particular historical and cultural locations, and which came up against everyday family practices, understandings of community and personal responsibility, and the various constraints which individuals faced both within and across families. We also draw out how the overall findings of our project speak to understandings (and imaginings) of family, relatedness, connections to community and institutions and how these understandings 'work' with wider public health imperatives and individuals' well-being. Future directions for research and policy are outlined, as well as the practice implications of our international study.

Conclusion

As you read through the chapters that follow, you will find our study has generated rich, interconnected and deep qualitative knowledge around the role of family practices across the world in mediating behaviour during a pandemic. How families have come together to cope and make sense of this period of heightened uncertainty is of deep concern to social scientists, both now and in the future – as well as to those in policy and practice, who seek to support families 'post' pandemic.

The significance of understanding family life in the study of infectious disease is clear. Combating a pandemic relies on all members of the family or household to uphold health guidelines in order to keep everyone safe. In turn, the range of stories shared by the many families taking part in our study show how the pandemic shaped family practices – focusing particularly on practices within cross-generational relationships – and how those relate to gender inequalities within the household. Given the range of behaviour changes within families, a lingering question to consider, therefore, is whether this period of upheaval will create lasting changes in family life. As Matthewman and Huppatz (2020) have reflected, the pandemic has the potential to lead to a 'reimagination of the social' (p. 682) in consideration of new forms of solidarity and collective action, in our case at the family level. Whether this 'reimagination' (rather than just retrenchment) has actually happened is something we document in this book in a range of geographical locations, reminding us once again of the importance of social science which is at once local *and* global in its endeavours. We hope you enjoy reading.

References

Agyemang, C., Richters, A., Jolani, S., Hendriks, S., Zalpuri, S., Yu, E., Pijls, B., Prins, M., Stronks, K. and Zeegers, M. P. (2021) 'Ethnic minority status as social determinant for COVID-19 infection, hospitalisation, severity, ICU admission and deaths in the early phase of the pandemic: A meta-analysis'. *BMJ Global Health*, 6:e007433. https://doi.org/10.1136/bmjgh-2021-007433.

Bacchi, C. and Goodwin, S. (2016) *Poststructural Policy Analysis: A guide to practice*. Basingstoke: Palgrave Macmillan.

Banks, J. and Xu, X. (2020) 'The mental health effects of the first two months of lockdown and social distancing during the Covid-19 pandemic in the UK'. *Fiscal Studies*, 4 (3). https://doi.org/10.1111/1475-5890.12239.

Barrios, J. M., Benmelech, E., Hochberg, Y. V., Sapienza, P. and Zingales, L. (2020) 'Civic capital and social distancing during the Covid-19 pandemic'. *NBER Working Paper 27320*. Cambridge, MA: National Bureau of Economic Research. https://doi.org/10.3386/w27320.

Bartscher, A. K., Seitz, S., Slotwinski, M., Siegloch, S. and Wehrhöfer, N. (2020) 'Social capital and the spread of Covid-19: Insights from European countries'. *IZA Discussion Papers, No. 13310*. https://www.iza.org/publications/dp/13310/social-capital-and-the-spread-of-covid-19-insights-from-european-countries (accessed 9 February 2023).

Beck, U. (1992) *Risk Society: Towards a new modernity*. London: Sage.

Beck, U. and Beck-Gernsheim, E. (2001) *Individualization: Institutionalized individualism and its social and political consequences*. London: Sage.

Benchekroun, R. (2022) 'Caring through a screen: Caring for kin under lockdown'. *Families, Relationships and Societies*, 11 (1), 3–18. https://doi.org/10.1332/204674321X16293510454010.

Benzeval, M., Bond, L., Campbell, M., Egan, M., Lorenc, T., Petticrew, M. and Popham, F. (2014) *How Does Money Influence Health?* York: Joseph Rowntree Foundation.

Berkhout, E., Galasso, N., Lawson, M., Rivero Morales, P. A., Taneja, A. and Vázquez Pimentel, D. A. (2021) 'The inequality virus: Bringing together a world torn apart by coronavirus through a fair, just and sustainable economy'. *Oxfam Briefing Paper*. https://doi.org/10.21201/2021.6409.

Blainey, K. and Hannay, T. (2021) 'The impact of school closures on spring 2021 attainment'. London: RS Assessment from Hodder Education and SchoolDash. https://www.risingstars-uk.com/getmedia/8181effc-58ef-48f7-9f78-94186578efa5/The_Impact_Of_School_Closures_May_2021 (accessed 24 January 2023).

Blundell, R., Cribb, J., McNally, S., Warwick, R. and Xu, X. (2021) *Inequalities in Education, Skills, and Incomes in the UK: The implications of the COVID-19 pandemic*. London: Institute of Fiscal

Studies. https://ifs.org.uk/inequality/wp-content/uploads/2021/03/BN-Inequalities-in-education-skills-and-incomes-in-the-UK-the-implications-of-the-COVID-19-pandemic.pdf (accessed 24 January 2023).

Boase, J. and Humphries, L. (2018) 'Mobile methods: Explorations, innovations, and reflections'. *Mobile Media & Communication*, 6 (2), 153–62.

Brown, S. M., Doom, J. R., Lechuga-Peña, S., Watamura, S. E. and Koppels, T. (2020) 'Stress and parenting during the global COVID-19 pandemic'. *Child Abuse & Neglect*, 110 (2), 104699. https://doi.org/10.1016/j.chiabu.2020.104699.

Bucknall, S. (2014) 'Doing qualitative research with children and young people'. In Clark, A., Flewitt, R. and Hammersley M. (eds) *Understanding Research with Children and Young People*. London: Sage, 69–84. https://doi.org/10.4135/9781526435637.n5.

Cowie, H. and Myers, C.-A. (2021) 'The impact of the COVID-19 pandemic on the mental health and well-being of children and young people'. *Children & Society*, 35 (1), 62–74. https://doi.org/10.1111/chso.12430.

Dawson, A. and Dennis, S. (2020) 'Social intimacy'. *Anthropology in Action*, 27 (3), 1–8. https://doi.org/10.3167/aia.2020.270301.

Dolby, T., Finning, K., Baker, A., Fowler-Dowd, L., Khunti, K., Razieh, C., Yates, T. and Nafilyan, V. (2022) 'Monitoring sociodemographic inequality in COVID-19 vaccination uptake in England: A national linked data study'. *Journal of Epidemiology and Community Health*, 76 (7), 646–52. http://dx.doi.org/10.1136/jech-2021-218415.

Douglas, M., Vittal Katikireddi, S., Taulbut, M., McKee, M. and McCartney, G. (2020) 'Mitigating the wider health effects of Covid-19 pandemic response'. *BMJ*, 369, m1557. https://doi.org/10.1136/bmj.m1557.

Eldén, S., Anving, T. and Alenius Wallin, L. (2022) 'Intergenerational care in corona times: Practices of care in Swedish families during the pandemic'. *Journal of Family Research*, 34 (1), 538–62. https://doi.org/10.20377/jfr-702.

Evans, S., Mikocka-Walus, A., Klas, A., Olive, L., Sciberras, E., Karantzas, G. and Westrupp, E. M. (2020) 'From "it has stopped our lives" to "spending more time together has strengthened bonds": The varied experiences of Australian families during COVID-19'. *Frontiers in Psychology*, 11, 2906. https://doi.org/10.3389/fpsyg.2020.588667.

Fancourt, D., Steptoe, A. and Bu, F. (2020) 'Trajectories of depression and anxiety during enforced isolation due to COVID-19: A longitudinal observational study'. *Lancet Psychiatry*, 8 (2), 141–9.

Ferreira, F., Sterck, O., Mahler, D. and Decerf, B. (2021) 'Death and destitution: The global distribution of welfare losses from the COVID-19 pandemic'. *LSE Public Policy Review*, 1 (4), 2. http://doi.org/10.31389/lseppr.34.

Finch, J. and Mason, J. (1993) *Negotiating Family Responsibilities*. London: Routledge.

Fraser, T., and Aldrich, D. P. (2020) 'Social ties, mobility, and COVID-19 spread in Japan'. *Scientific Reports*, 11. https://doi.org/10.1038/s41598-021-81001-4.

Gabb, J. (2008) *Researching Intimacy in Families*. Basingstoke: Palgrave Macmillan.

Gabb, J. and Fink, J. (2015) *Couple Relationships in the 21st Century*. Basingstoke: Palgrave Macmillan.

Golombok, S. (2020) *We are Family: What really matters for parents and children*. Melbourne: Scribe Publications.

Gray, C. and Hansen, K. (2021) 'Did Covid-19 lead to an increase in hate crimes toward Chinese people in London?'. *Journal of Contemporary Criminal Justice*, 37 (4), 569–88. https://doi.org/10.1177/10439862211027994.

Hewson, C. (2020) 'Qualitative approaches in internet-mediated research: Opportunities, issues, possibilities'. In Leavy, P. (ed.) *The Oxford Handbook of Qualitative Research* (2nd ed.). New York: Oxford University Press, 633–73.

Howes, S., Monk-Winstanley, R., Sefton, T. and Woudhuysen, A. (2020) *Poverty in the Pandemic: The impact of coronavirus on low-income families and children*. London: Child Poverty Action Group and Church of England. https://cpag.org.uk/sites/default/files/files/policypost/Poverty-in-the-pandemic.pdf (accessed 9 February 2023).

Kagitcibasi, C. (1996) *Family and Human Development Across Cultures: A view from the other side*. Mahwah, NJ: Lawrence Erlbaum Associates.

Kneale, D. and Bécares, L. (2021) 'Discrimination as a predictor of poor mental health among LGBTQ+ people during the COVID-19 pandemic: Cross-sectional analysis of the online Queerantine study'. *BMJ Open*, 11 (6). https://doi.org/10.1136/bmjopen-2021-049405.

Kneale, D., O'Mara-Eves, A., Rees, R. and Thomas, J. (2020) 'School closure in response to epidemic outbreaks: Systems-based logic model of downstream impacts'. *F1000Research*, 9, 352. https://doi.org/10.12688/f1000research.23631.1.

Lee, D. H. and Park, K. D. (2005) 신종 인플루엔자 대유행에 대한 우리나라의 대응방안 ['The preparedness plan for influenza pandemic']. Article in Korean. *Journal of Preventative Medicine and Public Health*, 38 (4), 386–90. https://koreascience.kr/article/JAKO200524717660962.page.

Lee, J. (2020) 'Mental health effects of school closures during COVID-19'. *Lancet Child and Adolescent Health*, 4 (6), 421. https://doi.org/10.1016/S2352-4642(20)30109-7.

Lupton, D. (2013) *Risk*. (2nd ed.). New York: Routledge.

Lupton, D. (2022) *COVID Societies: Theorising the coronavirus crisis*. London: Routledge.

Ma, Y. and Zhan, N. (2022) 'To mask or not to mask amid the COVID-19 pandemic: How Chinese students in America experience and cope with stigma'. *Chinese Sociological Review*, 54 (1), 1–26. https://doi.org/10.1080/21620555.2020.1833712.

Marc, A. G., Homan, P. A., García, C. and Brown, T. H. (2020) 'The color of COVID-19: Structural racism and the disproportionate impact of the pandemic on older Black and Latinx adults'. *Journals of Gerontology, Series B: Psychological Sciences and Social Sciences*, 76 (3), e75–80. https://doi.org/ 10.1093/geronb/gbaa114.

Marmot, M., Allen, J., Boyce, T., Goldblatt, P. and Morrison, J. (2020) *Health Equity in England: The Marmot Review 10 years on*. London: UCL Institute of Health Equity. https://www.health.org.uk/publications/reports/the-marmot-review-10-years-on (accessed 9 February 2023).

Matthewman, S. and Huppatz, K. (2020) 'A sociology of COVID-19'. *Journal of Sociology*, 56 (4), 675–83. https://doi.org/10.1177/1440783320939416.

McNeilly, H. and Reece, K. M. (2020) '"Everybody's always here with me!": Pandemic proximity and the lockdown family'. *Anthropology in Action*, 27 (3), 18–21. https://doi.org/10.3167/aia.2020.270304.

Mooi-Reci, I. and Risman, B. J. (2021) 'The gendered impacts of COVID-19: Lessons and reflections'. *Gender & Society*, 35 (2), 161–7. https://doi.org/10.1177/089124322110013.

Morgan, D. (1996) *Family Connections: An introduction to family studies*. Cambridge: Polity Press.

Morgan, D. (2011) *Rethinking Family Practices*. Basingstoke: Palgrave Macmillan.

Nazroo, J. Y. (2003) 'The structuring of ethnic inequalities in health: Economic position, racial discrimination, and racism'. *American Journal of Public Health*, 93 (2), 277–84. https://doi.org/10.2105/ajph.93.2.277.

Neal, S. and Murji, K. (2015) 'Sociologies of everyday life: Editors' introduction to the special issue'. *Sociology*, 49 (5), 811–19. https://doi.org/10.1177/0038038515602160.

Nguyen, V. M. (2020) 'Alone together: Intimacy and semi-mobility during Ho Chi Minh City's lockdown'. *Anthropology in Action*, 27 (3), 14–17. https://doi.org/10.3167/aia.2020.270303.

Office for National Statistics (ONS) (2020) *Coronavirus and How People Spent their Time Under Lockdown: 28 March to 26 April 2020*. London: Office for National Statistics.

Organisation for Economic Cooperation and Development (OECD) (2022) *The Unequal Impact of COVID-19: A spotlight on frontline workers*. Paris: OECD Publishing. https://www.oecd.org/coronavirus/policy-responses/the-unequal-impact-of-covid-19-a-spotlight-on-frontline-workers-migrants-and-racial-ethnic-minorities-f36e931e/ (accessed 9 February 2023).

Parreiras, C. (2021) 'The COVID-19 pandemic and the reconfigurations of domestic space in Favelas: Brief reflections on intimacies and precariousness'. *Anthropology in Action*, 28 (1), 52–6.

Pierce, M., Hope, H., Ford, T., Hatch, S., Hotopf, M., John, A., Kontopantelis, E., Webb, R., Wessely, S., McManus, S. and Abel, K. M. (2020) 'Mental health before and during the COVID-19 pandemic: A longitudinal probability sample survey of the UK population'. *Lancet Psychiatry*, 7 (10), 883–92.

Pink, S., Horst, H., Postill, J., Hjorth, L., Lewis, T. and Tacchi, J. (2015) *Digital Ethnography: Principles and practice*. London: Sage.

Prime, H., Wade, M. and Browne, D. T. (2020) 'Risk and resilience in family well-being during the COVID-19 pandemic'. *American Psychologist*, 75 (5), 631–43. https://doi.org/10.1037/amp0000660.

Risi, E., Pronzato, R. and Di Fraia, G. (2021) 'Everything is inside the home: The boundaries of home confinement during the Italian lockdown'. *European Societies*, 23 (sup1), S464–77.

Santomauro, D. F., Herrera, A. M. and 65 others. (COVID-19 Mental Disorders Collaborators) (2021) 'Global prevalence and burden of depressive and anxiety disorders in 204 countries and territories in 2020 due to the COVID-19 pandemic'. *The Lancet*, 398 (10312), 1700–12. https://doi.org/10.1016/S0140-6736(21)02143-7.

Shum, A., Skripkauskaite, S., Pearcey, S., Raw, J., Waite, P. and Cresswell, C. (2020) *Report 07: Changes in parents' mental health symptoms and stressors from April to December 2020*. London: Co-space study. https://cospaceoxford.org/wp-content/uploads/2021/01/Report_07_19JAN.pdf (accessed 24 January 2023).

Smart, C. (2007) *Personal Life: New directions in sociological thinking*. Cambridge: Polity.

Smart, C. (2011) 'Families, secrets and memories'. *Sociology*, 45 (4), 539–53. https://doi.org/10.1177/0038038511406585.

Tronto, J. C. (1998) 'An ethic of care'. *Generations: Journal of the American Society on Aging*, 22 (3), 15–20. http://www.jstor.org/stable/44875693.

Twamley, K., Doucet, A. and Schmidt, E. (2021) 'Introduction to special issue: Relationality in family and intimate practices'. *Families, Relationships and Societies: An International Journal of Research and Debate*, 10 (1), 3–10. https://doi.org/10.1332/204674321X16111601166128.

Vaterlaus, J. M., Shaffer, T., Patten, E. V. and Spruance, L. A. (2021) 'Parent–child relationships and the COVID-19 pandemic: An exploratory qualitative study with parents in early, middle, and late adulthood'. *Journal of Adult Development*, 28 (3), 251–63. https://doi.org/10.1007/s10804-021-09381-5.

World Health Organization (WHO) (2022) 'United States of America situation'. https://covid19.who.int/region/amro/country/us (accessed 24 January 2023).

Wu, C. (2021) 'Social capital and COVID-19: A multidimensional and multilevel approach'. *Chinese Sociological Review*, 53 (1), 27–54. https://doi.org/10.1080/21620555.2020.1814139.

2
Argentina: gendered effects of the COVID-19 lockdown and the transformations in well-being

Mariana de Santibañes and Gabriela Marzonetto[1]

Introduction

Shortly after the first coronavirus cases in Argentina were reported in March 2020, the Argentine government declared the state of Preventive and Mandatory Social Isolation (ASPO[2]).[3] This directive prohibited circulation, closed borders, and suspended all non-essential activities (see Figure 2.1 for timeline of public health measures). Families were forced to stay indoors for nine months, working and learning from home, resulting in multidimensional changes within households. Although implications varied according to members' role inside the family, household composition and socio-economic status, studies showed how women bore the brunt of the economic and social fallout of COVID-19,[4] aggravating existing gender inequalities (DNEIyG and UNICEF 2021). This was especially evident in how women organized and spent their time in terms of care responsibilities. Despite saving time on commuting and having both caregivers at home, research has revealed widespread gender discrepancies in COVID-19 time usage. Time-use surveys conducted during the first months of lockdown in the country revealed that, regardless of the gender of the household head, women perceived an increase of 48 percent over their usual care workload (UNICEF Argentina 2020).

Time-use survey studies focusing on time spent on necessities (for example, household chores and caretaking responsibilities) and leisure activities (for example, exercising, watching TV, reading) showed that

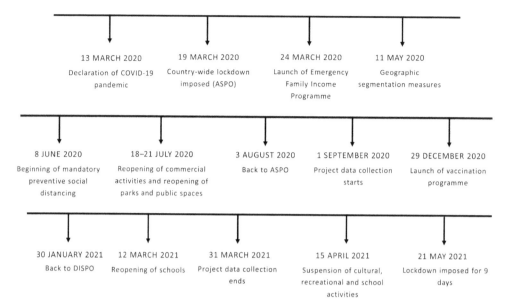

Figure 2.1 Timeline of COVID-19 in Argentina. Source: authors.

changes in how women, especially mothers, spent their time during the early months of the pandemic predicted a drop in women's subjective well-being (Giurge et al. 2020; UNICEF and CEPAL 2020; Zhou et al. 2020). However, while some women may have experienced the extra hours of care work as a burden that absorbed all their free time, others may have experienced it as a refreshing break from their pre-COVID routines. This can be explained in part by other dimensions of time that relate to the daily interactions in interpersonal relationships within the family group. Such interactions are also at the heart of social well-being and may thus affect the meanings and valorizations that women may project on their use of time.

With a focus on care, we conducted interviews between September 2020 and March 2021 with 35 women with school-age children from the Metropolitan Area of Great Buenos Aires (AMBA) and the province of Mendoza, to explore how confinement measures affected well-being, as adherence to such measures triggered changes in the use of time and social interactions. By addressing this question, we aimed to expand the understanding of women's experiences with and around care, and how these experiences affect their overall assessment of their happiness in a confinement context (Diener 2009; UN Women 2020; UN Women and CEPAL 2020).

Findings show that while, for many women, COVID-19 lockdown led to a decline in their subjective well-being, for others it brought an improvement in several aspects of their lives, especially for women from lower economic backgrounds. This situation has led to reflections or existential crises around women's interpersonal relations, occupations, careers, education and self-worth and a desire to act on and be consistent with these epiphanies, ultimately revealing the transformative potential of the pandemic.

Policy context

As a result of the declaration of Preventive and Mandatory Social Isolation (ASPO), circulation without authorization was punishable by law and could end in arrest.[5] Traffic restriction measures also put limitations on running errands and shopping freely, with families assigned certain days to shop based on the numbers on their identity documents. Yet, there was disparity in the extent to which people were able to remain at home and comply with ASPO norms. For instance, studies show socio-economic and spatial segregation in behaviour (Goicoechea 2020): those who had the opportunity to work remotely, make large groceries purchases, and had their own car found it easier to comply with sanitary measures than those in a more vulnerable position. Those living in overcrowded and small houses, with little access to resources and without their own means of transportation, did not have the necessary conditions to adhere to the lockdown requirements. Hence, among other societal aspects, ASPO and, later, the Preventive and Mandatory Social Distancing measure (DISPO) did not take into account the persistent inequalities within locations and population in the country. Such disparities also affected peoples' ability to access green areas, as it was forbidden to be in public areas such as parks, squares and playgrounds, so neglecting especially children and vulnerable population's rights.

ASPO was accompanied by support measures for the population, fundamentally the Emergency Family Income subsidy (IFE) for workers in the informal economy[6] and the Emergency Assistance Programme for Work and Production (ATP) which provided government payments to employers to help cover the salaries of registered workers. Despite this assistance, the economic crisis in which the country already found itself was exacerbated by the pandemic crisis, which only deepened the current state of social vulnerability. According to the National

Institute of Statistics and Censuses data (INDEC), in the first semester of 2020 poverty reached 40.9 per cent of the population, an increase for the third consecutive year. The negative impact was also evidenced in the reduction of 187,000 jobs in formal employment and a drop of 47 per cent in the informal employment rate between February and October 2020 (CIPPEC 2020). According to a survey carried out by UNICEF in July 2020, 45 per cent of households declared having a reduction in their income compared to prior to the pandemic. Families with children and adolescents were particularly affected, a situation evidenced in the increase in the poverty rate of these households from 43.4 per cent in 2019 to 50.3 per cent in the first half of 2020. Similarly, there was an increase of 5.4 percentage points in households with children and adolescents whose income was below the basic food basket value. This abrupt drop in income and employment brought with it other effects in terms of the living conditions of households, such as a reduction in food spending, loss of social security or school dropout (UNICEF Argentina 2020; CIPPEC 2020; UCA 2021).

Furthermore, in order to address the childcare crisis triggered by ASPO, a set of policies around care were implemented. In general, these measures were monitored by the Inter-Ministerial Roundtable on Care Policies created in March 2020 and were accompanied by the 'Quarantine with Rights' campaign on care co-responsibility. Among these policies, the following stand out: permission to circulate for people with paid or unpaid care responsibilities; paid leave for domestic workers during the time of ASPO; suspension of the duty to attend the workplace for those who were responsible for the care of children or adolescents for the duration of school closures (Decree 297/20; Res. 207/20). In addition, a law regulating remote work was enacted, establishing workers' right to have schedules compatible with their care responsibilities (and a reduction in working hours in consequence if necessary) without any salary reduction.

Although these measures were noteworthy for contemplating and protecting the right to give and receive care, most of them only covered workers in the formal sector or public employees, through the ATP programme. This means that they failed to cover the more than 46 per cent of the workforce that participate in the informal economy. Some measures were taken to counter this: social benefits were reinforced and domestic workers were included as recipients of the previously mentioned IFE subsidy; the National Commission on Domestic Work set a wage increase of 10 per cent and minimal monthly payments; job layoffs were banned during the isolation period and employers remained under an obligation to continue payments. This was considered as a paid leave and was supplemented by awareness campaigns on the importance of employers taking care of their employees and on domestic workers' rights (López Mourelo 2020).

Lastly, given the closure of schools, the national government implemented a set of strategies to complement the measures for children and adolescents' care, and to ensure the continuity of school activities. Mainly, a trans-media strategy was implemented, which included the distribution of educational booklets to populations with limited access to connectivity, a digital educational portal with activities, videos, books and materials for teachers and families, and virtual training programmes for teachers from all educational levels. Despite these efforts — as in the case of Pakistan — only one out of five schools had the capacity to offer online classes to their students, and more than 1.1 million students had dropped out of classes by December 2020 (Baratta 2021).

Theoretical framework

Time use and social interaction as measures of well-being

People's well-being is influenced by a variety of factors, including their income, emotional and sexual fulfilment, favourable social and environmental circumstances, and how they spend their time. This depends on the contributions of both market-related (paid) and non-market (unpaid) activity, whether it takes place in the realm of private relationships or social and communal organizations. These two aspects of work have been seen differently throughout history, with the majority of research concentrating on paid work, thus ignoring a wide range of activities aimed at personal, family and social well-being (Held 2005). Unpaid work has only recently been a topic of concern and research, as scholars aim to reconfigure the meaning of work to include the weight of unpaid labour, ensuring consistency with reality. The use of time thus serves as a tool for addressing both dimensions of work and is a significant indication of population health as well as social and gender inequities (Esquivel 2009; Jun 2020; Bauman et al. 2019; Vega-Rapun et al. 2020).

In this light, care work for household members merits special mention among the unpaid activities entrusted to household members, especially women, which promote well-being. It refers to those activities that are indispensable for satisfying the basic needs of people's existence and reproduction. It implicates the provision of physical and symbolic elements that enable people to live in society. It includes self-care, direct care of other people (the interpersonal activity of care), the provision of the preconditions in which care takes place (cleaning the house, buying and preparing food) and care management (coordinating schedules, commuting to educational centres and supervising paid care work at home, among others) (Rodríguez Enríquez and Pautassi 2014). Feminist scholars have shown how care relationships and care work are activities that are inherent to life and thus play an important role in people's well-being and subsistence (Carrasco 2003; Tronto 1987). Time-use surveys are instruments that enable this specific aspect of work to be addressed, ultimately making visible the sexual division of labour in families and the link between the many welfare-providing actors.

Broadly speaking, measuring time use allows one to identify how much time each person devotes to different activities, which are divided into four categories: 1) necessary time, which refers to the time required to satisfy basic needs such as sleep, eating and personal care; 2) contracted time, which is the time spent on regular paid work; 3) committed time, which includes activities associated with housework and care and 4) free time, the only time in this categorization that is not considered work time, and refers to activities associated with leisure (Vega Rapun et al. 2020, 20). From this, broad patterns of time use are inferred, and the amount of time people have for self-care, relaxation and leisure activities is studied in proportion to the time they spend on paid and unpaid work activities. From this perspective, leisure is considered a scarce commodity and, thus, not equally scarce for everyone (Stiglitz et al. 2009). However, given that there is an intrinsic relationship between free time and work time (either paid or unpaid), people's gender, economic and social relations also come into play. In the same way, these relationships not only condition the quantity but also the quality and content of this time. Furthermore, the so-called ethics of care – where taking care of others' needs is the highest moral imperative (Gilligan 1977) – constitutes a key constraining factor in women's leisure at any age (Henderson and Allen 1991).

The existing literature suggests that not having free time for enjoyment is detrimental for physical, psychological and spiritual health and well-being. Additionally, leisure activity contributes to enabling formation and affirmation, effective coping in stressful situations and in adverse events, and has positive influences on other domains of life such as work, family, and personal relationships (Mannell 2007). Lack of access to care services (both formal and informal) and changing work routines, among other factors, intensified care work within households, making leisure's quantity and quality a luxury for many and thus potentially having a negative effect on people's ability to have the kind of well-being that could alleviate the stress of confinement and provide a more pleasant experience during the pandemic.

In view of this, analysing women's use of time, and in particular their time for leisure, is vital to understanding their well-being, although, taken alone, use of time does not provide a sufficiently comprehensive view. Fundamental to social well-being are interpersonal connections and the dynamics of familial interactions to fulfil basic needs (which may range from socialization to emotional support). Interactions between family members were influenced by a number of factors in the pandemic, including the physical space within the home, the number of people residing in the home, the number of services available to all family members, the increased stress and anxiety caused by the health situation and the unpredictability of its duration, to name but a few. The social constraints prompted families to implement new relationships and intergenerational connections, affecting their daily lives, routines and habits and thus influencing the *meanings* attributed to the daily dynamics of coexistence.

As a result, our study incorporates a relational lens, expanding its focus to women's social interactions, understood as 'the bonds and interpersonal relations that we nourish (and) are an essential part of our daily lives'[7]. A lack of interaction with the outside world can negatively affect our care relations. It can lead to a lack of community and/or kinship nets to deal with either basic care chores (as examples, pick up children from school, clean the house, do groceries) as well as with the emotional aspects of care (share reflections, be listened to and listen to other's worries, accompany in grief processes, nourish personal relations, give and receive emotional support). Likewise, social isolation during the pandemic required families to remain in their homes, leading to the intensification of social interactions between household members. This kind of situation can have significant social, economic and psychological consequences that can be catalysts for stress and ultimately lead to violence (Peterman et al. 2020). Thus, both a lack of social interaction outside the household and the intensification of social interactions between family members can have a tremendous effect on the physical, mental and emotional burden of care, which relies mostly on women.

Methods

As with the wider study reported in this book, we aimed to broadly understand family experiences during the COVID-19 pandemic by specifically examining how adherence to governmental measures during lockdown changed women's use of time and social interactions, and affected their well-being. For this, we designed a qualitative study using an interpretive approach. We conducted online in-depth interviews over a six-month period with 35 women (a total of 175 interviews) and with children under 18 years of age, living in the Metropolitan Area of Great Buenos Aires and the province of Mendoza.[8] Although the call was extended to all family members, only 5 per cent of the participants were men or children, and we have thus focused on women's experiences only in this chapter. The monthly interviews lasted on average 50 minutes and sought to inquire about women's families' daily lives in the time prior to the pandemic and during the months of greater restrictions and isolation. We created flexible interview protocols that could capture the experiences of a very diverse group of women, with different care loads and occupations and living in different socio-economic conditions. Protocols varied from month to month and remained context sensitive. Conversations sought to delve into family and individual routines; material and emotional care work (both to *and* from other members of the household); time for self-care; care networks; (desires for) changes and continuities in routines and lifestyles; and challenges and emotions around the pandemic and government measures.

Analysis

There were multiple rounds of data analysis. The first round consisted of monthly virtual meetings with the field team where each researcher made a descriptive memo of the conducted interviews. We drew similarities and differences between these, identifying turning points and topics for deeper investigation. During these meetings, particular dynamics and experiences became salient, ultimately becoming the focus of analysis, as the team identified a cross-pattern of themes within the dataset. At the end of the data collection stage, the authors developed and wrote analytical memos on the topics associated with changes in care arrangements, social interactions, leisure and behaviours around measures.

The second round was a reflective process, focused on the analytical memos and transcripts of eight randomly selected women, in which we went back-and-forth between meaning units to ensure comparability across observations. Interpretive content analysis (Drisko and Maschi 2015; Krippendorff 2018) was the key analysis tool for this stage. We went beyond quantifying the most straightforward denotative (manifest) elements in the database, to focus on the interpretations of (latent) content (Ahuvia 2001). We arrived at connotative meanings (latent content) by combining individual elements in each interview to understand the meaning of the whole. The meaning units were identified and condensed into a description that was then abstracted and coded.

The third round of analysis was the stage of systematic coding of the interview transcripts using Atlas.ti 9 software with a codebook that resulted from the previous phase. In the fourth round, the team met to share insights of the first round of coding and make adjustments to the codebook accordingly in order to start a second round of collaborative coding based on the changes introduced. At this point, for example, we realized the key role of emotions in considering well-being, particularly those emotions triggered by the mental health of children in confined situations. Likewise, the need to also create a code for the wishes and projections or effective changes of direction in the professional and personal lives of interviewees was made clear.

Main themes and findings

How do participants understand and respond to social distancing measures?

The level of adherence to ASPO and DISPO varied according to the Argentine's political context. For instance, in the very early stages of ASPO, the fear of an unknown virus together with the expectations associated with the new president in rule showed a great degree of acceptance from families. As ASPO measures were extended, further limiting freedom of circulation and preventing school attendance, reactions, expectations, and adherence to measures started to decline, along with approval of the government. As time went by, attitudes towards government regulations were cross-cut with people's political preferences and those families who did not sympathize with the current government displayed greater frustration and resistance to measures.

Furthermore, measures imparted by the national and/or local governments were accepted and followed to a greater or lesser extent, dependent on fears that superseded those of getting or transmitting the virus to others. Findings show that those participants and families who most respected the new established norms were either: 1) those who felt overwhelmed by the ambiguity or constant changes in measures and were afraid of penalization; or 2) those from the lower-income bracket receiving state aid which, it might be argued, generated an extra sense of responsibility. This group also feared the consequences of being absent from work due to sickness without having access to health insurance.

For participants who were more reluctant to adhere to government measures, findings revealed that one of the main justifications for transgressing ASPO lay in their fears for the mental health of their children living in confinement. For example, many participants shared the anxiety and confusion generated by the 'countless' norms and guidelines released every week and by different governmental actors, as the odds of infringing them without even being aware of them increased every week. This particular situation affected the ability to plan family activities in the short and medium term. This was the case for Marcela, a dentist and university teacher, mother of an 11-year-old daughter and married to a war veteran husband who suffered from PTSD, when trying to plan a family vacation on the coast:

> It was different, it was weird because you saw that the beach was 'on fire', with young people spreading the virus … So, we did not know if [the local government would decide] to close the coast … we stayed tuned to the news, my husband could not unplug, he was super tuned to the news … He told me, 'we don't know if we are going to have to stay here or if we are going to be able to come back (home)' … at that time I was paying more attention to the news than during the rest of the year (Marcela, Mendoza, February 2021).

For many, this fear and anxiety led to inaction, disrupting the possibility of generating safe spaces in which new social and environmental interactions could take place, or limiting the possibility of enjoying free time, as in the case of Marcela and her husband spending a good part of their vacation period awaiting the news. On the other hand, in the case of participants concerned about the mental health of their children, the fear of the consequences that the confinement could have on their children's development and well-being inhibited the fear of contracting the virus or being detained by the police:

> Now I am fine, I am adapted, but what continues to [bother] me from the beginning is the discomfort of the kids. It's something I can't handle. The anguish generated by what the kids are going through is unmanageable, it has no end … [My neighbourhood] is quite residential … so we would go out carrying bags [as if we were] going to do the groceries – but everything was a lie … The police

> stopped me three times with the kids, shouting at me in front of them: 'You are putting your children's health at risk!' but the street was deserted (Julia, Buenos Aires, September 2020).

Julia works as a researcher in a private hospital, has two children (ages 10 and 14), and is married to a doctor who works in intensive care. This quote highlights the extra care burden for children brought by the pandemic. Many families reported – beyond their intuitive concerns – diagnoses of depressive and anxiety symptoms in their children and adolescents. In addition to using 'subterfuge techniques' to get children to be outdoors, other participants managed to set up meetings outdoors or at homes with their children's friends and thus promote their children's social interactions with peers. These examples show the extent to which attitudes toward government measures were deeply linked to women's (and their families') well-being, since measures had the capacity to negatively interfere with social interactions and the quality of leisure time.

Impact on family life: changes in women's well-being

This section is divided into two parts, representing the time both before and during the pandemic. In the first, we provide a general description of women and their families' routines, to serve as a baseline for reflection on the effects of COVID-19 measures on their standard of living. The second part deals directly with the months of strict confinement and is divided into three subsections, each addressing women's perceptions of their well-being based on changes in care responsibilities, social interactions and leisure.

Life before COVID-19

Participants' testimonies confirm the pre-existing inequalities in the country in regard to the social organization of care, both in terms of gender differences and socio-economic status imbalances (Faur 2014). While the vast majority of care work responsibility rested on women, families belonging to the highest income quintile almost completely outsourced their domestic and care work. The families of the poorest households, however, had practically no resources or opportunities to do this (Marzonetto et al. 2021). Julia's testimony allows us to imagine the rhythm of her routine and the dynamics within her family:

> Before the pandemic we got up at 6.20 a.m. We would prepare breakfast and food for the children. My husband would go to the hospital ... I would finish up getting everything ready, and drop

the kids at school and then I would go to the hospital. That whole commute left me at the hospital at 8.15 or 8.30 a.m., depending on the traffic … that's when my workday basically started … After that, the days that the boys practised sports outside school … I would leave the hospital, pick them up and bring them there. Other days they would also go to English classes, so they would come home, have a snack and then go to classes. Then we had some time to relax, to prepare dinner and to plan the next day … We had a person who helped us at home … She did not stay to sleep but was [at the home] 10 hours a day. Some days she picked up the boys at school, which gave us the opportunity to work until a little later (Julia, Buenos Aires, September 2020).

On the other hand, Valeria is a domestic worker, she lives with her six-year-old daughter and husband in the Conurbano Bonaerense (suburbs of the Metropolitan Area of Buenos Aires). She reported that:

From Monday to Friday [I got up] at 6 a.m., prepared my daughter for school, made her breakfast, took her to school, went back home, had breakfast, changed clothes and went to work … I would go to work on Mondays at 9 a.m. and leave at 1 p.m. I would go home, take my daughter to therapy and help her with homework, we would have lunch and I would go to a course I'm taking … Then on Wednesdays I worked in Ituzaingo, from 12 to 6 p.m. … Well, the same thing in the morning … take [my daughter], have breakfast, tidy up my house, and leave … On Thursdays I also worked, the same story … and on Fridays I relaxed a bit, I did not work … but yes, overall I was quite active: I would come and go all the time, didn't stop much (Valeria, Buenos Aires, September 2020).

These routines reflect similarities and differences in participants' experiences based on their income level, career and care responsibilities in their homes. In relation to the similarities, we observe profound exhausting pre-pandemic routines marked, among other aspects, by commuting time. On the other hand, we observe differences in their time use dynamics. For instance, in the daily routine of Julia and her family, we can see that they use part of their time for investing in skills, practising sports and in leisure activities, while the most instrumental dimension of care (domestic chores such as cleaning, cooking, decluttering and doing the laundry) are delegated and commoditized. Meanwhile, Valeria's routine depicts her as the main caregiver for her daughter, working in different places, and wasting a lot of time commuting. In terms of social interactions with family members, the previous testimonies also reflect the minimalist nature of family interactions during the week. The itineraries are basically made up of full days of work and schooling, with many more hours being shared with people outside the home than with family members. In this sense, Carina, a domestic worker who lives with her daughter and her husband in a multifamily house, says:

> For example, having breakfast together or having lunch were moments that we never spent together ... The only day that my husband didn't work was on Sundays, [so] the only day that we had breakfast and lunch together was on Sundays (Carina, Buenos Aires, November 2022).

On the other hand, thanks to the outsourcing of care work, most women from the more affluent social classes exhibited a relatively varied and dynamic social life, with weekly meetings with friends and partners and spaces for interaction outside of work, such as gyms, courses and workshops. This greater degree of social interactions also reflects the leisure time available to such women prior to the pandemic. In the following sections we will delve more into these topics and their transformation during the months of confinement.

The months of strict confinement

As previously described, while ASPO reduced public life to an essential minimum, it maximized private life. Families were forced to absorb the consequences of COVID-19 restrictions as they struggled to recompose and recreate the loss of spaces, activities, routines, and interactions with the 'outside' world. These efforts were ambivalent in nature. The lack of commute for school and work, unemployment, the relaxation of routines, structure, and dress requirements, expanded the availability of time and space for families. On the other hand, however, home-schooling, remote work, the shrinkage of care networks, and COVID-19 safety routines rapidly saturated those dimensions, increasing care loads and intensifying some social interactions while dissipating others. These effects varied across families, not only according to their socio-economic background but also based on family type and composition, number and age of children, internet access and availability of technological devices, occupation, employment status or coexistence with other elder adults or members with disabilities.

The emergence and disappearance of care responsibilities

Women from higher socio-economic groups reported relief at not having to rush out at 7.30 a.m. to drop their children off at school and then commute to work. In the first weeks of confinement their schedules were cleared from time spent commuting as well as travel time to after-school programmes, doctors' appointments or social commitments. Likewise, many saw their working hours shortened, and with this, they found a pause that allowed them to reconnect with their families, in particular, by investing in their emotional care:

> I have been able to be a calmer mother ... as luckily, I had to quit [seeing patients in] my private office. Thank God I can do that, it has allowed me to be a little calmer, speaking as a woman, right? I tell you as a housewife and everything, it has allowed me to be more connected with my family and not be on the run all the time (Marcela, Mendoza, September 2020).

Marcela is not only the family's sole worker but also manages all the care work of the house, either by observing and advising on her husband's tasks closely or by giving directions to the maid. This new reality has certainly been a break from a nearly relentless agenda.

On the other hand, the vast majority of participants from lower socio-economic groups were employed as domestic workers and had seen their activities suspended during the early stages of the pandemic (López Mourelo 2020). As a result, many were faced with complete work-free schedules for months on end, for the first time in their lives. At the beginning, this was a distressing and guilt-ridden prospect for them, as they feared that their bosses would stop paying them for not going to work (regardless of the restrictions on sacking workers). Rosario is an immigrant domestic worker from Bolivia who lives in Mendoza with her brother, his wife and their three children, who are 13, 11 and 6 years old. When asked about her new routine, she shares the following:

> Well in my house I started to throw away what was no longer useful ... and then I cleaned a lot. I really like pastry ... I make my own bread at home; we don't buy it any more. Cooking entertains me. And I keep my routine busy and I also play a lot with my nephew and nieces ... The truth is that without them I don't know what I would do, they are my fun. I was very active and then suddenly I found myself at home, and without my routine; although I used

to get up at 6 a.m., [now I sleep] until 8 a.m. (Rosario, Mendoza, September 2020).

Vanina, who is a single mother of a teenage boy, states:

> I'm more relaxed. With the garden and the little flowers. I try to cook something delicious for my son … spending time with him … Well, having the time, it is like you are looking for something to do and you keep everything neat, clean (Vanina, Buenos Aires, September 2020).

Similar to the first quote, both of these quotes not only reveal the emotional re-encounter with the dependents of the household, but also a deep reconnection with their homes, as separate dependent entities that have been involuntarily neglected because of long 12-hour workdays, 6 days a week. These entities are now inhabited, enjoyed and cared for. These experiences manage to connect with the emotional dimension of care (Held 2005), turning it into a source of gratification and indulgence, a condition of possibility to tune in with oneself and with the other, and a point of reference and stillness amid so much uncertainty and fear.[9] Indeed, caregiving is by nature an activity that takes place within the domestic and private sphere, and therefore involves relationships of esteem between those who give and receive care, and is therefore strongly influenced by feelings and emotions such as love, solidarity and dedication.

Nonetheless, this emotional dimension of care was not only a source of gratification but was also very taxing. Although concern for children is a constant in parents' lives, sudden changes to the social lives and daily routines of kids triggered new fears among adults. Unstable learning environments, prolonged isolation, lack of contact with nature and various other factors contributed to making children vulnerable to burnout. Interviewees have reported that their kids showed symptoms of physical or emotional exhaustion, adding an unexpected load of care to the pandemic equation. Carla, a biology teacher in a middle school and a single mother of a four-year-old boy, was currently living with her parents (both retired school teachers). She stressed that she was concerned by her son's regression during the pandemic:

> My son is now very afraid, afraid of everything. He fears going to the bathroom alone, fears [walking] in the hallway, going outside, everything. I thought he was going to get over it, but no … The other day, we had a telephone interview with the psychologist and she

told me not to let it go and that, although all the children have had problems because they have not experienced everything that a child (is supposed to) at that age, she says that we have to work on it. And the days go by and it's the same, I have tried everything. It must be this confinement, who knows, the lack of contact with other children as well (Carla, Mendoza, February 2021).

Although we could say that many interviewees and their families had experienced a smooth adaptation to (and even benefited from) the changes in routines triggered by the new restrictions, others – particularly those women from the wealthiest households – reported being faced with scenarios of chaos, anguish and saturation. Indeed, after the first two weeks of lockdown, many activities that could be done remotely had been adapted to the new scenario and had to coexist in the same place: suddenly homes were transformed into being simultaneously work, educational, recreational and family spaces. Work demands did not decrease (sometimes the opposite happened); the adaptability of the schools to support children and caregivers in an effective way was deficient, and grandparents, aunts and babysitters who did not live with the family were erased from the care map, as were domestic workers for household chores. In this context, participants saw themselves forced to assume the roles of teachers, cooks, cleaners, advocates for their children's education and psychologists or psychopedagogues, in parallel with their paid and previous unpaid care work. Following is the testimony of Julia who vividly describes this 'collapsed' reality:

The four of us started to have a bad time, but I think that ... I was the one who started having the worst. I would say that I did not have a good time. Especially because I love going out, going to work. And I stopped doing it. Then I spent 24 hours with the kids who, obviously, were also affected by the confinement. I realized that I did not finish what I had to do for work. That I had to clean, that I had to cook food, that I had to help them with their homework ... It took me four hours to answer an email. [I said] 'No, stop. This can't be!'. Well that lasted a month or so, which was like a silent war with my husband. I hated him deeply. I was really angry ... He is a super partner. I really love him a lot but [at that time] I hated him (Julia, Buenos Aires, September 2020).

This quote shows how this participant assumed by 'default' all the care work that was left vacant in the house and illustrates how the emotional relationship with labour participation is different for professional women compared to those in lower socio-economic groups. Professional women tend to feel empowered and satisfied with their paid jobs, and thus, when they perceive that these spaces of their 'own' are being threatened by elements of the private sphere, the instrumental dimension of family life becomes overwhelming for them. On the other hand, those forced to work in lower-category jobs due to the need for family subsistence, felt liberated when they were able to continue without those jobs, once financial support guaranteed a means of subsistence.

The intensification and the weakening of social interactions

Mandatory stay-at-home policies have abruptly forced participants to rely on their household members for their sense of overall social interactions, closeness and belonging. In this context, participants' experiences around social interactions were inscribed in a contradictory panorama. On the one hand, in light of the stressful and erratic nature of the pandemic and its worsening of the pre-existing social and economic crisis in Argentina, family units offered more instances for social connections and greater social support, both of which are associated with well-being (Reis et al. 2004). On the other hand, forced coexistence with family members, 24 hours a day 7 days a week, led to greater tension, conflict and a sense of invasion of personal space. This scenario, combined with psychological and economic stressors characteristic of the pandemic as well as potential increases in negative coping mechanisms, resulted in situations of family violence.[10]

Aldana, is a domestic worker and a single mother of a 15-year-old son. With regard to the increased closeness with family members, she shared the following reflexion:

> During the pandemic ... my son and I [started to] take care of each other, but previously it was [only] me taking care of him all the time. He used to mind his own business. We saw each other very little ... We didn't talk so much; we weren't so close. It was like: 'Ok, you ate, now go to school, here are your clothes'. Perhaps [our dialogue] was very infrequent ... And with the pandemic the care started to be mutual. We were together, he helped me with house chores ... Before, during the day, he would never send me a message. Now he sends me messages in the middle of the day (asking): 'Ma, how are you?' He is thinking of me. And when he arrived home, he hugged me. Before, he didn't. He asks me how my

> day was … There was a change for the better (Aldana, Buenos Aires, November 2020).

Likewise, Marisa, a paralegal lawyer who lives with her husband (an accountant) and their teenage son said:

> We even got to watch TV shows together with my husband, we took the dogs for a walk together, sometimes we cooked dinner together. We have started to do that now (Marisa, Mendoza, November 2020).

Both testimonies show the birth of new types of social interactions between women and their family members, which generated positive emotions and social connectedness, deepening and strengthening bonds of mutual care. Similar to discussion in the previous section of this chapter, many participants expressed gratitude for this kind of family re-bonding and were comforted by the possibility offered by the pandemic to 'understand' and 'learn' about the rhythms, qualities and internal worlds of their family members. Yet, while most of the evidence supports the well-being generated by the intensification of social connection within households, many participants shared the challenges associated with having their families compelled to spend all day together in close quarters, and how this affected many of their interactions and relationships. Carla describes the atmosphere in her home as follows:

> We felt a lot of tension. It seems to me that at the beginning there were more frictions, more moments of tension, and fights. It was like [everything was] exploding and then over time, when [the government] said that this was going to last for a long time, it's like we started to respect each other a little more and lower the level of violence that there was at one point (Carla, Mendoza, September 2020).

Likewise, the intensification of social interactions with family members led to the intensification of care. The following example comes from Ludmila, a married entrepreneur with a two-year-old daughter, who explains this mechanism as follows:

> The other day my friends got together at night and I arrived one hour and a half late because I couldn't put my daughter to sleep … I had to leave her crying and screaming with my husband, because

there came a time when it was impossible ... within the good of being together every day, dependency harmed me. What happens if I am not there or if I want to go out with my friends one night? Dependency, that, yes (Ludmila, Buenos Aires, October 2020).

Spending the whole day at home, without the help of third parties, led this and other participants to fulfil all (or most) care responsibilities. The result was that when it came to having a break from those responsibilities in order to get some leisure time, it was practically impossible because new care habits and dynamics had been generated, especially around babies and toddlers. We have seen how this type of situation usually led to the disruption of interactions with the rest of the family, triggering not only tensions but also feelings of resentment and being overwhelmed that threatened family bonds.

Overall, interviewees' living experiences allowed us to infer that the distribution of care work was closely linked to the levels of tension and friction experienced at home during ASPO. In this sense, we suggest that if the women had a positive *perception* of how care tasks were shared around the house, this contributed first to their general well-being and second to the well-being of family members and their social interactions. In the same way, a negative perception of the distribution of care fed the ill-being of women and consequently that of the members of the household, given that many of the interactions between them were brought about by exhaustion or resentment.

The rise and fall of leisure time: a room of one's own

Just as for some participants their care universe expanded or contracted due to COVID-19 measures, so did the time they dedicated to themselves. Professional women often had to give up a good deal in terms of the 'spaces' they'd previously inhabited for work or leisure. In lockdown, the type of activities they sought were mainly directed to help them 'switch off', (as opposed to more nurturing activities) to overcome the burnout of confinement:

[Going for a walk] is the only space that I have tried as much as possible not to lose. [It doesn't happen] as often as I would like to but you have to keep the axis somewhere because otherwise we would end up killing each other. We tried to [respect] something that was untouchable. In my case I chose that, to go out for a walk every day to clear up a bit (Marisa, Mendoza, October 2020).

On the other hand, although free time was partly devoted to typical leisure activities such as exercising, gardening or watching TV, it also had a strong productive component among lower-income women. No longer able to go to work, they found themselves swimming in uncharted waters – most could not remember ever having so much time for themselves. This was the case for Vanina and Miriam, domestic workers in the AMBA district:

> One of the things that I started to do, is a hairdressing course ... There I feel that ... frees my mind! And I do it with so much desire. It makes me happy ... Another good thing that happened to me this month is that I signed up to finish high school. [These things] are necessary and you need them more when you don't want to get stuck, and you want to move on, and you know you need to be educated (Vanina, Buenos Aires, October 2020).

> If I had [the space] I would do more things. I would like to do gardening courses. I would like to learn something, take courses. I'm doing Zoom. I like that. I did a choir workshop. Now I'm doing the second module of 'Approaching the Work World'. It is good, very good. You learn your rights regarding everything related to work (Miriam, Buenos Aires, October 2020).

These quotes show how, given the luxury of time, participants began to invest in themselves. In fact, circumstances triggered existential reflections among these women about the amount of time that their work demanded, as well as the type of work they did. Many shared their intention to either change their work field entirely (investing in training), find jobs closer to their homes, or renegotiate the duration of their working hours, given the time spent in commuting (for some, up to six hours a day, depending on traffic and bus availability).

Discussion and concluding reflections

Following our theoretical framework, we used time spent on paid and unpaid work, social interactions and leisure time as indicators of the changes in the self-perception of well-being in the women interviewed. We have found that each of these indicators reveals light and shade in about equal proportions. While in some cases the instrumental tasks of care have multiplied, leading to high stress levels for many women, emotional care has served as a space for reunion between women and their partners and/or children. Likewise, leisure time was mostly enjoyed by women from lower-income families, exempted from working for months, decided to dedicate that time to training in search of new work horizons. Conversely, now having to absorb all the care work that they used to outsource, women from middle and upper income brackets saw their free time highly decimated. In this sense, the highly feminized care trajectories that preceded the sanitary crisis triggered by the COVID-19 pandemic were either maintained or exacerbated, as in all cases women assumed 'by default' most of the care work that was left vacant by third parties. This exposes the deeply gendered nature of this new tacit 'arrangement', despite the urgent need to redistribute care work posed by a crisis of this magnitude.

In reference to the emotional aspects of care, we observed possibilities of reconnection and bonding between family members, and within individuals themselves, which led to rethinking interpersonal relationships and personal/professional projects in the post-pandemic future. However, isolation measures intensified participants' social interactions in both negative and positive ways, ultimately revealing the importance of women's *perception* of the care distribution within the home in defining the nature of some interactions. Women's perceptions of balance around care in its instrumental, emotional, temporal and relational dimensions, constitute a necessity for a minimum quality of life. All these alterations in participants' well-being have led towards profound existential reflection concerning their affections, their roles inside the home and their professional life. This may have happened to such an extent that, in at least one of these fields, the pandemic may have established a breaking point, from which in the short term there seems to be no return. On the other hand, the amount and nature of pandemic regulations brought constraints for families wanting to plan their daily activities. The constraints added an extra burden to women and their families, with the necessity to deploy all kinds of strategies to preserve the well-being of their family members.

One of this chapter's chief purposes was to contribute to making visible women's experiences of the pandemic, their defeats, efforts, struggles and conquests. The other purpose was to offer alternatives to the conventional understanding of gendered time-use dynamics during the pandemic. The inquiry into social interactions with family members and individuals outside the home, throughout the confinement months, enabled us to obtain a more nuanced depiction of participants' perception of their well-being. Illuminating the significance of these factors helps to contextualize the interaction between paid and unpaid labour, inside and outside of the family.

Lessons drawn from this study can assist us in initiating talks regarding the significance of leisure and social interactions in pursuit of well-being, more generally. Consequently, it is necessary to consider new possibilities for a more egalitarian use of time in the four categories outlined earlier in this chapter (necessary, contracted, committed and free time), not only in the larger community but also between men and women.

Notes

1. We want to give special thanks to our team of research assistants who worked *ad honorem* and with a great sense of commitment – without them this study would not have been possible: Melina Perez, Itatí Moreno, Ana Vinitsky, Lucio Marinsalda, Guadalupe Macedo, Sofía Benzaquen, Victoria Bestard Pino, Antonieta Priore, Paula Blodinger and Eugenia Peiretti.
2. This and other abbreviations or acronyms in the chapter are those used in Spanish.
3. The extended original name of the measure known as ASPO is Aislamiento Social Preventivo y Obligatorio (see Ciudad de Buenos Aires 2020).
4. Female labour participation in the country declined 45% according to an ECLAC (CEPAL) report (CEPAL 2021).
5. During 2020 arrests for the infringement of the ASPO directive was the second cause of arrest after the infringement of private property (National Penitentiary Office, November 2020). Fines range from AR$10,000 to AR$1,000,000 (from US$55 to US$5,000, approximately), and if the offender was a civil servant the penalty entailed the loss of their position.
6. The IFE Subsidy consisted of four payments of AR$10,000 (c. US$156) for informal workers, single tax payers for the lowest categories and beneficiaries of other social assistance programmes.
7. The APA Dictionary of Psychology definition of 'Social interactions', https://dictionary.apa.org/social-interactions (accessed 23 May 2022).
8. Access to participants was gained through contact with the Human Resources Department of the Hospital Italiano of the City of Buenos Aires and with school principals and unions of the Greater Mendoza area. In the case of most of the lower-income participants, contact was facilitated by the Union of Auxiliary Personnel of Particular Households (UPACP) and its Training School for Domestic Service Personnel. We obtained ethical approval for the study from the Institutional Review Board of New York University (IRB-FY2020-4390) and institutional support from Universidad Nacional de Cuyo (Argentina) and New York University (USA).
9. This is consistent with studies that have shown that although the negative psychological impact of the COVID-19 pandemic is readily apparent, some people did surprisingly well (Recchi et al. 2020; Okabe-Miyamoto et al. 2020).
10. The pandemic brought an unprecedented wave of family violence. According to the UN, reports of gender-based violence increased by 39 per cent in Argentina during the first part of the quarantine (Naciones Unidas, 2020).

References

Ahuvia, A. (2001) 'Traditional, interpretive, and reception based content analyses: Improving the ability of content analysis to address issues of pragmatic and theoretical concern'. *Social Indicators Research*, 54 (2), 139–72.

Baratta, M. V. (2021) *No esenciales: La infancia sacrificada*. Buenos Aires: Libros del Zorzal.

Bauman, A., Bittman, M. and Gershuny, J. (2019) 'A short history of time use research; implications for public health'. *BMC Public Health*, 19 (Supplement 2), 607. https://doi.org/10.1186/s12889-019-6760-y.

Carrasco, C. (2003) 'La sostenibilidad de la vida humana: ¿Un asunto de mujeres?'. In Magdalena, L. T. (ed.) *Mujeres y trabajo: Cambios impostergables*. Porto Alegre: Veraz Comunicação, 4–25. http://bibliotecavirtual.clacso.org.ar/clacso/gt/20101012020556/2carrasco.pdf.

CEPAL (2021) 'La autonomía económica de las mujeres en la recuperación sostenible y con igualdad'. https://repositorio.cepal.org/bitstream/handle/11362/46633/5/S2000740_es.pdf (accessed 9 February 2023).

CIPPEC (2020) *Impacto social del COVID-19 en Argentina: Balance del primer semestre de 2020*. Buenos Aires: Programa de Protección Social.

Ciudad de Buenos Aires (2020) 'Aislamiento social preventivo y obligatorio: Decreto 297/2020 Disposiciones'. [Preventive and mandatory social isolation. Decree297/2020 Provisions]. *Boletín Oficial de la República Argentina*,19 March 2020. https://www.boletinoficial.gob.ar/detalleAviso/primera/227042/20200320 (accessed 1 June 2021).

Diener, E. (2009) 'Subjective well-being'. In Diener, E. (ed.) *The Science of Well-Being: The collected words of Ed Diener*. Berlin: Springer Science, 11–58. https://doi.org/10.1007/978-90-481-2350-6_2.

Drisko, J. and Maschi, T. (2015) 'Interpretive content analysis'. In Drisko, J. and Maschi, T. (eds) *Content Analysis*. New York: Oxford University Press, 57–80.

Esquivel, V. (2009) 'Uso del tiempo en la Ciudad de Buenos Aires'. In *Seminario virtual de especialización en género, economía y desarrollo en el contexto de la crisis*. Buenos Aires: Universidad Nacional de General Sarmiento, 70.

Faur, E. (2014) *El cuidado infantil en el Siglo XXI: Mujeres malabaristas en una sociedad desigual*. Buenos Aires: Siglo Veintiuno editores.

Gilligan, C. (1977) 'In a different voice: Women's conceptions of self and of morality'. *Harvard Educational Review*, 47 (4), 481–517.

Giurge, L. M., Yemiscigil, A., Sherlock, J. and Whillans, A. V. (2020) *Uncovering Inequalities in Time-Use and Well-Being During COVID-19: A multi-country investigation*. Boston, MA: Harvard Business School.

Goicoechea, M. (2020) 'La (in)movilidad urbana como capacidad de respuesta desigual frente a la pandemia: Una mirada a escala metropolitana'. In Goren, N. and Ferrón, G. R. (eds) *Desigualdades en el marco de la pandemia: Reflexiones y desafíos*. Buenos Aires: Universidad Nacional de José C. Paz, 75–80. https://www.clacso.org/wp-content/uploads/2020/07/COVID-IESCODE-UNPAZ.pdf (accessed 9 February 2023).

Held, V. (2005) *The Ethics of Care: Personal, political, and global*. New York: Oxford University Press.

Henderson, K. A. and Allen, K. R. (1991) 'The ethic of care: Leisure possibilities and constraints for women'. *Loisir et societe/Society and Leisure*, 14 (1), 97–113.

Jun, J. (2020) 'Balance in time use and life satisfaction of older people in Korea'. *Journal of Time Use Research*, 15 (1). https://doi.org/10.32797/jtur-2020-3.

Krippendorff, K. (2018) *Content Analysis: An introduction to its methodology*. Thousand Oaks, CA: Sage.

López Mourelo, E. (2020) 'La COVID-19 y el trabajo doméstico en Argentina'. Organización Internacional del Trabajo (OIT). https://www.ilo.org/wcmsp5/groups/public/---americas/---ro-lima/---ilo-buenos_aires/documents/publication/wcms_742115.pdf (accessed 23 January 2023).

Mannell, R. C. (2007) 'Leisure, health and well-being'. *World Leisure Journal*, 49 (3), 114–28.

Marzonetto, G., Rodríguez Enríquez, C. and Alonso, V. (2021) *La intersección entre las desigualdades económicas y de género en América Latina*. Buenos Aires: Consejo Latinoamericano de Ciencias Sociales. https://www.clacso.org/wp-content/uploads/2021/03/V4-Conv01-Marzonetto-La-interseccion.pdf (accessed 25 January 2023).

Naciones Unidas (UN) (2020) 'La ONU y Argentina luchan con la otra pandemia del coronavirus, la violencia de género'. *Noticias ONU*, April 2020. https://news.un.org/es/story/2020/04/1473082 (accessed 26 January 2023).

National Directorate for Economy, Equality and Gender (DNEIyG) and United Nations Children's Fund (UNICEF) (2021) 'The impact of the pandemic on households with children and adolescents led by women'. Buenos Aires: DNEIyG/UNICEF. https://www.unicef.org/argentina/media/11301/file/The-impact-of-pandemic-households-with-children-and-adolescents-led-women.pdf (accessed 9 February 2023).

Okabe-Miyamoto, K., Folk, D., Lyubomirsky, S. and Dunn, E. W. (2021) 'Changes in social connection during COVID-19 social distancing: It's not (household) size that matters, it's who you're with'. *PloS ONE*, 16 (1), e0245009. https://doi.org/10.1371/journal.pone.0245009.

Peterman, A., Potts, A., O'Donnell, M., Thompson, K., Shah, N., Oertelt-Prigione, S. and Van Gelder, N. (2020) 'Pandemics and violence against women and children'. *CGD Working Paper 528*. Washington, DC: Center for Global Development.

Recchi, E., Ferragina, E., Helmeid, E., Pauly, S., Safi, M., Sauger, N. and Schradie, J. (2020) 'The "eye of the hurricane" paradox: An unexpected and unequal rise of well-being during the COVID-19 lockdown in France'. *Research in Social Stratification and Mobility*, 68, 100508. https://doi.org/10.1016/j.rssm.2020.100508.

Reis, H. T., Clark, M. S. and Holmes, J. G. (2004) 'Perceived partner responsiveness as an organizing construct in the study of intimacy and closeness'. In Mashek, D. J. and Aron, P. (eds) *Handbook of Closeness and Intimacy*. Mahwah, NJ: Lawrence Erlbaum, 201–25.

Rodríguez Enríquez, C. and Pautassi, L. (2014) *La organización social del cuidado de niños y niñas*. Buenos Aires: Centro Interdisciplinario para el Estudio de Políticas Públicas (CIEPP).

Stiglitz, J. E., Sen, A. and Fitoussi, J. P. (2009) *Report by the Commission on the Measurement of Economic Performance and Social Progress*. Brussels: European Commission. https://ec.europa.eu/eurostat/documents/8131721/8131772/Stiglitz-Sen-Fitoussi-Commission-report.pdf (accessed 9 February 2023).

Tronto, J. C. (1987) 'Más allá de la diferencia de género: Hacia una teoría del cuidado'. *Journal of Women in Culture and Society*, 12, 1–17.

UCA (2021) 'Efectos de la pandemia COVID-19 sobre la dinámica del bienestar en la Argentina urbana: Una mirada multidimensional acerca del impacto heterogéneo de la crisis tras una década de estancamiento económico (2010–2020)'. Documento Estadístico– Barómetro de la Deuda Social Argentina – 1ª ed. Buenos Aires: Educa.

UN Women. (2020) 'COVID-19 in Latin America and the Caribbean: How to incorporate women and gender equality in the management of the crisis response'. Panamá: UN Women. https://bit.ly/3jzu8C7 (accessed 25 October 2021).

UN Women and CEPAL (2020) 'Care in Latin America and the Caribbean during the COVID-19: Towards comprehensive systems to strengthen response and recovery'. Santiago, Chile: Coediciones CEPAL/NU. https://repositorio.cepal.org//handle/11362/45917 (accessed 25 October 2021).

UNICEF Argentina (2020) 'Encuesta de percepción y actitudes de la población: Impacto de la pandemia COVID-19 y las medidas adoptadas por el gobierno sobre la vida cotidiana'. Buenos Aires: Fondo de Las Naciones Unidas Para La Infancia (UNICEF). https://www.unicef.org/argentina/media/8056/file/Covid19-EncuestaRapida-InformeEducacion.pdf (accessed 9 February 2023).

Vega-Rapun, M., Domínguez-Serrano, M. and Gálvez-Muñoz, L. (2020) 'The multidimensionality of poverty: Time poverty in Spain'. *Journal of Time Use Research*, 15 (1). https://doi.org/10.32797/jtur-2020-2.

Zhou, M., Hertog, E., Kolpashnikova, K. and Kan, M. Y. (2020) 'Gender inequalities: Changes in income, time use and well-being before and during the UK COVID-19 lockdown'. *SocArXiv Papers*. https://doi.org/10.31235/osf.io/u8ytc.

3
Chile: pandemic, neoliberal precarity and social outbreak

Ana Vergara del Solar, Mauricio Sepúlveda,
Juan Pablo Pinilla, Daniela Leyton,
Cristián Ortega and Claudia Calquín

Introduction

This chapter reports the findings of an investigation carried out in Chile between 2020 and 2021, within the framework of the transnational study previously described in this book. The research was conducted by an interdisciplinary team consisting of anthropologists, sociologists and psychologists from six universities (Universidad Arturo Prat, Universidad de Valparaíso, Universidad de Santiago, Universidad Diego Portales, Universidad Tecnológica Metropolitana and Universidad de Concepción). [1,2]

The project aims at understanding the changes and challenges in the daily life of families, and the meanings and imaginaries that people ascribe to them. Likewise, it involves comparisons between the four regions in the study (Tarapacá, Valparaíso, the Metropolitan Region and Biobío), between families from different socio-economic groups (hereafter, SEGs) and of different composition, as well as between family members of different gender and age. In order to approach the subject matter in greater depth, in this chapter we concentrate on the families' shared experiences. At the same time, and following the general design of the book, we refer to how family members responded to the social and health measures derived from the pandemic, and the impact that the pandemic and such measures had on their daily lives.

In Latin America, the COVID-19 pandemic disrupted labour, domestic and care dynamics, especially affecting lower-income groups, informal workers, children and women (CEPAL/ECLAC 2020), thus laying bare the vulnerability and socio-economic inequalities that characterize our region. In the case of Chile, the precarity of life was already a matter of intense public debate, ever since the so-called 'social outbreak' that began on 18 October 2019, a few months before the pandemic's arrival in the country. On that day, high school students had jumped the subway turnstiles without paying, in protest against a fare hike, and this led to the spread of massive street protests against Chile's neoliberal development model – the earliest and most consistent and systematic application of the model worldwide (Harvey 2005; Taylor 2006). Given this context, a major interest of this study is to understand how the pandemic, social outbreak, and the precarity resulting from neoliberalization came to interlock in Chile. This is a cross-sectional analysis, carried out on a time scale that was short or conjunctural, to use Braudel's (1970) expression, since a deeper understanding of the structural phenomena involved, as well as of their transformations and links, would require the consideration of longer historical time periods.

In this chapter, we first briefly describe the national context in which the pandemic occurred, and then give an account of some theoretical coordinates that guided us in the production and interpretation of our findings. We then describe the methodological design of the study, and end with our main results and conclusions. As we observed, precarity sustained over time and social outbreak contributed to people's intense distrust in the action of the authorities during the pandemic and sense that they needed to take charge of their own economic and health protection and support. Although there are incipient processes of change in social subjectivity, the processes through which social and political problems such as the pandemic are understood by governments and people as collective, and confronted through strategies that go beyond individual and family responsibility for well-being, are still weak.

The context of Chile

The intensity with which the pandemic has affected Chile and its resulting economic crisis are directly linked to an economic model driven by the unrestricted accumulation of capital, and a state reluctant to intervene in the regulation of the market, including the labour market, and circumscribed in its role of providing welfare and ensuring social rights. In this regard, it should be remembered that neoliberal policies in Chile go back to the 1970s, and were initiated by a civil–military dictatorship

(1973–90) that also involved brutal repression and severe restriction of social participation. In 1980, when General Pinochet imposed a constitution without democratic participation, both the neoliberal model and a notion of a protected democracy were institutionalized, the latter with the aim of ensuring the permanence of the model when the dictatorship came to an end.

Post-dictatorial democratic governments have contributed to the consolidation of the neoliberal model. Although they have increased social spending and reduced absolute poverty, inequality has increased, with Chile now among the most unequal countries in the world (World Bank Group 2016). At the same time, incomes are very low, with a median monthly wage of 420,000 Chilean pesos (US$533) and with 69.4 per cent of workers earning less than 635,000 (US$806), while the income poverty line is 459,534 Chilean pesos (US$583) for an average household of four people (Fundación Sol 2021). To compensate for these low wages, 70 per cent of households have recourse to credit, with the total household debt at 50 per cent of GDP (Fundación Sol 2021). Although lower socio-economic groups experience more extreme living conditions, most of the population is exposed to low wages, precarious jobs and a condition in which access to health, education, social security and other social rights has been commoditized and depends on families' purchasing power. In this context, the social outbreak in opposition to this socio-economic model and the constitution perpetuating it took place against a background of massive social mobilizations, a sustained crisis of trust in the institutions and the political system, and a marked loss of government popularity. Even so, the intensity and duration of the protests was a surprise to all concerned.

So, in March 2020, when the first cases of COVID-19 became known, the country was already in the midst of an acute political crisis (see Figure 3.1 for a timeline of COVID-19 in Chile). With the implementation of lockdowns and measures of social isolation due to the pandemic, this intensity slackened and protests became more infrequent. Moreover, attention was now directed at the promise of a new constitution, made possible by a political agreement reached in November 2019, which involved the holding of a referendum in October 2020 and the formation of a Constitutional Convention in July 2021 that would be responsible for drafting the new constitution.

In epidemiological terms, the contagion and mortality figures of the pandemic in Chile were comparatively high during 2020 and much of 2021. For example, daily average infections on 10 June 2020 were at 6,754, placing Chile fifth in the world with the highest net figures, only

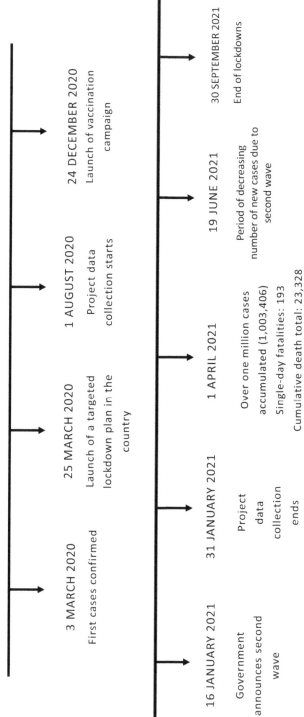

Figure 3.1 Timeline of COVID-19 in Chile. Source: authors.

surpassed in Latin America by Brazil (Worldometers data for 2020, Worldometers.info). This occurred within the framework of health, political and economic measures which, although formally part of a plan of action, in practice lacked sufficient coordination, showed little sensitivity to particular territorial and social realities, and were highly centralized, with little participation of regional authorities and civil society. In addition, there was a tendency to hold individuals responsible for becoming infected and allow the economic activities of large companies to continue, on the assumption that a number of lives would have to be 'sacrificed' in order to do so, especially those of poorer sectors. In this scenario, general mortality rose by 13 per cent compared to 2016–19, while the mortality rate observed due to COVID-19 was 114.2 per 100,000 inhabitants, thus becoming the first cause of death in the country in 2020 (DEIS 2021). The most extensively applied socio-sanitary measures have been those related to social distancing, a night-time curfew and the closure of educational establishments. At the same time, as part of a massive immunization drive, 87.03 per cent of the target population had been vaccinated by September 2021 (MINSAL 2021). Other measures, such as lockdowns and reductions of the allowed capacity in different types of establishments, have obeyed a selective logic that classifies phases of severity and type of measures according to the contagion figures of the country's different municipalities.

The vaccination process started in February 2021, and infections began to drop the following August. As of 9 September 2021, the cumulative incidence rate (per 100,000) of infections was 8,596 and that of deceased persons was 194, figures not so unlike those of Brazil, the country with the highest net number of cases in Latin America, with a rate of 9,813 and 274 respectively. The difference can be seen in the rate of new daily infections, which was 2.6 in Chile, compared to 14.4 in Brazil (Worldometers data for 2021, Worldometers.info).

As in other Latin American countries, the pandemic has deepened the economic difficulties of families, with effects on both income and employment. According to a United Nations study (UNDP 2020), the income of 59.4 per cent of Chilean households fell compared to the previous period, and unemployment reached 30 per cent of those who were employed. In mitigation, the government resorted to various economic measures, including direct cash transfers, monetary support and facilities for payment of basic services such as water and electricity, as well as access to an unemployment insurance that was originally not provided for this purpose. All such measures were insufficient. Against this background, the Chilean Congress approved the withdrawal of pension funds by individuals on three occasions, which only deepened the crisis of a highly privatized, ineffective and discriminatory pension system.

The pandemic has also had an impact on education, in the context of a highly segregated educational system. The availability of online classes has varied according to families' socio-economic stratum (MINEDUC 2021). For the lower social strata, even with the availability of online classes, gaps in the quality of internet connectivity have been decisive in access (SUBTEL 2017). Other effects of the pandemic in the country concern food insecurity (RIMISP 2021), the postponement of vaccination and health treatment for conditions other than COVID-19, and the worsening of an already critical mental health situation (ACHS 2021). In addition, the marked gender imbalances in domestic and care tasks have worsened (Bravo et al. 2020), while the family burden of care has intensified, in a country in which these activities generally have a 'familistic'[3] nature (Esping-Andersen 1990) to the detriment of state action and policies.

At the same time, the effect of structural determinants is that the impact of diseases are unevenly distributed among sectors of the population. In Chile, as in other countries, the highest burden of infection and deaths is found in sectors concentrated in cities and with lower incomes. For example, a study conducted in 2020 found that COVID-19 morbidity and mortality rates were higher in areas where there was a greater presence of overcrowded households and those with monthly incomes in the first four deciles (Fuenzalida 2020).

Theoretical framework

According to our main argument, it is important to consider three interconnected concepts: neoliberalization, precarization, and everyday life. By neoliberalization, we mean specific historical processes aimed at implementing the neoliberal model in particular contexts. Such processes of neoliberalization do not necessarily have a linear relationship with neoliberal doctrine since they are impure, heterogeneous, contingent and pragmatic. This is the case of the numerous monopolies that exist in Chile and of recurrent restrictions of public liberties, which contradict neoliberal theory but maximize the concentration of capital (Harvey 2005; Vergara del Solar et al. 2021).

The neoliberalization process is not only economic and political in nature but also involves the production of forms of subjectivation. One of its effects is the assignment to individuals and families of responsibility for social problems and another is the precarity of living conditions; these effects shape both public and private discourses, as well as the experiences of subjects (Castel 1997; Laval and Dardot 2013). On this point, we raise the question of whether the pandemic, as a social problem, was interpreted by people from an individualistic stance (for example, by attributing responsibility for contagion to the behaviour of individuals), as might have been expected in Chile prior to the social outbreak, or if the latter could have opened the door to greater politicization of the crisis, with less emphasis on individuals and more on the state and structural factors.

On the other hand, neoliberalization processes have made precarity an inexorable condition of our time (Rucovsky 2020). Thus, in neoliberalized contexts, precarity has ceased to be an exceptional circumstance and has become the norm, something to be found at the centre of political rationality (Rose 2012) and of the political regime (Bourdieu 2000). Precarity refers not only to lack of job protection (unemployment and underemployment) but is also embodied in lived experiences of insecurity, uncertainty and lacking the minimum socio-economic conditions needed to guarantee survival (Díaz and Insúa 2019). Thus, it includes work but overflows work's boundaries, and obliges us to live permanently with the unpredictable and contingent (Lorey 2016), reaching into hitherto unsuspected areas: the affective, the sexual, the perceptual, the bodily (Tsianos and Papadopoulus 2006). At the same time, precarity must be understood as an organizing category that designates the political, economic, and legal effects of a generalized precarious condition (Lorey 2016). It is also an analytical category that allows a situated description of the structures of human experience (Mayor 2020), to be understood as geo-localized and micro-politically located power relationships in everyday life.

At the same time, the government strategy in Chile of holding individuals responsible for social problems is far from new and has left a powerful imprint on people. In 2012, for example, a study carried out by the United Nations Development Programme (UNDP 2012) observed, in the discourses of the participants, how interpretations of a structural nature, in an economic and political sense, were absent from their discussion of the problems afflicting them, such as low incomes or unemployment. This was in a context in which the idea was promoted that individual effort was the key to achieving better living conditions and obtaining social recognition.

As mentioned, the social outbreak, and the social mobilizations preceding it, opened the door for the politicization of a series of issues. We understand such politicization as shifting into the public domain matters that had been treated, to all appearances, as purely private (Fernández Christlieb 2004). This was the case with issues such as social inequalities and problems of access to education and health. However, it is still unclear how people interpreted the effects of the pandemic.

As for daily life, there was recurring comment in the global press about how the pandemic had disrupted the routines of individuals and families. In the social sciences, meanwhile, notions such as that of the 'biographical disruption' caused by the pandemic period were suggested (Moretti and Maturo 2021, based on a concept by Bury 1982). As much as our results show that people experienced the pandemic as a 'storm', as we will describe later, we cannot take those results literally. This is because thinking of daily life prior to the pandemic as static and self-evident is highly debatable, both in general and for Latin America in particular.

Far from seeing everyday life as a hidden reservoir of meanings, routines and rituals so naturalized as to be unnoticed by people, it seems important to us to emphasize its dynamic and conflictive character, and its ability to reveal broader social contradictions (Lefebvre 1972; De Certeau 2000). This is particularly valid for countries like Chile, where it is difficult to find a pre-pandemic life in which public and private stability, predictability and social security was the norm. It is also valid for settings plagued by class, gender, age and ethnic conflict, among other categories, for which everyday life is already a space of uncertainty that requires finding a guiding ethic in circumstances that are never entirely pre-established.

In Chile, in addition, the experience of unpredictability is frequent in low and medium-low SEGs (UNDP 2012). In those groups, everyday life is experienced as a constant odyssey for survival. Furthermore, although the evidence suggests that better resourced groups experience periods of greater biographical stability than the most disadvantaged, the threat of precarity and the destabilization of life opportunities is present at every moment and in every action (UNDP 1998). By this process, the social outbreak in Chile accentuated an existing scenario of economic instability and disruption of daily routines; it showed that 'biographical disruption' would not be exceptional in Chile, nor could a radical contrast be drawn between a previous harmonious and stable life and a present one disrupted by the pandemic crisis. It was therefore a question of relative differences, not of absolute phenomena.

Data collection and sample

As in the case of the other countries participating in the transnational study, a qualitative ethnographic approach that seeks to understand in depth the way of life of a specific social unit (Rodríguez Gómez et al. 1999) was used for the research in Chile. In particular, a 'micro-ethnography' was carried out. Micro-ethnography studies certain situations and social problems via a complex understanding of small, apparently mundane scenes of everyday life, thus addressing macrosocial problems through the microanalysis of natural activity (Spradley 1980; Streeck and Mehus 2005).

Data collection was undertaken through in-depth interviews conducted with individuals and families. At the beginning of the fieldwork, the first of three interviews was conducted with the contact person in the household (usually a woman). The second interview was at an intermediate stage, conducted with the household as a collective, including adults, older adults when present, children and young people. The third and final interview took place at the end of the fieldwork with the family member who had been most active in completing the multimodal diaries, usually a child, young person or an adult woman. Digital videoconference platforms were used for the interviews, allowing each dialogue to be recorded in audio and video and later transcribed.

Indeemo, a mobile application for micro-ethnography, was used as a complementary technique in the case of Chile. Indeemo's *multimodal diaries* were recorded by two members of each participating family: a child or young person between 12 and 17 years of age, and an adult. The application enabled participants to capture their daily life through the use of multimedia resources available on their mobile devices. The research team was also able to communicate and interact directly with participants through the same application.

As a second, complementary technique, a demographic and socio-economic profile of the household was compiled via a questionnaire, completed by an adult member of the family and designed to obtain information on the household's composition in addition its economic and employment situation.

The study sample consisted of 38 families from 4 regions of the country: there were 10 families from Tarapacá (Northern Chile, 26.3 per cent), 10 from Valparaíso (the region of Chile's most important port, 26.3 per cent of the sample), 10 from Biobío (Southern Chile, 26.3 per cent), and 8 from the Metropolitan Region, which includes Chile's capital, Santiago, 21.1 per cent). Nineteen of the families were bi-parental (50 per cent), nine were single-parent (24 per cent), and 10 were extended (26 per cent). Nineteen families belonged, in socio-economic terms and according to the AIM Index (AIM 2019), to a low income or extreme poverty group (37 per cent), 11 to a medium-low SEG, (29 per cent) and 13 to a medium SEG (34 per cent). Three (8 per cent) were immigrant families from Venezuela, Ecuador and Bolivia, and six (16 per cent) belonged to indigenous peoples (Aymara and Mapuche). All families had at least one child or young person between 12 and 17 years of age, and the adults ranged in age between 18 and 78.

The research procedures received ethical approval from the University of Santiago, Chile. Analysis of the information gathered followed a socio-hermeneutical process consisting of the following stages: 1) a detailed reading of the transcripts of interviews and of the multimedia material collected in Indeemo; 2) coding and classification according to the research objectives; 3) the construction of family stories; and 4) analysis and interpretation of discursive systems from which conjectures were made regarding different spheres of people's lives and, within them, the everyday life that is of particular interest in this chapter.

Main findings

How do participants understand and respond to social distancing measures?

The study participants generally accepted the pandemic's existence and the need for social and health measures such as social distancing, the use of face masks and the suspension of face-to-face classes, largely because they observed that these measures were very similar to those applied in other countries. Furthermore, in many cases non-mandatory recommendations were followed by people in the study, such as disinfecting products brought from abroad or changing clothes when returning home from the street.

These actions were part of a strategy of 'safeguarding', a withdrawal of individuals and families into themselves, in which the ethical sense of caring for self and others prevailed, together with the perception that the social environment and the authorities did not provide sufficient security against the dangers of the virus. Thus, compliance with the measures was not based on trust in the authorities but, precisely, because of distrust in them. People had, to quote an expression used by participants in our study, to 'care for themselves'. In a family belonging to the middle SEG, for example, a 36-year-old woman reports:

> My mother tells me: 'you know what? This question is in the end just Moraga's Law'.[4] She tells me. 'Here, whoever gets the virus, just gets it, and unfortunately …' she tells me: 'here you have to work and if I get the virus I'll die, I'll just die, that's all'.

This quote also refers to the problem of lockdowns. As in the case just mentioned, in many families we were told that some of their members had been obliged to go out for work reasons during the lockdown. This was the product of a complex decision based on an impossible choice – such choices are frequent in a context of precarity – between self-exposure to contagion, directly affecting life and health, or self-deprivation, affecting the care and basic needs of oneself and one's loved ones due to the absence of family income. In the case of a family belonging to the low SEG, a 39-year-old man told us:

> [If] the government was to tell you 'Right, stay at home, drink, eat all this' … then we could be in lockdown for years, that could make you want to be in lockdown. But if you have nothing, whether you like it or not, you have to go out. There are people living here who have few resources. There are some ladies who are single mothers, who live alone with their little girls, imagine for them not being able to go out during the week. If they don't go out, they don't eat. That is the harsh reality.

As demonstrated in this book and happened in other countries around the world (Burns et al. 2021), many people were forced to move around the city for work, take public transport, or be in crowded spaces. In Chile, those who went out did so because their activities were considered essential according to government regulations. However, evidence suggests that many companies falsified the required permits in order to be in this category and thus maintain their staffing (Gonzalez 2020). To these must be added those who had to engage in informal commercial activities, a recurrent survival strategy in Latin America (Matus and Montes 2020). As Chilean studies of pandemic mobility show, the displacement of people in cities declined only slightly (no more than 30 to 40 per cent) even at moments of the strictest lockdown, with differences according to the socio-economic profile of the urban areas concerned (ISCI 2021). Those in our study who could stay at home, especially in the middle SEG (socio-economic group), expressed gratitude for this possibility which others did not have, as if it were a privilege.

Urban mobility also responded to the need to provide care to relatives or acquaintances, or to participate in solidarity activities such as soup kitchens (in Spanish, 'ollas comunes'[5]), a strategy historically frequent in Chile in times of deep economic crisis. Regarding care, many families were rebuilt during the pandemic by bringing back a relative who had not previously lived at home, but in other cases where this was not possible frequent journeys were necessary. Thus, families, understood not only as those living together but as a larger unit of mutual support and care, participated in decisions and arrangements regarding these requirements. We note, however, that this phenomenon is not new in Chile or in Latin America, where literature shows that the provision of care and social welfare have a 'familistic' character (Esping-Andersen 1990), as mentioned previously.

Even while trying to comply with the socio-sanitary measures of the pandemic, the participants were very critical of how the policies were implemented. The informants perceived application of the measures to be untimely, lax, or insensitive to the specific needs of the population, and some distrusted what was suspected to be a eugenic or 'social cleansing' motive. In a family from the low SEG, for example, a 19-year-old woman stated:

> ... the people who die are the people they see as least useful, the elderly, sick people, people with diabetes, people with hypertension, people who are overweight; it suits them that people like my father do not die, because they contribute [in taxes], it is money ...

Others saw in the measures an intent to contain the process of political change that began with the social outbreak. For example, the relaxation of lockdowns a couple of months before the plebiscite that, in October 2020 approved the constitutional reform made several participants suspect that it was a way to hinder the vote, by increasing infections.

Distrust of government action was also expressed in scepticism about the official morbidity and mortality figures, which was reflected objectively in the reasons given why the first minister of health involved in the pandemic (Jaime Mañalich) had to resign. In this scenario, many of the participants tried to find more trustworthy information on the internet, in foreign media or in their contact circles, as a kind of *counter-knowledge* (Foucault 2008). In this regard, in a family from the low SEG, a 43-year-old woman reported the following:

> My daughter got into the [web] pages and she told me: 'Look mum, this doctor is Korean and she is saying that if the country does not take the measures, everyone will be infected' ... And she was more concerned that if this disease spreads there will be great difficulty, various risks, about how the president does not take the proper measures or how they cannot find out if we go to a page and see the international news [because it is dangerous to do so].

On other occasions, distrust was generalized towards relationships with people outside the family, towards 'people' in abstract terms. Thus, as also happened in the UK (Twamley et al., Chapter 10 in this book), a dichotomy began to be built between 'us', identified as responsible, prudent and ethical people, and the 'others', representatives of those who are irresponsible, reckless and unconcerned about the consequences of their actions. We can interpret this finding in terms of an ethic of biological citizenship or bio-citizenship, which tends to exclude those who do not promote or protect health-related values (Rose 2012). In another family from the low SEG, a 71-year-old woman claimed that:

> For me this pandemic has been very difficult, and the hardest thing for me is to know that there are people who are healthy and who do not comply with things and that has done us more harm. Because we, I, at least, who have been locked up for seven months, locked up, uh ... I say, 'why don't people stop to think?' And that's what hurts me most.

Impact on family life

As we mentioned, the pandemic appeared in the lives of individuals and families suddenly and unexpectedly in March 2020. It was a moment when many families had recently returned from summer vacations in January or February, in debt and having to pay a series of expenses that accumulate in March (school expenses, car licences, and others). Thus, a 37-year-old woman from the medium-low SGE said that the pandemic found them 'in the raw'. By this she referred especially to the lack of economic resources, but also to a politically and subjectively more general feeling of defencelessness and fragility.

In addition, the pandemic brought with it a series of changes related to confinement in small living spaces – the majority in Chile have between

41 and 60 square metres in which to live (MINDES 2017) – and the need to ensure care in exceptionally difficult circumstances. The study participants described these changes as an upheaval, a shipwreck, an experience of invasion and chaos in their daily lives. The first few months in particular were marked by anxiety, insomnia and irritability, among other experiences. In this first moment of disorganization of daily personal and family life, not only were individual and collective routines upended, but also the objective and subjective bases that had made it possible to experience a degree of stability in the home.

Adults who mainly stayed at home report experiencing a feeling of time being suspended, of bewilderment at an unfamiliar experience, combined with the fact of confinement to the home. This experience was less intense among those who continued to go out for work or for other reasons, although fear of contagion increased and brought with it another change to normal timescales, an awareness of their finitude, of the possibility of their own death or the death of those whom they might infect.

Whether they should or should not go out to work, for adults the relationship between past, present and future was transformed by uncertainty and the impossibility of planning beyond the immediate, especially for economic or labour matters. This experience of destabilization is narrated by the interviewees as a continuity with what was experienced since the social outbreak. In a medium SEG family, for example, a 42-year-old woman commented that:

> Economic insecurity is also part of that storm – am I going to have any money? What about material things? Am I going to be able to pay the bills? You see what I mean? And then things start to happen in relationships. You begin to fight. I mean, we'd just had the scare of the social outbreak, then something just as chaotic came along.

After those first months, the participants tended to re-direct their attention towards the present, in an effort to stop worrying about what had been lost or what might happen in the future. In the testimonies, there is a greater emphasis on focusing on what is controllable rather than on what is not, together with a prolongation of the present moment, later to be expressed as a revaluation of the domestic environment, daily life and close affections. There was transition from a present empty of meaning to one revitalized by new personal and family projects, such as developing a new work activity, family members getting to know each other better and learning to accept each other, watching the children grow, learning English or to use computer technologies, improving one's skills in the kitchen, fixing the house, and so on. In a family from the medium-low SEG, for example, a 32-year-old woman stated:

> We have to be careful and live from day to day, because if we collapse, we feel miserable, and we were a bit *depre* (depressed). We were anxious, with mood swings, because you still unconsciously hurt the one next to you and a chain is generated ... We talked about that and said 'we are going to live from day to day and we are going to see ourselves as well off and as happy as possible, not thinking that next year I will have no job', because you are bound to ask yourself that at some point ... we will all try to work in tune with one another.

Children and young people took part in this re-composition of projects, especially in the value they attached to new activities, the creation of spaces for the family to get together or the cultivation of new opportunities for personal learning. However, their experience seemed a little different from that of adults: affected not so much by the 'collapse' of previous personal projects as by a feeling of suffocation and nostalgia for lost activities and sociability. In particular, they missed sharing with their classmates at school, participating in sports or cultural activities, going out to play in the park or square, or visiting friends. In children and young people, 'lockdown' and 'boredom' are more related to confinement and social and spatial isolation than to a feeling of emptiness or loss of the sense of time.

Children and young people also valued experiences shared with the family, those that take place around cooking, playing games or watching movies together. These activities intensify in them a feeling of belonging and accompaniment by their family, as expressed, for example, by a 15-year-old boy from a family in the low SEG:

> [With the pandemic] I have appreciated the family environment more. Because of the pandemic, like many people have died. We didn't really appreciate our surroundings, I feel that due to the pandemic everything is appreciated more; family, friends, everything. But when there was no pandemic, like everything did not matter; then you didn't really appreciate what you had around you. But now that there is a pandemic, you are kind of more aware of what you have.

In this quote, a kind of 'second look' at family and friends, a revaluation of ties can be observed, in a similar way to the UK (Twamley et al.,

Chapter 10 in this book). As in the case of other participants, this is part of the intensification of the present, mentioned before, and of a vitality in the face of death and vulnerability. A feeling of gratitude is also expressed for their parents' efforts, as in this comment of a 14-year-old boy from a family in the medium-low SEG, whose mother had to go out to sell second-hand clothes in street markets to support them:

> I sometimes go [with her], but the times I go it's still complicated, because there you can see the effort that my mother makes for us, getting up early every day, ironing all day so that the clothes are right, because clothes that look good like that are sold.

However, the feeling of gratitude and the appreciation of life and of 'what you have' is not limited to children and young people. Some adults express it by comparing themselves to those facing more difficult situations. In the Latin American context, this has been described in relation to other very adverse situations, such as sustained political violence in Colombia (Serrano 2000) or child workers in Central America (Woodhead 1999).

In a similar vein, the new situation provided an opportunity, in several cases, to spend more 'family time' together. People in Chile have long expressed difficulties in doing so (UNDP 2012; Vergara et al. 2019), due to long work and school hours, lengthy travel between work and home, and the precarity of public and institutional support for families and care tasks.

In terms of productive work, the pandemic revealed, time and again, living conditions and overexploitation that had enormous costs. Those who worked as employees had to face fears of dismissal or direct threats in this regard, or experienced longer shifts or working hours. Two primary school teachers, for example, belonging to a family from the medium-low SEG, told us how their online workday had increased to about 12 hours a day, between teaching and preparing online classes, supporting students with technical or comprehension difficulties, participating in meetings and other tasks. Many people who had built up independent economic activities, moreover, had to suspend them, as we described before, and faced not only the economic consequences but also the disappointment of an aborted personal project whose scope went beyond simple commercial activity.

On the other hand, quarantines and school closures, and the ending of some face-to-face jobs blurred the boundaries between home, school and work and generated either frenetic activity (Moretti and Maturo 2021) or a work continuum that produced an experience of temporal and spatial saturation. As far as domestic and care work were concerned, men and older children participated more than previously, although adult women continue to shoulder most of the burden in this regard, as was observed in other countries (Passerino and Trupa 2020),

Regarding schoolwork, children and young people did not feel comfortable with online classes, when they were able to access them. Their perception was that they learned little and were unable to maintain close relationships with their teachers and classmates. As we observed previously, there were also problems with the quality of the internet connection available for families living in more impoverished places. In the case of a family from the low SEG, for example, the children had to travel daily on public transport to an aunt's house, so risking contagion, just to use the internet (although this also exemplified the wider involvement of families to which we referred earlier). At the same time, Chilean education has historically had a dual character – inclusive, while also exclusive – for the lowest socio-economic groups. Its exclusive character emerged with greater force in the pandemic, with the resolution of problems left to parents, the children themselves or their teachers, the latter already overloaded by online classes and helping to solve students' connectivity problems, as seen earlier.

Discussion and final reflections

After nearly 50 years of neoliberal policies in the country, the pandemic, with its measures and its effects, only intensified the profound precarity of people's lives. The social outbreak that occurred shortly before the pandemic arrived in Chile, was a novel phenomenon yet, at the same time, one rooted in historical precedent. It reactivated forms of collective organization that had been relatively dormant and, simultaneously, illuminated the structural relationships that exist between different spheres, such as those related to government, health, education, welfare, the social organization of care and the provision of free time.

Moreover, the collective and individual resources deployed in the pandemic were not unusual in Chile but were the product of historical and cultural repositories that are activated in very adverse situations such as dictatorship, economic crises, natural and environmental disasters, and the COVID-19 pandemic. However, the imprint that neoliberalization processes have left on the construction of subjectivities and on the cultural individualization of Chilean society is not to be disregarded.

Overall, we observe a complex scenario. Families and their members put into play various arrangements and strategies to deal with the difficulties created and enable their decisions regarding daily life, its organization and the various forms of work involved. This entailed a complex decision-making process, involving not only cognitive judgement but also acts of faith about building a life that was liveable for themselves, their family and their environment. As mentioned before, one of the hardest decisions was the dilemma posed by the need for subsistence on one hand and the demand for confinement on the other. These two forms of life-affirmation came into conflict, as a contradiction that must be managed at a personal and family level as part of a logic of sacrifice. This constellation of action, ethics and decision – and the personal and collective repositioning it involved – speaks to the capacity for action of children, youth and adults. It generated in people a feeling of pride about their moral commitment to family and 'getting by' together, which motivated gratitude and self-gratitude.

Emphasizing such agency of this kind does not imply an assumption that people were able to negotiate repositioning to solve any difficulty, neither are we minimizing such difficulties, many of which could have been reduced if public responses and planning had been more coherent. It only implies that, as we might have assumed, people did not remain static or passive in the face of events. Even in structural frameworks of great precarity, they have tried to lead their own lives and those of their families as far as possible.

However, we cannot think of agency as disconnected from structural aspects. To a large extent, the material and emotional survival of families in Chile has rested on this ability of people to mobilize their own resources, even to the extreme of exhaustion. At the same time, although with less force than we expected, some study participants agreed with the attribution of individual and family responsibility for the control and consequences of the pandemic that the government has upheld as a media strategy and which goes back to earlier governments and different social agents.

What lies ahead after the pandemic remains uncertain. Even as the trend of a decline in infections continues, the pandemic, as a complex social phenomenon, may not end so quickly. Its effect on employment, economic activity, the loss of academic learning, people's mental health and other effects, has long-term implications. The social outbreak that coincided with the start of the pandemic has enabled a new Constitution to be drafted, in which the state has greater responsibility for welfare provision and the assurance of social rights; this also weakens the conception of a protected democracy by opening more spaces for social participation. However, constitutional change can be relatively cosmetic, as has happened in countries like Colombia, if it is not accompanied by other, deeper and more extensive transformations. Such is not an easy task in a global economy in which Chile occupies a passive position as a supplier of raw materials and is subject to pressure from international credit agencies and free trade agreements. The capacity of Chile and its people to recover from the pandemic depends also on the opening of a new political-economic context for the country.

Notes

1 The study was funded by ANID (Agencia Nacional de Investigación y Desarrollo/National Research and Development Agency, grant number COVID0341) and the University of Santiago. We are grateful for their support.
2 The following researchers also participated in the study: Félix Aguirre, Angélica Barra, Ketty Cazorla, Fabiola Ibáñez, Germán Lagos, Carolina Peixoto, José Antonio Román and Jorge Iván Vergara.
3 For Esping-Andersen (1990), a familistic welfare regime is one in which family units are assumed and required to bear the primary responsibility for the welfare and care of their members.
4 Colloquial expression in Chile, which alludes to a situation of misfortune which does not necessarily affect everyone. In its full version, as a rhyming pun, the expression is: *Ley de Moraga, el que caga, caga* ['Moraga's law: the one who shits, shits']. In this case, to shit means to get the worst of the situation.
5 A form of popular organization where food is provided to the impoverished and unemployed through the delivery of homemade meals with the participation of neighbours, friends and families (Apablaza 2021).

References

ACHS (Asociación Chilena de Seguridad) [Chilean Security Association] (2021) 'Termómetro de la salud mental en Chile ACHS-UC, Tercera Ronda, mayo de 2021'. https://www.achs.cl/portal/centro-de-noticias/Documents/Termometro_SM_version3.pdf (accessed 4 September 2021).
AIM (Asociación de Investigadores de Mercado, Chile) [Association of Market Researchers, Chile] (2019) 'Actualización Clasificación GSE AIM y Manual de Aplicación Chile 2019'. https://aimchile.cl (accessed 10 December 2019).
Apablaza, M. (2021) '"Ollas Comunes" in Chile in times of the "new normal"'. https://ddrn.dk/6734/ (accessed 5 January 2022).
Bourdieu, P. (2000) *Contrafuegos: Reflexiones para servir a la resistencia contra la invasión neoliberal*. Barcelona: Editorial Anagrama.
Braudel, F. (1970) *La historia y las ciencias sociales*. Madrid: Alianza Editorial.
Bravo, D., Castillo, E. and Hughes, E. (2020) 'Estudio longitudinal Empleo-COVID19: Datos de empleo en tiempo real'. Santiago: Universidad Católica-Centro de Encuestas y Estudios Longitudinales. https://www.uc.cl/site/assets/files/15455/estudio-empleo-covid19-datos-de-empleo-en-tiempo-real-diciembre2021.pdf (accessed 5 September 2021).
Burns, N., Follis, L., Follis, K. and Morley, J. (2021) 'Moving targets, moving parts: The multiple mobilities of the COVID-19'. In Lupton, D. and Willis, K. (eds) *The COVID-19 Crisis: Social perspectives*. London: Routledge, 27–38.

Bury, M. (1982) 'Chronic illness as biographical disruption'. *Sociology of Health & Illness*, 4, 167–82.

Castel, R. (1997) *La metamorfosis de la cuestión social: Una crónica del asalariado*. Buenos Aires: Paidós.

CEPAL [ECLAC – Economic Commission for Latin America and the Caribbean] (2020) 'El desafío social en tiempos del COVID-19'. *Informe Especial COVID-19*, No. 3. https://repositorio.cepal.org/bitstream/handle/11362/45527/5/S2000325_es.pdf (accessed 17 September 2021).

De Certeau, M. (2000) *La invención de lo cotidiano. 1. Artes de hacer.* Mexico City: Ibero-American University.

DEIS [Department of Statistics and Health Information] (2021) *Estadísticas de defunciones por COVID-19*. Ministry of Health, Chile. https://informesdeis.minsal.cl/SASVisualAnalytics/?reportUri=%2Freports%2Freports%2F357a72ec-43b7-4ca9-89cb-33f4818d2ab3&sectionIndex=0&sso_guest=true&sas-welcome=false (accessed 21 September 2021).

Díaz, V. and Insúa, P. (2019) 'Discursos sobre la precariedad: Consecuencias en la identidad y en la obra del artista'. *Revista de la Asociación Española de Neuropsiquiatría*, 39, 111–32.

Esping-Andersen, G. (1990) *The Three Worlds of Welfare Capitalism*. Cambridge: Polity.

Fernández Christlieb, P. (2004) *El espíritu de la calle: Psicología política de la cultura cotidiana*. Mexico City: Anthropos.

Foucault, M. (2008) *Defender la sociedad*. Buenos Aires: Fondo de Cultura Económica.

Fuenzalida, M. (2020) 'COVID-19 y las desigualdades territoriales al interior de Áreas Metropolitanas de Valparaíso, Santiago y Concepción, Chile'. *Espiral, Revista de Geografías y Ciencias Sociales*, 2, 79–89.

Fundación Sol (2021) 'Los verdaderos sueldos de Chile-2021'. *Fundación Sol* (blog). https://www.fundacionsol.cl/blog/estudios-2/post/los-verdaderos-sueldos-de-chile-2021-6796 (accessed 13 September 2021).

Gonzalez, T. F. (2020) 'Empresas fuera de control: El factor "Permiso Único Colectivo" en la propagación de la pandemia'. *Diario Universidad de Chile*, 22 June 2020. https://radio.uchile.cl/2020/06/22/empresas-fuera-de-control-el-factor-permiso-unico-colectivo-en-la-propagacion-de-la-pandemia/ (accessed 9 February 2023).

Harvey, D. (2005) *A Brief History of Neoliberalism*. Oxford: Oxford University Press.

ISCI (Instituto Sistemas Complejos de Ingeniería, Chile) [Institute for Complex Engineering Systems, Chile] (2021) *Reportes de movilidad en tiempos de Covid, 2021*. https://isci.cl/covidcat/reportes/ (accessed 15 September 2021).

Laval, C. and Dardot, P. (2013) *La nueva razón del mundo: Ensayo sobre la sociedad neoliberal*. Barcelona: Gedisa.

Lefebvre, H. (1972) *Crítica de la vida cotidiana*. Mexico City: Siglo XXI.

Lorey, I. (2016) *Estado de inseguridad: Gobernar la precariedad*. Madrid: Ediciones Traficantes de Sueños.

Matus, C. and Montes, M. (2020) 'Comercio informal en Santiago: Pistas etnográficas para el reconocimiento de una práctica urbana'. *Planeo*, 83, 1–14. http://revistaplaneo.cl/wp-content/uploads/Arti%CC%81culo_Matus-y-Montes.pdf (accessed 17 September 2021).

MINDES (Ministerio de Desarrollo Social y Familia, Chile) [Ministry of Social Development and Family, Chile] (2017) *Casen 2017. Síntesis de Resultados: Vivienda y entorno*. Santiago: Ministerio de Desarrollo Social. http://observatorio.ministeriodesarrollosocial.gob.cl/encuesta-casen-2017/Resultados_vivienda_casen_2017.pdf (accessed 9 February 2023).

MINEDUC (Ministerio de Educación, Agencia de la Calidad de la Educación) [Ministry of Education, Chile] (2021) 'Diagnóstico Integral de Aprendizajes'. https://diagnosticointegral.agenciaeducacion.cl/ (accessed 17 September 2021).

MINSAL (Ministerio de Salud) [Ministry of Health, Chile] (2021) 'Más del 87% de la población objetivo ha completado su esquema de vacunación contra SARS-CoV-2'. *MINSAL*, 10 September 2021. https://www.minsal.cl/mas-del-87-de-la-poblacion-objetivo-ha-completado-su-esquema-de-vacunacion-contra-sars-cov-2/ (accessed 20 September 2021).

Moretti, V. and Maturo, A. (2021) '"Unhome" sweet home: The construction of new normalities in Italy, during COVID-19'. In Lupton, D. and Willis, K. (eds) *The COVID-19 Crisis: Social perspectives*. London: Routledge, 90–102.

Passerino, L. and Trupa, N. (2020) 'Experiencias de cuidados y trabajo: Preocupaciones, malestares y emociones en contexto de pandemia de Covid-19 en Argentina'. *Revista Feminismos*, 8, 134–48.

RIMISP (Centro Latinoamericano para el Desarrollo Rural) [Latin American Centre for Rural Development] (2021) 'Pandemia y alimentación en los hogares de Chile: Resultados de la Encuesta de Seguridad Alimentaria y Alimentación'. https://www.rimisp.org/wp-content/uploads/2021/06/6-Chile.pdf (accessed 21 September 2021).

Rodríguez Gómez, G., Gil, J. and García, E. (1999) *Metodología de la investigación cualitativa* (2nd ed.). Malaga: Aljibe.

Rose, N. (2012) *Políticas de la Vida: Biomedicina, poder y subjetividad en el siglo XXI*. La Plata: Editorial Universitaria.

Rucovsky, M. De Moura (2020) '¿Cómo hacer sentido en la precariedad? *Bíos*-precario e vida sensible'. *Revista Bakhtiniana*, 15 (3). https://doi.org/10.1590/2176-457344046.

Serrano, J. (2000) 'Menos querer más de la vida: Concepciones de vida y muerte en jóvenes urbanos'. *Nómadas*, 13, 10–28.

Spradley, J. P. (1980) *Participant Observation*. New York: Holt, Rinehart & Winston.

Streeck, J. and Siri, M. (2005) 'Microethnography: The study of practices'. In Fitch, K. and Sanders, R. (eds) *Handbook of Language and Social Interaction*. London: Lawrence Erlbaum Associates, 381–404.

SUBTEL (Subsecretaría de Telecomunicaciones, Chile) [Undersecretary of Telecommunications, Chile] (2017) *IX Encuesta de acceso y usos de Internet*. https://www.subtel.gob.cl/wp-content/uploads/2018/07/Informe_Final_IX_Encuesta_Acceso_y_Usos_Internet_2017.pdf (accessed 23 September 2021).

Taylor, M. (2006) *From Pinochet to the 'Third Way': Neoliberalism and transformation in Chile*. London: Pluto Press.

Tsianos, V. and Papadopulus, D. (2006) 'Precariedad: Un viaje salvaje al corazón del capitalismo corporeizado'. *Transversal Texts*. https://transversal.at/transversal/1106/tsianos-papadopoulos/es (accessed 10 September 2021).

UNDP (United Nations Development Programme) (1998) *Desarrollo Humano en Chile: Las paradojas de la modernización*. Santiago: UNDP.

UNDP (United Nations Development Programme) (2012) *Desarrollo Humano en Chile: El desafío de repensar el desarrollo*. Santiago: UNDP.

UNDP (United Nations Development Programme) (2020) *Impactos Socioeconómicos de la Pandemia en los Hogares de Chile: Resultados de la Encuesta Social COVID-19*. https://www.estudiospnud.cl/wp-content/uploads/2020/11/202001110_pnud_covid-1.pdf (accessed 17 September 2021).

Vergara, A., Sepúlveda, M. and Salvo, I. (2019) 'Being a parent and being a child in Chile today: The relational construction of subject positions in a context of neoliberalisation'. *Subjectivity*, 12, 371–88.

Vergara del Solar, A., Llobet, V. and Nascimento, M. L. (2021) 'South American childhoods since the 1990s: Between neoliberalisation and the expansion of rights: An introduction'. In Vergara del Solar, A., Llobet, V. and Nascimento, M. (eds) *South American Childhoods Since the 1990s: Neoliberalisation and children's rights*. London: Springer/Palgrave Macmillan, 1–43.

Woodhead, M. (1999) 'Combatting child labour: Listen to what the children say'. *Childhood*, 6 (1), 27–49.

World Bank Group (2016) *Poverty and Shared Prosperity 2016: Taking on inequality*. https://openknowledge.worldbank.org/bitstream/handle/10986/25078/9781464809583.pdf (accessed 17 September 2021).

Worldometers 'Coronavirus'. https://www.worldometers.info/coronavirus/#countries (live updated site, accessed 10 February 2023).

4
Pakistan: families in Karachi recalibrating care during COVID-19

Safina Azeem, Shama Dossa, Asiya Jawed, Ayesha Khan, Mahnoor Mahar and Faiza Mushtaq

Introduction

Our study was motivated by an expectation that the pandemic was an opportunity for the government, communities and families to adjust the institutional and social structures that produce care work to be more equitable. We examine reflections from 27 families in Pakistan's largest city, Karachi, to ask how care was recalibrated during the crisis and if there were any changes in gendered roles or family norms as a result.

Most Pakistani families are patriarchal and patrilineal (Sheikh 1973). Families usually live in extended and multigenerational households (Baig et al. 2014). One home may comprise parents, young children, grandparents, married sons with their spouses and children, as well as unmarried or divorced adult offspring. Other elderly relatives, nieces and nephews, may share the same home. Adolescents who live in joint families may have improved resilience and social adjustment (Us-Sahar and Muzaffar 2017). Research conducted before the pandemic finds the gendered division of roles and responsibilities within the family is linked to a better quality of life for men and boys in families, irrespective of family structure (Lodhi et al. 2021). There is limited research on the negative physical, psychological and professional impact on care-givers within families (Irfan et al. 2017). Domestic care work was found to substantially reduce time and opportunities for women's employment, education and skill development (NCSW et al. 2020; Masood 2019).

The start of the pandemic in Pakistan provided an opportunity to study the impact of this new disaster on families and communities. Emerging findings from other research indicated some problem areas. A quantitative study found the increased parental concern brought on by the new financial burdens and caring for children was linked with negative parenting practices, with mothers and low-income families at a higher risk of stress (Zafar et al. 2021). Families with healthy internal dynamics and an active coping style enjoyed greater psychological well-being during the pandemic than those with unhealthy dynamics (Ahmad et al. 2021). A study with COVID-positive individuals in the city of Lahore found high levels of community stigmatization forced some to move to different localities (Jafree et al. 2020). Infected individuals found solace in faith as a coping mechanism for anxiety, stress and guilt over worrying loved ones (Mansoor et al. 2020). Household members occupied their homes with increased constraints due to limitations of space and the level of autonomy they enjoyed. As in other contexts with highly gendered household space, women and girls were primarily responsible for caring for the sick, children and elderly. With family members spending more time together indoors under lockdown, women's domestic work burden increased significantly (Nepal Research Institute and CARE Nepal 2020).

We begin the chapter by situating the study in the context of the COVID-19 pandemic in Pakistan, followed by a description of our theoretical framing and research methodology. Next, we present our findings to answer the two guiding research questions of this study: first, how participants understood and responded to government guidelines around social distancing measures and, second, the impact on family life. We show how families recalibrated their care practices to cope with an upended world, although without lasting shifts in gendered roles.

The spread of COVID-19 in Pakistan

The first two cases of COVID-19 in Pakistan were detected in the cities of Karachi and Islamabad on 26 February 2020. The first lockdown was imposed a month later by the Sindh government, in the province where Karachi is located. By the end of October 2021, Pakistan had 1.27 million confirmed cases and over 28,000 deaths (Government of Pakistan 2021). Throughout the course of the pandemic, the ruling party and Sindh government brought forward different policies regarding the lives and livelihoods of Pakistani people. On 23 March 2020, a countrywide lockdown was imposed, which continued until 9 May. This was followed by a strategy based on 'smart lockdowns', that is, sealing areas with infected cluster populations while easing restrictions on economic activities with adequate safety guidelines. Figure 4.1 shows the timeline of COVID-19 spread and government response measures in Pakistan.

June 2020 saw a peak of COVID-19 cases in Pakistan with 6,825 new cases being reported in a single day. Cases began to fall by August 2020 and the burden on hospitals eased. Schools and universities which had remained shut since March finally resumed in September 2020 with a hybrid teaching system (online and in-person). The national and provincial governments issued Standard Operating Procedures (SOPs) to protect against COVID-19 infection amongst the population. These advisories included social distancing and masking measures in markets, private events and large public congregations. The measures were not fully observed or effectively enforced, leading to a second wave of infections in November 2020 (Khan et al. 2020) when the increased hospitalizations strained existing health systems. However, policies such as partial lockdowns in infected localities helped to mitigate the burden of disease. Finally, in February 2021 the vaccination campaign was launched with supplies from China (SinoPharm, SinoVac and CanSino) and Russia (Sputnik V). This led to the government easing SOPs but retaining the use of smart lockdowns to control local outbreaks.

The country entered its third wave in March 2021 and a fourth wave, led by the Delta variant of COVID-19, in July 2021. By the end of October, nearly 18 per cent of Pakistan's population were fully vaccinated and 31 per cent of the population had received their first dose. The number of new cases and death rates slowly declined as the government required everyone to be vaccinated and the programme was rolled out to children over 12 years old.

Theoretical framework

Our framing for this chapter draws on conceptualizations of both care work and emotional work. There is limited literature around care work within families during COVID-19 in Pakistan and the region (Nanthini and Nair 2020). Research from the region indicated women increasingly felt burdened by their domestic care responsibilities, such as looking after elderly in-laws in joint family households (Narasimhan et al. 2021; Sarker 2020). Women received limited practical help in daily tasks from their

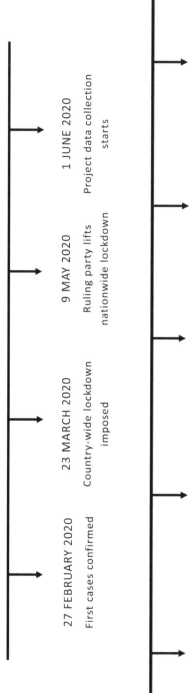

Figure 4.1 Timeline of COVID-19 in Pakistan. Source: authors.

husbands, but women and girls did four times as much work as men (Deshpande 2020). A popular online petition in Mumbai (India) urged the Indian Prime Minister to encourage more men to share in housework during the first year (BBC 2020). Global findings concurred that the added burden of domestic and child care work fell on women, irrespective of their employment status (Andrew et al. 2020; Boca et al. 2020; Collins et al. 2020).

To understand intra-family practices and dynamics with more depth we make use of Folbre's formulation of 'care work' as that in which the quality of service is affected by the workers' concern for the well-being of the care recipient. This includes care provided in diverse locations, such as home, community and a variety of paid work environments (Folbre 2012, 598). It involves a combination of intrinsic motivation, such as parental responsibility towards children, and extrinsic motivation, such as care work which is paid. In unpaid care work, gender norms and expectations of reciprocal care by adult children towards parents in old age may motivate the work (Folbre 2012, 600). The extent to which the state provides welfare services that reduce the burden of unpaid care, particularly on women, can transform the exploitative nature of care work within families (Folbre 2008).

An important dimension of care work involves emotional labour, which can be commodified in the marketplace (through value ascribed to producing emotional states) but is also performed within families in innumerable 'actions that go unnoticed but are critical to the construction of the family itself' (Steinberg and Figart 1999, 23). Research to explore how individuals may feel about the emotional work they may be obligated or wish to perform may illuminate the ambivalence and tensions they may experience in their roles as care-givers (Garey and Hansen 2011). Feelings themselves, as 'patterned expectations of what people are supposed to feel, or not feel, in particular situations' (Garey and Hansen 2011, 10), are situated in specific cultural and family contexts. The pandemic, therefore, presented possibilities for new feelings to emerge as specific family contexts came under unique strain.

Framing our analysis through a care lens, therefore, serves two purposes. First, it fills a gap in the empirical literature about intra-family care practices in Pakistan, and second, it permits us to foreground how the families in our research imbued the everyday coping strategies of life during the pandemic with meaning through the enactment of care.

Methods

Data was collected from August 2020 to July 2021, spanning the pandemic and initiation of vaccinations. Due to lockdown and safety considerations for participants and the research team, our longitudinal qualitative study relied on remote digital platforms for data making. Digital ethnography literature (Pink et al. 2015) provided methodological grounding to shape the techniques and processes through which we reconceptualized 'the field' and 'qualitative research practices and ethics', and accounted for how digital, methodological, practical and theoretical dimensions overlap (O'Reilly 2012). Instead of 'direct' contact with the participants, we took a 'mediated' contact approach in which 'listening' may involve reading or sensing and communicating through digital media like voice notes, video, photographs and visuals (Pink et al. 2015, 3).

Participants were recruited through an open call on social media (Facebook, Instagram, Twitter) and word-of-mouth to participate in the study. Families were selected to participate based on the following criteria: recruited families were Karachi-based since the pandemic began, with access to smartphones, and included at least one household member below age 25. Our sample included 27 families (173 individuals). A total of 57 family members responded to bi-weekly prompts (Table 4.1). As this was a qualitative exploratory study, we were not looking for data saturation or statistical generalizability, rather, our focus was capturing multiple emerging perspectives. Little prior research had been conducted on this topic and we hoped the study would identify further areas for research.

The families lived in 16 different neighbourhoods, including low, middle and upper socio-economic localities. The collective income of the poorest household was US$270 per month as compared to the country's

Table 4.1 Number of research participants by gender and age in Pakistan study.

Sex	Age (years)				Total
	13–18	19–25	26–55	>55	
Male	3	6	11	4	24
Female	4	11	16	2	33
Total	7	17	27	6	57

per capita income of US$1089 (World Bank 2020), while the wealthiest family owned multiple businesses and properties. The families were from diverse ethnic backgrounds: Sindhi, Punjabi and Urdu-speaking migrants from India (known as Muhajirs). Most were Sunni Muslim, reflective of the national demographics, with one Hindu and one Christian family.

Interviews were recorded using telephone, WhatsApp or Zoom. We transcribed, and inductively coded them using Atlas.ti 8 software. In group workshops the research team triangulated the coding structure and findings. Monthly prompts were sent to all participants via WhatsApp, the most widely used communication tool in Karachi among those with smartphones. These prompts were sent in both Urdu and English through both text and voice notes, so as to reach participants who were less literate. Individuals responded using text, audio, videos or images. In-depth interviews at the beginning and end of the research period were held with one member from each household who was identified as a key informant. Only three key informants dropped out of the study before the end. To gain insight into youth experiences, from March to May 2021 we conducted six online interviews via Zoom with adolescents from the families already included in the study.

The study was approved by the Pakistan government's National Bioethics Committee. All participants were provided with pseudonyms to protect their confidentiality. Our all-women team of feminist researchers extended space, empathy and compassion during the data-collection process. Some participants reported that the in-depth interviews felt cathartic while for others the monthly prompts encouraged reflection about the pandemic's impact on their lives.

Data was managed through password-secured files that were only accessible to the research team and stored using designated pseudonyms. Data for each prompt was transcribed if it was a voice note or the text was pasted in the designated prompt file along with any photographs received. We used reminder calls and designed colourful visual posters to motivate participants' responses (Figures 4.2 and 4.3).

Findings

We present our findings in two sections. First, we analyse how our families responded to the institutional messaging offered by the state to 'care' for its citizens, and the role of media and workplaces in enhancing or undermining that messaging. Second, we explore how the enactment of care in family life was impacted.

Figure 4.2 Prompt 5 sent to participants in Pakistan, 16 November 2020. Source: authors.

The government of Pakistan is launching the COVID-19 vaccination drive across the country. How do you feel about this? Will you or will you not take the vaccine when it becomes available to the general public? We would like to know your views. Let us know through a text message, voicenote, or video.

حکومت پاکستان نے اعلان کیا ہے کہ پاکستان میں کووِڈ ۱۹ ویکسی نیشن ڈرائیو شروع ہونے والی ہے۔ اس سے متعلق آپ کے کیا خیالات ہیں؟ جب عام عوام کو یہ ویکسین دستیاب کی جائے گی تو آپ اسے حاصل کرنا چاہیں گے یا نہیں؟
ہمیں اپنا جواب میسج، وائس نوٹ یا ویڈیو کے ذریعے بھیجیں

Figure 4.3 Prompt 8 sent to participants in Pakistan, 9 February 2021. Source: authors.

How did participants understand and respond to social distancing measures?

The families who participated in our study experienced the pandemic while embedded in, and interacting with, multiple other social institutions. Different institutions emerged as trusted sources of information, material and symbolic resources, and other forms of support for different families and helped mediate the crisis situation for them in different ways. Three categories emerged as most significant: the government, the media and the workplace.

Government

The Pakistani government responded to the public health emergency through a series of lockdowns and issuing of social distancing guidelines which did not find widespread compliance amongst the population. Matters were complicated further because of the tussle between Prime Minister Imran Khan's government at the centre and the provincial government in Sindh, where Karachi is located, which were frequently at odds with each other. Participants in our study expressed ambivalent attitudes about the measures taken by the government, praising some actions while being sceptical about others. Perceptions of the government's performance in handling the crisis were shaped powerfully by individuals' pre-existing political opinions, loyalties towards specific political parties and history of experiences with state institutions. Many participants had low levels of trust in the government's ability or interest in providing care to citizens, which undermined the effectiveness of the state's COVID-19 response measures.

Arif Ahmed (age 41, businessman) runs a small leather company. He said the Sindh government had been very good with tracking and following up on COVID-19-positive individuals in the early months of the pandemic. His overall assessment, however, was that the provincial government took the precautions too seriously 'under the influence of the West' (31 August 2020). He was especially critical of the strict lockdown policy and its potential to 'ruin' the country, while stating that 'the policy of the federal government was correct: some strictness but also using a carrot'. Fizza Tahir (32, mother and homemaker) also said she was happy with Prime Minister Imran Khan's leadership and that a complete lockdown was impossible. Other participants echoed this sentiment, which corresponds to the federal government's position in defence of its strategy of targeted, 'smart' lockdowns to avoid large-scale business shutdowns and save livelihoods.

Zarish Husain (43, mother and teacher) was impressed with the federal government's response to the pandemic, saying, 'They are caring for their people'. She contrasted this approach with previous elected governments run by other political parties. When asked to elaborate, she cited the free provision of vaccines, a social protection programme for low-income families, 'transparency', and an 'easy process to get the vaccine. They've really tried to make it easy for people'. Although most of her positive experiences were the result of Sindh government services and programmes, like other participants, she nonetheless gave the credit to the federal government.

Participants offered a range of assessments and opinions about official institutions and representatives of the state based upon their day-to-day interactions. Many praised the testing, treatment and vaccination services provided by public hospitals in Karachi and contrasted them favourably with privately-run healthcare facilities. Police and law enforcement received mixed reviews. Some noted that police presence in markets and other public areas was the only thing that compelled people to wear masks, with lax attitudes otherwise prevailing towards social distancing guidelines.

Others were critical of the police for trying to enforce government orders haphazardly without any real understanding of the situation. The Ehsan family suffered through a police barricade of their street for more than a fortnight while they were dealing with a COVID outbreak in their home. They perceived this as an unnecessarily punitive action which, rather than showing care for them in a time of illness, instead created fear and made neighbours and relatives stay away, thus depriving the family of other sources of care and support. The family's COVID-positive status was shared with authorities and published in a government gazette during the first wave, when measures to control local outbreaks were new. The family felt stigmatized within their community, a source of stress that further eroded their trust in the government.

Media

There was variation within and across households in how information about COVID-19, its spread and risks, and preventive strategies was received. Some participants mentioned that they looked up specialized sources of scientific information, such as the websites of international health organizations or medical journals. These individuals often had a doctor or other medical professional in the family. The generational divide was salient for usage of media and determining which sources of news were considered trustworthy. Older participants relied heavily on television coverage of the pandemic, placing their confidence in mainstream media organizations and the expectation of receiving timely, accurate information from them, while young people were far more likely to be sceptical of such sources and instead preferred to receive their updates through social media.

Eeshwar Kumar (62, activist), a grandfather from the Hindu community living in the lower middle-income neighbourhood of Lyari, noted that the whole family watched television news regularly, while his sons also looked up information on Google. His granddaughter had begun taking health and safety precautions on her own after she started online school and was able to carry out her own research. Many young adults in our study found that COVID-19-related news on Twitter, Instagram, YouTube and Facebook helped them to feel informed and therefore more in control. They shared new information with family members as a way to demonstrate care and concern. Still, many younger participants also reported feeling overwhelmed by the ceaseless reporting of infection rates, fatalities and other sombre news, eventually cutting back on the amount of time they spent online.

Kinship networks, community organizations and neighbourhood-level associations played an important part in the circulation of information during the pandemic, often in digitally mediated forms. These sources included valuable support and resources, but also scientifically inaccurate claims and rumours. Word of mouth and messages circulated through WhatsApp were cited by young and old alike as significant sources of information.

Some individuals actively used social media to disseminate information they thought might be useful for members of their community. Aliya Ahmed (31, mother and homemaker) said that when her husband contracted COVID-19 early in 2020, he had posted the news on Facebook as a public service message. He let everyone know 'if they had been in contact with him over the past 6–7 days, they should get tested' (31 August 2020). She said many people praised him for not hiding his COVID-19-positive status.

Workplace

The countrywide lockdown and closure of businesses during the first wave of the pandemic had a major impact on the economy, with only a partial recovery having taken place after this. Between April and July 2020, 20.7 million people lost their jobs and 53 per cent of households across the country faced reduced income (Pakistan Bureau of Statistics 2020). Participants in our study also shared their concerns about varying levels of job security, fluctuating incomes and work conditions during this time period.

Multigenerational families with more than one income-earner were better able to weather the economic insecurity. Many of the Kumars were unemployed during the pandemic months, but the steady income and benefits of one son with a job at a government medical college kept the household afloat. School and university teachers, doctors and employees of banks and pharmaceutical companies were among those who kept working and receiving salaries throughout the lockdowns and ensuing economic downturn. Participant Zarish Husain's job as a college lecturer did not pay much, but it gave her peace of mind to know that it was secure. Her husband, on the other hand, owned an animation and post-production studio where new projects stopped coming in as the economy took a downturn. Arif Ahmed, meanwhile, was forced to close down his leather apparel workshop briefly during the initial lockdown, but he was soon back in business with the boom in online shopping and increased access to international buyers.

Employers did not always have adequate protections in place during the crisis and the demands placed upon employees occasionally became a source of anxiety for participants. In addition to cancelling annual salary increments or imposing pay cuts, some workplaces were not receptive to employee requests for flexible work hours or special provisions due to health considerations. Very few offered any help with the cost of COVID-19 tests or compensation for missed days of work.

Sumaiya Osmani (28, corporate brand manager) reported that her work–life balance was badly affected during the pandemic, with late night Zoom calls and little time to spend with family. Her firm treated her as an essential worker and insisted on daily attendance, even when other staff followed hybrid attendance. The expense of daily commuting and fears of infecting her elderly parents caused her stress. She expressed her discomfort to the human resources department but found little sympathy. 'It did occur to me that I should just quit and that, you know, nothing is more important than your life and health. But they [employers] just play on your insecurities … [They] know you will not find another job because of the pandemic' (13 September 2020). Sumaiya eventually left this job and moved to a philanthropic hospital because it offered a more caring work environment.

Employment issues were more acute for blue-collar workers and those relying on the informal economy. The majority of households in our study had one or more domestic staff members before the pandemic, to help with cooking, cleaning, laundry, driving or gardening. The first lockdown led many domestic staff to be temporarily laid off. Some of our participants reflected on the privilege they normally enjoy in their day-to-day lives and expressed gratitude for their domestic help. Many reported that they continued to pay salaries until staff members were able to return to work, and also provided support as and when medical needs arose, but this was not uniformly practiced.[1]

Given the scant enforcement of labour laws or minimum wage regulations, the goodwill of employers and habits of charitable giving are the only protections available for vulnerable social groups. The Pakistani government announced a slate of economic relief and stimulus policies that included cash grants, subsidies and tax incentives (IMF 2021). However, the relief package was slow to be disbursed and the stimulus measures appeared to benefit the country's elites, while the economic crisis continues to imperil the most marginalized. This, once again, heightened the scepticism of citizens towards the intentions and abilities of the state to provide care for them. The informal mechanisms through which care and support is channelled within society instead got reenergized as a result of the COVID uncertainties.

Impact on family life

We present our findings on the impact of COVID on family life by first examining how caring 'for' within the family changed. Second, we explore methods of self-care; that is, how our participants perceived their own needs and acted to meet them. Finally, we show that caring 'with' others in the community enhanced individuals' perception of personal well-being during this stressful period. Within families, individuals varied in their perceptions of risk and their enthusiasm for following safety precautions depending upon what sources of information they trusted and their relationship with institutions like the government, media, workplace and community. This led to negotiations and tension within families, often exacerbated along gendered and generational lines as the findings here show.

Caring 'for'

Care roles and division of work within the home during the lockdown were deeply gendered. In extended family households the number of individuals ranged from nine to almost thirty. Those families who could afford domestic staff managed without their support. Women balanced the demands of new norms of online work and study with the increased burden of health-related care and concern for the well-being of loved ones. Mothers reported an earlier start to the day, to meet increased demands for three cooked family meals in a full house, alongside overseeing children's schoolwork.

To cope without the support of domestic staff sent home during lockdown, Yasmeen Farooq (32, mother and homemaker) and her sisters-in-law ended their tradition of late-night family dinners and closed the kitchen earlier. After a brief hospitalization with COVID, she said her mother-in-law expected her to resume cooking immediately, and Yasmeen's optimism was shadowed by this ambivalence about the expectations of her as a care provider:

> Sadly [my mother-in-law] didn't feel that COVID was tough on us in any way. I got back to kitchen duties after two days. I always say I don't expect anything in return, but I don't know, I was kind of emotionally drained (Yasmeen, 3 September 2020).

Only a few participants said that men contributed to domestic work. The daughters-in-law at the Kumars never enjoyed the support of staff. Alisha Kumar (35, mother and homemaker) would wake at 6 a.m. to start cooking, while the men slept until 11 a.m. every morning, without any routine during lockdown. The women cleaned each of the six rooms in the flat, one by one, during the day. Unable to visit their own families, Alisha says the sisters-in-law grew closer as together they juggled the burden of childcare and domestic labour.

The additional care work had implications for children; in some families they stepped in to support their mothers and provide the emotional and domestic work required to keep the family functioning during the crisis. Girls contributed to domestic work as an extension of their responsibilities. Sisters looked after younger siblings and cousins, keeping with family expectations. Yasmeen's daughter Nimra Farooq (13, student) said she 'enjoyed the responsibility' (27 March 2021) of caring for her little sisters when the extended household contracted COVID and those children who'd escaped infection were quarantined for their own protection. She managed to feed, bathe and console her distraught youngest sister, only a toddler, who struggled to comprehend why her parents were unable to attend to her needs. In other homes, some younger sons helped with limited chores, aware of the increased workload on their mothers.

Some women resented the emotional work required to cope with the new stresses. While women noted the gendered nature of their additional care work, they avoided directly critiquing it. One exception was Batool (21, student) who, in an excerpt from a university essay shared with the interviewer, observed how women managed without domestic staff while men's behaviour remained unchanged:

> In this new reality, the gendered roles seem to be even more distinguishable, with the once working-women like my mother, now without the help of ... house-workers, having to transform into a super-human (10 September 2020).

When most of Zainab's (45, mother and homemaker) family contracted COVID during the first wave, she became their sole care-taker in the absence of domestic help. But when she, too, fell ill her mother and sisters sent over boxes of food. She recalls no one in her own home 'took responsibility' for her initially and she cooked porridge for herself in an upstairs kitchenette during isolation. Days later, her sons began to bring food (12 December 2021).

Batool noted the consequences of how poorly men coped:

> expectations of masculinity and a stigma towards mental illnesses means that most men aren't talking about how they feel.

Batool told of her domestic maid, stuck at home, 'now physically abused repeatedly in front of her children with not even her work to escape to', and of a friend 'who lives on edge waiting for her father to decide whether she and her mother can stay in the house that day' (27 February 2021).

Zainab also observed her own family:

> I felt like everyone was dealing with high blood pressure ... no one was calm. And I had to deal with the situation because if I got angry at the men of the house, the household atmosphere would get completely disturbed (12 December 2021).

Yasmeen insisted the pandemic brought her large joint family closer. She admitted 'both pros and cons' to their new lives, but tried to remain positive. Thus, she fine-tuned her inner emotional life to ensure harmony within the home during the crisis:

> ... we all are there for each other, but then on the other hand I don't – I don't interfere in anybody else's personal thing – until and unless they ask for it. You know, no free advice until asked (3 September 2020).

New areas of conflict emerged due to the concerns over maintaining safety from infection. Batool observed that her mother Hadia (50, mother and health worker) tended to COVID patients and maintained careful hygiene practices to protect her family from infection when she came home. In contrast, her father socialized every evening without observing social distancing, and his mood swings damaged the home environment.

Families used new creative strategies to care for their children. The Kumars found ways to make this added emotional work entertaining. They made up stories to explain why it was impossible to order take-out from favoured eateries, so the children would not worry excessively about COVID-19, and devised countless arts and crafts projects to entertain them during long afternoons and evenings under lockdown. Two girls learned to play football in the living room, and their proud father shared pictures with us to show how they kept themselves cheerful during this period. Yasmeen recalls that when 21 of the 25 members of her household came down with COVID-19, her healthy young children were isolated for their own protection in the basement. She coined the term 'corona huggy' to describe a virtual embrace she gave her toddler at the window each night. One mother from a privileged upper-middle class background said her 14-year-old daughter's mental health crisis was triggered by prolonged isolation and difficulties adapting to online education. After consulting a psychologist, she temporarily withdrew her daughter from school.

Older youth from higher socio-economic backgrounds were more vocal than others from less educated homes in articulating their mental health challenges and feelings of isolation. Batool, a more affluent teenager, recognized her privilege in being able to 'disconnect' from the outside world and consciously avoided reading COVID-19-related messaging on her digital media: 'If I'm being uncomfortably honest, I don't want to read about people starving and dying and losing their friends and family to the virus'(10 September 2020). Some said that their parents' loss of livelihoods negatively affected their well-being. To counter the isolation, young people used digital technology to reach out to relatives and friends living within the city and in other countries. Technology helped them to maintain old friendships and make new friends through online platforms – but only if they enjoyed the luxury of easy internet access.

Some young participants grew to appreciate the time they could now spend with their parents, grandparents and other relatives in extended households. Lockdown strengthened their bonds with some older relatives and siblings, somewhat mitigating their loneliness. Some mentioned reviving connections with family members in other cities or abroad, drawing on a shared experience of the pandemic. Young people repeatedly expressed fears of their parents and grandparents getting COVID-19, as if a dimension of care responsibilities had become apparent to them for the first time. This new sense of responsibility added to their burden of emotional work. A young man who works in a medical college used his up-to-date health knowledge to convince his parents to adopt SOPs at home. Anxiety around protecting against infection led to enormous relief when an elder recovered from COVID-19, or to new feelings of loss and grief upon losing a loved one. Adil Paracha (16, student) remembered the turmoil eventually settling down: 'Slowly it got to [be] like okay, I can go see my friends, you know as long as I made sure we were safe, and I am safe' (23 April 2021).

Self-care

Each individual developed a personalized set of strategies to ensure some level of self-care. A few women said their deep faith helped to counter waves of anxiety. Reaching out to loved ones for virtual chats helped to cope with isolation, and television provided escape amongst the more privileged. Despite the extra domestic workload, young Sonam Kumar (age 14, student) valued the time her family spent 'talking together' and reassuring her not to absorb too much 'tension' over the virus (16 April 2021). Self-care strategies revolved around nurturing close relationships through appreciating human connection.

Many younger participants missed their physical activities and routines. They displayed a variety of coping mechanisms to care for their own well-being. Those without access to online classes entertained themselves by playing games with their siblings or cousins, getting a pet, or arts and crafts. When asked what practices helped during the spring lockdown, Batool mentions Zoom calls to 'hangout virtually' with cousins (20 November 2020), and going 'up to my roof and listening to music for a few hours, keeping a music diary for doodling, colouring and writing about songs I love and how they make me feel' (21 September 2020). She occasionally wrote music and poetry, too but 'didn't have the energy to do this regularly or often' (21 September 2020). It was easiest to re-watch favourite television shows.

Batool spent more time with her teenage brother, Adil, developing a closeness impossible in busier times. When asked if any relationship with a family member changed, Adil spoke of his sister:

> Even though the lockdown kind of boxed us in together ... it gave us more time to talk about the more important stuff – emotional stuff

and mental health ...That's an awesome boundary to cross with a sibling or with anyone really (23 April 2021).

His mother, Hadia, on the other hand, felt increasingly concerned for his psychological well-being. She suspended her careful adherence to SOPs and allowed him to visit the gym.

The need for individual privacy within the home required delicate negotiation as the months wore on, particularly amongst joint families. The Farooq's joint family household decided to limit their time together in the TV lounge. Yasmeen developed her own combination of Netflix, *namaz* (prayer) and late-evening walks alone in her neighbourhood to cope with her changed life. Another young woman used reflective journaling and smoking cannabis in her room to cope with loneliness, losing her father to COVID-19 and a fraught relationship with her step-mother.

Care 'with' the community

Across their varied socio-economic levels, those participants who joined in social work benefited from engaging 'with' others to improve overall well-being. The Kumars are an intergenerational household of 17 people sharing one flat. The oldest man is head of the household; his wife, unmarried adult daughter, and four married sons live together with their families. One son, Dhruv (31, insurance surveyor) found it difficult to stay at home during lockdown and joined his father in distributing ration packs to community members. Dhruv's view was that as a 'political worker', he was 'providing services to mankind ... when you feed the hungry, you feel inner satisfaction' (6 October 2020). His father similarly recounted that helping wage labourers who had lost daily earnings was a first priority. His relatives disagreed, which negatively impacted their relationship.

Hadia volunteered time at Karachi Central Jail to raise awareness about COVID-19 amongst young prisoners. In another role as a volunteer healthcare provider she offered guidance on COVID-19 management in a tele-health service. She said these roles led to personal growth through the many 'meaningful relationships' and empathy the work generated. Combined with her deep faith it became a source of personal sustenance, countering the pandemic-related anxiety at home.

The impact of COVID-19 on education presented complex challenges along with new opportunities to support students. The start of online education forced students to adjust to new modalities of learning while navigating Karachi's constant electricity shortages and unreliable internet connections. Students within the same household learned to 'take turns' in watching their individual recorded lectures, borrowing equipment or using their parents' mobile phones to attend classes. Many parents bought mobile phones to support their children with online classes given the high cost and market shortage of computers. Some low-income schools were closed for over six months because online learning was not feasible; teachers were not trained to conduct online classes and families had no access to the internet. Nauman Chaudhary (age 33, teacher) worked in a non-profit school for lower-income students. He was concerned that as a consequence of school closures many of his older students were made to work in factories, perform manual labour or work at home. When schools reopened during 2021, the families expected their children to continue this paid work. Chaudhary's concerns led him to make attempts to convince such students to return to education and offer them free tuition to prepare them for their examinations – as a gesture of community care.

Young people may have developed an expanded sense of care as a state of relating to the world around them. They feared the impact of the next wave on their daily lives. Raza (13, student) said he found the situation 'somewhat depressing … but it's now normal … [We] must be careful but we can't finish this immediately, we have to live with it'. Although dealing with uncertainty became the new normal, Sonam (14, student) said she wanted an end to the burden of care it had brought, so that:

> … we can have peace … and parents are able to go back to their jobs, so poor people can have money and can run their houses and kids can pursue their passions and complete their education (16 April 2021).

Discussion

Our research provided a unique opportunity to gain insight into individuals' interpretations of real-time changes in their care responsibilities, and observe the subtle recalibrations of caring 'for' and caring 'with' in their everyday lives. Family members experienced the government, media and workplaces as more or less reliable sources of information and support, depending on their varying levels of trust. Changes in care work within the family and community revealed that alongside the increased gendered burden on women, individuals used care practices to develop a sense of meaning in an unprecedented situation. Our findings on the recalibration of care and related emotional work (Garey and Hansen 2011) contribute to the emerging literature on the impact of care work amongst family providers in Pakistan (Zafar et al. 2021; Irfan et al. 2017).

The government's inconsistent handling of the pandemic (Khattak 2020) and the official public information campaign did not adequately convey the risks or convince the population to make significant behavioural modifications. Our findings show how many people disregarded social distancing guidelines and mask mandates, especially after the first wave subsided and death rates remained low. Government messaging on adopting precautionary measures worked when people felt both cared for and connected with parties or individuals representing government positions. Other research finds a correlation between the 'civic culture' of communities and the likelihood of their voluntary compliance with government-imposed social distancing measures (Durante et al. 2020). Participants in our study demonstrated their understanding of civic culture when they shared information (or misinformation) with others in the community and family networks, often through digital media, as a way to care for them and build confidence. Many men, and a few women, engaged in community-based care practices to offer different forms of support to deprived households, out-of-school students and prisoners. This empathy contrasted sharply with some instances of community stigmatization when COVID-19 infection was detected. While none of our research participants were forced to move to another locality (Jafree et al. 2020), as mentioned previously, one family was stigmatized by a heavy-handed government measure to isolate their home once infection was detected there.

There is an ongoing debate in the literature regarding how well the democratic or authoritarian attributes of governments explain the effectiveness of their responses to emergency situations like the COVID-19 pandemic (Frey et al. 2020; Petersen 2020). Our observations show more complex patterns of state–society relations, developed over long periods of time, shaping the responses of families and communities. People's perceptions about the performance of various levels of government largely conformed to their pre-existing political beliefs amid a highly polarized political climate. Even where leaders earned praise or escaped criticism, cynicism about state institutions manifested itself through the circulation of conspiracy theories, vaccine hesitancy and lack of trust in official figures, the latter routinely questioned in public discourse.

COVID-19 added to the gendered division of care work (Folbre 2012) amongst the families in our sample. These findings confirmed global research findings on the added burden of care work on women (Andrew et al. 2020; Boca et al. 2020; Collins et al. 2020; Sarker 2020; Nepal Research Institute and CARE Nepal 2020). Only a few men engaged in domestic work they did not previously perform or increased their level of contribution, reinforcing previous research findings that men enjoy higher qualities of life within families (Lodhi et al. 2021). For some women, the added burden deepened pre-existing constraints to paid work or pursuing interests (NCSW et al. 2020).

Individuals holding jobs experienced their employers through the lens of care practice, appreciating those which tried to care for their employees by allowing them flexibility to work at home or offering additional support. Sumaiya decided to move from an employer that disregarded its care obligation towards employees. Instead she joined a philanthropic organization that had demonstrated greater concern for protecting its employees from COVID-19, suggesting a reorientation of her career. Hadia devoted more of her professional skills to the care and emotional work of counselling patients and inmates to soothe their concerns over infection.

While there were women in our sample who critiqued the unequal gender burden of their care work, others emphasized opportunities the pandemic afforded to care 'for' others through greater bonding across generations or extended families. The added physical and psychological challenges necessitated greater emotional work through actively demonstrating empathy and understanding for grandparents, amongst sisters-in-law and between siblings. The lockdown created time and opportunity to nurture relationships, master new digital technologies and explore new learning modalities together. The Kumars and Farooqs, with healthy family dynamics (Ahmad et al. 2021), recalibrated their care and emotional work to focus on keeping the mood light and engaging younger children in creative activities, online schooling and community work. However, men's high-risk behaviour undermined the effectiveness of caring practices within a family. Their dismissive attitudes towards social distancing may reflect masculine norms valorizing bravery and strength, along with a desire to evade increased care responsibilities by leaving the house (Umamaheswar and Tan 2020).

Individuals, across gender and age, displayed an enhanced understanding that caring 'for' included self-care during this crisis. Some women found solace in faith to cope with emotional and psychological stresses, as Mansoor et al. (2020) also demonstrate. We further show how they also paid increased attention to personal health and well-being practices, such as going for walks or connecting with loved ones online. Both men and women also discovered that caring for others enhanced their self-care practices by improving their mood and generating a sense of meaning out of the crisis.

Adolescents in our sample living in joint families may have benefited from additional emotional support, as Us-Sahar and Muzaffar (2017) had found pre pandemic. The need to shield elderly parents within the home, as a dimension of young adult's care responsibilities, featured strongly in our data. Our young caregivers did not explicitly voice being conflicted between their traditional roles requiring adult protection and caregiving situations where they are expected to act adult. Indeed some children (particularly girls) were proud of caring for their siblings and supporting their parents. However, they repeatedly voiced stress and fear about a loved one falling ill or dying. We do not exclude the possibility that care practices may have, on occasion, led to a reversal of the functional or emotional roles between parents (and grandparents) and children. Some theorists have termed this reversal 'parentification' (Watson 2017). This has implications for quick transitions to adulthood which need to be explored further. Some research finds caregiving responsibilities teach life skills and promote independence while other studies suggest such responsibilities at a young age could be emotionally and mentally destructive to child development (Watson 2017). This would be an important area to explore in future to expand the limited research on family care-givers in Pakistan.

Conclusion

Our research saw evidence of both government and families recalibrating their understanding of care responsibilities due to the pandemic. The state enacted, with mixed effect, a policy of caring for the well-being of its citizens to protect them from COVID-19. Within families, individuals began to engage in more self-care practices as a dimension of caring 'for', and expressed a new appreciation for care-giving professional roles. The recalibrated understanding of the value of emotional work extended to children as they assumed new responsibilities. Both men and women gave increased time to care 'with' the deprived within their communities. Future research on the impact of COVID-19 on families may benefit from using an expanded and recalibrated notion of care to adequately account for their experiences.

Note

1   We were unable to interview domestic staff.

References

Ahmad, S., Nasreen, L., Batool, S. and Khalid, S. (2021) 'Family functioning and psychological well-being: The mediating role of coping strategies during COVID-19 lockdown in Pakistan'. *Polish Psychological Bulletin*, 52 (2), 162–71. https://doi.org/10.24425/PPB.2021.137259.

Andrew, A., Cattan, S., Costa Dias, M., Farquharson, C., Kraftman, L., Krutikova, S., Phimister, A. and Sevilla, A. (2020) 'The gendered division of paid and domestic work under lockdown'. *IZA Discussion Paper, No. 135000*. http://ftp.iza.org/dp13500.pdf (accessed 7 March 2023).

Baig, N.-A., Rehman, R. R. and Mobeen, N. (2014) 'A parent-teacher view of teens behaviors in nuclear and joint family systems in Pakistan'. *The Qualitative Report*, 19 (67), 1–12.

Boca, D. D., Oggero, N., Profeta, P. and Rossi, M. C. (2020) 'Women's and men's work, housework and childcare, before and during COVID-19'. *Review of Economics of the Household*, 18, 1001–17.

British Broadcasting Corporation (BBC) (2020) 'Coronavirus in India: "PM Modi, please make men share housework!"'. *BBC News*, 21 July 2021. https://www.bbc.com/news/world-asia-india-53469696 (accessed 31 May 2022).

Collins, C., Landivar, L. C., Ruppanner, L. and Scarborough, W. J. (2020) 'COVID-19 and the gender gap in work hours'. *Gender, Work & Organization*, 28 (51), 101–12. https://doi.org/10.1111/gwao.12506.

Deshpande, A. (2020) 'The COVID-19 pandemic and gendered division of paid and unpaid work: Evidence from India'. *IZA Discussion Paper, No. 13815*. http://ftp.iza.org/dp13815.pdf (accessed 31 May 2022).

Durante, R., Guiso, L. and Gulino, G. (2020) 'Civic capital and social distancing: Evidence from Italians' response to COVID-19'. *Vox, CEPR Policy Portal*, 16 April 2020. https://voxeu.org/article/civic-capital-and-social-distancing (accessed 30 January 2023).

Folbre, N. (2008) 'Reforming care'. *Politics & Society*, 36 (3), 373–87. https://doi.org/10.1177/0032329208320567.

Folbre, N. (2012) 'Should women care less? Intrinsic motivation and gender inequality?'. *British Journal of Industrial Relations*, 50 (4), 597–619. https://doi.org/10.1111/bjir.12000.

Frey, C. B., Chen, C. and Presidente, G. (2020) 'Democracy, culture, and contagion: Political regimes and countries responsiveness to COVID-19'. https://www.oxfordmartin.ox.ac.uk/downloads/academic/Democracy-Culture-and-Contagion_May13.pdf (accessed 30 January 2023).

Garey, A. I. and Hansen, K. V. (2011) 'Introduction: An eye on emotion in the study of families and work'. In Garey, A. I. and Hansen, K. V. (eds) *At the Heart of Work and Family: Engaging the ideas of Arlie Hochschild*. New Brunswick: Rutgers University Press, 1–14.

Government of Pakistan (2021) *Pakistan Cases Details*. https://COVID.gov.pk/stats/pakistan.

International Monetary Fund (IMF) (2021) 'Policy Responses to COVID: Pakistan – IMF'. https://www.imf.org/en/Topics/imf-and-covid19/Policy-Responses-to-COVID-19#P (accessed 30 January 2023).

Irfan, B., Irfan, O., Ansari, A., Qidwai, W. and Nanji, K. (2017) 'Impact of caregiving on various aspects of the lives of caregivers'. *Cureus*, 9 (5), e1213. https://doi.org/10.7759/cureus.1213.

Jafree, S. R., Momina, A. and Naqi, S. A. (2020) 'Significant other family members and their experiences of COVID-19 in Pakistan: A qualitative study with implications for social policy'. *Stigma and Health*, 5 (4), 380–9. https://doi.org/10.1037/sah0000269.

Khan, A., Khwaja, A. and Jawed, A. (2020) *Navigating Civic Spaces During a Pandemic: Pakistan Report*. Karachi: Collective for Social Science Research. https://opendocs.ids.ac.uk/opendocs/handle/20.500.12413/16543 (accessed 30 January 2023).

Khattak, D. (2020) 'Pakistan's confused COVID-19 response'. *The Diplomat*, 9 June 2020. https://thediplomat.com/2020/06/pakistans-confused-COVID-19-response/.

Lodhi, F. S., Rabbani, U., Khan, A. A., Raza, O., Holakouie-Naieni, K., Yaseri, M., Farooq, U. and Montazeri, A. (2021) 'Factors associated with quality of life among joint and nuclear families:

A population-based study'. *BMC Public Health*, 21 (1), 234. https://doi.org/10.1186/s12889-021-10265-2.

Mansoor, T., Mansoor, S. and Zubair, U. bin (2020) '"Surviving COVID-19": Illness narratives of patients and family members in Pakistan'. *Annals of King Edward Medical University*, 26 (Special Issue), 157–64.

Masood, A. (2019) 'Influence of marriage on women's participation in medicine: The case of doctor brides of Pakistan'. *Sex Roles*, 80, 1–18. https://doi.org/10.1007/s11199-018-0909-5.

Nanthini, S. and Nair, T. (2020) 'COVID-19 and the impacts on women'. *NTS Insight. No IN20-05*. Singapore RSIS Centre for Non-Traditional Security Studies (NTS Centre). Singapore: Nanyang Technology University. http://www.jstor.org/stable/resrep26875 (accessed 30 January 2023).

Narasimhan, H., Chittem, M. and Purang, P. (2021) 'Pandemic times in a WhatsApp-ed nation: Gender ideologies in India during COVID-19'. In Manderson, L., Burke, N. J. and Wahlberg, A. (eds) *Viral Loads: Anthropologies of urgency in the time of COVID-19*. London: UCL Press, 362–83. https://doi.org/10.2307/j.ctv1j13zb3.25.

National Commission on the Status of Women (NCSW), Ministry of Human Rights and UN Women (2020) *Gendered Impact and Implications of COVID in Pakistan*. Policy Brief. Islamabad: Government of Pakistan.

Nepal Research Institute and CARE Nepal (2020) *A Rapid Gender Analysis on COVID-19 Nepal 2020*. UN Women Asia and the Pacific. https://asiapacific.unwomen.org/en/digital-library/publications/2020/11/a-rapid-gender-analysis-on-covid-19-nepal-2020 (accessed 10 February 2023).

O'Reilly, K. (2012) *Ethnographic Methods*. London: Routledge.

Pakistan Bureau of Statistics (2020) *Special Survey for Evaluating Socio-Economic Impact of Covid-19 on Wellbeing of People*. Islamabad: Government of Pakistan. https://www.pbs.gov.pk/sites/default/files//other/covid/Manual%20of%20Instruction%20covid-19.pdf (accessed 30 January 2023).

Petersen, G. (2020) 'Democracy, authoritarianism, and COVID-19 pandemic management: The case of SARS-CoV-2 testing'. *American Political Science Association Working Paper*. https://doi.org/10.33774/apsa-2020-wbhfk.

Pink, S., Horst, H., Postil, J., Hjorth, L., Lewis, T. and Tacchi, J. (2015) *Digital Ethnography: Principles and practice*. London: Sage.

Sahar, N-us. and Muzaffar, N. (2017) 'Role of family system, positive emotions and resilience in social adjustment among Pakistani adolescents'. *Journal of Educational, Health and Community Psychology*, 6 (2). http://doi.org/10.12928/jehcp.v6i2.6944.

Sarker, M. R. (2020) 'Labor market and unpaid works implications of COVID-19 for Bangladeshi women'. *Gender, Work & Organization*, 28 (Supplement 2), 597–604. https://doi.org/10.1111/gwao.12587.

Sheikh, M. A. (1973) 'Child rearing in Pakistan and its effects on family welfare'. *Journal of Child Clinical Psychology*, 2 (2), 26–7. https://doi.org/10.1080/15374417309532506.

Steinberg, R. J. and Figart, D. M. (1999) 'Emotional labor since the managed heart'. *Annals of the American Academy of Political and Social Science*, 561, 8–26.

Umamaheswar, J. and Tan, C. (2020) '"Dad, wash your hands": Gender, care work, and attitudes toward risk during the COVID-19 pandemic'. *Socius: Sociological Research for a Dynamic World*, 6, 237802312096437. https://doi.org/10.1177/2378023120964376.

Watson, L. (2017) 'Young people who care for a family member with physical or mental health problems: Can research better reflect the interests of young carers?'. In Harding, R., Fletcher, R. and Beasley, C. (eds) *Revaluing Care in Theory, Law and Policy: Cycles and connections*. London: Routledge, 81–96.

World Bank (2020) 'GDP per capita (current US$) – Pakistan'. https://data.worldbank.org/indicator/NY.GDP.PCAP.CD?locations=PK (accessed 30 January 2023).

Zafar, N., Naeem, M., Zehra, A., Muhammad, T., Sarfraz, M., Hamid, H., Enam, K., Moaz, M., Shah, B., Ishaque, S. and Muhammad, N. (2021) 'Parenting practices, stressors and parental concerns during COVID-19 in Pakistan'. *Child Abuse & Neglect*, 130 (1), 105393. https://doi.org/10.1016/j.chiabu.2021.105393.

5
Russia: life, learning and family agency under COVID-19

Maria Dobryakova, Elizaveta Sivak and Olesya Yurchenko

In this chapter we analyse how the life of Russian families with schoolchildren changed under COVID-19. Russia offers a story of the pandemic in a country with relatively mild and lightly enforced restrictions. Its only lockdown was comparatively brief (two months in 2020), and mostly affected major cities.

We conducted ethnographically oriented observations and online interviews with 38 families from across Russia. The major and persisting change in family routines was the abrupt switch to home-based schooling – universal for all regions of Russia – in the middle of March 2020, which, after the summer holidays, for many pupils in Years 5–9 lasted until winter 2021.

We analysed families' behaviour in the context of the pandemic with a special focus on their instances of agency: (1) how people acted in different situations (which restrictions they complied with and which they ignored) and (2) how they were able to turn the challenges of the period into an opportunity. We found that parents' occupation shapes their responses to and experiences of school closures. Those from non-routine professional backgrounds engaged with more agentic behaviour in everyday and schooling routines under COVID-19 than those in more routine-based occupations.[1] Those engaged in non-routine professions had more room to exercise agency in their jobs and they had a higher agentic capacity. It made their transition to home-based schooling smoother, and it is this same capacity which made families feel more confident under the pandemic. In conclusion we consider some of the long-term implications of this finding for teaching and learning more generally, as well as the needs of children of parents in routine-based occupations.

Introduction

Russia offers a story of the pandemic in a country with a peculiar combination of national features. Geographically, its territory is vast and regional development is uneven — hence the question of policy coherence (Zubarevich 2013; Zubarevich and Safronov 2020; Tóth-Czifra 2020; World Bank Group 2020). Socio-culturally, it has been under the long shadow of its Soviet past — hence the question of trust and values (for example, Klicperova-Baker and Kostal 2018, especially p. 29; Kulin and Meuleman 2015). Politically, it claims a position of an ambitious and strong international player — hence an issue for policy choices and vaccine development (Yaffa 2021; World Bank Group 2020). An interplay of these features underlies the country's responses to the challenges of the pandemic and should be kept in mind, even though the data we discuss in this chapter are of a smaller scale.

We explore life in the pandemic at the household level, looking into the coping practices of families with school-age children. We chose this focus for our analysis for two reasons. On the one hand, learning from home during the lockdowns was one of the biggest impacts of the pandemic in Russia. This is partly due to the notable poverty rate, coupled with the obvious fact that families' experience of home-schooling to a large extent depended on their resources, including 'hardware': whether a family had enough spare rooms and electronic devices to facilitate home-based learning. Although the official poverty rate in Russia (12.7 per cent) seems to be comparable to that of Germany (10.4 per cent), and lower than that of the United States (17.8 per cent), sociological data suggest that almost one third of the Russian population is affected by poverty[2] (Brand 2021; for an overview of students' conditions and environments for home-schooling prior to the crisis see OECD 2020).

On the other hand, as educational researchers we had a hunch that difficulties faced by families were partly rooted also in the schooling habits and traditions that had long gone unquestioned but — when challenged by the crisis — led to profound school failures.

Our aim in this chapter is to explore families' response to the pandemic, with an emphasis on their schooling attitudes and strategies. We focus on two research questions:

- How do families react when an unexpected major change — such as the uncertainty and threat of COVID-19, and inconsistent government regulations — disrupts their established social practices in everyday life and schooling?

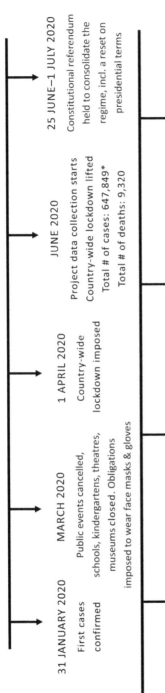

Figure 5.1 Timeline of COVID-19 in Russia. Source: authors.

- What kind of factors affect families' home-schooling experience? In what way may parents' non-routine professional experience support families' capacity to cope with learning?

The pandemic in Russia: country context and key facts

The mass spread of the coronavirus in Russia started in the middle of March 2020. The country was in national lockdown between late March and early June 2020. At later stages, there were no major lockdowns, restrictions referred mostly to working and learning from home. Masks and gloves were mandatory in public from March 2020 (see later, on how people reacted to this). School closures were regulated by regional authorities, with mostly Years 5–9 learning from home until winter 2021.

Daily new cases in Russia were at approximately 8,100 on 27 April 2021;[3] the total number of cases since the start of the pandemic had reached 4.8 million, with a 2.28 per cent fatality rate[4] and Moscow accounting for the largest number of cases.

The first anti-COVID-19 measures were introduced in Russia in mid-March 2020 (for a comprehensive list of Russia's government measures in response to COVID-19, see KPMG 2020). Conventional face-to-face instruction at schools, vocational and higher educational institutions was overwhelmingly replaced with distance learning. Russian regions varied significantly in their schools' capacity to stream lessons online (Saprykina and Volokhovich 2020; Kosaretsky et al. 2022). Some schools offered online lessons, some gave out only homework and instructional materials for children. Most kindergartens were closed for about two months (from the end of March to the end of May 2020). At the end of March, the government announced a series of non-working days throughout the country; paid holidays lasted until mid-May 2020. Only essential workers (those working in healthcare, the food industry, public transportation, etc.) formally remained at their working places. Figure 5.1 on the previous page shows the timeline of COVID-19 spread and government response measures in Russia.

At the same time, a significant number of people in fact switched to work from home. Ministry of Labour data shows that 6.5 million people (3.5 per cent of the labour force) worked remotely after the beginning of the pandemic, as compared to 30,000 people before the pandemic (Ministry of Labour and Social Protection 2021). These are only the official numbers (accounting for those people who were transferred to distance work, as stated in their labour contracts); the actual number of people who worked remotely during the lockdown was probably much higher. According to population polls, the pandemic caused a drop of income for every second Russian citizen (51 per cent) (Olson 2021).

In most Russian regions, commuting restrictions were in effect from the end of March 2020 until the beginning of June 2020. Local authorities passed stay-at-home orders forbidding people to leave the house, except for traveling to work; people were allowed only to seek emergency medical care (in case of a direct threat to health), to shop at the nearest store and/or pharmacy, to take out the rubbish, and to walk pets no further than 100 metres away from their house. Shopping malls, cafes, cultural centres, and sports and entertainment venues were all closed. By the end of March, the passenger traffic in the Moscow underground had decreased by 82 per cent compared to the same period of the previous year.[5] However, this regime of self-isolation was strictly enforced primarily in the larger cities, where police were monitoring compliance with the restrictions.[6] In small cities and rural areas, people were able to spend time outside despite the lockdown.

In general, everyday life was affected most during the 2-month March–May 2020 lockdown. During this period, compliance with the anti-COVID-19 measures (share of people reporting that they wore face masks, limited contact with their friends, observed social distancing requirements, etc.) was the highest (80 per cent); in Autumn 2020, the compliance rate was 60 per cent (Olson 2021). In May 2020, everyday practices began to shift to their usual ways: people gradually resumed face-to-face social contacts and returned to the streets. However, those who had switched to telecommuting continued to work from home. Schools remained closed till the end of the academic year at the end of May. Later, in some regions, secondary and high school students studied remotely in October–December 2020.

The lifestyle of urban residents (especially in large cities serving as major transport hubs, with the highest number of detected cases of infection) was affected by the coronavirus pandemic more significantly, than that of people in smaller towns and rural residents. (For an overview of economic trends of the pandemic and its effects for the Russian labour market, see also World Bank Group 2020.)

Theoretical framework

The pandemic led to serious disruptions in families' everyday life; people found themselves in an unknown, highly uncertain situation – as part of their historical situation and through the communicative context at large.

Coping with the uncertainty implied selection and evaluation of information, making choices. At the same time, families' reactions to the disruptions, and their behaviour in the new context, ranged from complying with government regulations to defiance and protest.

Trying to explain these variations, we analyse families' practices as instances of their agency, influenced by their past experience and future projections. We rely on the model of agency developed by Emirbayer and Mische (1998), but extend it to include the external context of action perceived as framing (Bernstein 1990, 2000).

> Human agency is 'the temporally constructed engagement by actors of different structural environments – the temporal-relational contexts of action – which, through the interplay of habit, imagination, and judgment, both reproduces and transforms those structures in interactive response to the problems posed by changing historical situations (Emirbayer and Mische 1998, 970).

> Framing refers to the principle regulating the communicative practices …Where framing is strong… the transmitter controls the selection, organization, pacing, criteria of communication, posture, and dress of the communicants, together with the arrangement of the physical location (Bernstein 1990, 36–7).

Our analysis starts when people face a dilemma, a choice, a conflict, or an unpredictable situation fraught with some danger. In our case, there are two major dimensions of such an initial dilemma: the initial outbreak of the pandemic (highly unpredictable, with no yet known safe routes to navigate through it) and remote learning (familiar ways of schooling suddenly collapsed and turned upside down).

The official framing (communicative principle) of the governmental response to the pandemic was strong: the state, at the national or regional level, imposed restrictions that regulated even the 'dress' of the communicants (face masks, gloves). As for schooling, its framing has traditionally been strong in Russia: teachers possess the greatest control over the selection, sequencing, pacing and evaluation of the knowledge of the learner. Within the same context, the overall reaction of people varied greatly. Some people felt more confident when given clear guidance and perspective, while others preferred to rely on their own judgement.

So what was there in families' past experience and future projections that led them to different choices? Of course, the socio-economic status of households seems to be a key differentiating factor. However, in a highly uncertain situation — such as life and learning under COVID-19 — one's ability to deal with uncertainty can become a source of strength. Therefore, we also differentiated our participants by their experience of exercising control in the workplace, where some respondents had greater autonomy and scope for decision-making. Our participants differed in terms of their autonomy (personal freedom) in the workplace, currently or in the past: their right to plan work for themselves and someone else, to control and judge it, as well as their freedom to deal with 'clients' of any sort. To do this, we grouped occupations of our participants in two large pools of 'routine' and 'non-routine' labour.

To attribute our participants' employment experience to 'routine' or 'non-routine' categories, we used definitions of occupational tasks suggested in the influential work on the changing task composition of the US labour market (Autor et al. 2003; Autor and Price 2013). Autor, Levy, and Murnane ('ALM') refer to tasks as routine 'if they can be accomplished by machines following explicit programmed rules' and 'non-routine' when 'the rules are not sufficiently well understood to be specified in computer code and executed by machines', and where tasks involve 'adaptability to accepting responsibility for the direction, control, or planning of an activity' (ALM 2003, 1283, 1323).

Routine tasks mainly refer to manual occupations and routine cognitive occupations such as book-keeping and data entry. Non-routine tasks are primarily characteristic of 'professional, managerial, technical, and creative occupations, such as law, medicine, science, engineering, marketing, and design' (ALM 2003, 2). When talking to our participants, we asked them to describe their professional routines and relied on their descriptions, rather than on the formal naming of their occupations.

Therefore, in addition to conventional socio-economic status, we also explored parents' professional background and dispositions based on their work experience. This allowed us to reach a subtler understanding of the relationship between the nature of parents' work and families' subjective well-being during the pandemic.

Sample and method

Our research methods rely on phenomenology (for example, Van Manen 2014; Moustakas 1994) and digital ethnography traditions (for example, Hutchinson 2011) which allow exploration of deeper aspects of practices and attitudes that usually fall through the net in mass surveys. In our analysis, we combine two sets of data about family life, learning and supporting practices in the pandemic: digital ethnographic observations (conducted in October–November 2020 and March–May 2021) and in-depth online interviews (in June–August 2020 and May–June 2021). To grasp a broader family context, we asked the families about their usual routines and pastimes, asked the parents about their own schooling experience and about their professional life, and asked the children about their interests, hobbies, relations within family and with friends. We conducted interviews with 38 families (79 respondents) from 9 regions of Russia; 20 families took part in the digital ethnography.

When selecting participants for our study, we tried to look for representatives of diverse experience: geographically, they came from megapolises and small towns from across Russia; socio-culturally, they belonged to different educational and professional backgrounds. At the same time, we limited the scope of our analysis to a specific demographic group – families with schoolchildren. On the one hand, this large demographic group (there are 16.3 million schoolchildren in Russia) embraces very diverse families in terms of their socio-economic status. On the other hand, learning from home was, according to many surveys (Kosaretsky et al. 2022), a very difficult indirect – as not directly involving health – effect of the pandemic for many families, with severe consequences for some (Shmis 2021).

The average age of our participant parents was 43 years. Seven families in our sample had three or more children; one third of the families had two children, others had one child; the children's ages ranged more-or-less evenly across all years of study, from secondary to high school. In twenty participant families both parents were employed; other families had only one working adult; in one family, there were no working adults. Most families had an average income; four families had below-average income and five families had above-average income. However, in our sample, the impact of these diverse sociodemographic characteristics was negligible, compared to participants' professional activities. This is why, when referring to the interviews, we include only those details that differentiated respondents within the context of the study's focus.

When recruiting respondents, we asked them about their occupation/profession, trying to balance existing representations of 'routine' and 'non-routine' labour. However, in some cases, participants' personal descriptions of their daily professional routines led us to re-attribute them. For example, according to the ALM classification, a cook is a representative of 'non-routine manual labour', but our respondent in this profession described her work as 'routine':

Researcher: Does it ever happen at your work that you do something in a different way, maybe in a new way, a way not expected from you?

Tatiana: No, everything is very stable… My superiors may come. We have a menu; anyone can see it. So I must cook only what is there on the menu, no steps to the side (Tatiana, cook at a canteen; routine tasks).

There were other contradictory professional locations with people employed in preschool education, cleaning services, housing and communal services, or clerical work. Their own professional self-portrait in their own words was decisive for us. Routine workers described their usual day as monotonous, repetitive, lacking any autonomy at their working place:

> All my working days are alike. Well, there might be minor deviations, maybe within some 10 per cent. But essentially it is always the same. Counting money, spending money, cash inflow, cash outflow (Regina, accountant; routine tasks).

> Maintenance requests arrive. I do what is there in a request. Fix what needs to be fixed. I'm a maintenance technician. It's easy, I do it all the time. Manual work, have been doing it all my life. A matter of habit. (Anton, plumber; routine tasks).

Non-routine work involved at least some scope for self-regulation (direction, control and planning of activities). Professional routines were defined by our respondents as solving complex problems in their own way, with a general reference to organizational norms and professional ethics:

> I'm in charge of student mobility, both Russian and international students …They apply, I advise them on various issues … We organize exhibitions …I do the interpreting. If a foreign delegation comes to visit, I meet them at the airport, help them with accommodation, make sure everything is alright with them (Violet, international affairs manager at a regional university; non-routine tasks).

In our sample, we had two formally unemployed housewives, but they both had had some professional experience and turned out to be active self-employed small entrepreneurs. One mother in our sample had lost her job at the beginning of the pandemic, we asked her about her recent professional experience.

We used WhatsApp and Telegram messaging software[7] to collect digital ethnographic data. Each of our participants could choose either WhatsApp or Telegram, as it was important for us that they use an application they were well familiar with. Three of us moderated individual chats with each of the participants; we sent them tasks and prompts on their daily routines with the aim of discovering the participant's dispositions and emotions. For example, we asked them:

- What is your favourite place at home these days? Why?
- Can you picture two to three items that distract you/your child from studies or help you concentrate?
- Can you try to remember up to five questions you asked your child today/your parents asked you today? What were they about?

We used Zoom, Skype or WhatsApp to conduct the interviews; and MaxQDA software to analyse the data. Last but not least, with this research framework, we followed individuals' reactions to the pandemic in social media (Facebook, Instagram, VKontakte, Telegram). Ethical approval was granted by the Institutional Review Board of the National Research University Higher School of Economics (IISE IRB).

Findings

How do participants understand and respond to social distancing measures?

The information about COVID-19 was conflicting and constantly changing during the first stage of the pandemic. Most of our participants were sceptical about government guidelines around COVID-19. They were more frustrated by the psychological aspects of the lockdown and the way things were explained, rather than by the actual threat to their life and health. They did not protest overtly or demonstrate any defiance, but rather made their own individual adjustments to the formal requirements.

Our participants were confused by the news and official public policy guidelines for safety: stay-at-home orders, social distancing, wearing face masks in public. We tried to explore how respondents dealt with the confusing policy and information and how they were choosing their own patterns of behaviour to protect themselves from the virus.

Almost all respondents stated that they felt anxious and distressed at the outbreak of COVID-19. They felt that they could not protect themselves and the ones they loved. Describing their psychological condition, many participants used such words as 'uncertainty', 'fear' and 'anxiety':

> As if the whole world has become dangerous. Our entrance has been plastered with some hysterical leaflets. Must be our maintenance office to have scattered these silly posters. I was reading them and couldn't help wondering — what is it? a plague?! … It felt like all the curtains were drawn and the verdict announced — 'there will be no dawn for humankind' (Elvira, engineer; non-routine tasks).

> It was a state of unpleasantness, discomfort, you know… And the city looked absolutely deserted, dead. People were either absent altogether, or shied away from each other, avoided each other, it was unpleasant. Even now, it is summer, we already go out into the street, but I remember that feeling, I would never want it to come back (Anissa, software tester; non-routine tasks).

To reduce distress, some respondents refrained from watching TV or reading news on the internet as the constant stream of disturbing news only escalated their fears. In some families, there was one person who gathered essential news and data (the number of COVID-19 cases per region, per country, and so on) and then shared it with the family. Men were more often in charge of choosing trusted sources of information:

> … my husband is very good at browsing information, just don't ask me where he finds it, I have no idea, it's him, he is good at it. He's so good at critical thinking. I usually just ask him (Anissa, software tester; non-routine tasks).

> My husband is responsible for the internet, he reads and communicates a lot there. I only watch the federal news, the First Channel news on TV. My husband is trying to comprehend. Well, to be honest, there's still a lack of understanding … some kind of uncertainty. What kind of virus is it, where does it come from, how does it spread, there are so many versions. It's still not clear where it came from. Why such a great country, such a developed world cannot create a vaccine … (Maria, nursery teacher; routine tasks).

All our respondents greeted the lockdown initiatives with some caution. Least of all they trusted information coming from municipal authorities (other ethnographic studies from Russia support this observation: Kholyavin 2020; Tartakovskaya 2021). The latter were often judged as incompetent, and measures they introduced were often associated with political gain. This is why many of participants searched for 'non-official' trustworthy sources of information to be able to clarify for themselves what precautions they should take to stay safe.

The major factor of the scepticism seems to be rooted in the past (Soviet) experience, where it became a habit to observe the discrepancy between slogans and reality. The way of avoiding an undesirable strong framing was, thus, familiar – 'pretend you agree and then do it your way'.[8]

As for the future projections of the pandemic, they were highly uncertain, on the one hand, and seemed to be no worse than other existing diseases, on the other. This also supported the attitude of scepticism (in our sample, we had no overt COVID-19-dissidents, but they are not rare in the country in general, as our analysis of social media reveals).

> It's just a usual flu. Why all the restrictions? Ah, it's just an act for show (Anton, plumber; routine tasks).

> I believe, the dangers are exaggerated … I absolutely don't understand why we must be wearing gloves. I couldn't find a plausible explanation. Masks, okay, I would wear a mask, if there is a rule, no need to break it, it's not too difficult for me to comply. But then it became clear that it's just a formality, nothing more, I saw people make masks out of shirts, pillow cases, it makes no sense, gives you no protection whatsoever! If you are not allowed to enter a shop without a mask, okay, let it be, say, an old shirt mask (Liz, owner of a small tourist business; non-routine tasks).

We discovered that attitudes towards government guidelines differed considerably, depending on families' involvement with routine versus non-routine work. People in routine occupations relied more on circulating hearsay, referring to their friends and local community. They seldom felt it necessary to look for alternative information other than that provided by federal and local TV channels.[9] They often felt confused trying to prioritize sources of information:

> You don't know who to trust: either TV, or people. On TV they say one thing, but people around, they say something else, well, on the street ... You still don't understand who is saying what ... People, they all are saying something different. Some say: this is all nonsense ... As far as I know, none of my friends has yet gotten sick (Anton, plumber; routine tasks).

> They escalated the situation a lot, this is why there is such a gap between what they say in the news and what we have here in real life. And this causes a kind of distrust, I think (Regina, accountant; routine tasks).

Those in non-routine occupations searched for more robust information about strategies for staying safe, deliberately combining diverse sources and comparing them for consistency. They mentioned an array of mass media and specialized sources such as WHO recommendations, online-newspapers (*RBK-daily*, *Meduza*, *Vedomosti*), medical media (*The Lancet*), medical groups in the social networks (including public accounts of trustworthy doctors, heads of COVID-hospitals). Non-routine workers also often mentioned professionals (doctors, microbiologists, virologists) whom they personally knew as important sources of information:

> We have a chat of St. Petersburg parents, it's called Littleone, there are lots of interesting threads. I have friends there. There is, for example, a thread of 'Doctors United' ... And this information from them, from those mothers-doctors, it's most trustworthy. They are parents themselves, but someone is a doctor in this hospital, someone is a nurse, and they share first-hand news from the inside (Olga, employed in the communal services; non-routine tasks).

> A very good friend of mine is a biologist; he sells personal safety wear. He's been doing it all his life. So, he said, and there couldn't be two minds about it, that face masks cannot help anyone. He said this when we still did not know anything, but everything [in his shop] had already been sold out. He said no masks can help anyone, because of the size of this virus, it cannot be held by usual face masks, their weaving is too large, you need to wear respirators or reinforced masks, but they are not suitable for an untrained person, you just won't be able to wear them. Well, okay, we are told to wear face masks, so we do (Liz, owner of a small tourist business; non-routine tasks).

The first month of the lockdown (March 2020) was the period when most participants in our research abided by the recommendations and restrictions. On the one hand, it was the time of utmost uncertainty, and participants did what they were told by the state and healthcare authorities. On the other hand, it was the period when the state authorities strictly controlled how the public guidelines were followed. In a month, pronounced differences could be observed in behaviour patterns of individuals within their households and the community.

People from routine occupations tended to ascribe responsibility for protection against the virus to external authorities (that is, were drawn to the external locus of control). At the early stage, they followed the public policy rules, as they feared fines or worried about their own health and their family. However, when looking at their neighbours in the local community they realized that some dared to violate the restrictions, and started doing the same:

> And so, probably, for the first month we strictly observed [the rules], did not leave the house, and then … we all started to go out … Because after all, everyone was going out, somehow everyone was relaxed about it … You still relax sooner or later. We have not heard of any cases in the area. We all communicate with each other here. We have such a compact neighbourhood; we all know each other. If someone got sick, we would quickly spread it. We still wear masks when we go shopping, but only because it is forbidden to pay at the checkout without masks (Tatiana, cook at a canteen; routine tasks).

> At the very beginning, of course, we followed the rules, but even then we did so only because it was mandatory, and not because we were afraid of something… (Regina, accountant; routine tasks).

The most controversial and heated debate was about face masks: who should be wearing a mask and where, whether masks really protect and whether they may harm.

> If it were not for the fines, I would not wear a mask, I see no protection against this. These masks, they don't protect against this disease, that's my opinion. Because they just cause even more dirt. You pull it with your hands constantly, and it's all this summer heat, you sweat, it slips, you sweat, so it causes even more dirt (Anton, plumber; routine tasks).

There were numerous reports of aggressive behaviour in public transportation when a passenger refused to wear a mask; aggression might be towards either a person without a face mask or someone who is asking her co-commuters to put on a mask.[10] It was a widespread practice to wear a mask under/around the chin: 'I don't care but if you insist let's pretend we play this game …'. This *faire-semblant* behaviour on behalf of many citizens was coupled with a *laissez-faire* style of enforcement on behalf of the authorities that resulted in a lack of trust towards government initiatives and prescriptions, including vaccination.

Non-routine workers tended to demonstrate a more active social stance and sought to rationalize their choices pertaining to the pandemic daily routines. They tried to make informed decisions by evaluating the risk–benefit balance. For example, some chose to get up early in the morning and go for a walk while the streets were still empty because staying constantly indoors, in their opinion, was in the long run fraught with more risk:

> We ordered everything in, didn't go shopping at all. Didn't communicate with anyone. But it would've been insane to stay indoors all the time, not to go for a walk at all, that was driving me crazy (Anissa, software tester; non-routine tasks).

Overall, non-routine workers resorted to more complicated safety routines: they used hand sanitizers regularly, cleaned their groceries with an antiseptic, washed their clothes after coming home and some even bought a pulse oximeter to monitor their blood's oxygen saturation. They explained their routines as follows:

> All our measures and precautions, they are entirely our own decision. I mean, we read about all this stuff on the WHO website and figured out what we can do, what we cannot do… If we went out, we then, of course, disinfected everything and everywhere. We have a chlorine spray, we keep it near the front door, so that everyone coming from outside could spray the things. I immediately sewed face masks for all of us. We just didn't have time to buy a pulse oximeter (Violet, international affairs manager at a university; non-routine tasks).

Another important difference in social attitudes towards public safety recommendations which manifested along our routine/non-routine cleavage was that of the 'relevant other'. The health of other family members was the prime concern for people involved in routine occupations. Whereas those involved in non-routine occupations tried to envisage – at least in what there were sharing with us – a safer position for both their immediate family and wider society, taking into consideration more vulnerable senior citizens:

> Yes. Because a mask is not only a way to keep yourself safe, but also a way not to infect anyone else. So this is, let's say, such a double responsibility. For myself and for others, too (Violet, international affairs manager at a regional university; non-routine tasks).

> As I say, it's better to overdo it than to miss it. And then, if we look at it from the point of view of elderly people. Suppose I was a carrier. I used to communicate a lot, I've always had a very large circle of friends ... I will not argue about efficiency, because I am afraid we still understand little at all in this whole story (Ann, accompanist to young musicians; non-routine tasks).

'Responsible citizenship' seemed to be an important aspect of their identity for some people during the pandemic (Kislyakov and Shmeleva 2021; Kholyavin 2020; Tartakovskaya 2021). In our sample, non-routine workers explained that they voluntarily followed public guidelines and were careful not to put others at risk (thus adhering to the WHO ethics: 'no one is safe until everyone is safe'). According to the participants in this subgroup, as far as it was technically possible, they took steps to ensure that they did not harm others and, as a behavioural model, continued to stick to the same 'responsible' values they had been used to before the pandemic (sorting waste, supporting charities, etc.). In their interviews, our participants referred to 'staying at home' as an instance of their agentic behaviour and rational choice. They clearly put themselves in opposition to those who ignored public guidelines for safe behaviour.

Impact on family life and learning from home routines

Family life changed a great deal during the pandemic. School closures brought an increase in parents' involvement in childcare and their child's education. At the same time, the switch to remote working and social isolation measures meant that some fathers, especially, were more exposed to increased family needs, simply because they were spending more time at home.

In our interviews, we asked the informants how and, in particular, who was involved in their children's distance learning. Our results suggest that there was only a moderate increase in fathers' involvement in childcare and children's education, despite the drastic rise in the need for parental help, especially during the first weeks following school closures. We found that irrespective of mothers' and fathers' work arrangements, mothers were primarily responsible for organizing distance learning. They controlled the whole process on a daily basis: helped the child with different tasks (doing homework, solving technical problems with the online-learning platforms); controlled whether the child was attending their online-lessons, whether they uploaded homework on time; communicated with the school, arranged for assistance from others (teachers, father); and tried to support the child's learning motivation. Mothers were also responsible for the emotional labour, necessary to facilitate successful learning:

> What is my role on their studies? Well, it is their overall emotional [state], it depends on me. If the ambiance is calm, everyone at home is calm, then the child is calm and comfortable (Xenia, beauty therapist; non-routine tasks).

In contrast to this, fathers were usually involved only as temporary assistants in childcare and education: every now and then they helped with school subjects (especially some difficult homework in maths or sciences), if the child or the mother asked them to. Typically, these were situations where the mother could not help, or where the father had a special interest or professional background in the subject.

> Our dad is a programmer, and there are topics that only dad can help him with. So yes, we hear it all the time: 'Dad, what is this?'. I mean, it is interesting for [my son] and he understands that his dad can give it to him, so he corners him, demands (Regina, accountant, routine tasks).

Researcher:	Do you control [your son's] studies?
Anton:	Well, no, it's mostly my wife, she does.
Researcher:	Studies, that's mostly her sphere of control, right?
Anton:	Yes. Yes. Yes, that's hers.
Researcher:	Does she ever ask you to help with anything related to their studies?
Anton:	Sure. When she is away at work and I'm at home, I can help with some questions if they ask (Anton, plumber; routine tasks).

In our sample of 38 families, most fathers were not involved in the learning process on any regular basis and typically were not in charge of home-schooling. The change brought about by the pandemic was discernible but did not change existing behavioural patterns. Although there was an increase in fathers' involvement in their children's education during the lockdown, it mainly had to do with the frequency of occasional assistance, rather than in sharing a more general responsibility for managing children's studies.

Similarly, there was no evidence in our interviews that the division of parents' labour pertaining to childcare duties was questioned and reconsidered within families during the lockdown. Rather, it seems that mothers automatically took on the additional responsibilities brought about by the lockdown. As before, they were responsible for their children's education and well-being.

In general, the three most frequent complaints around home-schooling (other than those related to 'technical' problems and lack of devices) mentioned by families were as follows:

- Children lacking the skills necessary to support self-regulated learning, including planning one's time and setting priorities ('My son/daughter couldn't do anything without me, I had to keep reminding and assisting', was typical of comments from mothers.)
- A lack of teacher's guidance in the presentation, explanation or revision of the disciplinary knowledge ('We were left on our own, no support whatsoever, *content was not delivered.*')
- A mismatch between learners and their textbooks ('Textbooks are too difficult to comprehend, I cannot grasp what the main idea is' was a recurrent complaint, even from avid readers.)

The first complaint, about parents' forced involvement in the management of their children's studies, is also recurrent in quantitative surveys (for example, Knopik et al. 2021). With the latter two, however, we are entering a new domain.

We looked at these through the prism of the scope of control that teachers and students have over learning, and their agency in response to changing situations (Emirbayer and Mische 1998; Bernstein 1990). What kind of disruptions might explain the recurring complaints? Were they new disruptions brought about by the pandemic? Or were they already-existing disruptions, only revealed by the pandemic?

In Russia, the usual framing of schooling is very strong, which means that teachers possess the greatest control over the selection, sequencing, pacing and evaluation of the learner's knowledge. Teachers emphasize 'the correct way' of performing a task (Russia is not an exception here). School life is structured by bells, classrooms, lessons and textbooks, with homework taking two to three hours every day. Teachers tend to encourage discipline: in most schools, children are not expected to ask questions during lessons. The children from our sample mentioned that they rely heavily on textbooks. Their tasks are focused on the repetition and memorization of important facts and classifications, or mastering a method (like column division). For example, homework in history, geography and biology would usually include reading and reciting a paragraph from a textbook. Homework is almost always graded, which makes some children cheat. They confessed that they often copy and paste ready-made answers from special databases.

All in all, many children in our sample found their studies boring, tiring and stressful (at least in many of the disciplines). Given this, they needed an external motivation to keep going: the strong framing (control) comes from school and is further supported by parents who control formal aspects of studies, such as timing and grades.

During the periods of learning from home the general situation with schooling did not change. In most cases, neither textbooks nor learning tasks offered by the teachers were engaging (just as in the normal schooling). Many children could not understand textbooks (that is, informational texts) and did not know how to use the internet for general educational tasks. Both parents and children mentioned that they were struggling with textbooks:

> It seems to me that it [the textbook] is not very convenient. Everything is somehow not highlighted, your gaze does not even focus on some rule … And the child is stupidly staring at the page and can't concentrate (Regina, accountant; routine tasks).

> It is very difficult for me to make sense of what our textbooks say. I get lost in their words, all those official sentences, official language. I just don't understand anything. It feels like [opening] our constitution and starting to read it. I can't comprehend it, if it is not translated. I don't understand: are there Chinese hieroglyphs or Russian Cyrillic characters (Lily, 16-year-old school student).

In the absence of children's internal motivation, many parents had to provide an alternative enforcement of framing. Parents helped their children scrape through and make meaning of textbooks, reminded them of their timetable, uploaded homework. It is not surprising that so many found it exhausting.

> Home-schooling is not learning … nothing just entered his head, no doubt … it's been just total mess. [His mum] was constantly sitting with him … It's his mum, she studied more than he did. They asked such questions, such questions, you yourself don't know the answers to these questions (Anton, plumber; routine tasks).

> I have never been so involved in my children's studies. They constantly need my help, I constantly had to control them … I would absolutely not want to go online again, absolutely not (Liz, owner of a small tourist business; non-routine tasks).

> [The main problem with distance-learning is that it] makes children very relaxed, … no discipline… They get up late, don't have meals at their usual times… Online-learning makes them lazy (Victoria, office-manager; routine tasks).

But this was not true for all the families. We noticed an important difference between parents from routine and non-routine occupations. Let us remind the reader here that routine labour in our approach is not about fixed working hours but rather about the repetitive and predictable nature of labour, as described by our participants.

Parents from routine occupations tried to copy the strong school framing (the formal part of it), to resurrect the usual routines: they controlled what their children did and uploaded every bit of homework in time, made sure they got good grades, read all the paragraphs from the textbooks they were asked to read. On the other hand, 'non-routine' parents often attempted to explore alternative ways to organize their children's studies, designed for their specific circumstances and preferences. Such parents were able to find advantages in home-based learning they would like to keep for their children's studies in general, such as a more flexible timetable, being able to choose priorities and using additional online resources.

Non-routine parents managed to work out an alternative – weaker – framing for their children's learning, which made the children feel more responsible for their own studies and learning. This approach proved more efficient and sustainable. Such families expressed much more confidence, satisfaction and optimism when describing their experience of distance learning:

Distance learning? Well, not bad with us, it was fine... Of course, you can't go anywhere ...why we accepted these conditions, we adapted ... perhaps it was even more comfortable and took less time ... it seemed that everything could be done faster, somehow there was more fun. And she liked the novelty ... some kind of new experience. Children are always interested in it, to try something new ... I do not interfere with her lessons ... she is a responsible child (Julia, manager in cleaning; non-routine tasks).

Distance learning suits us perfectly to make our own timetable ... We realized that it is just a perfect option for us. It is so wonderful when we can do everything that needs to be done but we do it according to our own timetable (Liz, owner of a small tourist business; non-routine tasks).

My son has been quite happy about it. He felt comfortable. Usually he doesn't like his school, just doesn't like anything about it ... and during their distance learning he had a choice: I can do this today and I can do that tomorrow. He was able to steer his studies himself – when you do something... So there are more options, more choice. That is, he was comfortable. And it is much easier for me, too, when he is comfortable, morally easier (Inma, lawyer; non-routine tasks).

Discussion and conclusions

Our most important observation from this study was the difference in coping strategies between parents from routine and non-routine professional backgrounds, respectively. Their workplace experience tends to be a key differentiating factor for both of our research questions. This difference is not limited to parents' socio-economic status as described by their level of income and formal education (although there is an association, of course). It also has to do with the nature of their accumulated professional experience: whether it has involved flexible and non-standard work routines; tolerance and adaptability to uncertainty; a certain degree of control over choices and decision-making – in whatever sphere that may have been.

The framing of new everyday routines under the pandemic restrictions introduced by the state was strong. However, at the family level, people could on an individual basis either break, ignore or follow the rules. Their response to this changing historical situation was defined by the interplay of habit (past professional experience), imagination (scope considered relevant for decision-making), and judgement (diversity of sources, their reliability).

Those from mostly routine backgrounds tended to rely on their immediate circle of friends, neighbours and colleagues, and seldom questioned official sources of information about the virus. Whereas participants with a non-routine background sought to expand the range of sources, to find first-hand professional expertise rather than second-hand administrative recommendations. Their own re-imagining of the new situation involved greater control over the selection, organization, and communication arrangements during the lockdowns and imposed restrictions.

With schooling and learning from home the situation was similar. With the outbreak of the pandemic, when schools were closed and children had to learn from home, the school could no longer sustain its strong framing. Schools tried to transfer their usual ways online 'as is' but mostly failed: some had poor internet connection, some 'lost' children behind turned-off cameras and organizational disruptions. What was there left to reach out to children and keep them learning? It could either be activities triggered by children's internal motivation or an alternative enforcement of framing.

For those families who usually delegate full control to the school and have little experience of acting in new and uncertain environments (a disposition we associated with routine occupations), home-schooling experience was more difficult. Such families were easily left behind. When separated physically from their teachers (who could no longer guide them and help select aspects of meaning, or organize and pace learning), many children were not able to learn, and their parents did not know how to support them, even if they wanted to.

At the same time, our results suggest that the problems that families encountered in home-based learning are not new. They are rooted in the pre-existing strong framing of schooling, in which there is no room for learners' agency, both children and their parents are not given opportunities to gain experience of independent learning. This trend is largely overlooked in Russian mass education, but stands in sharp contrast with the general shift in many national systems of education, at least at the level of their intended curricula.

In the late 1990s to early 2000s, a number of countries started to actively transform their education systems to adjust their school graduates' competences to the demands of the changing labour market and, more broadly, 'global challenges'. Simultaneously, schools have been experiencing pressure from new technological and informational opportunities to change their formats of teaching and learning. The general global shift in education is associated with an enhancement of the learner's role (this is very well captured and reflected in the OECD Future of Education and Skills 2030 project[11]): the former compliant passive recipient is now turning into an active agent who controls the selection, organization and pacing of knowledge. When this becomes the case, learners are less vulnerable when left on their own without daily teacher's guidance.

Therefore, from a longer-term perspective, sustainable solutions seeking to mitigate the painful experience of schooling disruptions should look deeper than access to the internet and the number of electronic devices per family – which are crucial but not sufficient. A weaker framing offering some room for the learner – in the design of learning situations, tasks and choice of textbooks – would stimulate self-regulated learning skills and internal motivation; the system would then remain sustainable even without external enforcement.

Notes

1. In making this distinction between 'non-routine' and 'routine', we draw on the terminology of Autor, Levy and Murnane (2003), which we discuss further in the section 'Theoretical framework'.
2. '…more than a third of households cannot afford to buy each family member two pairs of comfortable, seasonally appropriate shoes, and over half cannot cope with unexpected spending' (Brand 2021, 146). These are official government data. However, Russian independent demographers and economists have consistently argued that the real scale of the crisis was much larger and that officials manipulated the statistics. The interplay of the major political events and quarantine restrictions on the timeline also indirectly support this charge. For more detail see, e.g., https://www.washingtonpost.com/world/europe/russia-covid-count-fake-statistics/2021/10/16/b9d47058-277f-11ec-8739-5cb6aba30a30_story.html and https://www.nytimes.com/2020/05/11/world/europe/coronavirus-deaths-moscow.html.
3. https://www.statista.com/statistics/1102303/coronavirus-new-cases-development-russia/.
4. Data from Johns Hopkins University of Medicine, see https://coronavirus.jhu.edu/map.html, https://coronavirus.jhu.edu/region/russia (accessed 8 March 2023).
5. https://www.mos.ru/news/item/71882073/?onsite_molding=2.
6. For example, stopping cars to check if the driver and the passengers had obtained a special permit; stopping dog owners and joggers in parks reminding them that they were not supposed to walk there. As this sort of enforcement did not make much sense (violators were remaining in the open air and keeping their distance, or were in their private cars), it made people question other restrictions imposed by the authorities.
7. We did not use any professional software for the digital ethnography due to research budget restraints.
8. A simple example may help understand the roots better. Many of the Russians who lived under the Soviet regime, remember slogans 'Long live the Communist Party of the USSR!' on buildings, walls, fences – any place to which legible letters could be stuck. For most people, it was no more than a decoration that you do not pay much attention to. Ironically, this does

not mean that Russians are immune to propaganda. It means that many of them are focused only on their private life (as a result of propaganda) and do not interfere with the state, while the latter does not invade their private lives until they interfere with the state. For a subtler analysis of state–society relationships in Russia see Forrat 2017.
9 Most Russian citizens (83% in urban areas, 72% in rural areas) have access to the internet (Statista 2020); the choice of sources of information is defined mostly by their personal preferences.
10 In Saint Petersburg, a passenger was stabbed to death on the bus after a quarrel over face masks. https://www.reuters.com/article/us-health-coronavirus-russia-murder-idUSKBN2801KE.
11 https://www.oecd.org/education/2030-project/.

References

Autor, D. H., Levy, F. and Murnane, R. J. (2003) 'The skill content of recent technological change: An empirical exploration'. *Quarterly Journal of Economics*, 118 (4), 1279–333.

Autor, D. H. and Price, B. (2013) 'The changing task composition of the US labor market: An update of Autor, Levy, and Murnane (2003)'. https://app.getsphere.com/david-autor/articles/the-changing-task-composition-of-the-us-labor-market-an-update-of-autor-levy-and-murnane-2003 (accessed 8 March 2023).

Bernstein, B. (1990) *Class, Codes and Control*. Vol. 4: *The structuring of pedagogic discourse*. London: Routledge.

Bernstein, B. (2000) *Pedagogy, Symbolic Control and Identity*. Revised ed. London: Routledge.

Brand, M. (2021) 'The OECD poverty rate: Lessons from the Russian case'. *Global Social Policy*, 21 (1), 144–7.

Emirbayer, M. and Mische, A. (1998) 'What is agency?'. *American Journal of Sociology*, 103 (4), 962–1023.

Forrat, N. (2017) 'The Infrastructure of Authoritarianism: State–society relationships, public sector organizations, and regime resilience in Putin's Russia'. Doctoral dissertation, Northwestern University, Evanston, IL.

Hutchinson, K. (2011) 'Homework through the eyes of children: What does visual ethnography invite us to see?'. *European Educational Research Journal*, 10 (4), 545–58.

Kholyavin, A. O. (2020) 'Социальное бездействие на ранних этапах пандемии COVID-19' [Social inactivity in the early stages of the COVID-19 pandemic]. Article in Russian. *Sotsiologicheskie issledovania*,11, 139–48. https://doi.org/10.31857/S013216250010722-7.

Kislyakov, P. A. and Shmeleva, E. A. (2021) 'Prosocial orientation of Russians during the COVID-19 pandemic: Caring for others and yourself'. *Frontiers in Psychology*, 12, 629467. https://doi.org/10.3389/fpsyg.2021.629467.

Klicperova-Baker, M. and Kostal, J. (2018) 'Democratic values in the post-communist region: The incidence of traditionalists, skeptics, democrats, and radicals'. In Lebedeva, N., Dimitrova, R. and Berry, J. (eds) *Changing Values and Identities in the Post-Communist World*. Cham: Springer, 27–511.

Knopik, T., Błaszczak, A., Maksymiuk, R. and Oszwa, U. (2021) 'Parental involvement in remote learning during the COVID-19 pandemic: Dominant approaches and their diverse implications'. *European Journal of Education*, 56 (4), 623–40. https://doi.org/10.1111/ejed.12474.

Kosaretsky, S., Zair-Bek, S., Kersha, Y. and Zvyagintsev, R. (2022) 'General education in Russia during COVID-19: Readiness, policy response, and lessons learned'. In Reimers, F. M. (ed.) *Primary and Secondary Education During COVID-19*. Cham: Springer, 227–61. https://doi.org/10.1007/978-3-030-81500-4_9.

KPMG (2020) 'Government and institution measures in response to COVID-19: Russia'. https://kpmg.com/bg/en/home/insights/2020/05/government-and-institution-measures-in-response-to-covid-19.html (accessed 10 February 2023).

Kulin, J. and Meuleman, B. (2015) 'Human values and Welfare State support in Europe: An East–West divide?'. *European Sociological Review*, 31 (4), 418–32.

Ministry of Labour and Social Protection (2021) *Remote Work Perspectives* (in Russian). Ministry of Labour and Social Protection. https://mintrud.gov.ru/employment/72 (accessed 10 August 2021).

Moustakas, C. (1994) *Phenomenological Research Methods*. Thousand Oaks, CA: Sage.
Olson, A. (ed.) (2021) *Sociology of the Pandemic: Corona FOM Project*. Moscow: Institute of the Public Opinion Foundation (in Russian). https://media.fom.ru/fom-static/ФОМ%20-%202021%20-%20Книга%20-%20Социология%20пандемии_Проект%20коронаФОМ.pdf (accessed 8 March 2023).
Organisation for Economic Cooperation and Development (OECD) (2020) *School Education During COVID-2019: Were teachers and students ready? Country Note: Russian Federation*. https://www.oecd.org/education/Russian-Federation-coronavirus-education-country-note.pdf (accessed 23 August 2021).
Saprykina, D. and Volokhovich, A. (2020) 'The problems of transition to distance learning in the Russian Federation through the eyes of teachers'. *Education Facts*, 4, 29.
Shmis, T. (2021) 'The pandemic poses a threat to academic progress of Russian school students'. *World Bank Opinion*, 10 May 2021. https://www.worldbank.org/en/news/opinion/2021/05/10/the-pandemic-poses-a-threat-to-academic-progress-of-russian-school-students (accessed 3 August 2021).
Statista (2020) 'Share of households with internet access in Russia in 2020, by area'. https://www.statista.com/statistics/255129/internet-penetration-in-russia/.
Tartakovskaya, I. (2021) 'Trust in the face of the pandemic' (in Russian). *Sociologichesky Journal*, 27 (2), 68–89. https://doi.org/10.19181/socjour.2021.27.2.8087.
Tóth-Czifra, A. (2020) 'The malaise of the Russian regions'. *Institute of Modern Russia (IMR)*, 4 May 2020. https://imrussia.org/en/analysis/3106-the-malaise-of-the-russian-regions (accessed 23 August 2021).
Van Manen, M. (2014) *Phenomenology of Practice: Meaning-giving methods in phenomenological research and writing*. London: Routledge.
World Bank Group (2020) 'Russia's Economy Loses Momentum Amidst COVID-19 Resurgence; Awaits relief from vaccine'. *Russia Economic Report no. 44*. December 2020. https://openknowledge.worldbank.org/bitstream/handle/10986/34950/Russia-Economic-Report-Russias-Economy-Loses-Momentum-Amidst-COVID-19-Resurgence-Awaits-Relief-from-Vaccine.pdf (accessed 15 September 2021).
Yaffa, J. (2021) 'Russia beat the world to a vaccine, so why is it falling behind on vaccinations?'. *The New Yorker*, 12 April 2021. https://www.newyorker.com/news/daily-comment/russia-beat-the-world-to-a-vaccine-so-why-is-it-falling-behind-on-vaccinations (accessed 15 September 2021).
Zubarevich, N. (2013) 'Four Russias: Human potential and social differentiation of Russian regions and cities'. In Lipman M. and Petrov N. (eds) *Russia 2025*. London: Palgrave Macmillan, 67–85. https://doi.org/10.1057/9781137336910_4.
Zubarevich, N. and Safronov, S. (2020) 'Russian regions in the acute phase of the coronavirus crisis: Differences from previous economic crises of the 2000s'. *Regional Research of Russia*, 10, 443–53. https://doi.org/10.1134/S2079970520040115.

6
Singapore: families living in and through the pandemic

Vineeta Sinha, Pooja Nair,
Narayanan Ganapathy and Daniel Goh

Introduction

In the wake of the confounding spread and persistence of COVID-19 globally, the virus has left a catastrophic impact. However, the deeply ingrained structural inequalities that mark societies mean that individuals, communities and societies experienced the virus and its effects differentially, unequally and unjustly. For Singapore too, an account of how the country coped with the virus, cannot be a uni-dimensional, singular narrative. This project was part of a larger research agenda which interrogates how different Singapore-based communities have been impacted by the pandemic, shifting the lens onto social, cultural and political landscapes, to highlight embedded fault lines and blind spots, which determine how the virus has impacted everyday lives and how individuals have coped. A key register in this chapter rests on the issue of 'inequalities' which has surfaced as a crucial part of Singapore's narrative on COVID-19 management.

In this chapter we present how Singapore's middle-class families have experienced the COVID-19 virus and how they have responded to government-instituted measures and policies. One of the first responses of the Singapore government to the outbreak of the virus was to announce a 'circuit breaker' period from 7 April to 1 June 2020, along with introducing the COVID-19 (Temporary Measures) Bill on 7 April (Lam 2020). Multiple support packages were introduced to address the various impacts of the evolving pandemic on the state's economy and society, through aiding households and businesses. During this period, only essential services remained open, work-from-home and home-based learning were the default positions, individuals could only leave the house for exercising and masks in public places were mandatory. While these measures were instituted to stem the transmission of the virus, they were also hugely disruptive and have changed how Singaporeans live, work, eat and play. Drawing on the everyday life experiences of living with the virus, this chapter argues that the moments of lockdown only conveyed an illusion that life was 'on hold' and that 'everything had stopped'. On the contrary, our data confirm that everyday life has its own rhythm, is dynamic and not suspended for anything, not even for a virus.

This chapter discusses the repercussions of the pandemic and its disruption on the everyday lives of families living in Singapore against the backdrop of government policies. Through a qualitative, longitudinal, ethnographic study with 28 middle-class families over a one-year period, we document the experiences of individuals living through moments of lockdown and beyond. For this study we conducted interviews and regular follow-ups via messaging platforms such as WhatsApp to document the everyday lives of our interlocutors and their families, and to understand their experiences of living through COVID-19. Specifically, we demonstrate that while the pandemic-related changes indeed reconfigured work and family life and individual mental and emotional well-being, the enduring nature of social relationships and gendered division of labour remained intact, even under very particular circumstances of a global pandemic. In capturing those moments of transformation, our data allow us to speak of the emergence of the contours of a 'new normal', where it seems the tendency is that women bear the brunt of pandemic-related changes in the familial space; it remains to be seen how permanent this state will be. A timeline of COVID-19 in Singapore is shown in Figure 6.1.

Country context

With a high population density of 7,810 persons per square kilometre, families and residents in Singapore predominantly live in high-rise flats. In total, 78.7 per cent of the population live in Housing and Development Board (HDB) flats (apartments), which are subsidized public housing, of which 'nearly 1 in 3 households [indicated living] in a HDB 4-room flat' in 2020 (SingStat 2020). A typical HDB four-room flat in Singapore has a floor area of approximately 90 square metres, with three bedrooms and two bathrooms (Yohannan 2020). Another 16 per cent of the population reside in private condominiums/other apartments, and 5 per cent of the

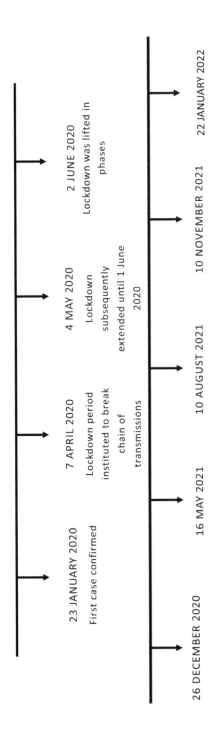

Figure 6.1 Timeline of COVID-19 in Singapore. Source: authors.

population lives in houses (SingStat 2020). Concepts of space and its intersectionality with gender therefore inevitably become critical when considering the implications of the pandemic on the everyday lives of Singaporean families and residents, given that the burden of care-giving falls on the women in patriarchal Singapore and this logic is deeply entrenched. As then Prime Minister Goh Chok Tong once pointed out:

> In a largely patriarchal society, minor areas where women are not accorded the same treatment should be expected so long as the welfare of women and of the family is protected (quoted in Ganapathy 2002, 182).

Such deeply rooted logic manifests in how space and gender intersect and enables us to consider the implications of the pandemic in a deeper manner.

In 2020, 'households comprising of at least one family nucleus – formed by a married couple, or one parent with never-married child(ren) – accounted for 78.0 per cent of resident households, a decrease from 82.9 per cent in 2010' (SingStat 2020). In total, 52.5 per cent of all married couples formed dual-income households (SingStat 2020). While nuclear families remain the dominant family structure within Singapore, it is key to acknowledge both the growing number of married couples not having children and the rise in divorce rates. As of 2020, divorced/separated couples constitute 4.3 per cent of the total population (SingStat 2020). Further, due to the 'prevalence of dual-income parents and a rapidly ageing population', many households have been experiencing a growing need for a domestic helper, where 'every fifth Singaporean household hires a [helper]' (Awang and Wong 2019). The hiring of domestic help has become a necessity rather than a luxury for several residents in Singapore. With the 'Asian ideal' of care work of elderly parents often falling onto women, the increasing number of Singaporean women in the labour force has dictated a need for these domestic helpers to aid in lessening the burden of care work (Huang et al. 2012). Recognizing the existence of diverse family units, as well as the presence of a domestic helper (if any) within the home is essential in contributing to a more nuanced understanding of the individual's experience in coping with the pandemic.

Singapore reported its first case of COVID-19 on 23 January 2020. As of 25 August 2021, Singapore has reported a total of 66,692 cases and 50 fatalities. With the surges in Delta and Omicron variants in the second half of 2021, as of 30 January 2022 Singapore had reported a total of 348,330 cases and 854 deaths from the virus. To the outside world,

Singapore appeared to have managed the pandemic extremely effectively, with relatively lower cases and fatalities. This was made possible by several factors, including Singapore's prior experience of dealing with the SARS virus in 2003 and the public health plans and policies instituted for dealing with future pandemics – specifically the logic and mechanism for tracking and tracing effectively cases of infection across the island. In addition, Singapore's public healthcare infrastructure is world-class. Singapore treated all those who were infected with the COVID virus free of charge, and class background or lack of financial resources were not factors in deaths from the virus. These achievements and successes, notwithstanding, our argument is that at everyday life levels, Singapore residents experienced challenges that cannot be mitigated by the overall 'positive report card' that Singapore received externally.

The government implemented a 'circuit breaker' (CB) for a period of close to two months, from 7 April to 1 June 2020 (see Figure 6.1). The term was carefully curated by the government to signal that the strict measures were meant to *break* the transmissions within the community whilst allowing essential services to continue. This was in essence a period of lockdown whereby residents were only allowed to leave their homes if they worked in the essential services sectors, or to buy groceries or exercise. During this period, Parliament passed the COVID-19 (Temporary Measures) Act, which prohibited social gatherings of all sizes in both public and private spaces. All non-essential retail stores and services were closed, and dining-in at restaurants was not permitted, heavily restricting the movement of individuals. Under this law, the wearing of face masks was compulsory for all residents in Singapore, with exemptions for those engaging in strenuous exercise and children below the age of two years old. Excluding essential services and key economic sectors, most workplaces were closed, and students shifted to a full, home-based learning.

While Singapore was viewed as a model for curbing the spread of the virus during the initial stages of the outbreak, it became apparent that the government underestimated the vulnerability of low-wage migrant workers, which led to a surge of approximately 1,000 daily cases among migrant workers living in dormitories. The cases in the dormitories formed the bulk of Singapore's COVID-19 infections in 2020.

With the end of the CB, Singapore has been striving to gradually reopen its economy in multiple phases (Phases 1, 2 and 3). However, the onset of new waves of community infections delayed the reopening of the economy and businesses, with the enactment of subsidiary phases such as Phase 2 (Heightened Alert), Phase 3 (Heightened Alert) and vaccinated-differentiated safe management measures (see Figure 6.1). During these periods, there was a reversion of measures in attempts to control the number of community cases in Singapore. During Phase 2 (Heightened Alert) period, for instance, dining-in at restaurants ceased and social gatherings were limited to two people. The escalation of infections was attributed to the emergence of new and contagious variants of the virus, such as the Delta, Alpha and Omicron variants.

Nevertheless, the National Vaccination Programme, which has been rolled out in phases since December 2020, has been critical in the reopening of the Singapore economy. Vaccinations have remained voluntary and universally available to all residents in Singapore, free of charge, including to all migrant workers. As of 30 January 2022, 92 per cent of the eligible population and 88 per cent of the total population had received two vaccines and 58 per cent had also received their booster shot. Vaccination-differentiated COVID-19 restrictions were introduced in early August 2021, whereby only fully vaccinated individuals could dine-in at restaurants, in groups of up to five people, and food consumption was permitted in vaccinated-only cinema halls. From 14 February 2022, completion of the booster vaccine was required for residents to maintain their 'fully vaccinated' status. Residents were generally compliant with taking the vaccine, and the country did not encounter much resistance in terms of this although, as with most other countries, there were some initial concerns over the efficacy of the vaccine.

To aid with contact tracing, a national digital check-in system, *SafeEntry*, was put in place whereby individuals had to scan a QR code or their identification cards before entering and leaving public venues and workplaces. In September 2020, *TraceTogether* tokens, a small device that expedites contact tracing through tracking the locations individuals have visited, became available for collection nationwide. In May 2021, the use of the *TraceTogether* mobile application and token for check-ins were made mandatory and replaced the existing *SafeEntry* system, to reduce the average time taken to contact trace from four days to one and a half days.

Multiple financial packages and subsidies were instituted by the government to support Singaporeans through the pandemic. The schemes were focused on assisting industries impacted by COVID-19, lower- and middle-income families, and individuals who experienced job losses and pay cuts, among others. Singapore aimed to move towards approaching the pandemic as an *endemic* disease in the second half of 2021. The rationale was that, as more people got vaccinated, the state could begin to ease regulations such as border restrictions and safe management measures, moving forward with a new state of normalcy.

Theoretical framework

The analytical framing for this research rests on two pivots: 'everyday life' and 'ethnography', both of which we approached as theory and method. The former approaches the everyday, ordinary, taken-for-granted world we live in as an object of scrutiny. Applying this lens to the current project we asked the following analytical questions: How can a sense of everyday-ness be sustained in situations where certainty and predictability are absent? How do individuals and families, living through moments of disruptions to a given social order (as in a pandemic), engage in acts, processes of interaction and sense-making to achieve normalcy? What new modalities and registers of everyday-ness emerge through these transformative experiences? Indeed, what new everyday norms, ethos and practices were produced as families lived through the COVID pandemic? Against this backdrop, we embarked on a research project that operationalized the research questions we listed earlier thus: How does everyday life unfold for individuals and families in moments of lockdown, with constraints on their physical movements, enhanced social isolation and altered modes of social interaction? What shape does everyday life take for various categories of individuals in families – living in and through COVID-19 times? In performing a range of everyday practices that are needed to accomplish daily life, what are the emotional and mental states of these individuals? Our ethnography responds to these queries, by eliciting human, social and cultural details of living with the virus and providing a focused analysis.

Rather than assume a single family type, we problematized the notion of 'family' by acknowledging the following family arrangements, so as to capture the diverse and contrasting everyday experiences of living with the pandemic: nuclear families with children, extended, intergenerational families, single parent families with children and elderly people living alone or with a caregiver. In this, the normative gendered division of labour, embedded in patriarchal notions and firmly defined roles for men and women emerge as an analytical pivot in this project.

Sample and data generation

Even in ordinary circumstances, the intimate nature of everyday life excludes ethnographers from intense participatory observation, so researchers often use 'socially distant' methods such as periodic interviews to peer into everyday life practices. During the COVID-19 outbreak, the restrictions on movement and social lockdowns implemented by authorities to contain it posed additional challenges. The first challenge was the recruitment of research subjects. We were unable to approach potential subjects face-to-face in their natural social settings to gain their trust and willingness to participate in the research. The second challenge was data generation, as we were unable to interact with subjects to observe and interview them in a dynamic way to capture in-depth qualitative data about their everyday lives. The third challenge was to generate data over an extended period, as ethnography entails the embedding of the researcher into communities to continuously collect data about the meanings of practices, which cannot be gleamed in a one-off data generation event. The move to using digital technologies as a research tool is not new (Beneito-Montagut et al. 2017; Hine 2015; Hobbis 2020; Pink et al. 2015), and we used social media platforms and smart phones as a means of accessing interviewees and generating data. In recruiting Singaporean middle-class families as research participants, we used a combination of education, salary, occupation and accommodation to gauge a sense of 'middle-classness'. For families with the main subject or at least one parent being a Singapore citizen, we recruited research subjects in the following four categories: (a) nuclear families with child/children; (b) extended, intergenerational families with child/children; (c) single parent families with child/children; (d) elderly people living alone, or with a caregiver.

We recruited 28 families in the four categories above, using our own social networks of trust, and friends and associates who were able to link us to suitable individuals. We respected the privacy of individuals and only made contact when there was mutual consent. Nuclear families (19) formed the largest subset in our sample, with five single-parent families, two from extended/intergenerational families, and the remaining two being elderly individuals living alone or with a caregiver. All but two of the families we recruited had children, whether in nuclear or single or extended family groups. Most of these families had children who were either in primary (aged 6–12) or secondary schools (aged 13–16), while some of our older interlocuters had children who were already in the workforce or in tertiary education. A majority in our sample had a highest educational qualification of diploma or above, and formed middle-class households, except for two elderly interlocutors who had no formal education. Of these, ages ranged from 31–60 years, while two were young adults in the age range 21–30, and two were over 70 years old. We spoke to 24 women and 4 men, even though we attempted to recruit multiple family members from the same family for interviews. But doing so was a huge challenge. Women in our pool were most willing to speak with us, and indeed 'found' time to do so. When we asked to speak to their male partners, some women were unwilling to share contacts, while others declared that their partner was too busy with work. We are aware of the gendered nature of our resulting data, with a heavy focus on women. Interestingly, the fact that it was largely women who responded to our requests for multiple rounds of interviews and regular updates on their daily lives reinforces the gendered division of labour argument we make here. We argue, thus, that during pandemic conditions, the scope of 'women's work' expanded considerably – it would seem to even include being a research interlocutor.

For data generation, we set up a research mobile phone line with WhatsApp downloaded to be used as the main data collection app. WhatsApp allowed for a broadcast list of contacts through which we could send out periodic research information, invitations for vignettes and so on to individual research subjects. The end-to-end message encryption feature of WhatsApp also ensured greater protection of any confidential data shared by research participants; this aided the creation of a safe space and platform for participants to express their thoughts/emotions, and share their experiences with us. Research subjects were able to send us responses and vignettes through WhatsApp, directly and individually, without others seeing their responses. Furthermore, WhatsApp is widely used in Singapore. Indeed, the authorities struggled to fight COVID-19 pandemic misinformation that 'went viral' through WhatsApp messaging. This reflects the fact that Singapore residents across all ages are very comfortable in using WhatsApp as an everyday social communication tool. Therefore, WhatsApp provided us with a readymade platform that was already a familiar everyday communication tool, enabling us to overcome the difficulties posed by the lockdown in conducting sustained ethnographic data collection (Kaufmann and Peil 2020; Kaye et al. 2018).

Due to the social distancing measures that were enacted, we were unable to meet our interlocuters in person. We wondered about whether the research could be designated 'ethnographic', given the need to turn to digital methods, rather than engage in sustained face-to-face interactions. An added concern was to ensure the privacy, confidentiality and integrity of our interlocutors. After several rounds of digitally-mediated interactions via WhatsApp and, especially, in Zoom interviews, we felt confident that these methods generated rich data. We also felt we were making human connections, preserving the empathetic element of our interactions and relationships we forged – core elements of ethnography. We were gratified that our interlocutors shared their pandemic-related everyday experiences candidly. We ensured that our encounters were not invasive. We appreciated the silences and delays to our request for updates as we did not intrude with multiple and repeated requests for responses. Given that we were primarily using WhatsApp, which demands quick/accelerated response in real time, we were extra mindful that we did not pressurize our interlocutors, who were already leading challenging lives. We also ensured that the data generated were protected and accessible only to the research team.

There were three phases in our data generation process: the initial interviews, the follow-up messages or calls and the final interviews. We conducted initial interviews with 26 of our research subjects through video or audio calls in August/September 2020. The initial interview consisted of questions such as 'Could you tell us about your living arrangements?', or 'How did you and your spouse decide on this division of responsibilities?', among others. We arranged face-to-face interviews, adhering to all safe management measures, with the remaining two elderly participants who preferred speaking to us in person. Interviews were conducted in English, except for the ones with Mme Brooke and Mme Annie, the elderly participants, which were conducted in Tamil and Malay respectively. After the initial interviews, we sent out three rounds of follow-up messages in September, October 2020 and January 2021 respectively. To facilitate the collection of data, we provided our research subjects with several ways of responding to our prompts: text messages, recording audio messages on WhatsApp, sharing photos or video clips, or scheduling a quick phone call with us to share their responses.

To conclude this phase, we conducted the final interviews with our participants from June to August 2021. The final interviews took longer to complete as it was challenging to contact participants and schedule video or audio calls with them – a situation which we had anticipated, given the prolonged duration of the research, compounded by our informants' struggles with the pandemic. To encourage greater participation in the final interviews, we set up a Google survey form with questions we had prepared, to provide an alternative means for participants to share their experiences with us. We managed to collate responses from 21 of our research participants in this final phase. Questions asked included 'How have you and your family been coping with the abrupt shift to the Phase 2 (Heightened alert) measures?' and 'How has your mental health been throughout the past one to two months or so?', among others. All research data were anonymized, and pseudonyms were randomly assigned to maintain the confidentiality of participants.

Findings

How participants understood and responded to government guidelines around COVID

One way to interpret the response of Singapore families to state-imposed safeguards and regulations is to note a demonstrable general compliance and understanding towards the tedious and draconian measures. These measures included the mandatory wearing of face masks and strict control of gatherings, which the general Singapore population, including those we interviewed, observed even though they were challenging and disrupted not only everyday life but also important festivities and social events (see Figure 6.2). Typically, external observers noted the conformity

Figure 6.2 During the pandemic, Archana and family, masked, and on an outing to Pulau Ubin, a small island off Singapore. Source: authors.

and acquiescence of Singaporeans towards such safe distancing measures. In addition, however, Singapore residents themselves also understood the need for these safeguards in the face of a pandemic and expressed a sense of civic consciousness and social responsibility towards the larger community, particularly towards its vulnerable members.

Our research confirms that residents in Singapore showed tremendous resilience and adaptability in the face of a public health crisis and followed the necessary COVID-19-related government guidelines. Our participants acknowledged feeling 'lucky' and grateful for being in Singapore, highlighting that their finances and access to basic amenities/resources had not been significantly affected – an observation that was a function of the sample group's generally middle-class background as well as the government support that was offered to Singapore residents. A recent Rajaratnam School of International Studies research study involving a sample of 6,000 individuals confirmed that 80 per cent of those surveyed expressed 'high levels of support for circuit breaker measures' (Baharudin 2021b). The same study also found that those with lower incomes, earning less than S$1,000 and between S$1,000 and S$2,900 reported financial challenges in making ends meet during the pandemic. Conversely, those with higher incomes had very different experiences, such that 'four in 10 households earning between S$8,000 and S$9,900 and fewer than three in 10 households of those earning between S$10,000 and S$14,900 reported disruptions to incomes' (Baharudin 2021b). The median salary of women in Singapore for 2020 was S$4,374 and for men in the same year was S$4,719.

Impact on family life

Our year-long research generated rich and nuanced qualitative data from the 28 middle-class families we followed and interacted with in 'socially distant' modes over this period. Given the brief of this chapter, we are only able to present three themes in detail with supporting narratives and everyday life vignettes shared by participants. These are, the intersecting rhythm of personal and professional time and lives in the home, the entrenchment of the regnant gendered division of labour in the home and the challenges of staying connected with family members, especially the elderly given the CB period and the restrictions on the numbers of individuals who were permitted to interact face-to-face (which varied during the period between two, five and eight persons).

Intersecting rhythms of personal and professional lives

Many of the women and men we interviewed admitted to not knowing when they should stop working, and were in fact working past their stipulated hours. According to Samuel, these prolonged periods of work time which were productive were nonetheless physically and mentally draining:

> [The] first few weeks [were] terrible, because you just don't know when to stop work. So, it's like you're working and working and working and you get really exhausted…so I realized that you have to be disciplined about putting in place some time to take a break (Samuel, 55, father, living in a condominium, nuclear family).

This was exacerbated when interlocutors were unable to draw a clear line between their personal lives and work lives. Such work-from-home arrangements have dismantled 'temporal and geographical barriers that separate home and work roles' and the public sphere from the private sphere (Ford 2011). Typically, work is presumed to happen within the public sphere whilst the home, the private sphere, is considered a space for leisure. However, as Ford's (2011) work asserts, the relationship between the public and private is no longer dichotomous; 'public and private are… enmeshed. They are continually renegotiated and redefined, always in relation to one another'. The work-from-home system has brought into close contact these different aspects of individuals' lives such that the lines between what is 'public' and 'private' has become ambiguous. As such, navigating through these spatial boundaries has demonstrably been a challenge for many. Daniella shared the following strategy to address this issue:

> I've always told my husband that the bedroom is for sleeping… and we don't have a work station or anything in the bedroom… anything educational or work-related always happens in a communal space… it actually helped because when you step into your room, it kind of creates that boundary between your work space and your home space… [because] now… your work is inside your home, so you need to have some kind of boundary there (Daniella, 36, 4-room HDB flat, nuclear family).

Furthermore, a number of our research participants highlighted that their work arrangements had become 'more flexible' such that they could take breaks during the day, to engage in household chores, for instance, or spend time with their children, if there were no meetings scheduled or urgent deadlines to be met. For instance, Benjamin acknowledged that his working hours were mediated by his children's routines:

> I can do (my work) later in the evening or night, so sometimes I just play with the kids in the meantime… if there's no meeting (Benjamin, 38, father, 5-room HDB flat, extended family).

Benjamin elaborated on how these work arrangements allowed him to look after his mother:

> I saw more of the kids and I'm able to help out, lah, more with the, you know with the some of the work at home, help take care of the kids, if not my, my mum … we need to take care of her, she has um some epilepsy condition so we can't leave her alone, all alone, so usually my mother in-law comes over in the morning … to help out but now she doesn't have to do that, lah, because I'm here.

Fitness instructor Jane explained how having a domestic helper had made it easier for her to conduct her online fitness lessons at home:

> My helper [does the cooking]. Outsource already [laughs]. Ya, anyway ah actually without her, I can't do any of my Zoom classes at all, honestly speaking. So, for those … people in my line, if they don't have additional help, I, I find it hard for them… it'll be very tough for them if they have to look after kids, if they don't have helper or they don't have anybody to help them you know (Jane, 48, mother, condominium, nuclear family).

As such, performing other responsibilities such as care work, housework and even recreational work within the household during the working day seem to have contributed to the 'longer' working hours experienced by informants. Even when they were not working their regular jobs, many were preoccupied with parenting and household duties; this was less apparent in the cases of individuals who had employed foreign domestic workers (FDWs), who were charged with doing household chores.

Altered, reconfigured gendered roles in the 'new normal'?

Even as Singapore residents supported circuit breaker measures and accepted work-from-home arrangements, coupled with home-based learning for school-age children, as the 'new normal', the care of the household and its various members and their needs proved to be onerous, more so for the women in the household. While many women in our sample took on a larger, disproportionate share of household and childcare commitments, some rationalized their behaviour by addressing their partner's lack of expertise, competency and experience in carrying out these tasks. Accordingly, our research sought to explore the reproduction of traditionally masculine or feminine identities and roles during a global pandemic. While COVID-19 disrupted and dramatically altered existing indices of normalcy, witnessed in a sustained period of work-from-home and home-based learning, our research reflects the prevailing gendered divisions of labour and its salience within the wider socio-cultural context of Singapore.

Whilst the overall caregiving and household responsibilities had increased for all during the CB period, we gathered from our interviews that conventional gendered division of labour persisted within nuclear family households, where both parents were working. Often, the fathers would engage in playing and having fun with the kids when they had time off work whereas the mothers were focused on their schoolwork and home-based learning and had to keep an eye on them even while juggling their own non-home-based work. A relatively common response from women was that their spouses were usually busier with work; asked about this, Quin (46, mother, condominium, nuclear family) remarked that '[her husband] will play with them … whenever he's free'.

In some families, fathers became more actively involved in caring for the children or teaching them as they spent more time at home. Some of the women noted that their children grew closer to fathers from 'seeing' them around at home during work-from-home. However, Taylor, like others, observed that part of the 'work' of fathers during their time at home was to discipline children:

> That is the part which they don't like, cos they are always being disciplined now, which he, he wasn't around most of the time, he has less, there's one less disciplinarian at home, but now there's one always at home [laughs]. They get disciplined more (Taylor, 39, mother, house, extended family).

Rebecca expressed similar views and even excused her husband's inability to help out more:

> I think my husband is not used to… dealing with domestic life and dealing with work in the same environment. I think that's stressful… my helper does more of the chores, I do more of the parenting… or

> the teaching and stuff like that (Rebecca, 40, mother, HDB flat, nuclear family).

The women's acceptance of these circumstances and situations as in this instance allows us to recognize how 'gendered spaces themselves shape and are shaped by daily activities' and compels us to rethink the meanings ascribed to 'public' and 'private' spaces (Spain 1992). Indeed we also sensed that the women we spoke to were very aware of the stress their partners were under and did not want to aggravate the situation by highlighting the gender imbalance vis-à-vis division of labour in managing the home and in care work. Margaret in her final interview indicated that the greatest challenge living through a pandemic was ensuring her husband did not go 'crazy' working at home with the kids around:

> Although I um, I am working, but um when the kids and everybody is at home, I have to manage their conflicts more, ya… because he has to um, he has to meet his work commitments uh, ya I mean someone has to you know (chuckles) make sure everything is still running smoothly so uh, ya, so for him it's his work lah, so for me it's making sure the kids' schedules uh, conflicts are handled quietly so that he can work. (The greatest challenge for me has been) making sure that uh my husband doesn't go crazy (laughs) because of you know, I said, uh, the youngest son will be very noisy lah, ya… so sometimes you know, can see my husband getting very uh annoyed, ya. So, have to manage that while I'm working, you know sometimes when I'm not at home, I still have to uh make sure, ya the noise doesn't get to him (Margaret, 46, mother, house, nuclear family).

The division of labour within the household did become a point of contention among some couples, but not necessarily only when one partner was unemployed. Kim (45, woman, living in an HDB flat, nuclear family) and her husband experienced some struggles managing the household when he was unemployed and at home during the pandemic:

> In the past… he's not around most of the time … I take charge, right, and I'm quite okay doing that when he's not around and I don't have an issue. But because he's so free, so free ah [laughs] during this period of time, he wants to take charge, and, and, so when that happens, I say okay, you take charge then, I'll just

focus on my work ... and you're right in the sense that sometimes, a little bit of tension ah, because ... I'm used to running it my way, and he, he's used to doing it his way. He likes very advanced planning whereas I'm okay you know, because I've never had to worry about him being around or not around, so impromptu like you know, dinner tonight I can just decide in the afternoon, okay let's do this, ya, but he plans a week ahead [laughs] which sometimes drives me a bit crazy... [we have] different styles of managing the household.

This then seems to reinstate 'the existing gender stratification system that [relegates] women to the private sphere' (Spain 1992). The stay-at-home period during the CB highlights and exposes that the home remained a gendered space where women are expected to perform duties as mother, wife even as they continue with their outside jobs and somehow achieve some balance between these two, whereas men can still predominantly focus on their day job and 'help out' with the kids *if* there is time left over and they are 'available'. Yet, perhaps unsurprisingly, many mothers *did not* express any concerns vis-à-vis the division of responsibilities with their husbands in terms of childcare; rather, they were mostly supportive and understanding of their spouse's work schedules, even though they had their own jobs to perform as well.

Staying connected with relatives

Personal family circumstances, in addition to the disruptions caused by the pandemic, shaped the mental well-being of families. Some nuclear families reported being able to spend more time with their husbands and children, during the pandemic. For example, Olivia (45, mother, condo, nuclear family), like many others in our sample, noted that there was certainly 'more family time' – socializing more, playing games and eating together – the list of activities had expanded to fill the entire day. Similarly, Hazel (45, mother, house, single parent) admitted to being able to see her kids more as a result of work-from-home arrangements, as she would normally have been busy working in the office.

Yet, in other ways, families struggled to keep in touch with their elderly parents and in-laws during the CB and many, like Olivia, were concerned about their social isolation:

Uh, ya, I think we were quite concerned that my mother-in-law would feel quite lonely, 'cos she was staying alone ... can be very

> isolating for the seniors ... same with my family as well actually, but my dad and my mum, at least it's two of them, ah ... definitely I think they don't get to see the grandkids, so they do miss them, ya. At the same time, for them as well church et cetera, they couldn't go, ya. And then when they had to meet over Zoom, like my mother-in-law had like Zoom sessions for bible study once in two weeks, but when she wasn't quite familiar with how to use it... it would get a bit frustrating for her. Ya, so we had to like help her...teach her how to use Zoom so that she could then Zoom with other people (Olivia, 45, mother, condo, nuclear family).

Our 80-year-old woman Tamil-speaking interlocutor Mme Brooke, who lived with her helper acknowledged her reliance on technology during the lockdown period to cope with the isolation. Our transcribed description reads:

> A typical day for Mme Brooke during the CB period would begin with her simple morning exercises at home when she wakes up at 6 a.m. After that, she would listen to the news on the radio at 8 a.m. and watch the news on TV too. Then, her helper would go out to buy groceries and they would contemplate on what dishes to cook for the day. After lunch, she would sleep for a while in the afternoon and then wake up at about 4 p.m. and watch TV...She spent most of her time watching TV and talking on the phone to check in with her friends and family, both in Singapore and abroad. She noted that it would have been much harder to pass her time without these devices (described from conversation with Mme Brooke, 80, 3-room HDB flat).

Similarly, Yousef, a single parent living with his children shared that regular communication with his family and friends provided him with a sense of comfort during the CB period:

> Uh, I talk to them over the phone every day, every day I talk to them, if I don't talk to them, they will call me, they will find out what's happening, how am I doing, and then during the restricted time you know they, they will check whether I have my meals, do I have food, or if not my sister will send my brother in-law you know, he will drive down to my place to pass me food and all that you see, so, so uh communication is still uh active every day between us lah (Yousef, 59, father, 2-room HDB flat, single-parent family).

Full-time homemaker and recently divorced interlocutor Phoebe emphasized the significance of spending time with her children during this period of change:

> So basically uh we were still trying to adjust to our life, a new life before circuit breaker, so this COVID thing came about, I mean we, while we were adjusting to our new life, we already didn't go out as much already, uh so, when…the new, new circuit breaker came about, we just continued to… basically adjust to our new living condition but by being more at home…Um, for the time being, I think the kids do need me because I'm, I'm considered their, their source, the, the single parent, ya, so I do want to make sure that their needs are taken care of more because, because our financial needs are kind of okay for now (Phoebe, mid-40s, mother, rented condo, single-parent family).

Not surprisingly, over the one-year period, some of our interviewees were noticeably weary as a result of the prolonged restrictions and the uncertainty of what was going to happen. When asked if she and her family were better prepared to cope with the restrictions in her final interview, Zoe said:

> There's a sense of sort of like learnt helplessness, like kind of like uh, it is what it is, like even if you're not okay with it, it's not that you can do anything about it anyway. So… it's just pointless to have an issue with it because you can't do anything about it unfortunately, this is just our reality, um and I guess it's very frustrating… (Zoe, 25, maisonette HDB flat, nuclear family).

Olivia too reported feelings of anxiety through this prolonged pandemic, even as she saw the positives in the moments of self-reflection about what is important in life:

> Mmm, I think I didn't expect COVID to last so long, ya…at this point, a bit of fatigue, lah, I guess with keeping up with all the measures…I mean I wasn't depressed or anything but I did feel like a certain sense of grief I guess with everything that had to stop, but I think that it was also perhaps… something that was necessary for us to pause and reflect and re-evaluate on what's most important… because a lot of the peripherals are stripped away right…no longer need to dress up, so you don't need to spend so much on shopping [laughs] (Olivia, 45, mother, condo, nuclear family).

Taylor similarly expressed feelings of anxieties in the initial periods of the pandemic followed by boredom after that. In her first interview, on her emotional state during circuit breaker, she said:

> Starting was more of fear, more of fear, as in like, the numbers are rising and stuff, um I think now, I think looking at the community numbers, I mean it was like going down, single digit, then not so scared, we're not so scared currently. Just any other day anyway so, didn't have much of like a drastic change um but now I think it has been quite a period so, boredom kind of like sets in a little, it's like ugh [chuckles] like I want to go out sometimes (Taylor, 39, mother, house, extended family).

Our data brought a third key theme to the surface – the high levels of anxiety and mental health and well-being concerns experienced by our research participants, particularly amongst women – which we recognized as being crucial but are unable to fully explore this theme here.

Discussion

Our research aimed to interrogate the impact of the COVID-19 pandemic on individuals and communities, through a focus on everyday lives of families in Singapore. A qualitative approach was invaluable in eliciting narratives of these day-to-day experiences, even as current circumstances of lockdown and social distancing challenged us to conceive novel modes of conducting qualitative, ethnographic research and generating rich, in-depth data. Under pandemic conditions, the turn to digital technologies was inevitable, to access remotely the complexities of experiences and voices of middle-class families in Singapore society.

We also witnessed the emergence of a new everyday as novel practices (wearing a mask, washing hands, using hand sanitizers, more home cooking, more leisure activities, Zoom meetings and social events – birthdays, commencements, parties) became common under these altered living conditions (Figure 6.3).

At the same time, older everyday practices (walking, exercising, cooking, etc.) were reconfigured. Taylor, in her first interview, soon after the start of the CB, observed that a large part of the day was devoted to eating and preparing food for the family:

> Mm, time to experiment more variety of cooking uh, so we, we try to come up with new dishes, or we, I, I bake more and stuff, or and,

Figure 6.3 Kamala family celebrating daughter Neha's sixth birthday, with cake cutting via Zoom, while keeping to restricted numbers for social gatherings. Source: authors.

> since they are always home, they want tea break, lunch break, tea break, again, so they forever eating like that. Ya, so, so I also bake, so I think we used up like maybe 20 packets of bread flour ... during the whole circuit breaker (laughs). Flour hoarders, we are flour hoarders (Taylor, 39, mother, house, extended family).

Cooking at home emerged as a dominant new activity for many of the families in our sample. Several of our interviewees took to experimenting with new dishes and cuisines, baking emerging as a top favourite. Women and helpers who were largely responsible for food provision in the home also 'complained' that they spent more time in the kitchen. Given that more people were at home for longer periods meant more demands for in-between snacks in addition to breakfast, lunch and dinner. This is a striking contrast to pre-COVID-19 eating practices, when 7 out of 10 Singaporeans typically and regularly ate outside the home.

New family or couple routines were formed, especially during the circuit breaker, such as taking walks together or doing other leisure activities (like playing board games and card games, movie nights, etc.) at home on a regular basis. In a multi-religious Singapore society where almost 85 per cent of the population declare themselves to be religious,

religious and cultural activities typically undertaken as a family were affected. Religion has a strong and deep presence in Singapore society with active participation in the festival and ritual calendars of multiple faiths as well as the physical frequenting of places of worship, sometimes on a daily basis. As the pandemic unfolded and social distancing became the norm, families, including elderly members, turned to digital technologies – like Zoom, Facebook and WhatsApp - to keep in touch with extended family and elderly parents and grandparents. For families with young children, parents, and especially mothers, became the facilitators in their children's academic and social life. Even if teachers provided instructions, parents had to help out and explain how to do things. Parents also facilitated the maintenance of young children's friendships by organizing online sessions and communicating with other parents (as the children were too young to do it themselves).

Ideally, it would be critical to also ask how the impact and experiences of the pandemic are mediated by sociological variables like class, gender, nationality, age and ethnicity. The middle-class families we spoke to acknowledged that vulnerable members of society who need social support services have been impacted differently by the pandemic. They recognized that the lack of access to crucial support translates directly into differentiated, unequal and unjust impacts of the pandemic. At the level of the family as a social institution we mapped gendered experiences in the home to unpack normative arguments about 'natural' division of labour in homes. A large part of this research was invested in capturing the rhythm of everyday life during this pandemic and asked how everyday life has been transformed in this moment of crisis, where routinization, predictability, and certainty are tenuous if not missing. Our interlocutors were extremely patient through this long research period, but some did express uncertainties about whether their updates and responses would be too mundane, boring and repetitive. This certainly reflected how they perceived their own current lives, which many we spoke to described as 'boring' and where 'nothing was happening'.

Conclusion: towards a 'new normal'?

All societal domains, including, healthcare, family life, employment, housing, education, and criminal justice systems, have been recalibrated in Singapore with the aftershocks of the COVID-19 pandemic. Over a period of over two years, the world had witnessed the tragic loss of vulnerable human lives to the virus. Those with greater economic and social capital, including the middle-class families from Singapore enjoyed the luxury of physical/social distancing and the privileges this bestowed, with the option of working and learning from home and protection from disease and possible death. The Singapore middle-class families in our sample demonstrated a high degree of compliance with government-initiated measures. There were no public shows of resistance against pandemic mandates. Rather, Singapore residents displayed considerable patience and resilience in adhering to government guidelines, even though frustration and fatigue set in and many were jaded, given how long the social distancing measures and their disruptions had lasted. Prime Minister Lee, in a national address on the COVID-19 situation, suggested that the arrival of a 'new normal' would be signalled by the easing of restrictions with light safe management measures being retained, while COVID-19 numbers remained stable on a daily basis without exponential growth (Ong 2022). This was a rather nebulous prospect for the average individual to take on board, given a lack of individual control over the outcome, and bound to create fatigue in the compliance of social distancing mandates and care roles. Furthermore, since most mandates were lifted as of 26 April 2022 (Lin 2022) it would be interesting to study the shift in mindsets towards this new normal.

Evidence from other research in Singapore shows that the ongoing pandemic brought definite mental and emotional exhaustion. Concerns about the financial costs and economic losses of the pandemic have been expressed by local businesses, economists and the government. Relatively speaking, far less has been done thus far about the distressing 'cost' in terms of emotional health and well-being of individuals, although the latter have been finally acknowledged. Singapore society will need to not just acknowledge but also mitigate fears of individuals and communities through allocation of appropriate and adequate resources to address these anxieties concretely. Ultimately, through this research our aim is to inform social policy and local responses to the COVID-19 pandemic. The larger remit of the project will enable inter-country comparisons, while retaining the integrity of specific contexts and the research insights emerging therefrom.

References

Awang, N. and Wong, P. T. (2019) 'The Big Read in short: S'pore families' dependence on maids and the issues that need addressing'. *Today*, 2 November 2019. https://www.todayonline.com/big-read/big-read-short-spore-families-dependence-maids-and-issues-need-addressing (accessed 23 February 2023).

Baharudin, H. (2021a) 'Lower-income folk worst hit by S'pore's Covid-19 circuit breaker: Study'. *The Straits Times*, 24 August 2021. https://www.straitstimes.com/singapore/lower-income-folk-worst-hit-by-spores-covid-19-circuit-breaker-study?utm_source=emarsys&utm_medium=email&utm_campaign=ST_Newsletter_AM&utm_term=Lower-income+folk+worst+hit+by+S%E2%80%99pore%E2%80%99s+Covid-19+circuit+breaker%3A+Study&utm_content=24%2F08%2F2021&utm_source=whatsapp&utm_medium=social-media&utm_campaign=addtoany (accessed 23 February 2023).

Baharudin, H. (2021b) 'Study finds high levels of support for Singapore's Covid-19 circuit breaker measures'. *The Straits Times*, 24 August 2021. https://www.straitstimes.com/singapore/rsis-study-finds-high-levels-of-support-for-circuit-breaker-measures?&utm_source=whatsapp&utm_medium=social-media&utm_campaign=addtoany (accessed 23 February 2023).

Beneito-Montagut, R., Begueria, A. and Cassián, N. (2017) 'Doing digital team ethnography: Being there together and digital social data'. *Qualitative Research*, 17 (6), 664–82. https://doi.org/10.1177/1468794117724500.

Chia, S. (2023) 'What is the average salary in Singapore and are you earning enough?'. *SingSaver*, blog, 16 February 2023. https://www.singsaver.com.sg/blog/average-income-median-salary-singapore.

Ford, S. M. (2011) 'Reconceptualizing the public/private distinction in the age of information technology'. *Information, Communication & Society*, 14 (4), 550–67. https://doi.org/10.1080/1369118x.2011.562220.

Ganapathy, N. (2002) 'Rethinking the problem of policing marital violence: A Singapore perspective'. *Policing and Society*, 12 (3), 173–90.

Hine, C. (2015) *Ethnography for the Internet: Embedded, embodied and everyday*. London: Bloomsbury Academic.

Hobbis, G. (2020) *The Digitizing Family: An ethnography of Melanesian smartphones*. Basingstoke: Palgrave Macmillan.

Huang, S., Yeoh, B. S. and Toyota, M. (2012) 'Caring for the elderly: The embodied labour of migrant care workers in Singapore'. *Global Networks*, 12 (2), 195–215.

Kaufmann, K. and Peil, C. (2019) 'The Mobile Instant Messaging Interview (MIMI): Using WhatsApp to enhance self-reporting and explore media usage in situ'. *Mobile Media & Communication*, 8 (2), 229–46. https://doi.org/10.1177/2050157919852392.

Kaye, L. K., Monk, R. L. and Hamlin, I. (2018) '"Feeling appy?" Using app-based methodology to explore contextual effects on real-time cognitions, affect and behaviours'. In Costa, C. and Condie, J. (eds) *Doing Research in and on the Digital: Research methods across fields of enquiry*. London: Routledge, 11–29.

Lam, L. (2020) 'Necessary for Singapore to fast-track COVID-19 laws amid unprecedented situation: Lawyers'. *CNA*, 13 April 2020. https://www.channelnewsasia.com/singapore/singapore-fast-tracks-covid-19-laws-unprecedented-situation-763471 (accessed 23 February 2023).

Lin, C. (2022) 'Relief, revival as Singapore scraps its COVID curbs'. *Reuters*, 26 April 2022. https://www.reuters.com/world/the-great-reboot/relief-revival-singapore-scraps-its-covid-curbs-2022-04-26/ (accessed 23 February 2023).

Ong, J. (2022) 'The new normal: How can Singapore move beyond COVID-19?'. *The Straits Times*, 7 May 2022. https://www.straitstimes.com/singapore/politics/moving-beyond-covid-19-how-can-singapore-find-a-new-way-forward-in-a-more-challenging-landscape?utm_source=emarsys&utm_medium=email&utm_campaign=ST_Newsletter_AM&utm_term=Moving+beyond+COVID-19%3A+How+can+S (accessed 23 February 2023).

Pink, S., Horst, H. A., Postill, J., Hjorth, L., Lewis, T. and Tacchi, J. (2015) *Digital Ethnography: Principles and practice*. London: Sage.

SingStat (Singapore Department of Statistics) (2020) *Census of Population 2020. Key Findings*. https://www.singstat.gov.sg/-/media/files/publications/cop2020/sr2/findings2.pdf (accessed 23 February 2023).

Spain, D. (1992) *Gendered Spaces*. Chapel Hill: University of North Carolina Press.

Yohannan, R. (2020) 'Types of HDB BTO Flats in Singapore – Floor space, prices, and who can apply'. *The Smart Local*, 28 March 2020. https://thesmartlocal.com/read/bto-hdb-types-singapore/ (accessed 22 February 2023).

7
South Africa: COVID-19 and family well-being

Sadiyya Haffejee, Anita Mwanda and Thandi Simelane

Introduction

South African families are accustomed to disruptions. The COVID-19 pandemic presents yet another shock to the well-being of families already disturbed by apartheid and the HIV and AIDS epidemic. These earlier disruptions significantly altered family life, and the impact of them is still felt today. During the period of apartheid, the creation of homelands, the migrant labour system, influx control and Pass Laws[1] fostered the geographical separation of family life and employment, rupturing the family system (Knijn and Patel 2018). Similarly, the HIV and AIDS epidemic, initially marked by government denialism and subsequent inaction, disrupted the family systems' capacity to care for and support each other, resulting in compromised household security, significant loss of life and a sharp increase in the number of child-headed households (Sebola et al. 2020). The contemporary South African family is characterized by heterogeneous living and caregiving arrangements, including many female-headed and multigenerational family systems and varied marital patterns (Mokomane et al. 2019). Many families continue to be marked by ongoing challenges, including socio-economic difficulties, high family and community violence levels, and poor access to resources.

Against this backdrop of historical challenges and complex family systems, we frame our discussion of risk and resilience in South African families during COVID-19. We do this by applying a family resilience perspective that recognizes the effects of multiple stressors on family functioning and the potential of every family in mitigating or decreasing exposure to adversity and mobilizing resources and protective processes to enable adaptive coping (Masten 2011). In this study, we are interested in how pre-existing and co-occurring risks, like poverty, unemployment and poor service access, increased risk for families and how families have reorganized, adapted and coped during this period. The family resilience framework draws on a systemic approach and positions family vulnerability, risk and resilience in the context of multilevel recursive influences when dealing with a stressor of this magnitude (Walsh 2021).

In the following sections, we provide a brief glimpse into the structural context of COVID-19 in South Africa and describe the multimodal methods, including digital diaries, telephone calls and individual interviews, that we employed in our study. The data collected over the course of eight months, from 26 June 2020 to the end of March 2021, provided rich, nuanced and intimate insights into the struggles and resources of each family. This allowed us a privileged insight into the everyday realities of South Africans during this surreal time. Here we focus on three key areas: firstly, how families, and individuals within these families, responded to and experienced the pandemic and the resultant safety regulations; secondly, the specific risks posed to families as a result of the pandemic and the lockdown, and thirdly, how individuals and families adapted. Findings show that, to a large extent, participating families were compliant with COVID-19 lockdown rules. However, for some, socio-economic challenges made total compliance difficult. The economic and educational fallouts caused by the pandemic exacerbated pre-existing adversities and required concerted efforts to reorganize and adapt. Families did this by searching for meaning and focusing on the positives. Through this discussion on adversity and attempts at adaptation, we draw attention to the resilience processes our families engaged in. Our findings provide insight into how contextual and cultural realities influence resilience processes, and in this, we contribute to evolving understandings of resilience.

South Africa country context

Available statistics suggest that South Africa has been the worst hit by the pandemic on the African continent, with 2,913,880 positive cases and 88,464 deaths reported between March 2020 and mid-October 2021 (Department of Health, Republic of South Africa n.d.). This was despite an evidence-informed and decisive response from the government.

'The cure is worse than the disease' (Muller 2020) was a sentiment expressed by many South Africans in response to the government's rapid move into a hard lockdown at the end of March 2020. The lockdown resulted in a national curfew, prohibition on travel nationally and internationally, and the closure of schools, businesses and places of worship. The sale of alcohol and tobacco was also prohibited (Egbe and Ngobese 2020). This prohibition on alcohol was instituted to dissuade people from congregating at bars and taverns. At the same time, the sale of tobacco was banned to prevent the spread of the virus through sharing cigarettes (Manyoni and Abader 2021). The prohibition of alcohol, while contentious, resulted in other public health benefits, such as a decrease in hospital admissions due to alcohol-related injuries (Van Hoving et al. 2021, 480). During the initial lockdown period, the government deployed the military in certain areas, monitoring movements and taverns and warned of harsh fines for those that were not compliant (Manderson and Levine 2021).

Between March and November 2020, lockdown levels gradually de-escalated as the situation eased and in response to urgent calls to reopen the economy. After that, measures became somewhat fluid in response to increases in cases and the emergence of new variants. For example, in December 2020, the 'South African' or Beta variant of the COVID-19 virus was detected, colliding with the second wave of the pandemic, which resulted in the reinstatement of tighter lockdown levels (Tegally et al. 2021).

Critiques of government response may be understood against the historical and prevailing socio-economic conditions facing South Africa. The pandemic arrived in March 2020 amid a technical recession, with 29 per cent of the workforce unemployed and youth unemployment rates at over 50 per cent. Food prices were increasing, and more than a third of South African families were in debt (Naidu 2021). The situation was compounded by fiscal irregularities, funds mismanagement and state departments' corruption (Naidu 2021). In this context, it was unsurprising that the hard lockdown initiated by the government was met with concern and criticism. Many asserted that South Africa could not sustain such safety measures. These assertions were verified when newspaper headlines announced growing hunger and job losses in the country within days of the pronouncement (Dawson and Fouksman 2020). However, the swift action from the government signalled signs of learning from mistakes made in handling the HIV and AIDS epidemic; then, the government's refusal to acknowledge scientific evidence and subsequent lack of action had resulted in the senseless deaths of millions (Ross 2020). In contrast, with COVID-19, there was greater reliance on emerging scientific knowledge and a willingness by the government to engage with experts.

Acknowledging concerns regarding the welfare of the majority of the population, the South African government introduced several social welfare initiatives to aid and buffer individuals and families during the lockdown period. These included a 500-billion-rand[2] COVID Relief Fund, enabling increases in existing welfare grants, the provision of a new temporary COVID-19 social relief grant and the distribution of food parcels for those in need (Mudeau 2022). In addition, those affected by temporary closures at work or who lost employment due to the lockdown could access the Temporary Employment Relief Scheme (TERS) or claim from the existing Unemployment Insurance Fund (UIF). The latter was only applicable to workers registered with the fund. To remediate the loss of learning time, the National Department of Basic Education (DBE) also prepared online and broadcast support resources (Fouché et al. 2020).

However, the number and magnitude of the challenges facing citizens meant that these alleviation measures were insufficient (Bridgeman et al. 2020). Efforts were further hampered by the mismanagement of resources and poor service delivery systems (Staunton et al. 2020). In the weeks following the announcements of these provisions, anecdotal reports and social media posts suggested that access to food parcels, grants and business bailouts was not happening soon enough. Many, like those working in the informal sector, were excluded from accessing support. Between April and May 2021, approximately 10 million people, including 3 million children, lived in a household affected by hunger (Spaull et al. 2021). School closures meant a lack of access to food for 9 million children who received a meal at school as part of the National School Nutritional Programme (Seekings 2020).

Similarly, access to education, for some, was severely impacted. The digital divide meant that most children attending public schools had limited, if no, access to learning, while children attending fee-paying, private schools had access to online learning forums, suffering minimal disruption to their educational progress (Soudien et al. 2021). During this period, over half a million children between the age of 7 and 17 dropped out of school, most of them from poorly resourced areas (Spaull et al. 2021). High dropout rates and poor educational access contribute to ongoing cycles of poverty in South Africa, hampering growth and entrenching inequities (Patel et al. 2017). Research conducted during this period shows that those most likely to have ongoing work, albeit remote, were likely to be non-black, living in a house/flat (as opposed to living in informal housing[3]), and have higher educational levels, favouring those in higher socio-economic categories (Nwosu et al. 2021).

Families in South Africa, like families globally, have been confronted with additional caregiving responsibilities during this period; women, in particular, appear to have borne the brunt of this. In South Africa, approximately 37.9 per cent of households are female-headed; these households are more vulnerable to poverty, have more child dependents and experience higher unemployment rates (Nwosu and Ndinda 2018). The pandemic impacted many of these families, with research showing that women accounted for two-thirds of the estimated three million job losses reported in the first three months (Casale and Posel 2020). This research also showed that twice as many women as men found that caring for children negatively impacted their ability to work (Casale and Posel 2020).

As the pandemic continued, and the country rode out a third wave and the addition of the Delta COVID-19 variant, the emphasis shifted to vaccine rollout, schools reopened, and there was a move to Alert Level 1 lockdown, which meant significant easing of restrictions on curfews and social gatherings (Mahase 2022). However, many of the challenges continued to deepen, and the full impact of the pandemic is yet to be discovered. The timeline (Figure 7.1) provides an overview of COVID-19 in South Africa.

Theoretical framework

Given the multitude of problems facing families in South Africa, it would be easy to pathologize and focus on how the ecology harmed the individual/family and vice versa (Ungar 2021). However, this does not convey the breadth of experiences and responses. In South Africa and elsewhere, we see continual attempts at recovery and adaptation and, ultimately, resilience (Chang et al. 2020). How is this possible? What facilitates this shift? How do we meet challenges like COVID-19 and respond in ways that are equitable and sustainable (Ungar 2021)? In South Africa, as with countries globally, the experience and impact of COVID-19 cannot be divorced from the multitude of other adversities experienced daily. The family, as a system, is nested within other systems and is influenced by national policies and contexts, interacting throughout its life cycle with the surrounding ecology and changing resources (Gritti 2020). The family and the social system are bound in an interlocking system, each influencing the other (Gritti 2020). This then raises the

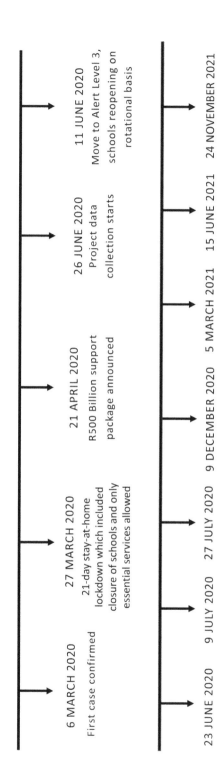

Figure 7.1 Timeline of COVID-19 in South Africa. Source: authors.

question of what can be done at a policy and systemic level to bolster and promote family resilience.

Family resilience refers to the family's capacity as a functional system to overcome adversity (Walsh 2021). This draws on Masten's (2014) well-recognized definition of resilience as 'the capacity of a dynamic system to adapt successfully to disturbances that threaten system function, viability, or development'. These definitions highlight the presence of one or multiple stressors and the system's ability to adapt and recover. Our focus here is on the family system, exploring how it adapted to the pandemic and the regulations imposed. In drawing on a resilience framework, we move from a risk-saturated view to one that invites action and change. This approach is grounded in both a systemic and developmental perspective and provides a comprehensive approach to understanding family well-being (Isaacs et al. 2020). In her overview of the family resilience framework, Walsh (2003, 2016, 2021) reminds us that every family's experience of the pandemic had both standard and unique features; for example, in South Africa, social distancing, curfews and mask-wearing were shared as 'standard', while economic status, geographical location and race created a difference. Walsh (2021) identifies several transactional processes that are instrumental in facilitating family resilience and organizes these into three mutually interactive and synergistic domains. These domains include shared belief systems (that is, meaning-making, positive outlook, transcendence and spirituality), organizational resources (that is, flexibility, connectedness, social and economic resource mobilization) and communication processes (clarity, open emotional sharing and collaborative problem solving), all of which make up the core processes. Drawing on Walsh's framework, we consider how different families experienced the pandemic, how families made sense of and understood this experience and the resources they drew on to reorganize and negotiate new rules and confined spaces, all against the backdrop of multiple pre-existing and complex challenges.

Methods: data collection and sample

To get a glimpse into the everyday experiences of families during this unprecedented period, we employed a mixed-method qualitative ethnographic design. Longitudinal data was generated through the digital dairies of 20 families between June 2020 and March 2021 and was supplemented by one-off telephonic interviews with 21 individuals. COVID-19 spurred an interest in alternate forms of data collection and the use of digital diaries, though not in itself new, was most suitable for capturing data in real-time while providing rich contextual information and insight into family life over an extended period (Grinter and Eldridge 2001). This method positions participants as data collectors, giving them the power to choose the most suitable means of communication (photo, text, video) and allowing them to edit their responses if they wish (Jarrahi et al. 2020). Importantly, it also enabled remote data collection.

Digital platforms were initially accessed to recruit participants. Details of the study were shared over social media platforms, such as the Centre for Social Development in Africa's Facebook page and community WhatsApp groups, and interested participants were invited to contact the research team. Since the response rate through these avenues was poor, researchers also accessed pre-existing community networks and community partners. Approximately 21 families responded to this initial call; of these, one family exited due to time commitments. The total number of participants that began the study was 44. Invitations to participate were shared again to increase participation numbers and accommodate interested individuals who could not commit to the diary entries. Participants were invited to one-off telephone interviews. By these means, a further 21 participants were recruited. The total number of South African participants thus included in the study was 64: 16 children (11 girls and 5 boys) and 48 adults. All participants resided in Gauteng province, and just under a third of the adult participants were unemployed. Participants represented high, middle and low socio-economic status (SES) households and different racial groups. The lowest level of education for participating adults was Grade 8 (secondary education). Five of the children in the sample were in primary school, ten in high school and one in tertiary. Most of the participating families had access to electricity, piped water and sanitation; two families had no regular electricity access, and one did not have a flushing toilet. Most families lived in brick houses, and three lived in informal housing.

For the diary entries, the mobile application WhatsApp was used. Access to computers and laptops is limited in the South African context; WhatsApp, by comparison, is more readily available and cost-effective, making it a viable option for participants. A data allowance was supplied to all participants to ensure that participation in the study did not cause additional strain. Participants were sent prompts which focused on various aspects of their pandemic experiences and were invited to respond with a text, voice message and/or a video or image. Researchers TS and AM were in regular contact with the participants, and if and when participants failed to respond, they followed up with a text reminder or a call. A total of

11 prompts were sent out during the data collection period. Initially, it was envisaged that the prompts would be sent out weekly and then fortnightly to all participants; however, as the research team accommodated participants' schedules, the prompts were structured around individual response times. In instances where participants could not respond via WhatsApp messaging, TS and AM engaged with participants by telephone (with their consent and at a time convenient for them). These phone discussions were recorded and later transcribed. Once all prompts were sent out, and responses were received, additional check-in telephone calls were conducted at two time points (December 2020 and March 2021).

The in-depth individual interviews with participants were conducted by phone, again at pre-arranged and convenient times. A semi-structured interview schedule was designed based on the diary prompts. Interviews were approximately 60 minutes long and were recorded with the participants' permission. Diary prompts and the interview schedule was developed considering the participants' age. For example, questions were adapted for children/young people to be age and context appropriate.

Ethics

Ethics approval was obtained from the Faculty of Humanities, Research Ethics Committee at the University of Johannesburg. All ethical guidelines were adhered to, including informed consent for adults, assent for children, voluntary participation, confidentiality and anonymity. Family names are pseudonyms.

Data Analysis

The data set consisted of 278 texts and/or voice messages, 350 images and 45 videos, and the transcripts of the 21 individual interviews. Both weekly tasks and interviews were primarily in English. Nonetheless, a few respondents chose to respond in their mother tongues, for example, isiZulu, SeSotho or isiXhosa. As a result, any multilingual texts were transcribed from vernacular to English, and all transcripts were analysed in English. All textual and audio/video data were transcribed verbatim and analysed using thematic analyses (Braun and Clarke 2006), and Atlas.ti 9 was used to manage data. Data were separately coded by both AM and TS and reviewed by SH. Regular meetings were held to discuss the data, and consensus discussions were used to identify and resolve discrepancies where coding was not unanimous.

Findings

We focus on three broad themes: experiences and responses regarding pandemic and safety regulations, impact, and adaptation. In sharing how participants in our study experienced and responded to the safety regulations imposed by the government we touch on the influence of contextual factors. Then, drawing on a resilience lens, we focus on the intensification of vulnerabilities and the adaptive responses, which includes how families reorganized and adapted to accommodate pandemic changes.

How did participants understand and respond to social distancing measures?

In South Africa, unlike in many other countries in the Global North and despite vocal criticism of the regulations from many sectors, most of our families appeared to comply with the restrictions imposed, at least in the initial months of the lockdown. All our families were aware of and understood the safety measures imposed and had a sense of what was expected. In one of the quotes below, a participating mother describes the efforts she and her children adopted, and a participating father shares his perceptions of the protection that the safety measures provided for him:

> Me and my kids have been exercising the rules and making sure that we sticking to it, that we need to wash our hands regularly and put on masks, and we carry sanitisers in our bags (mother, 36, Protea family, high SES; diary extract, August 2020).

> We've always been wearing masks, washing our hands, I think though that act, it might have maybe saved me because at one point I came into contact with someone that had Corona, if it wasn't for me washing my hands I maybe I would have gotten the virus… so I think those safety measures were actually on point, if those measures could be followed you might be clear or free of the virus you know (father, 29, Rhino family, middle SES; diary extract, September 2020).

Although many saw the necessity of the regulations, this was weighed against an awareness of hardship and intensifying difficulties, as demonstrated by this young person from the Blue Crane family:

> I think the lockdown was a good method to help stop or decrease the spread of the virus. Even though it brought job loss in many families,

> but it helped to save lives (daughter, 18, Blue Crane family; diary extract, July 2020).

The following excerpt from an adult participant encapsulates the South African experience of lockdown:

> I think lockdown is a good thing if you have the money for it, it's hard for people that don't have the money for it (mother, 49, Hadeda family, high SES; diary extract, July 2020).

This awareness of the impact of disparate circumstances emerged consistently. Participants living in poorly resourced areas described daily challenges, and participants living in more resourced or privileged circumstances were aware of the challenges facing the majority of South Africans.

The presence or absence of additional and pre-existing challenges influenced the extent to which participants chose or were able to comply with safety measures. For participants living in poorly resourced communities, lack of running water meant sanitation difficulties. For others, lack of power or frequent power outages increased daily difficulties. For some, this meant they were forced to disregard social distancing rules. For example, with no electricity, one participant maintained that she was forced to go to neighbours to charge her phone. She said:

> Yoh we are struggling guys because we have to cross the street, knock at people's doors to get our phones charged. Uh anyway we will adapt to it (mother, Peacock family, low SES; diary extract, July 2020).

For one participant, no electricity meant an early night. For others, the lack of electricity was inconvenient, limiting entertainment options and encouraging non-adherence, as seen in the following quotes.

> If the TV was on then at least we would watch the TV. But now because we don't have electricity I cannot just stay home (mother, 33, Ostrich family, low SES; interview, July 2020).

Similarly, another participant highlights that no electricity meant frequent shopping trips, increasing exposure.

> We can stay at home but … for example to us living in the settlement we don't have electricity so in order to have food and other thing, is

to go to the shop. No one will come to you unless you go out there (mother, 35, Springbok family, low SES; diary extract, July 2020).

She also spoke of her fears of exposure to COVID-19, as a result of an inability to social distance when living in an informal settlement:

The space thing is what makes me worried because we don't have much space, we are living in a shelter so there's no space where we can practice social distancing

In addition to socio-economic and resource constraints, compliance was also affected by confidence in government and individual compromises on safe socializing versus unsafe socializing. Some participants shared doubts and distrust about the efficacy of the restrictions, which seemed to be a result of a general lack of confidence in government, as demonstrated by this quote:

I think people don't believe that COVID is real … there's so many myths about it. Even when it started, people were saying a lot of things about the government. Now it's even worse that there is corruption in government. People say, 'you see these people wanted to just make money' (mother, 39, Dove family, low SES; diary extract, September 2020).

For others, the lack of consistency regarding regulations also increased suspicions and justified flouting of regulations. A young adult from the Kudu family said:

Not being allowed to visit family, it boggles how 10 of my family members can decide that we are going to eat at a restaurant, but then I can't visit one of them … it doesn't make sense, so it's hard to abide by them because you actually think they are nonsense, you know (daughter, 24, Kudu family; diary extract, August 2020).

Another questioned not being able to travel to see her elderly parents but being allowed to shop:

I think that was very, very hard. You know what, the thing is if you are allowed to go to a shop, why aren't you allowed to go to your parents' house? Even if you are sitting outside in the car with a mask, you know (mother, 42, Mongoose family, middle SES; interview, September 2020).

The following quote reflects how a few participants rationalized decisions to comply or not; some social interactions were perceived safe and others not:

> We have been quite strict on social distancing, we do not socialize or have people over, and I haven't seen my elderly parents since February as they are high risk. We have chosen one or two families and allow play dates with those families only (mother, age not shared, Crocodile family, high SES; diary extract, July 2020).

As is apparent, while compliance in general appeared to be high, this varied over time and was influenced by family circumstances and personal assessments of safety and necessity.

Lockdown as challenging was a common sentiment. For most participants, the social distancing and business closures were particularly difficult. This adult from the Springbok family says of her experience:

> Social distancing is very difficult, especially if you don't understand. I won't lie for me at first, but when I start to adjust, I learned about it and start to practise it, and know why we must do social distancing. And lockdown is very, very frustrating if I must say so because most of the jobs are closed, including the place where I work, so nothing you can do (mother, 35, Springbok family, low SES; diary extract, July 2020).

For many women participants in our study, the pandemic meant additional care duties, increased financial concerns, job losses and, for a few, the responsibility of ensuring family compliance. The Springbok mother says:

> I find it more difficult because everything is on me, and the children when they are hungry, they won't go to their father, but they will come to me, so it's making me think that I'm no longer supporting them the way I use to... (July 2020).

She adds in a later activity, 'Yes, their dad helps with what he wants. So, what I learnt is that a woman, she's the one who takes care of the family' (August 2020).

Across the sample, parents' experiences of lockdown were coloured by their concern over children's welfare. Concerns about school closures, child safety, and general well-being dominated discussions about children. One mum noted the difficulty in keeping children indoors during the lockdown period:

> It's just that kids are kids. You will find them in the streets. Even though you talk to them, they don't understand. They want to play, so yeah (mother, 32, Blesbok family, low SES; interview, August 2020).

This was an important observation and contrasted with the experiences of our families residing in more affluent areas; in these contexts, children were occupied with online learning and appeared to have minimal in-person social interaction.

For many parents, resource constraints meant no access to education or online programmes made available through the media channels. In the following quote, a mum talks about her children's boredom and lack of access to learning platforms:

> Even though we know that it's very risky, but I feel like they are losing out. They are bored here because we don't have electricity. If maybe we have electricity because there were channels (on television), they told us that children can catch up on schoolwork, but because we don't have electricity for us, it's a challenge (mother, 28, Gemsbok family, low SES; interview, July 2020).

To ensure access to better resources and a continuation of learning, this family chose to separate by sending their child to live with extended family members in another area:

> In terms of her, she is struggling because we don't have electricity, sometimes we don't have water. I had to take the chances of taking her to my younger sister to stay there so that she can study there (mother, 43, Peacock family, low SES; diary extract, July 2020).

Children from participating families located in poorly 'resourced' areas echoed parents' awareness of financial strain and resource constraints. While experiences of boredom were common for all children in the sample, for some, like this child from the Springbok family, it was intensified by financial difficulties:

> It is getting boring now because there is nothing exciting anymore about staying at home because we are behind with schoolwork. Everyone in my family also get bored because some do not have jobs anymore. They are just staying home with us, and we just want to have clothes again (son, 11, Springbok family; diary extract, August 2020).

From these quotes, we can see how lack of access to basic resources compounded the difficulties that some families experienced, so increasing risk.

Increasing risk as a result of the safety regulations

Acute stressors or a cascade of stresses unsettle family functioning, which causes shocks throughout the relational network (Walsh 2016). The pandemic and resultant lockdown heightened threats to family well-being due to increased financial insecurity, caregiving burdens and confinement-related stress (Prime et al. 2020). For most of our families, safety regulations impacted family finances, increased concerns related to poverty, employment and hunger, halted educational learning and progress, and increased mental health challenges – all of which increased exposure to risk factors. One participant captured both the opportunities and the risks, saying:

> Because I am not working at the moment, I have been spending quite a bit of time with the children, which has been good and bad in a way. We get to spend much more time with each other, quality time, but at the same time, it's mouths to feed. So, it's sort of like a double-edged sword (father, 27, Lion family, middle SES; diary extract, August 2020).

Many of the participants in our study suffered job losses or loss of earning potential due to the pandemic.

> But I think the negative part of lockdown is the unemployment. I mean, I had a thriving catering and events business before lockdown, and with the start of lockdown, my business was the first to close (mother, middle SES, Lion family; diary extract, June 2020).

As a result of job losses, some families struggled with buying food and other necessities. This mum, who ran an early childhood learning centre, says about her experience:

> Another thing is I used to work, and it was much better because I could put food on the table. As a single parent, when you work like me, I could buy food for the house. I have two children, and we could survive on the school fees money. So now that we are in lockdown, I can't work because we have closed, and there is no income for the house. So, it is difficult to survive with my children (mother, 43, Blue Crane family, low to middle SES; diary extract, July 2020).

She added at a later point that although family members have stepped in to assist, she sometimes feels uncomfortable asking for more when the food runs out:

> So, it is very difficult; I am not coping at all because even the little food my family bought for us, it is challenging for me to go back and ask for more if, for example, my sugar or salt is finished. I am now relying on help from my family, and I am not used to this life. It's rough (July 2020).

For children, the pandemic resulted in the loss of learning time. One young person speaks of her difficulty in understanding course material without access to teachers:

> They [trial exams] are going well, but I am not coping well because I missed out on some things because, during the lockdown, we were forced to self-study at home. So, some of the things I didn't understand well (daughter, 18, Blue Crane family; phone call diary extract, October 2020).

Added responsibilities combined with access to fewer coping resources, financial worries, genuine fears of hunger, loss of learning time, and unemployment resulted in mental health challenges.

> I tell myself this too shall pass. I think I am probably coping the worst. Trying to hold it together for everyone and also having to experience self-absorbed teens who only want to interact with their friends (mother, age not shared, Crocodile family, high SES; diary extract, August 2020).

Impact on family life: reorganizing around change

Family resilience theory suggests that significant life events, like the pandemic, impact the entire family unit, as described previously, for example, in terms of education and employment; vital transactional processes may be activated, and this provides opportunities for adaptation for individual members and the family (Walsh 2016). The family system makes both internal and external adjustments to balance its needs, relational resources and external demands (Heath and Orthner 1999). Our findings show how individuals in the family mobilized essential resources and strengths, both internal and external, from within the family system and through their social interactions to adapt to the sudden changes and challenges brought about by the pandemic. These efforts included attempts at meaning-making, reorganizing to meet the demands of home-schooling, facing job losses or working remotely, reconnecting with each other and enhancing communication patterns, all of which allowed for positive adaptation. For some participants, the pandemic and the resultant impositions were viewed positively, and they chose to see it as a moment to reflect, take stock and develop new competencies.

> For me personally, lockdown has been a positive and a negative experience. I have chosen to make it as positive as possible. I've appreciated the time off. I'm using the time to reconstruct my life… I've thoroughly enjoyed that I don't have to get up and be anywhere at a particular time. For me, that's been the most positive thing, and it's given me time to recover from previous negative things that have happened in my life, so that's good… I am also looking at it as opportunity to change direction because I got a psych degree, but I can't do anything with it and, so I was thinking of doing my psych honours and then my psych master's, so I am processing that at the moment (mother, 49, Hadeda family, middle SES; diary extract, July 2020).

The lockdown presented an opportunity to reconnect, communicate and enhance relationships for all families. The following quote shows how family relationships benefited from time together without external distractions and demands.

> It's very good. I think spending time together and being able to talk … more often actually made the relationship so, so much better. Because like before, everybody just did their own thing because we knew that it's not like we are going to have to be stuck together at some point, you wake up tomorrow you go to work, so I don't have to deal with you the whole day. But our relationship has improved quite a lot, we spend time together, you know we communicate well

> together now, and I think we appreciate each other a lot more than we did before. So yeah, I think our relationships overall here in the house have really improved (daughter, adult – age not shared, Eland family, middle SES; interview, October 2020).

For one family, the lockdown enabled the introduction of a new ritual and increased family time. In this instance, the family began watching a television series together. The mother says,

> My husband and I loved this series in our younger years, so, on day 1 of lockdown, we started watching it again with the kids, and they love it!! We have watched one episode every night since lockdown. It's become a ritual (mother, age not shared, Crocodile family, high SES; diary, July 2020).

For another participant, the lockdown positively impacted her relationship with her husband. Their relationship improved as he was more present and shared childcare duties with her, something he did not do before.

> With my husband, the lockdown period has also affected us in a positive way. I say so because we now spend more time together grooming our children. Before COVID-19, my husband never was spending time at home. During the week, he would come home in the evening tired; he will eat, bathe and sleep. Friday evenings, he would go out and come home when everyone is sleeping. The next day that will be Saturday, he will go out as well as Sunday. We hardly would spend time with him. This caused a lot of suffering in the house. Now he spends his time with family even if his salary was cut, at least that little comes home.

She adds:

> I got the satisfaction I needed. Yes, some will argue with me looking at finances that we were affected negatively… but I needed my family (mother, 45, Impala family, middle SES; diary extract, August 2020).

For one family, lockdown created an opportunity for the family to be reunited. Pre-COVID-19, the dad had always worked and lived in another province but moved back home during the lockdown. The daughter says, 'with my dad we have bonded much because he is not staying in this province, so for the lockdown, he was here with us' (daughter, child – age not shared, Gemsbok family, low SES; interview, October 2020).

While many households saw a shift in care duties, often with more duties absorbed by maternal figures and/or women members of the household, for some mums, it meant a sharing of duties, which facilitated better family relations. For example, this mum describes sharing household duties with her daughter:

> When we wake up before, we would leave some of the work for the weekend, but now we know how to share the responsibility. When I cook, the firstborn washes the dishes. We swap; sometimes, she cleans. Before the responsibility was not shared because after school, they would focus on their homework (mother, 43, Blue Crane family, low to middle SES; diary extract, July 2020).

For a few, the pandemic and the difficulties required them to mobilize external resources or make resources available to others. For example, this mum says of accessing food parcels:

> …we actually got some food parcels from a company… They are a non-profit organization. So, at least with those food parcels, we can eat for that 3 months duration (mother, 27, Hartebeest family, middle SES; interview, August 2020).

For others, as demonstrated in the excerpts, being able to offer support to those in need was necessary. It not only helped them cope but also facilitated the resilience of those in need:

> There's a squatter camp about, I think, maybe five minutes, six minutes from my house when you're driving. To think about them not having food and then here, I have got a lot of food here in the house, and I can't go to them. It was quite a very difficult period in my life during this COVID-19, and I was so torn between what I should do. It was only when started sitting down and started planning how I am going to start giving them food. We started with going with the car and opening the boot for them to pick up bread. Slowly we started figuring out safer ways that we can get the food across to them (mother, 36, Protea family, high SES; diary extract, August 2020).

Discussion

Family life in South Africa is complex and in constant flux. Historical, structural, epidemiological, political and social forces drive change and demand adaptation (Goldberg 2013). COVID-19 presented one more challenge to family well-being and stability. In the face of and following such a major stressful event, families may struggle with an accumulation of prior or concurrent stressors emanating both from individual family members and from the family system and/or community (Brown-Baatjies et al. 2008). In South Africa, historical and co-occurring hardships include poverty, unemployment and poor access to resources and services. The family resilience framework focuses on strengths under strain. It determines functioning in context (Brown-Baatjies et al. 2008), offering opportunities to improve family functioning and individual well-being (Isaacs et al. 2020).

In tracking family well-being during the pandemic, we found that, in general, compliance with safety regulations was high over the course of eight months. This is consistent with findings from an online survey with almost 20,000 South Africans conducted in the first month of lockdown. Dukhi et al. (2021) found that most of those surveyed stayed home and only left in order to buy essential items or collect a social grant. Less compliant groups included those living in poorer-resourced areas and crowded spaces (Dukhi et al. 2021). Similarly, non-compliance mostly appeared to result from structural and spatial factors for families in our study. Living in small, tightly packed dwellings with intermittent access to electricity meant that lockdown and social distancing regulations were ignored when individuals were forced to 'borrow' electricity and access a grant or a food distribution site. Social distancing was easier to maintain for those with greater economic and social capital and readily available resources. The varied ways in which families in our study responded to and experienced the pandemic draws attention to how geography, politics, and privilege intersect, furthering disadvantaging some (Ross 2020). Levine and Manderson (2021) offer one explanation for the relative ease with which South Africans accommodated lockdown rules. Their greater compliance may, in part, be attributed to the militarization of lockdown and reliance on tactics reminiscent of apartheid. Cowed by images of armed forces and fear of punishment ensured that individuals and families tried to adhere to lockdown regulations to some extent. Other possible explanations may include the risk of contracting the virus or a sense of social responsibility. Findings from our data suggest that for most of our participants, compliance could be attributed to fear of punishment and fear of becoming ill.

Deepening socio-economic difficulties impacted most families, either through direct experiences with unemployment and poverty or through an awareness of the financial crisis unfolding in the country. Emerging research from South Africa suggests that socio-economic risks intensified as the pandemic continued (Spaull et al. 2021), further entrenching systemic inequalities. As researchers peering into the lives of families, we too were drawn into the daily struggles of many of our families; requests for assistance with obtaining food parcels and narratives of hunger brought home the challenges facing South Africans and created an ethical and moral dilemma. We questioned our responsibility towards participating families and to the surrounding community, exploring ways in which we could mobilize resources and facilitate resilience. Walsh (2016) suggests that researchers practice resilience in overcoming the conceptual and methodological challenges to advance knowledge, focusing on what can be learned and accepting what is beyond control. Our methodological approach provided an opportunity for individuals and families to reflect on both their difficulties and their coping strategies. Indeed, feedback from a few participants suggested that participating benefited them.

While some families reported increased relational difficulties and caregiver strain, the changing nature of families meant that accommodations were made to adapt to the new reality. Depending on their resources, challenges and values, each family forged a different pathway to resilience (Walsh 2016). Participating families in our study looked for meaning to understand this extraordinary time; some found possibilities for individual growth and a moment to stop and take stock. Many saw it as an opportunity to reconnect, draw closer to each other, be grateful and appreciate time together. In some families, enforced time together called for better communication and problem-solving. Families mobilized resources through relatives and community support to aid them through the challenges, while a few who had resources were motivated to share. These processes of adaptation mirror the core transactional processes identified in the family resilience framework (Walsh 2003, 2016) and offer a starting point from which to consider possible interventions to enhance family well-being.

Conclusion

As with every discussion highlighting the resilience of individuals, families and communities, the challenge is not to celebrate the enduring strength of individuals while dismissing the prevailing factors that increase risk and vulnerability. COVID-19 and the resultant lockdown have undoubtedly intensified existing challenges, increasing the vulnerability of thousands of families. In this chapter, we have touched on the differential impacts of the pandemic on families, which replicated political, spatial, social and economic fault lines. Identifying resilience processes does, however, present opportunities to assess family functioning and develop appropriate, contextually relevant, multilevel interventions that decrease vulnerability while strengthening functioning. Inherent in the definition of resilience is the process of change from disarray to processes of recovery, or system-wide transformation, before, during, and after exposure to adversity; this recognition of system-wide evolution emphasizes the responsibility that surrounding systems have in facilitating well-being for individuals and families (Ungar 2021).

In South Africa, historical and contemporary challenges mandate a systemic response to family well-being, since monosystemic interventions are unlikely to have a significant impact. Thus, while COVID-19 has devastatingly highlighted systemic failings, it has also offered insight into the needs and capacities of families. South African families require access to essential, basic services like running water and electricity, equitable access to education, employment opportunities and functional health services. Multilevel intervention and prevention programmes are needed to support families at risk and enable family and individual well-being. The pandemic and its aftermath present an opportunity to transform social policies to respond to the historical, biological, social and environmental factors that impinge on family well-being (Walsh 2016).

Notes

1. Influx control was a way to restrict and control the number of black South Africans living, working and entering urban areas. According to the Pass Laws, black South Africans over the age of 16 were required to carry their pass documents, referred to as dompas, at all times (Hindson 1985).
2. Approximately US$31,528,635.
3. Informal housing refers to makeshift structures that have not been erected according to approved plans and planning regulations, typically on land that has been unlawfully occupied.

References

Braun, V. and Clarke, V. (2006) 'Using thematic analysis in psychology'. *Qualitative Research in Psychology*, 3 (2), 77–101.

Bridgeman, G., Van der Berg, S. and Patel, L. (2020) 'Hunger in South Africa during 2020: Results from Wave 2 of NIDS-CRAM'. *Working Paper No. 3. National Income Dynamics*

(NIDS) – Coronavirus Rapid Mobile Survey (CRAM). https://cramsurvey.org/wp-content/uploads/2020/09/3.-Bridgman-G.-Van-der-Berg-S.-_-Patel-L.-2020-Hunger-in-South-Africa-during-2020-Results-from-Wave-2-of-NIDS-CRAM.pdf (accessed 11 February 2023).

Brown-Baatjies, O., Fouché, P. and Greeff, A. (2008) 'The development and relevance of the resiliency model of family stress, adjustment and adaptation'. *Acta Academia: Critical Views on Society, Culture and Politics*, 40 (1), 78–126.

Casale, D. and Posel, D. (2020) 'Gender and the early effects of the COVID-19 crisis in the paid and unpaid economies in South Africa'. *Working Paper No. 4. National Income Dynamics (NIDS) – Coronavirus Rapid Mobile Survey (CRAM)*. https://cramsurvey.org/wp-content/uploads/2020/07/Casale-Gender-the-early-effects-of-the-COVID-19-crisis-in-the-paid-unpaid-economies-in-South-Africa.pdf (accessed 11 February 2023).

Chang, R., Varley, K., Tem, F. and Munoz, M. (2020–22) 'The COVID Resilience Ranking: The best and worst places to be as we learn to live with Delta'. *Bloomberg*, 24 November 2020, final update 29 June 2022. https://www.bloomberg.com/graphics/covid-resilience-ranking/.

Dawson, H. and Fouksman, L. (2020) 'Why South Africa needs to ensure income security beyond the pandemic'. *The Conversation*, 30 April 2020. https://theconversation.com/why-south-africa-needs-to-ensure-income-security-beyond-the-pandemic-137551 (accessed 11 February 2023).

Department of Health, Republic of South Africa (n.d., ongoing live data) 'COVID-19 daily updates and cases'. https://sacoronavirus.co.za/covid-19-daily-cases/.

Dukhi, N., Mokhele, T., Parker, W., Ramlagan, S., Gaida, R., Mabaso, M., Sewpaul, R., Jooste, S., Naidoo, I., Parker, S., Moshabela, M., Zuma, K. and Reddy, P. (2021) 'Compliance with lockdown regulations during the COVID-19 pandemic in South Africa: Findings from an online survey'. *The Open Public Health Journal*, 14, 45–55.

Egbe, C. O. and Ngobese, S. P. (2020) 'COVID-19 lockdown and the tobacco product ban in South Africa'. *Tobacco Induced Diseases*, 18, 39. https://doi.org/10.18332/tid/120938.

Fouché, A., Fouché, D. F. and Theron, L. C. (2020) 'Child protection and resilience in the face of COVID-19 in South Africa: A rapid review of C-19 legislation'. *Child Abuse & Neglect*, 110 (2), 104710. https:// doi.org/10.1016/j.chiabu.2020.104710.

Goldberg, R. E. (2013) 'Family instability and pathways to adulthood in Cape Town, South Africa'. *Population and Development Review*, 39 (2), 231–56.

Grinter, R. E. and Eldridge, M. A. (2001) 'y do tngrs luv 2 txt msg?'. In Prinz, W., Jarke, M., Rogers, Y., Schmidt, K. and Wulf, V. (eds) *Proceedings of the Seventh European Conference on Computer-Supported Cooperative Work ECSCW '01*. Heidelberg: Springer Netherlands, 219–38.

Gritti, P. (2020) 'Family systems in the era of COVID-19: From openness to quarantine'. *Journal of Psychosocial Systems*, 4 (1), 1–5.

Heath, D. T. and Orthner, D. K. (1999) 'Stress and adaptation among male and female single parents'. *Journal of Family Issues*, 20 (4), 557–87.

Hindson, D. C. (1985) 'Orderly urbanization and influx control: From territorial apartheid to regional spatial ordering in South Africa'. *Cahiers d'études africaines*, 401–32.

Isaacs, S. A., Roman, N. and Carlson, S. (2020) 'Fostering family resilience: A community participatory action research perspective'. *Child Care in Practice*, 26 (4), 358–72.

Jarrahi, M. H., Goay, C., Zirker, S. and Zhang, Y. (2021) 'Using digital diaries as a research method for capturing practices in situ'. In Symon, G., Prichard, K. and Hine, C. (eds) *Research Methods for Digital Work and Organization: Investigating distributed, multi-modal, and mobile work*. Oxford: Oxford University Press, 107–29.

Knijn, T. and Patel, L. (2018) 'Family life and family policy in South Africa: Responding to past legacies, new opportunities and challenges'. In Eydal, G. B. and Rostgaard, T. (eds) *Handbook of Family Policy*. Cheltenham: Edward Elgar Publishing, 249–60.

Levine, S. and Manderson, L. (2021) 'Proxemics, COVID-19, and the ethics of care in South Africa'. *Cultural Anthropology*, 36 (3), 391–9.

Mahase, E. (2022) 'Omicron: South Africa says fourth wave peak has passed as it lifts curfew'. *BMJ*, 2022; 376:o7. https://doi.org/10.1136/bmj.o7.

Manderson, L. and Levine, S. (2021) 'Militarising the pandemic: Lockdown in South Africa'. In Manderson, L., Burke, N. J. and Wahlberg, A. (eds) *Viral Loads: Anthropologies of urgency in the time of COVID-19*. London: UCL Press, 47–66. https://doi.org/10.14324/111.9781800080232.

Manyoni, M. J. and Abader, M. I. (2021) 'The effects of the COVID-19 lockdown and alcohol restriction on trauma-related emergency department cases in a South African regional hospital'. *African Journal of Emergency Medicine*, 11 (2), 227–30. https://doi.org/10.1016/j.afjem.2020.12.001.

Masten, A. S. (2011) 'Resilience in children threatened by extreme adversity: Frameworks for research, practice, and translational synergy'. *Development and Psychopathology*, 23 (2), 493–506. https://doi.org/10.1017/S0954579411000198.

Masten, A. S. (2014) 'Global perspectives on resilience in children and youth'. *Child Development*, 85 (1), 6–20. https://doi.org/10.1111/cdev.12205.

Mokomane, Z., Roberts, B., Struwig, J. and Gordon, S. (2019) *South African Social Attitudes: Family matters: Family cohesion, values and strengthening to promote wellbeing*. Cape Town: HRSC Press.

Mudeau, P. (2022) 'The implications of food-parcel corruption for the right to food during the Covid-19 pandemic in South Africa'. *ESR Review*, 23 (2). https://hdl.handle.net/10520/ejc-esrrev-v23-n2-a2 (accessed 8 March 2023).

Muller, S. M. (2020) 'COVID-19: The cure could be worse than the disease for South Africa'. *The Conversation*, 23 March 2020. https://theconversation.com/covid-19-the-cure-could-be-worse-than-the-disease-for-south-africa-134436 (accessed 11 February 2023).

Naidu, S. (2021) 'The impact of COVID-19: The conundrum of South Africa's socio-economic landscape'. *ACCORD*. https://www.accord.org.za/analysis/the-impact-of-covid-19-the-conundrum-of-south-africas-socio-economic-landscape/ (accessed 11 February 2023).

Nwosu, C. O., Kollamparambil, U. and Oyenubi, A. (2021) *Socioeconomic Inequalities Inability to Work from Home During the Coronavirus Pandemic: The case of South Africa. Wave 5, Working Paper 9*. National Income Dynamics (NIDS) – Coronavirus Rapid Mobile Survey (CRAM). https://cramsurvey.org/wp-content/uploads/2021/07/9.-Nwosu-C-Kollamparambil-U.-Oyenubi-A.-2021-Socioeconomic-inequalities-in-ability-to-work-from-home-during-the-coronavirus-pandemic-The-case-of-South-Africa.pdf (accessed 11 February 2023).

Nwosu, C. O. and Ndinda, C. (2018) 'Female household headship and poverty in South Africa: An employment-based analysis'. *Working Paper 761*. Cape Town: Economic Research Southern Africa.

Patel, L., Knijn, G. C. M., Gorman-Smith, D., Hochfeld, T., Isserow, M., Garthe, R., Chiba, J., Moodley, J. and Kgaphola, I. K. (2017) *Family Contexts, Child Support Grants and Child Well-Being in South Africa*. Johannesburg: Centre for Social Development in Africa, University of Johannesburg.

Prime, H., Wade, M. and Browne, D. T. (2020) 'Risk and resilience in family well-being during the COVID-19 pandemic'. *The American Psychologist*, 75 (5), 631–43. https://doi.org/10.1037/amp0000660.

Ross, F. C. (2020) 'Of soap and dignity in South Africa's lockdown'. *Corona Times*, 8 April 2020. https://www.coronatimes.net/soap-dignity-south-africa-lockdown (accessed 11 February 2023).

Sebola, E., Ntuli, B. and Madiba, S. (2020) 'Maternal AIDS orphans and the burden of parenting in youth-headed households: Implications for food security in impoverished areas of South Africa'. *The Open Public Health Journal*, 13 (1), 144–51. https://doi.org/10.2174/1874944502013010144.

Seekings, J. (2020) 'Feeding poor people: The national government has failed but civil society, provincial and local governments have tried to fill the gap'. *Ground Up*, 2 June 2020. https://www.groundup.org.za/article/feeding-poor-people-national-government-has-failed/ (accessed 11 February 2020).

Soudien, C., Reddy, V. and Harvey, J. (2021) 'The impact of COVID-19 on a fragile education system: The case of South Africa'. In Reimers, F. M. (ed.) *Primary and Secondary Education During COVID-19*. Cham: Springer, 303–25.

Spaull, N., Daniels, R. C., Ardington, C. and 35 others (2021) 'Synthesis Report, NIDS-CRAM Wave 3'. *Working Paper 1. National Income Dynamics Study (NIDS) – Coronavirus Rapid Mobile Survey (CRAM)*. https://cramsurvey.org/wp-content/uploads/2021/02/1.-Spaull-N.-Daniels-R.-C-et-al.-2021-NIDS-CRAM-Wave-3-Synthesis-Report.pdf (accessed 11 February 2023).

Staunton, C., Swanepoel, C. and Labuschaigne, M. (2020) 'Between a rock and a hard place: COVID-19 and South Africa's response'. *Journal of Law and the Biosciences*, 7 (1). https://doi.org/10.1093/jlb/lsaa052.

Tegally, H., Wilkinson, E., Giovanetti, M. and 44 others (2021) 'Detection of a SARS-CoV-2 variant of concern in South Africa'. *Nature*, 592, 438–43. https://doi.org/10.1038/s41586-021-03402-9.

Ungar, M. (2021) 'Introduction: Why a volume on multisystemic resilience?'. In Ungar, M. (ed.) *Multisystemic Resilience: Adaptation and transformation in context changes*. New York: Oxford University Press, 1–5.

Van Hoving, D. J., van Koningsbruggen, C., de Man, M. and Hendrikse, C. (2021) 'Temporal changes in trauma according to alcohol sale restrictions during the South African national COVID-19 lockdown'. *African Journal of Emergency Medicine*, 11 (4), 477–82. https://doi.org/10.1016/j.afjem.2021.08.001.

Walsh, F. (2003) 'Family resilience: A framework for clinical practice'. *Family Process*, 42 (1), 1–18. https://doi.org/10.1111/j.1545-5300.2003.00001.x.

Walsh, F. (2016) 'Family resilience: A developmental systems framework'. *European Journal of Developmental Psychology*, 13 (3), 313–24.

Walsh, F. (2021) 'Family Resilience: A dynamic systemic framework'. In Ungar, M. (ed.) *Multisystemic Resilience: Adaptation and transformation in context changes*. New York: Oxford University Press, 255–70.

8
Sweden: everyday family life during COVID-19

Disa Bergnehr, Laura Darcy and Annelie J. Sundler

Introduction

The Swedish national response to COVID-19 was unique in comparison with other European countries, with a strong emphasis on individual responsibility (Claesson and Hanson 2021). Instead of enforcing public lockdowns the authorities gave advice and recommendations. The national handling of the pandemic was built on principles of responsibility. Overall, there is a strong trust in authorities in Swedish society where the public tend to follow recommendations.

The first case of COVID-19 was registered at the end of January 2020. There were few infected people and few national measures taken prior to the school mid-term break in March, when the number of infected people increased rapidly. Initially, Sweden had high infection rates of COVID-19 and related deaths, for instance, compared with its Nordic neighbours Denmark, Finland and Norway. Old age and low socio-economic status markedly increased the risk of serious illness and death from the disease (Bartelink et al. 2020).

This chapter explores how Swedish adolescents, parents of dependent children and grandparents experienced the COVID-19 pandemic – how they understood and responded to pandemic policies and described changes in life. The analyses were based on interviews and written replies to open-ended questions with participants of varying national origin and socio-economic status. The data were collected between June 2020 and June 2021 across the country. We found that everyday life was influenced by continuous risk assessment and individual participants acted in different ways depending on their care and concern for the well-being of family members and relatives as well as for their own mental health. Risk assessment was also understood and managed in relation to children's education. Changes in life due to the pandemic policies were more prominent for some age groups than for others.

Country context

Swedish families and family policies

Sweden is a Scandinavian country with almost 10.5 million inhabitants, of which 20 per cent are migrants, born abroad.[1] The older population is increasing, with 20 per cent being 65 years old or older (Statistics Sweden 2021c). However, Sweden's fertility rate is among the highest in Europe (Statistics Sweden 2021b). Most families with dependent children are nuclear families, and 75 per cent of all children age 17 or under reside in a household with both their parents (Statistics Sweden 2021a).

In Sweden, the government provides generous universal support to families with children, as part of what is known as the Nordic welfare model. The Nordic model strongly values the right to health and healthy living for all, and the human rights perspective (Esping Andersen 1999; Goldscheider et al. 2015). Families benefit from free healthcare for pregnant women and children, paid parental leave insurance for over a year, subsidized and available childcare and after school care, free education (including higher education), financial compensation when parents stay home from work to tend sick children, a general monthly child allowance, and the right to reduced working hours for parents with young children (Wells and Bergnehr 2014). Family policy reforms have evolved along with gender equality and labour market policies since the 1930s; in Sweden, women and men, mothers and fathers, are encouraged to participate in paid labour to the same extent and to share domestic duties and the care of children equally (Björnberg 2002). Fathers have become more involved over the years, although there are still differences between men and women in time spent on paid labour and childcare (Duvander and Johansson 2019).

Overall, Swedish contemporary parenting ideals are in accordance with practice and are characterized by a child-centred family life with mothers and fathers who spend much time and resources on their child's upbringing (Bergnehr 2008, 2020; Bäck-Wiklund and Bergsten 1997; Forsberg 2009; Johansson and Andreasson 2017), often with practical and emotional support from grandparents (Eldén et al. 2021). The majority of children aged 17 and under grow up in nuclear family arrangements while 25 per cent have parents who do not reside together, in most cases due to divorce or separation. Almost 30 per cent of the children of divorced/separated parents share their time equally between the parents, but the most common arrangement is to reside only or most of the time with the mother (Statistics Sweden 2018, 2021c). Single mothers generally provide for themselves through paid labour, but approximately 20 per cent are dependent on social assistance (Stranz and Wiklund 2011). Overall, Swedish families with dependent children are well-off financially. There have been considerable improvements in living conditions for families during the past 20 years; poverty among households with children has decreased drastically, and two-thirds of all families have a good or very good standard of living. Families at risk of poverty are single-mother and/ or migrant-parent households (Save the Children 2018).

Pandemic policies

All support that Swedish families are granted through the welfare system continued as usual during the pandemic. Swedish society had no lockdown and the pandemic policies were based on recommendations rather than legal restrictions. After the outbreak, the National Public Health Agency (in Swedish, 'Folkhälsomyndigheten') and the government recommended higher education, adult education and upper secondary schools should change to online teaching, which they did. Higher education was conducted mainly online until autumn 2021. Upper secondary schools opened in August 2020 but went online or partly online in November 2020, which continued (with local variants) also during spring 2021. Preschools (caring for children one to six years of age) and compulsory school for 6–16-year-olds (grades 0–9) stayed open with some local exceptions during shorter periods, as did many leisure activities for these younger children. There were shorter periods of online education at home for some younger pupils at some schools and municipalities, in periods of transmission outbreaks. Figure 8.1 on the following page shows the timeline of COVID-19 spread and government response measures in Sweden.

Visits to care homes for the elderly were forbidden for six months in 2020 (April to October). This policy was criticized for being implemented too late, as the spread of COVID-19 was high in care facilities, especially at the start of the pandemic. Work-from-home for those who had a job that allowed this was recommended from April 2020 to 29 September 2021, and the numbers that could attend public events were restricted; many

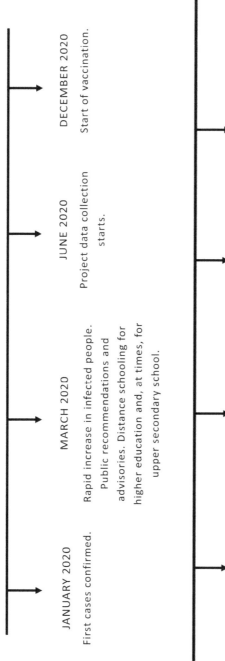

Figure 8.1 Timeline of COVID-19 in Sweden. Source: authors.

activities such as theatre shows, concerts and sport events were cancelled. In summer 2020, the number of COVID-19 cases declined but rose again during autumn and winter. In January 2021, a temporary pandemic law was implemented that gave the government legal rights to take further actions to limit the spread of the virus. Several formal restrictions were then implemented, such as shorter opening hours for restaurants and limiting the number of visitors at shops and malls. Many restrictions were eased, although not removed, on 1 July 2021 and remained in effect until the end of September 2021 (krisinformation.se). Some restrictions (for example, social distancing at restaurants, shops, and cultural/sport events) and recommendations (for example, working from home, social distancing) were then put into effect again from late December 2021 to February/March 2022, due to a high rise in the number of infected.

In Sweden, all people have a common and personal responsibility to prevent the spread of infections, according to the Swedish Infectious Diseases Act 2004:168 (Socialdepartementet 2004). The main recommendations to the public from the government and national authorities during the pandemic were: wash the hands frequently, keep social distancing, cough and sneeze into the elbow, avoid touching the eyes, nose and mouth, and stay at home when having symptoms. Those aged 70 or over were asked to self-isolate and to keep the amount of physical contact to a minimum. In December 2020, the vaccination programme started, with the elderly and at-risk groups first in line. From October 2021, children from 12 years of age were offered vaccination. At the beginning of January 2022, 82 per cent of the population aged 12 or over had received two shots of COVID-19 vaccine (Folkhälsomyndigheten 2022). From January onwards, a third shot of the vaccine was offered to all. Vaccination was offered at no cost for the individual, but the availability and procedures regarding vaccination varied somewhat across the country.

Previous research on COVID-19 in Sweden

Families with low socio-economic status, of which most are migrants, faced a higher risk than natives (by which we mean here as having two parents born in Sweden) and middle-class families of being affected by serious illness and death from COVID-19. Low socio-economic status groups also had an increased risk of unemployment and poor living conditions due to the pandemic (Drefahl et al. 2020; Folkhälsomyndigheten 2021a; Bartelink et al. 2020). Presumptions have been made that socio-economically disadvantaged children will suffer short-term and long-term consequences from the pandemic, such as learning impairment and health issues (IFAU 2021), but the risk for children of facing severe illness or death from COVID-19 was shown to be minimal, despite preschools and schools having stayed open (Ludvidgsson et al. 2021). Moreover, keeping schools open appears to have contributed to only a small increase in infection among parents (Vlachos et al. 2021).

Previous Swedish research on children's and parents' experiences of family life, well-being and schooling under the pandemic show somewhat varying results. One panel survey with almost 1,800 adolescents aged 15 to 19, conducted soon after the pandemic began, in June to July 2020, showed that the majority reported that they had complied with governmental recommendations. Most did not report any changes in their psychosocial functioning, but some that had experienced online schooling did. It was quite common for adolescents to report that the pandemic had affected their mental health, and a significant number reported less time spent with peers and more conflicts with parents (Kapetanovic et al. 2021). However, these results are contradicted by a follow-up panel study with mid-adolescents (approximately 13 years old at baseline, and 15 years old at the follow-up) that compared mental health and health behaviours of a control group that had not been exposed to COVID-19 (that is, answered the questions prior to the pandemic) to a group of youths that had been exposed (that is, answered the questions during the pandemic, in 2020). The study does not indicate any differences in the longitudinal changes reported on mental health, relationships with peer and parents, and health behaviours between those exposed to the pandemic and those who were not (Chen et al. 2021).

A panel survey on how the pandemic affected adolescents' well-being and everyday life suggests a stronger negative impact on women but that most young people adapted well to the changes to everyday life (Kerekes et al. 2021). When asked about concerns and worries caused by the pandemic, many children affirmed that they indeed felt worried, mainly about themselves or their relatives being infected or dying, but were less concerned about future consequences (Folkhälsomyndigheten 2021b; Sarkadi et al. 2021). Asked at the end of 2020, only one in ten children aged 11 to 15 reported that the pandemic had had a negative impact on their school work, while 25 per cent reported that it had restricted their socializing with peers, and 50 per cent reported being less engaged in leisure time activities than before the pandemic (Folkhälsomyndigheten 2021b).

To our knowledge, and at the time of the writing, work on how the COVID-19 pandemic has influenced Swedish families is scarce, and little is known about how children and parents experienced and responded to national restrictions and recommendations over time. However, there are a few exceptions. Eldén, Anving and Alenius Wallin (2021) investigated intergenerational care practices before and during COVID-19 through analyses of interview narratives from 30 grandparents, 12 parents and 12 children. They concluded that intergenerational care and involvement in everyday life are reciprocal and much valued. Grandparents, for instance, provide help to their adult children and their grandchildren in practical matters, as well as emotional support, but also gain much from their involvement. During the pandemic, the recommendations for older generations to self-isolate altered the opportunities for practical care and physical meetings but brought about 'new' ways to keep in contact, such as through video calls. The notion that social distancing would be only for a short time and was therefore bearable appeared in many narratives, although a longing for physical contact was also repeatedly expressed. However, for some people, the risk of infecting elderly relatives or of being infected was set in opposition to other risks, such as mental health issues, and the urgent need for physical meetings and practical support led them to defy the recommendations and continue with or take up physical meetings. For others, such as grandparents who prior to the pandemic had spent much time and energy on helping children and grandchildren in their everyday activities, the social distancing recommendations could actually be somewhat of a relief, providing a legitimate reason to step back from being so heavily involved (Eldén et al. 2021).

Another study explored how resettled refugee men from Syria experienced their fathering and adapted their parenting practices during COVID-19. The findings were based on individual interviews with 11 fathers, conducted in September and October 2020. The work reveals that the pandemic has had different consequences on family life, depending on the children's age and whether a child had periods of online education from home. However, fathering during the pandemic was experienced as being more intense and demanding but, by some, also more rewarding. This was due to the family confinement that made the fathers more involved in the care for children and the household. However, some said that this 'brought upon fathering' caused a sense of frustration and social isolation. The fathers were ambivalent towards the Swedish COVID-19 policies, in particular the decision to keep preschool and schools open, and some expressed uncertainties regarding what information about the disease they could trust (Wissö and Bäck-Wiklund 2021).

Theoretical framework

It has been argued that 'few areas of everyday life have been left unchanged in the wake of the emergence of this new infectious disease' (Lupton and Willis 2021, 4). Here we explore 'the social responses to risk' (Lupton and Willis 2021, 3); more specifically how adolescents, parents and grandparents understood the risks of COVID-19 and responded to the policies that were introduced due to the pandemic. 'To call something a "risk" is to recognize its importance to our subjectivity and well-being' (Lupton and Willis 2021, 21). Risk and *risk assessment* are conceptualized as social and cultural processes that are formed interdependently with others in the specific societal context, which make them open for re-interpretation and negotiation. It therefore becomes relevant to explore how different individuals understand and negotiate risk in different ways, and ambivalently oppose and/or affirm public policies and other people's interpretations of risk (Lupton 2013).

Our focus is family life, including *personal life* – a term proposed by Smart (2007, 188) to be more inclusive than the concept *family* in that it 'incorporates all sorts of families, all sorts of relationships and/or intimacies'. *Personal life* denotes agency and 'the centrality of the individual' but 'retains notions of connectedness and embeddedness in and with the social and the cultural'. In the analytical process, we found that well-being, care and risk assessment ran through the participants' narratives, and these concepts have thus been central to our analyses. *Well-being* and *care* are experienced and contingent on the individual's personal life, including the social and societal context in which the individual's relationships are embedded (Stoppard 2000; Noddings 2013). The concepts of care and well-being are related. To care for others and to receive/accept care is a natural part of our being in the world as socially interconnected individuals; care is essential for our well-being (Eriksson 1987; Larsson et al. 2013). Well-being relates to lived experiences of harmony and balance in life (Healey-Ogden and Austins 2011), and 'a maintained state of being generally comfortable despite brief moments of distress' (Bergnehr 2018, 4).

Methods

In our study we used a qualitative approach to explore how the risk of COVID-19 was understood, interpreted and acted upon by Swedish families. The data, based on reports from interviews, focus groups and written answers to open-ended questions, were collected over one year, but each study participant answered the questions only once, so there is no follow-up or longitudinal approach reported here.

Ethics

In Sweden, the Swedish Ethical Review Act (SFS 2003:460) regulates research involving humans. The present project's methods and design have been approved by the Swedish Ethical Review Authority (Dnr 2020-02155; Dnr 2020-04648).

All study participants received written and verbal information before they consented to participate. They were informed that their participation was voluntary and that they could opt out at any time for no specific reason. Children under the age of 15 who wished to participate had to receive consent from their guardians, according to Swedish research ethics. All names in this chapter are pseudonyms, and information that could reveal the participant's identity has been deleted or changed.

Participants and data collection

In total, 95 adolescents (55 female, 38 male and two unknown; 14 to 19 years of age),[2] 17 parents (15 mothers and two fathers; 32 to 48 years of age), and five grandparents (two grandmothers and three grandfathers; 68 to 82 years of age) participated in this study. between them, participants encompassed people of foreign (mostly refugee) and native origin and from a variety of socio-economic groups and family structures. These participants represented almost 120 households.

Early on in the pandemic, media, national authorities and research studies reported that people in disadvantaged areas with low socio-economic status were more prone to contract the disease, and to get seriously sick or die from it (for example, Bartelink et al. 2020). For this reason, we decided that we would actively try to recruit parents and children from such areas, as well as participants from middle-class families.

Data were collected between June 2020 and June 2021 through written replies to open-ended questions (N = 66 children; N = 7 parents; N = 5 grandparents), interviews or focus group interviews (N = 9 with, in total, 29 children) and individual interviews (N = 10 with parents). The mobile application Indeemo was used by a few participants to answer the open-ended questions, but the majority answered through a one-time questionnaire with open-ended questions. Some participants were recruited through social media (Facebook, advertising) and social networks. Most children were recruited through schools.

A few children (N = 4) and parents (N = 7), and all grandparents (all native and middle-class), answered questions during the summer of 2020. Individual interviews with other parents (Syrian and Iraqi refugees with residence permits) were conducted by telephone in November 2020 by a multilingual research assistant. Four focus group interviews (1–4 participants in each), and one individual interview with upper secondary school students (native, all from mid or high socio-economic status) were conducted online in December 2020 to January 2021 (N = 11 participants). Four focus groups with secondary school students, 15 to 17 years of age, in grade 9 (foreign origin, most with a refugee background, residing in a disadvantaged area) were conducted face-to-face in June 2021 (N = 18 participants); and, 62 children, 15 to 16 years of age, in grade 9 (of varying origin and socio-economic status but primarily middle-class natives) gave written replies to open-ended questions in June 2021.

The questions that the participants answered centred on their experiences of the pandemic: about their family life, school/work, leisure, well-being, and social relationships. Retrospective questions on how the pandemic had changed (or not changed) everyday life over time were asked.

Analysis

Data were analysed with a thematic approach (Braun and Clarke 2006; Sundler et al. 2019). Initially, the analyses started with an open-minded reading of the interview transcripts and written answers, with sensitivity to meanings in the participants' narratives. As the analytical process progressed, meanings identified in the written and spoken narratives were related to each other and coded to find overall patterns. Through the coding, themes emerged that showed how individual responses to policies and impact on family life overlapped with different aspects of family life such as daily chores, occupation, school, social relationships and leisure time. Detailed analysis of the themes made clear that risk assessments, well-being and care were central to understanding the participants' experiences of the pandemic and how they had responded to government recommendations and guidelines.

Findings

Understanding of and responses to government guidelines around COVID-19

Family life is largely structured around parents' occupation and children's schooling. In the present study, the parents in the households with dependent children had varying types of occupations; some were studying or unemployed, some had work that during the pandemic was mainly or only conducted from home, and others went to work as usual, for instance healthcare personnel, teachers, preschool staff and taxi drivers. For those who worked from home, everyday life became easier in some respects, as single mother Marion (46, native, university degree) noted: '[Life under] COVID-19 has resulted in a better balance for me between work and household duties but I miss the dynamic and catching up with people at work' (written note, September 2020).

Those who had to go to work that involved physical meetings, or had relatives in this situation, raised concerns about getting infected or infecting others. The recommendation to wear masks in public places or in certain kinds of jobs was introduced late in the pandemic, and in general masks were not used to a great extent in Swedish society. A 16-year-old boy, Samir (migrant background), brought up his and his father's concern about the father not being allowed to wear a mask by his employer, despite him working as a taxi driver and being exposed and exposing others to the risk of infection. Samir expressed frustration:

> My father works as a taxi driver, and for some time he was allowed to wear a mask, but then the company started saying 'You are not allowed to wear a mask. It frightens the customers'. They got fined if they wore a mask, despite them driving elderly people and sick people to the hospital and such (Samir, 16; focus group interview, FG2, June 2021).

The vagueness of the government guidelines – the vast possibilities for companies and individuals to interpret the recommendations and the varying ways to act – caused frustration as well as concerns for how to protect oneself and others from getting infected. Family members' risk assessment and behaviour could count for 'nothing' if any or both parents' work contained high risks of contracting COVID-19. Thus, at times participants assessed that there were risks, while employers (as in the example given before) and the government, for instance by running the schools much as usual, downplayed risk, or raised other risks such as low educational achievement levels.

There were parents that were made redundant or had a hard time making their businesses profitable due to the recommendations of social distancing, although shops and restaurants were allowed to stay open (with some restrictions) during the pandemic. Others were unemployed at the beginning of the pandemic and continued to look for work. Obviously, unemployment or the risk of becoming unemployed caused stress in these families. However, since society was kept open with no lockdown, many could keep their jobs or business, and those who were unemployed continued to apply for jobs. Adnan, a father who was unemployed also prior to the pandemic, was positive about Sweden having had no lockdown, referring to his occupational status: 'You have to try hard and life goes on. Had they closed down everything it would have been harder to find a job but now I have been to job interviews' (Adnan, 39, migrant; interview, November 2020). The findings in this chapter show how different risks are assessed and compared, such as, for instance, the risk of infection and the risk of unemployment and low income. Risk and risk assessment include ambivalence (Lupton 2013).

Daily life and routines changed for most during the pandemic. The recommendations on social distancing and hand washing were evident in the study participants' reports about washing fruit and vegetables more carefully, keeping social distance and being hesitant to visit shops. Stress about getting infected and/or transmitting the disease to others through work or school was apparent. However, many continued to meet relatives such as grandchildren or older parents, but to a greater extent outside and not as often. New ways to socialize with family and peers were described; family dinners were replaced with walks and social activities that were outdoors in order to follow government guidelines. As Eric, a grandfather, reported:

> We try to keep a (physical) distance from others and we visit our son and daughter only outdoors, outside their house. It feels a little bit sad, not being allowed to go inside and sit down, but we have to manage and it feels important to persevere and make sure to follow the current restrictions (Eric, 76, native, university degree; written note, June 2020).

But social distancing and not meeting one's relatives or friends was hard for many, and the study participants' narratives indicate that this affected their well-being. Due to this, as time went by, many appeared to start to 'bend the rules' about social distancing. This was justified by saying that physical meetings were necessary for one's and/or the relatives' mental health. Lulu, a mother of four, answered the question on whether COVID-19 had changed the family's socializing as follows:

> At the beginning, when Corona started, we did not meet my parents-in-law because they have got diabetes and high blood pressure so we were afraid to see them. But then we realized that this situation would go on for a long time, and that we could not go on like this, not visiting them. My parents-in-law said to us that if you don't visit us, we will die of loneliness (Lulu, migrant, on parental leave; interview, November 2020).

Lulu's narrative illustrates a common way to reason: the risk of contracting COVID-19 and infecting others is assessed in relation to the risk of isolation that can cause mental health issues. In this juggling of different kinds of risks, the risk of mental health problems was considered greater and more pressing than the risk of infecting others or of being infected. This way to assess different risks is also exemplified by Lilly, a mother of four whose elderly parents lived in another city. She explained why she took the family to see her parents regularly although her parents were older and thus more at risk of becoming seriously ill if they contracted COVID-19:

> I really love my mother and I miss her. If I can't see her, I feel bad and they (the parents) feel bad. At the same time, I'm afraid, but I can't stop seeing them, and you never know what's going to happen, my father is old and loves his grandchildren and my children love to visit them (Lilly, 35, migrant, cleaner; interview, November 2020).

The social embeddedness of people's agency, and how their personal life (Smart 2007) affected pandemic practices were evident when analysing the participants' reports on how they interpreted and acted upon government guidelines. The importance of face-to-face contact with close relations comes across as central and connected to their and other's well-being (Stoppard 2001). Although the ideas of individual responsibility and having trust in the authorities were apparent in the narratives, government guidelines were negotiated and re-interpreted over time. In a focus group discussion (FG1, June 2021) where adolescents talked about why they socialized with peers outside school, 15-year-old migrant girl Bahar remarked, 'You can't really take it anymore, it's been going on for such a long time.'

Most study participants approved of the government's decision to keep society open with no lockdown, but some criticized governmental recommendations for being too vague and open to interpretation and thus hard to follow, or too general. As Sven, a grandfather, wrote about the matter:

> I'm very critical about the Public Health Authority's recommendation regarding the group they call 70+ ... It is not a homogeneous group in any way except the age. Sure, many in this group are at higher risk but there are many at higher risk in other (age) groups as well ... I try to follow the recommendations ... but I didn't care about the earlier rule of not travelling more than two hours away (from your house) when it came to visiting my partner ... Overall, I think the strategy in Sweden has made sense. Total lockdown can't be good (Sven, 82, native, university degree; written note, summer 2020).

Sven's narrative illustrates how recommendations were negotiated in relation to one's social relationships. Sven diverged from the general recommendations for elderly people to self-isolate, to be able to visit his partner, and he opposed the recommendation that people over 70 years of age should isolate themselves from others. To him, the Swedish way to keep society open accorded with his opinion, but he felt targeted due to his older age.

Sven reported on his experiences rather early on in the pandemic, during the summer of 2020, as did Annie (48, native, university degree), a mother of two adolescent children. Annie, in contrast to Sven, did not raise any substantial criticism towards government guidelines. Being younger, she was not affected in the same way by the recurrent public announcements to self-isolate if 70 or older. To her, the vague recommendation to maintain social distancing was easy to adapt to, and her life did not seem to have changed much because of the pandemic. Also, she noted that the members of her family had the same view on how to adjust to the guidelines and agreed on how to interpret and act upon recommendations. Like many others, she connected her well-being to her having close social relationships to family and friends.

> I have full respect and understanding for the demand for social distancing. It has not been difficult to accept and adapt to.

> In our family we have the same view and act in the same way ... I have been feeling quite well during the pandemic, and that's probably because life has still been relatively ordinary. I also have many close friends and my family to talk to (Annie, 48; written note, summer 2020).

The quote from Annie is yet another example of how people's understandings and responses to government guidelines depend on their social relationships; the importance of being able to physically meet close family and friends influenced how they acted upon the guidelines and assessed risk. Care, in this sense, is not only about avoiding getting infected and infecting others with COVID-19 but also about being able to show care on an everyday basis through social, face-to-face contact. Care is to care for as well as to be cared for, as it is played out in physical encounters (Noddings 2013).

School is a central part of children's everyday life that influences family routines and parental practices. Swedish children experienced the pandemic differently depending on their age. Organized leisure time activities and school were recommended to continue with physical meetings for children younger than 16 (Grade 9). Out-of-home activities were cancelled and school was organized online from home for several months for children and youths aged 16 to 19. Most children whose schools continued as usual were positive about the schools being kept open. They talked about it being good for their educational achievement and for their contact with peers. For instance, Carl, 15, reported: 'I think it's great [that the school stayed open], because I would have gone mad staying at home every day'. He also noted that 'it would be hard to do school work at home because all my family are there' (written note, June 2021).

Meeting friends at school was brought up as something of great importance; open schools meant that peer relationships were not dramatically affected by the social distancing guidelines. 'My way of socializing with my friends has not changed considerably since we hang out as usual at school', Tanya, 15, stated (written note, June 2021). Moreover, spending time with friends at school made it hard to justify social distancing outside of school. Liza, 15, wrote: 'My friends go to the same school as I do, most of them in the same class. Therefore, I spend time with them as usual [after school], since we would infect each other anyway at school' (written note, June 2021). Thus, for many children who met peers face-to-face on a regular basis at school, the recommendation to not spend time with friends after school hours seemed illogical.

However, children with family members that were at risk of becoming severely ill with COVID-19 described a more restricted life, with little peer contact outside of school, as they tried to avoid contracting the disease and thereby risk infecting family and relatives. There were also other children who were sceptical about keeping schools open as they were before the pandemic. They emphasized the risk of them becoming infected at school, or on the bus to school, and in turn infecting family members and/or vulnerable groups such as the elderly. Maria wrote:

> I think it's totally sick that school has stayed open when it's obviously a place where the infection can be transmitted. When the rest of the world takes things seriously and tries to stop it, Sweden does nothing. We pupils may infect high risk groups with Corona, and many may die because of this (Maria, 16; written note, June 2021).

Impact upon family life

The impact of the pandemic upon family life depended in part on the parent or parents' occupation and whether the child went to school or had online schooling at home, and to some extent on how individuals understood and responded to government guidelines. Working from home had pros and cons: it saved time and money for those who commuted, and it gave more flexibility in terms of being able to do some daily chores during the day (for example, shopping and preparing food, washing clothes, picking up children from day-care). But work from home could also cause tension between family members: Kelly, 15, reported on her father working from home: 'My father has been more at home and has become more irritated with me about certain things' (written note, June 2021). More time together in close proximity when work or studies had to be conducted at home was thus a potential trigger for irritation and conflict.

Parents who were working from home or enrolled in studies that went online during the pandemic brought up the dilemma of having to be home all the time. Not only did they miss out on social contact and face-to-face learning but had to care for children who were at home. Alice, a mother of two who was enrolled in higher education, wrote:

> It has been hard to study since the children have been home [from school] every now and then due to a mild cold, and now my oldest daughter has school [from home] online (Alice, 42, native; written note, January 2021).

Several migrant mothers who studied Swedish for Immigrants raised difficulties with learning the language when studying online from home. As Fatima stated:

> I don't learn as much now as when I'm at school. When I am at school, I listen to my classmates and to the teacher when they talk Swedish but being at home, I don't hear anyone who speaks Swedish (Fatima, 32, migrant; interview, November 2020).

Not learning the Swedish language can reduce these women's employment possibilities and consequently may affect the family's future financial situation.

Although changes in daily family routines were affected by the parents' occupation and children's school situation, a general pattern emerged showing that most families restricted their social contact with friends and family outside the household. Parents, grandparents and children reported that they tried to keep social distance and spent more time at home. Safa, a single mother of two children, answered the question of whether life had changed during COVID-19 the following way:

> Safa: Yeah totally
> Interviewer: In what ways?
> Safa: Like before we spent time with relatives and had really nice times together, and we went to fun parks, but now we don't go there because of Corona. Corona has changed a lot, you feel stressed all the time because some cousins got infected last week, and my sister's husband is a teacher and he got Corona and now all the family is stressed, so there's stress all the time. You can't relax, and you need to wash your hands, and I have to tell the children when they get back home [after school] to wash their hands and to use disinfection; yeah, like there are huge differences ... (Safa, 38, migrant, unemployed; interview, November 2020).

Safa's report exemplifies a common way to reason: the social distancing recommendation and the risk of getting infected or infecting others resulted in fewer physical meetings with relatives and friends, which particularly changed how family members spent time after work and school. The quote also illustrates that the pandemic heightened the awareness of risk and everyday concerns about others falling ill or even dying. Moreover, the risk awareness increased the overall stress in life and involved different ways of trying to avoid COVID-19 infection. The notion of risk affects personal life (cf. Smart 2007) – it is formed and played out interdependently with others (Lupton 2013) and connected to caring for others and oneself (cf. Noddings 2013).

That government guidelines and the continuous risk assessment influenced everyday life were raised recurrently by parents as well as grandparents and adolescents. Not being able to take part in the same activities as before, or to meet and socialize with others to the same extent, stand out as being what were most missed. However, although many negative aspects of the pandemic were raised, positive aspects of the new daily routines were also referred to. Marion, for instance, a single mother of two children, reported pros as well as cons with social distancing and working from home:

> The restrictions have resulted in me not meeting colleagues, parents and some friends as much. Everyday life becomes more boring since concerts have been cancelled and museums have closed. But like so many others, I have experienced spring and summer out in the open air, I have been at home when the children get home from school, I have restricted my socializing but have had time to meet my close friends more. I have had time for gardening, and for a kitten. I am sure one will remember this year as a lovely year that gave one more time at home with fewer demands. But right now, it feels a bit boring and limited (Marian, 46, native, university degree; written note, September 2020).

Marion restricted her face-to-face contact with her elderly parents in accordance with government guidelines; she worked from home and had only online contact with colleagues. But she continued to socialize with her closest friends, although outdoors. She referred to life under COVID-19 as 'more boring', with fewer social events, but also as something positive – a time for new experiences which had led to new interests such as gardening and a pet, and more time spent in nature. Furthermore, everyday life became less stressful, and she was always at home when the children got back from school. Marion reasoned that possibly people would look back at the pandemic with many good memories, as 'a lovely year that gave one more time at home with fewer demands'. The effects of the pandemic on everyday life and well-being thus come across as double-edged in Marion's report, which is similar to how other participants spoke on the same subject. Both negative and positive impacts on well-being and personal life were raised.

Childcare facilities, preschool and primary and middle school (up until the age of 15 to 16 years old) remained open during the pandemic, as did many of these younger children's out-of-school activities. But several of the migrant parents that resided in disadvantaged areas raised issues about letting their children go to school during the COVID-19 outbreak. Amira, a mother of three, put it this way:

> I kept my children at home for five weeks… I was worried something would happen to me or their father… You know that when your children go to school, and meet other children all the time and play, children forget to keep social distance, and when your daughter takes the bus to school and meets her friends at school there's not much you [as a parent] can do. You ask them to use disinfectant and then it's in the hands of God (Amira, 42, migrant, studies Swedish for Immigrants; interview, November 2020).

Amira, like others, kept her children at home for weeks because she was worried that they would be infected and then infect other household members.[3] This risk assessment strategy was also mentioned by other families living in disadvantaged areas. When the interviewer asked Amira why the children were sent back to school, she said: 'I realized that this [pandemic] would go on for a long time and life had to continue like before.' Parents that kept their children at home were contacted by the school after some time. Home schooling is not an alternative in Sweden, and parents can get fined when children do not attend school. Since children that reside in disadvantaged areas with low socio-economic status have a greater risk of school failure than other children (Statistics Sweden 2020), the migrant parents' risk assessment strategy to keep children home from school due to the risk of COVID-19 infection may thus have increased the risk of low educational achievement.

Swedish pandemic guidelines were presented as recommendations, and people interpreted and adapted to the guidelines in varying ways. Some of the parents in the present study mentioned difficulties when trying to restrict their children's socializing with peers since different families had different rules, for instance, some allowed children's friends in their house while others did not. Also, since the younger children went to school and had daily physical contact with friends, and many also met in leisure time activities, restricting peer socializing at home was not always easy for parents to justify. Alice, a mother of primary and secondary school children, wrote: 'Peer pressure got me last week and I let the children meet their friends indoors since we found out that most of the children's friends had socialized during the Christmas break but mine hadn't met anyone' (Alice, 39, native, on sick leave/university student; written note, January 2021).

The older adolescents in upper secondary school experienced months of online schooling at home and no organized out-of-school activities. In the present study, the older adolescents described themselves as taking the pandemic and social distancing seriously. While they still socialized with peers, they did so less and with fewer individuals. But being responsible and following national guidelines had costs: the restrained personal life appeared to have affected their mental well-being (cf. Smart 2007; Stoppard 2001). Social life was referred to as being 'on hold' due to the pandemic. Clara, expressed her frustration:

> In some ways, we are the ones who sacrifice the most ... These three years (in upper secondary school), many of us would say ... are the best time of our lives. We are expected to sacrifice these years sitting indoors (Clara, 17, native; interview, January 2021).

Moreover, some expressed concerns about not learning as much as they would at school. Online education from home made it harder for some to maintain daily routines, such as getting a good night's sleep, having proper meals and taking exercise. Others reported that they found learning more difficult with no face-to-face contact. Linda said:

> They [the teachers] rely on us, that we understand everything, which can be quite difficult through a computer, particularly if you have a trouble with the internet connection ...It's just hard to see, to understand, when you don't interact in the same way [as face-to-face] (Linda, 18, native; interview, December 2020).

However, some described mixed feelings about home schooling; although they worried about their and their peers' psychological well-being due to the social isolation, they also, as Sarkadi and colleagues (2021) noted, described how school online could be positive, since no time or energy had to be spent on commuting and it was easier to avoid unwanted peer contact. Once more, the examples illuminate how pros as well as cons with how pandemic policies affected well-being and personal life were raised. The impact has varied for different people in different ways.

Concluding discussion

The risk and responsibility related to the COVID-19 pandemic influenced the personal life of Swedish family members. Meaningful relationships and physical contact was emphasized as significant, having an impact on individual's well-being and adolescents' learning (cf. Smart 2007). Family members acted in relation to their individual responsibility and a continuous risk assessment which they interpreted differently in relation to care and concern for themselves and others (cf. Noddings 2013). To define something as potentially harmful for health and well-being is to define it as a risk, but the definition can be open to re-interpretation and negotiation (Lupton 2013; Lupton and Willis 2021). The present study shows that family life was characterized by increased risk awareness and a continuous risk assessment during the COVID-19 pandemic, and the dynamics of risk become clear in the analysis. The study participants' understanding of risk and their responses to government guidelines were impacted by the structures of their everyday life, such as occupation and education, as well as by their social relationships, care for others, and the notion of well-being. The analyses show that pros and cons of social distancing recommendations were experienced. More time at home could lead to frustration and conflicts but also to a sense of increased intergenerational closeness. For some, more time at home was overwhelmingly positive, while for others it was mainly negative. Although there were general patterns, different individuals experienced the pandemic in different ways (see also Wissö and Bäck-Wiklund 2021).

The study participants of all ages reflected on their own responsibility to try to avoid transmission of the virus. Although many demonstrated trust in national authorities, many also raised critical points about the policies and how the pandemic had been handled by the decision-makers. It has been pointed out that Swedes in general have had great trust in the national pandemic policies (Weman Josefsson 2021). However, the present study suggests that it was rather common to oppose or to re-interpret social distancing recommendations in order to reduce other risks. It is important to note that there were several risks to consider during the pandemic: the risk of COVID-19 had to be juggled in relation to risks such as mental health problems, educational failure and unemployment. Different risks were often contradictory and caused dilemmas and ambivalence, as previously suggested (Lupton 2013).

Our findings show that family structure (single, nuclear) and patterns of socializing with older generations before the outbreak of the pandemic (for example, contact with grandparents) affected responses to government guidelines. Over time, the recommendation of social distancing was re-negotiated and opposed in many families; to continue to physically meet relatives was deemed more important than adhering to social distancing. We found that intergenerational face-to-face contact thus continued to play a great part in many families' lives, also a prominent result in Eldén et al.'s work (2021). The need for practical and emotional support made family members oppose government guidelines that recommended elderly persons self-isolate and there was no physical contact between households.

Non-household members – such as relatives and friends – were repeatedly mentioned in the study participants' reports. This stresses the importance of acknowledging the individual's *personal life*, that is, that she/he is embedded in 'all sorts of relationships and/or intimacies' (Smart 2007, 188), and that care practices involve people that do not live in the same household. Care – to care for others and to be cared for – is a central aspect of life which is imperative for our well-being (Eriksson 1987; Noddings 2013; Larsson et al. 2013), and care includes family and relatives, as well as friends. Concerns and care for the well-being of family members and relatives come across as central in how risk was understood and managed in the present work. Open schools made it hard for children to avoid the risk of contamination and potentially transmitting the disease to family members and others. The desire to care for and protect others was thus difficult for many to act upon even when the risk of spreading the virus by social contact was very much agreed upon. At the same time, most study participants were positive about schools being open; in their reasoning, open schools benefited their educational achievement as well as their psychological well-being. Consequently, they experienced both pros and cons with no lockdown and open schools.

The findings of the present study support other work (Chen et al. 2021; Kerekes et al. 2021) which suggest that adolescents, overall, adapted well to the changes that the COVID-19 pandemic brought about and showed resilience and good coping skills. However, adolescence is a transitional period into adulthood that can be challenging; for instance, adolescents are vulnerable to mental health problems and peer relationships are of great importance to their well-being (Larsson et al. 2013). Therefore, we need to widen our understandings of how social distancing affects adolescence in the long run. A subject raised by all the study participants, regardless of age, was that physical contact matters: meaningful relationships, care for others and being cared for, effective learning, and psychological well-being are connected to meeting other people face-to-face. The most difficult experience for individuals and families during COVID-19 appears to have been the decline in face-to-face contact.

It has been suggested (Kerekes et al. 2021) that besides the socio-economic resources of a country, cultural, political and relational factors should be considered in future studies focusing on the impact of COVID-19. More knowledge is needed on how pandemic policies have affected different families and family members, and possibly will continue to affect families and family life in a post-pandemic world.

Notes

1 As used in this chapter, however, the term 'migrant' can also include children who have foreign-born parents.
2 It was very hard to recruit families, so the research team ended up contacting schools where some parents consented to participate in an individual interview and several 15-year-olds consented to participate in focus groups or by writing down their answers to open-ended questions. We have no information other than age and sex (and some did not tick the box about sex) on the youth that participated by writing their answers to open-ended questions.
3 There might be several reasons why (low socioeconomic status) migrant parents reported to us about keeping their children at home from school at the beginning of the pandemic while middle-class parents did not. We do not want to speculate here about the reasons, with such a limited number of study participants.

References

Bäck-Wiklund, M. and Bergsten, B. (1997) *Det moderna föräldraskapet: En studie av familj och kön i förändring*. Stockholm: Natur och Kultur.

Bartelink, V., Tynelius, P., Walander, A., Burström, B., Ponce de Leon, A., Nederby Öhd, J., Hergens, M. P. and Lager, A. (2020) *Socioekonomiska faktorer och covid-19 i Stockholms län. Rapport 2020:10*. Stockholm: Centrum för epidemiologi och samhällsmedicin.

Bergnehr, D. (2008) *Timing Parenthood: Independence, family and ideals of life*. Linköping: Linköping University Press.

Bergnehr, D. (2020) 'Adapted fathering for new times: Refugee men's narratives on caring for home and children'. *Journal of Family Studies*, 28 (3), 934–49. https://doi.org/10.1080/13229400.2020.1769708.

Björnberg, U. (2002) 'Ideology and choice between work and care: Swedish family policy for working parents'. *Critical Social Policy*, 22 (1), 33–52.

Braun, V. and Clarke, V. (2006) 'Using thematic analysis in psychology'. *Qualitative Research in Psychology*, 3 (3), 77–101.

Chen, Y., Osika, W., Henriksson, G., Dahlstrand, J. and Friberg, P. (2021) 'Impact of COVID-19 pandemic on mental health and health behaviors in Swedish adolescents'. *Scandinavian Journal of Public Health*, 50 (1), 26–32. https://doi.org/10.1177/14034948211021724.

Claesson, M. and Hanson, S. (2021) 'COVID-19 and the Swedish enigma'. *Lancet*, 397 (10271), 259–61.

Drefahl, S., Wallace, M., Mussino, E., Aradhya, S., Kolk, M., Brandén, M., Malmberg, B. and Andersson, G. (2020) 'A population-based cohort study of socio-demographic risk factors for COVID-19 deaths in Sweden'. *Nature Communications*, 11 (5097), 1–7.

Duvander, A.-Z. and Johansson, M. (2019) 'Does fathers' care spill over? Evaluating reforms in the Swedish parental leave program'. *Feminist Economics*, 25 (2), 67–89.

Eldén, S., Anving, T. and Alenius Wallin, L. (2021) 'Intergenerational care in corona times: Practices of care in Swedish families during the pandemic'. *Journal of Family Research*, 34 (1), 538–62. https://doi.org/10.20377/jfr-702.
Eriksson, K. (1987) *Vårdandets Idé* [The Idea of Caring]. Stockholm: Liber.
Esping-Andersen, G. (1999) *Social Foundations of Postindustrial Economies*. Oxford: Oxford University Press.
Folkhälsomyndigheten [Public Health Agency of Sweden] (2021a) *Folkhälsans utveckling: Årsrapport 2021*. Östersund: Folkhälsomyndigheten.
Folkhälsomyndigheten [Public Health Agency of Sweden] (2021b) *Skolbarns vardagsliv under COVID-19 pandemin*. Östersund: Folkhälsomyndigheten.
Folkhälsomyndigheten [Public Health Agency of Sweden] (2022) 'Statistik för vaccination mot covid-19'. https://www.folkhalsomyndigheten.se/smittskydd-beredskap/utbrott/aktuella-utbrott/covid-19/statistik-och-analyser/statistik-over-registrerade-vaccinationer-covid-19/. (accessed 4 January 2022).
Forsberg, L. (2009) *Involved Parenthood: Everyday life of Swedish middle-class families*. Linköping: Linköping University Press.
Goldscheider, F., Bernhardt, E. and Lappegård, T. (2015) 'The gender revolution: A framework for understanding family and demographic behavior'. *Population and Development Review*, 41 (2), 207–39.
IFAU [Institute for Evaluation of Labour Market and Education Policy] (2021) 'Swedish children and youth during the COVID-19 pandemic: Evidence from research on childhood environment, schooling, educational choice and labour market entry'. *Working paper 2021, No. 3*. Uppsala: IFAU.
Johansson, T. and Andreasson, J. (2017) *Fatherhood in Transition: Masculinity, identity, and everyday life*. Basingstoke: Palgrave Macmillan.
Kapetanovic, S., Gurdal, S., Ander, B. and Sorbring, E. (2021) 'Reported changes in adolescent psychosocial functioning during the COVID-19 outbreak'. *Adolescents*, 1 (1), 10–20. https://doi.org/10.3390/adolescents1010002.
Kerekes, N., Bador, K., Sfendla, A., Belaatar, M., El Mzadi, A., Jovic, V., Damjanovic, R., Erlandsson, M., Nguyen, H. T., Nguyen, N. T. A., Ulberg, S. F., Kuch-Cecconi, R. H., Meszaros, Z. S., Stevanovic, D., Senhaji, M., Ahlström, B. H. and Zouini, B. (2021) 'Changes in adolescents' psychological functioning and well-being as a consequence of long-term COVID-19 restrictions'. *Environmental Research and Public Health*, 18 (16), 8755. https://doi.org/10.3390/ijerph18168755.
Krisinformation.se (n.d.) *Krisinformation.se* [Emergency information from Swedish authorities]. https://www.krisinformation.se/detta-kan-handa/handelser-och-storningar/20192/myndigheterna-om-det-nya-coronaviruset. (accessed 20 December 2021).
Larsson, M., Sundler Johansson, A. and Ekebergh, M. (2013) 'Beyond self-rated health: The adolescent girl's lived experience of health in Sweden'. *Journal of School Nursing*, 29 (1), 71–9.
Ludvigsson, J. F., Engerström, L., Nordenhäll, C. and Larsson, E. (2021) 'Open schools, COVID-19 and child and teacher morbidity: A nationwide study'. *New England Journal of Medicine*, 2021 (384), 669–71. https://doi.org/10.1056/NEJMc2026670.
Lupton, D. (2013) *Risk* (2nd ed.). London: Routledge.
Lupton, D. (2021) 'Contextualising COVID-19: Sociocultural perspectives on contagion'. In Lupton, D. and Willis, K. (eds) *The COVID-19 Crisis: Social perspectives*. London: Routledge, 14–24.
Lupton, D. and Willis, K. (2021) 'COVID-society: Introduction to the book'. In Lupton, D. and Willis, K. (eds) *The COVID-19 Crisis: Social perspectives*. London: Routledge, 3–13.
Noddings, N. (2013) *Caring: A relational approach to ethics and moral education*. Berkeley: University of California Press.
Sarkadi, A., Sahlin Torp, L., Pérez-Aronsson, A. and Warner, G. (2021) 'Children's expression of worry during the COVID-19 pandemic in Sweden'. *Journal of Pediatric Psychology*, 46 (8), 1–11. https://doi.org/10.1093/jpepsy/jsab060.
Save the Children (2018) *Barnfattigdom i Sverige: Rapport 2018*. Stockholm: Rädda Barnen/Save the Children.
Smart, C. (2007) *Personal Life*. Cambridge: Polity Press.
Socialdepartementet [Ministry of Health and Social Affairs] (2004) 'Smittskyddslag (2004:168)' [Infectious disease Act (2004:168)]. *Socialdepartementet*. https://www.riksdagen.se/sv/

dokument-lagar/dokument/svensk-forfattningssamling/smittskyddslag-2004168_sfs-2004-168 (accessed 12 February 2023).

Statistics Sweden (2018) 'Nära tre av tio barn bor växelvis'. *Statistical News from Statistics Sweden*, 7 November 2018. https://www.scb.se/hitta-statistik/statistik-efter-amne/levnadsforhall anden/levnadsforhallanden/undersokningarna-av-levnadsforhallanden-ulf-silc/pong/ statistiknyhet/barns-boende-2016-2017/ (accessed 19 November 2018).

Statistics Sweden (2020) *Living Conditions for Children with a Foreign Background*. Stockholm: Statistics Sweden.

Statistics Sweden (2021a) '215 000 barn har en bonusförälder'. *Statistics Sweden Brief Analysis*, 9 March 2021. https://www.scb.se/hitta-statistik/artiklar/2021/215-000-barn-har-en-bonusforalder/ (accessed 4 January 2022).

Statistics Sweden (2021b) 'Sverige bland de länder i Europa som har högst barnafödande'. *Statistics Sweden Brief Analysis*, 16 March 2021. https://www.scb.se/hitta-statistik/artiklar/2021/ sverige-bland-de-lander-i-europa-med-hogst-barnafodande/ (accessed 4 January 2022).

Statistics Sweden (2021c) 'Så väntas Sveriges befolkning växa till 2070'. *Statistics Sweden Press Release*, 28 April 2021. https://www.scb.se/pressmeddelande/sa-vantas-sveriges-befolkning-vaxa-till-2070/ (accessed 24 January 2022).

Stoppard, J. M. (2000) *Understanding Depression: Feminist social constructionist approaches*. London: Routledge.

Stranz, H. and Wiklund, S. (2011) 'I välfärdssamhällets marginal – om socialbidragstagande bland ensamstående mödrar av svensk och utländsk härkomst'. *Socialvetenskaplig tidskrift*, 1, 42–62.

Sundler, A. J., Lindberg, E., Nilsson, C. and Palmér, L. (2019) 'Qualitative thematic analysis based on descriptive phenomenology'. *Nursing Open*, 6 (3), 733–9.

Vlachos, J., Hertegård, E. and Svaleryd, H. B. (2021) 'The effects of school closure on SARS-CoV-2 among parents and teachers'. *PNAS*, 118 (9), e2020834118. https://doi.org/10.1073/ pnas.2020834118.

Wells, M. and Bergnehr, D. (2014) 'Families and family policies in Sweden'. In Robila, M. (ed.) *Handbook of Family Policies Across the Globe*. New York: Springer, 91–107.

Weman Josefsson, K. (2021) 'Perspectives of life in Sweden during the COVID-19 pandemic'. *Journal of Clinical Sport Psychology*, 15 (1), 80–6.

Wissö, T. and Bäck-Wiklund, M. (2021) 'Fathering practices in Sweden during the COVID-19: Experiences of Syrian refugee fathers'. *Frontiers in Sociology*, 6. https://doi.org/10.3389/ fsoc.2021.721881.

9
Taiwan: a unique trajectory of the pandemic as both blessing and curse

Ching-Yu Huang, Fen-Ling Chen and An-Ti Shih

Introduction

Despite the geographical, socio-political and economic proximity of Taiwan and China, Taiwan managed to contain the spread of the pandemic well and thus never entered into a national lockdown. Therefore, compared to some other countries investigated in this book, Taiwan is an unusual case. The success in containing the spread of the pandemic relied heavily on the Taiwanese government's early and strict precautionary actions taken against the pandemic, which was informed by its previous experiences with SARS in 2003 (Chen et al. 2005).

In this chapter, we draw on longitudinal interview data from 22 families with school-aged children in Taiwan to explore how the pandemic affected their lives between June and December 2020. Our findings showed that the extent to which the families were affected was in accordance with employment sectors, and how the families negotiated and responded flexibly to the ever-changing pandemic situation, as well as the support government provided to different industries and to families in need. Generally, participants were compliant with various pandemic preventative measures and felt grateful to the government for its actions to keep the citizens safe (compared to some other countries around the world). Nevertheless, some also expressed concerns regarding the success of Taiwan's containment of the pandemic as being both 'a blessing and a curse': a 'blessing' because citizens in Taiwan remained safe and lives in Taiwan went on as normal, seemingly unaffected, just as before the pandemic; a 'curse' because that seemingly unaffected lifestyle is itself so different from that of other countries in the world, potentially making

Taiwan further isolated from the global economy. We discuss these findings within the social ecological approach (Thomeer et al. 2020), and consider their implication for participants' overall responses to the pandemic's impacts on family and professional lives. See Figure 9.1 for a timeline of COVID-19 in Taiwan.

Taiwan country context

Taiwan, an island nation 81 miles off the south-east coast of mainland China that hosts 23 million people, went through a unique trajectory during the COVID-19 pandemic. Due to its close geographical, economic and socio-political ties with China, Taiwan was expected to have the second highest number of cases of COVID-19 (Gardner 2020). Out of the 23 million Taiwanese citizens, 850,000 resided in and 404,000 work in China (Directorate General of the Budget and Accounting 2019; Pan and Yeh 2019). In 2019, 2.71 million visitors from China travelled to Taiwan (Wang and Lin 2020). As such, Taiwan had been on constant alert and ready to act on epidemics arising from China ever since the severe acute respiratory syndrome (SARS) epidemic in 2003. The SARS outbreak in Taiwan caused 668 probable cases with severe deterioration of pulmonary function and 181 deaths, which had prompted the Taiwanese government to develop pandemic control measures including isolation of patients, contact tracing, quarantine of contact persons, fever screening for inbound and outbound passengers at the airport, and hospital infection control (Chen et al. 2005). Additionally, fever screening for inbound and outbound passengers at the airport had remained a standard practice since 2003. With this experience, the Taiwanese government took a proactive approach for COVID-19 prevention by promptly integrating data from the national healthcare system, immigration, and customs authorities to aid in the identification and response to the virus (Wang et al. 2020). Preventative measures derived from previous SARS experiences (international travel suspension, mandated quarantine for anyone entering Taiwan, isolation of patients, contact tracing, quarantine of contact persons and strict hospital infection control protocol) were enforced immediately.

Perhaps partially due to the previous experience of SARS in 2003, the Taiwanese public were vigilant and immediately cooperative with the pandemic control measures proposed by the government from the very beginning. For instance, before the World Health Organization (WHO) was first alerted to the COVID-19 outbreak by Chinese authorities on

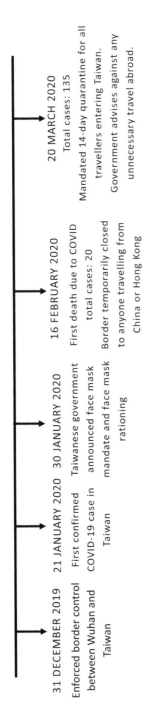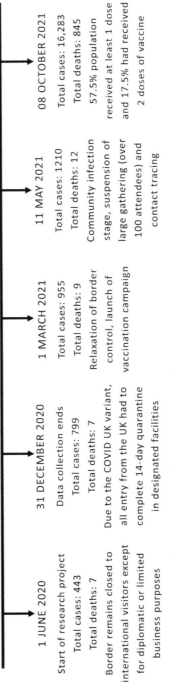

Figure 9.1 Timeline of COVID-19 in Taiwan. Source: authors.

31 December 2019 (World Health Organization 2020), the Taiwanese government had already enforced travel restrictions, border control between Wuhan and Taiwan, as well as mandatory PCR tests for passengers coming from Wuhan. By 30 January 2020, when the WHO declared COVID-19 a Public Health Emergency of International Concern (PHEIC), Taiwan had 10 COVID-19 cases, and the Taiwanese authority had enforced a range of COVID-19 prevention policies, including face mask rationing, suspending all flights between Wuhan and Taiwan, advising against travel to China, quarantine and contact tracing.

By the time the WHO declared the COVID-19 a pandemic on 12 March 2020, Taiwan had fewer than 50 COVID-19 cases (with one death) and had already engaged in 124 discrete action items to prevent the spread of the virus (Wang et al. 2020). Preventative measures at this point included contact tracing, border control, mandatory face mask-wearing, face mask rationing and cancelling large gatherings etc. Starting 19 March 2020, foreign nationals were barred from entering Taiwan with only some exceptions, such as those holding valid Alien Resident Certificates, diplomatic credentials or other official documentation and special permits (Chang et al. 2020). All who were admitted into the country were required to complete a 14-day quarantine upon arrival,[1] except for business travellers from low or moderate risk countries, who were subject to 5- or 7-day quarantines and were required to have had a COVID-19 test.

Overall, in 2020, the pandemic had a smaller impact in Taiwan than in most other industrialized countries, with a total of seven deaths and less than 800 COVID-19 cases (see Figure 9.2). The number of daily new cases in this first wave peaked on 6 April 2020 at 307, the overwhelming majority of which were imported, and the country never entered any form of lockdown; schools, and most businesses were operating as usual. However, travel, the hospitality industry and showbusiness were suspended between March and July in 2020. Daily lives within Taiwan were very much unaffected, except for the face mask mandate in public areas and transport and restrictions on international travel. Although there was no lockdown, large group gatherings were suspended and avoidance of crowded areas, as well as social distancing, were advised. The success of Taiwan's handling of the COVID-19 outbreak received international praise for its effectiveness (Baron 2020; Reuters 2020).

However, an outbreak in late April 2021 followed by a sharp surge in cases in May 2021 shattered the 'false sense of security' in the public. Total case numbers, which had been below 1,300 before May 2021, surged to more than 3,100 in the span of a week (Zennie and Tsai 2021).

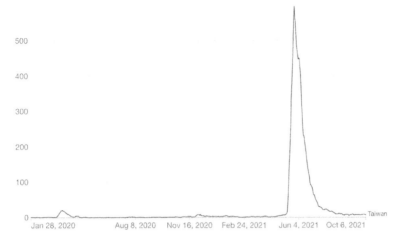

Figure 9.2 Daily new confirmed COVID-19 cases in Taiwan, 28 January 2020 to 6 October 2021. Source: Our World in Data (open access data at https://ourworldindata.org/coronavirus/country/taiwan).

The surge in cases had brought underlying problems to the surface regarding the low testing rate, enforcement of pandemic prevention measures among airline crew members, and the slow progress of the vaccination campaign. Yet, it also overturned the Taiwanese residents' hesitation to get vaccinated, due to the previously low case numbers. The vaccination rate had reached 55 per cent for the first dose, compared to only 1 per cent before the surge in May 2021 (Our World in Data 2021). Fortunately, this wave was controlled and by the end of June 2021 average new daily cases had reduced to double digits. By the end of August 2021 zero new daily cases were observed for the first time since the spike in May 2021 (Davidson 2021). As of 8 October 2021 (when this chapter was written), there was a total of 16,283 confirmed cases and 845 deaths (Taiwan Centers for Disease Control 2021).

Theoretical framework

Families are a key social factor and unit shaping health outcomes and health disparities at the population level (see Umberson and Thomeer 2020), and were particularly important in shaping health outcomes during the COVID-19 pandemic. Thomeer, Yahirun and Colón-López's

(2020) social-ecological approach suggested the following three tenets to understand the impacts of COVID-19 on health inequalities. First, the risks of specific pandemic outcomes as well as other health problems were unevenly distributed across families. Second, how families affected health outcomes during the pandemic would be subject to the influence of public policies, organizational decisions and concurrent events. Finally, several health inequalities driven by classism, sexism, racism and other forces would be amplified during the pandemic, yet the extent to which this occurred was shaped by families and by the wider public policies, organizational decisions, and concurrent events that also impact families and health. Therefore, in line with the overall approach in this book, we used families as a unit and followed the lives of 22 families (married couples with at least one school-aged child) between June and December 2020, with in-depth interviews to explore how their lives had been affected by the pandemic.

Our methodological approach was grounded in the sociology of everyday life, taking the everyday, taken-for-granted daily lives that we live in as an object of scrutiny (Kalekin-Fishman 2013). Thus our investigation and exploration pivoted around the topics surrounding how individual practices and thought processes contribute to the perpetuation of society, especially during the time of rapid change resulting from the pandemic. As such, the interview questions as well as later analyses were largely organized around the way in which the pandemic affected the participants' daily lives, through which we could explore how participants' understanding of daily lives and perception of normalcy had been affected by the daily practices during the pandemic. We sought to understand how individuals and families, living through moments of great disruption such as the pandemic, managed to achieve a sense of safety and health in their everyday lives. In what follows we first provide some background information about both the pandemic situation in Taiwan and the families who participated in the study. Thereafter, we illustrate the findings regarding how families responded to government guidelines and explore how family lives were impacted according to their levels of being affected by the pandemic. Finally, we discuss our findings according to the social ecological approach proposed by Thomeer et al. (2020) before concluding.

Data collection and sample

Our study was a mixed-methods longitudinal study, using a combination of online surveys and interviews conducted over six months. The study was reviewed and approved by the Research Ethics Committee of the School of Psychology at Keele University before its commencement (ethical approval number: PSY-200134). Our families were interviewed between June and December 2020, when Taiwan had only 799 COVID-19 cases (of which 671 had recovered and 7 died) by 31 December 2020. As the majority of families in Taiwan are led by heterosexual married couples (National Statistics Bureau Taiwan 2021), we targeted this group as our participants. Moreover, we wanted to explore how the pandemic affected parent–child relationships, thus one of our inclusion criteria was that there was at least one school-aged child (7 to 17 years old) in the family. The data was collected between June and December 2020. We recruited 22 families with children living in various parts of Taiwan through social media, university participant mailing lists, personal connections and outreach organizations. We purposively sampled participants for maximum socio-economic status (SES) diversity.

The interviews were conducted via phone calls, online or in person (at the time it was safe and allowed in Taiwan to meet face to face). Each family was interviewed four times within a three-month period, with the first two interviews conducted within the first month, the third in the second month and the fourth in the third month. Some example questions participants were asked include: How has the pandemic affected your daily lives (to be described in as much detail as possible)? What precautions did you take if you went out of the house/home? How is the pandemic affecting your relationship with your spouse/children? All the interviews were conducted in either Mandarin or Taiwanese, depending on the participant's preference. The interview recordings were then transcribed into Mandarin for analysis using thematic analysis techniques (Braun and Clarke 2006). We used matrix tabulations for comparisons across groups.

We divided the families into four categories defined by the extent of the economic impact of the pandemic on their lives: high, moderate, some or little economic impact. The high category included those who had lost their sources of income or been put on furlough due to the pandemic (six families); the moderate category included those whose work or income had been affected noticeably because of the pandemic and their job security in some cases also threatened (five families); the some economic impact category included those whose job security was unaffected, but their income may have decreased (four families); and the little economic impact category included those whose job security or income were unaffected, but there were changes in their work arrangement or workload (seven families). In the following Findings section, we explore family lives in each group to illustrate a) how participants responded to and understood government guidelines and b) the impact of the pandemic and relevant government guidelines on family life. Please refer to Table 9.1 for a summary of the participating families, who was interviewed, and the levels of economic impact the pandemic had on them.

Table 9.1 Summary of participating families in Taiwan and the levels of economic impact the pandemic had on them.

Family no.	Number and age (years) of children	Interview participants and profession	Level of economic impact
Family 1	3 children 22, 20, 17	Husband: Flight captain Wife: Home maker	High
Family 2	2 children 18, 4	Husband: Business manager Wife: Home maker	High
Family 6	1 child 15	Husband: Interior designer Wife: Air freight industry	High
Family 11	3 children 8, 6, 3	Husband: Ship captain Wife: Retired flight attendant	High
Family 12	2 children 11, 9	Husband: Taxi driver Wife: p/t Clerk	High
Family 20	2 children 12, 6	Husband: Tour guide Wife: Online business	High
Family 3	2 children 15, 13	Husband: Medical doctor Wife: p/t Lecturer	Moderate
Family 7	3 children 12, 9, 6	Husband: Nursing-home owner Wife: Higher education	Moderate
Family 13	1 child 8	Husband: Food industry Wife: p/t Medical industry	Moderate
Family 19	2 children 7, 5	Husband: Rehabilitation home Wife: Accountant	Moderate

Family no.	Number and age (years) of children	Interview participants and profession	Level of economic impact
Family 21	2 children 16, 8	Husband: Restaurant manager Wife: Medical industry	Moderate
Family 4	3 children 12, 9, 6	Husband: Coffee shop owner Wife: Coffee shop co-owner	Some
Family 8	2 children 11, 4	Husband: Bakery owner Wife: Bakery accountant	Some
Family 18	3 children 19, 18, 14	Husband: Security guard Wife: Social service	Some
Family 22	2 children 25, 17	Husband: p/t Technician Wife: Higher education	Some
Family 5	2 children 10, 6	Husband: Telecommunication Wife: Civil servant	Little
Family 9	2 children 11, 9	Husband: Social service Wife: Education	Little
Family 10	2 children 9, 5	Husband: Social service Wife: Social service	Little
Family 14	2 children 13, 8	Husband: Engineer Wife: p/t Education	Little
Family 15	2 children 13, 11	Husband: Telecommunication Wife: Education	Low
Family 16	3 children 22, 19, 16	Husband: Civil servant Wife: Medical industry	Low
Family 17	1 child 9	Husband: Research Wife: Education	Low

Findings

How participants responded to and understood government guidelines

As described in the introduction, the Taiwanese government had enforced meticulous pandemic control swiftly by integrating data from the national healthcare system, immigration, and customs authorities (Wang et al. 2020). Perhaps partially due to the previous experience of SARS in 2003, as already mentioned, the Taiwanese public were vigilant and immediately cooperative with the strict pandemic control measures, even if such measures were strongly impacting on their everyday lives. As such, it was not surprising that the strong endorsement and adherence to government guidelines on pandemic control came through the data, which we describe in this section.

As an example of adherence to government guidelines, one of the pandemic control measures was related to the strict international border control as well as to strict safety measures around contact with foreigners (such as disinfecting items and shoes, wearing face masks and social distancing). These precautions were well-understood and followed, even when such precautions caused additional stress during work. For instance, a father who works as a ship captain described how they had followed the pandemic control measures during their cruise:

> Our shipping cruise lines were between some designated ports between Taiwan (Keelung, Taichung and Kaohsiung) and China (Ningbo and Shanghai) once a week. At the beginning of the pandemic, we started to forbid the crew members to disembark in China, which was a big challenge psychologically. Because during the cruise, crew members were at work 24/7, so getting off the ship at the ports used to be the only chance for the crew members to unwind. This was no longer possible during the pandemic; therefore it has been more stressful for everyone. It also affected our interactions with the workers at the Chinese ports, because they were not very vigilant at the beginning of the pandemic outbreak and thought that we were over-reacting. We asked all of them to disinfect their shoes, wear face masks, reduce contact and only discuss work on the deck or via phone … if they had to board the ship, we would disinfect anything they had touched… the level of stress we had experienced during the pandemic had grown exponentially… I could see that the stress had taken a toll on their

emotional health and work performance (father, Family 11, high economic impact).

The closure of international borders as well as the governmental order on the suspension of certain industries (such as travel industry) in the beginning of the pandemic also directly affected some participants' employment immediately and their future career prospects. Thus, another theme that came through the data was participants' worries about job security, especially with those industries significantly limited by pandemic prevention guidelines. For instance, a father who worked as a tour guide, an industry suddenly suspended due to pandemic control, said:

> The shock to the travel industry was similar to what we had previously experienced in 2011 after the Japan Tōhoku earthquake and tsunami and the financial crisis in 2008 … Last time [in 2011] it was mostly affecting travels to and from Japan, other areas for travel and travels to China were still intact. The impacts of the financial crisis in 2008 was only temporary, and the sector was back to normal very quickly. But this time, it felt like you cannot see the light at end of the tunnel; you just don't know when it will end, and the impact is global (father, Family 20, high economic impact).

Moreover, international border closure was especially significant for those who previously travelled frequently between Taiwan and China. For example, the husband in Family 2 was a sales manager for a Taiwanese shoes company which had its factory and production line in China. Before the pandemic, he used to live and work in China most of the time while his wife and children lived in Taiwan. So he used to travel frequently between China and Taiwan. This is common for many Taiwanese companies, who set up their production lines in China due to the cheaper operational costs there. However, the strict border control between China and Taiwan during the pandemic meant this kind of lifestyle became no longer possible, affecting job security and prospects for many workers.

> I do worry about unemployment. We used to only have one day off per week, it became two days off per week with no payment for the additional day off, which is the company policy. Because of the pandemic, I was put on leave without pay. This was applied to all of the Taiwanese employees working in China, so we literally have lost

four days' payment per month. I got notified that our salary will be cut by 20 per cent, and this applies to all those above the managerial level. So in total, my salary was [reduced] by approximately 35 per cent (father, Family 2, high economic impact).

For some in other families, working in areas such as the medical or food industry, their work (but not necessarily income) was significantly affected by the pandemic, although their job security was not affected. The daily lives of those working in the medical profession were especially affected. These participants not only commended the governments' efforts and strict pandemic control, but they also even elaborated on these by developing an 'enhanced hygiene protocol' at home. Take Family 3 for example, where the father is a medical doctor and the mother a part-time lecturer in a higher education institution. Due to the father's line of work, the family had to reorganize how they went about their day-to-day life, to mitigate any risk of contracting the virus. For instance, his wife reported how they had come up with a protocol for him to come in and out of the home without jeopardizing the other family members' (her, and their two children) health. She said:

> The master bedroom is at the back side of the house. Therefore we consider letting him come in and out through the back entrance. However, if he comes in through the back entrance then he must pass by the kitchen. I have been cooking at home all the time then, so if anything gets into the kitchen, it's dangerous for me too. But this route [through the back entrance] poses the least threat to the children, and the least impact on us, because these are not the main spaces used by the rest of the family. In the end, I set our camping tent up at the main entrance, I even measured it to make sure the size is okay. So when he came home, he would leave his shoes outside, enter through the door, go directly into the tent where his slippers are located, then he would move inside the tent into our room (with my help). There is a ventilator in our master bathroom which pumps the air outside, so he asked me to block the ventilator, so the air would not go out. If he opens the bathroom window, the air from the bathroom would come into the house. Therefore he told me not to turn the ventilator on. And if I need to go into the room to deliver some food for him, I will wear the longest raincoat we have at home, a shower cap, and googles.... And when I come in, he will keep quiet and not talk (mother, Family 3, moderate economic impact).

This kind of 'enhanced hygiene protocol' after coming home from work was also reported by two other families (Family 7 and Family 19, both moderate economic impact), where the father in both worked in medical or care institutions.

As for families involved in the food industry (Family 13 and Family 21), both described how restaurant and other food industries had to diversify or think of other creative ways to buffer the effect of their lower customer number, showing their resilience by swiftly shifting their businesses to work with the government pandemic regulations. For instance, one father said:

> Now with the reduced business in the restaurant, we had to think about other ways to get more income. The first one, which was adopted by many companies, was to 'go out'. Such as going to sell bento boxes outside, or sell snacks. In the meantime, we produced some new products that we had been too busy to develop in normal (pre-pandemic) times, such as frozen food. We also produced some instant noodles during this new period of pandemic. So it is about how we can face and solve problems in difficult time (father, Family 21, moderate economic impact).

Although daily lives and the domestic market in Taiwan had not been affected too much and restaurants were still open for business during the pandemic, people did not go out to dine in restaurants as often as before the pandemic (even though, at the time of data collection, Taiwan had never entered a national lockdown, staying at home and avoiding crowded areas was advised by the Taiwan Centres for Disease Control). The restaurant that one father worked at had observed a 30–40 per cent reduction in business, and he expressed increased stress related to his work situation:

> It's been really stressful and tiring. When the income decreased, the boss would want us to come up with other ways to gain income and come up with some (health and safety) policies. And we will have to constantly test whether these policies are practically possible, and these are changing all the time. So physically it's not more tiring, but mentally, it is (father, Family 21, moderate economic impact).

The two families (Family 4 and Family 8, both some economic impact) where the parents ran the family business together both mentioned that they had to diversify their ways of marketing or operation during the pandemic to maintain their business. Family 4 owned a coffeeshop combined with a hand-made clothing shop. Before the pandemic, the business was very much reliant on face-to-face interactions as well as tourism, as many customers were from China and Japan. Because of this, at the beginning of the pandemic, their shop had a sharp drop (50 per cent) in income. However, they were resilient and managed to use this opportunity to transfer their business online:

> Since the pandemic, we started our website and sell things online, which soon contributed to 50 per cent of our profit. Not only did we make up for the 50 per cent of the loss from the beginning of the pandemic, but we also even reached new customers this way … The pandemic had facilitated our transition to online business. The time when our sales slowed down, it was the time to improve and transform ourselves. So we built our website and we even hired a Japanese teacher to teach us Japanese, that the beginning of our improvement. We also hired another teacher to teach us all these social media and online platforms used by Japanese people, including Japanese Twitter and Instagram … Our ethos was that, when the market is down, our effort and work in marketing should not be less than normal times. We should make even more effort to make our products more visible via the internet to the customers who are staying at home … A crisis is also an opportunity (Family 4).

The way they handled the pandemic crisis demonstrated their tremendous ability to adapt to change and respond to the government guidelines constructively. Similarly, Family 8 owned a bakery and had to change their bread production (incorporating enhanced health and safety measures) and sales (working with delivery platforms such as Foodpanda) in response to the pandemic. Fortunately, their lives were not that much affected beyond these changes. They also mentioned the interconnectedness of their work and family lives since they have co-owned the family business, and the particular challenges they may face because of this. The father said:

> Well, it's apparent to me that our physical health, money, and family are all interconnected. You cannot afford to lose any of them. If you do not have good family lives, you cannot focus on work. If you cannot make money, your family will suffer. If you have no health, you cannot enjoy the money you make either… so I think these three are all connected. You cannot live without one of them (father, Family 8, some economic impact).

Impact on family life

Although the pandemic was relatively well-contained in Taiwan, family lives were inadvertently affected. Many families said that their daily lives were not much affected beyond the adjustment at work, and they were well-adapted to the pandemic control restrictions (such as travel restrictions and wearing face masks), but the level of stress caused by the fear of exposure to the virus and the additional strict health and safety measures had impacted on the participants at a personal level. Such emotional impact was especially noticeable in those working in the medical professions. For instance, the woman who described the 'enhanced hygiene protocol' at home because her husband worked as a medical doctor also described the emotional impact the pandemic had on her husband:

> He wants us [family] to be safe, and I also know that he wants to feel cared for and be respected. Our neighbours know that he is a medical doctor, and he had told me several times he noticed that the neighbours were trying to keep a safe distance from him, this had made him a little upset … well, for the public, the pandemic may cause a short period of stress, but the stress on the medical professionals are really the most intense and lasting (mother, Family 3, moderate economic impact).

Effect on intergenerational family connections

Family interactions with grandparents were affected beyond the personal, emotional level. Traditionally in Taiwan, grandparents are actively involved in caring for their grandchildren (Yi et al. 2006), so families' relationships with grandparents in Taiwan were very close before the pandemic. Pandemic restrictions affected these. For instance, one father said:

> We haven't visited my parents since the pandemic started. We used to see them every weekend … But now they are worried, and we are also concerned … we don't want to pass anything on to them … and they don't go out that often anymore (father, Family 7, moderately affected).

Children's lifestyle and learning

Other than the pandemic's impact on the participants' emotional well-being and their reduced opportunity to directly interact with their parents, parents also commented on the pandemic's influence on their children's lifestyle and learning:

> On the one hand, I think the pandemic is restricting children's exploration to the outside world, because children cannot go outside [of Taiwan]. The less opportunity they had to explore, the less imagination and understanding they would have about the global society …But on the other hand, their teachers are guiding them to explore and think about how the pandemic around the world is affecting Taiwan, which was really positive (mother, Family 13, moderate economic impact).

The same participant also mentioned her son's complaints about how COVID-19 had affected his fitness due to the reduced time he could engage in outdoor sports.

> The less they go out, the less opportunity they have to do exercise … My son had complained that he could not go out and play basketball, so he had put on weight and couldn't jump as high as he used to!

Such impacts on children's social life and learning were not surprising given the global pandemic situation. Although the schools were open as usual during this study's data collection period, educational institutions responded to the pandemic by having additional health and safety measures. These included taking the body temperature of students before they entered the school gates, and sending home those with a temperature above 37°C and following up on sick students to ensure their health was monitored. A mother who worked in higher education, described her institution's health and safety responses:

> Starting from the pandemic, we had taken on additional work as educators. For instance, we are tasked with additional caring responsibilities for students who are in quarantine, such as international students … we had to text them every day to check up on them, asking how they are physically, and whether they need any assistance from us … We even needed to collate information about their body temperature every day to report to the health centre of the university, and act as the point of contact for them … I've been dealing with these issues the whole week. It really increased my workload… We had a COVID case on campus, so during the time of that case being reported, everyone was panicking. Wherever the [COVID-19-positive] person had been to for class or the gym, everyone would avoid. At the

time, many students even gave apologies because they did not want to risk being exposed to the virus ... We had to reassure them that it's all okay, and we had the UV disinfectant device here that we can help to kill all the virus on their personal items. It's really stressful for all of us (mother, Family 22, some economic effect).

While additional health and safety measures increased workloads and put stress on educational staff members, the pandemic also facilitated technology-mediated education. One father said:

I think the school is doing well with this (technology). My child had used video calls to attend speech contest ... and the teacher would coach him on how to present in front of the computer, such as using some gestures and looking at the camera so the audience would think that you are speaking to them (father, Family 9, little economic impact).

Unfortunately, we did not collect data from the children themselves, thus we could not report what implications such measures and use of technology in schools had on pupils themselves.

Move to online social and business interactions

For most, the aspect of their lives they found most affected by the pandemic was their social life. All of them mentioned reduced opportunities to see friends and extended family members in person during the pandemic, which they saw as something that is necessary to keep everyone healthy and safe. But their social interactions had changed from in-person to online. For instance, one family's participation in the church was changed due to the pandemic:

I think the area that was affected most obviously is our weekly church gathering. So during the pandemic, this had been shifted online. We usually have Bible reading groups for married couples, so we would have a Bible reading and praying session together with two other married couples before the pandemic. So this Bible reading group had been suspended for some time, until it was transitioned online. So now we meet with them online. It took us some time to get used to it, but now we think it's working well ... We don't need to go out of the home, and people take turn in a more organized way in the online meetings [compared to the face-to-face meetings] ... So in the online meetings we could stay more focused (Family 14, little economic impact).

In addition to the digitization of educational and social lives, digitization was also happening in peoples' professional lives. A father mentioned how virtual meetings were replacing face-to-face meetings at work:

So basically all the meetings during the pandemic have been moved online, there is no more face-to-face meetings in the office. Even if you are only 30 metres away from your colleague, the meeting will be held online. And you are required to install all such video conferencing software on your computer or mobile phone ... The meeting time has shortened as a result, because many topics are difficult to discuss when we are not face-to-face. I think virtual meetings will be the future, it's unavoidable. I think in the future, any meetings for things that are not particularly important issues will be discussed virtually, no need to travel physically anymore. For work organizations, it's also cheaper, because you don't need to pay for travel expenses anymore (father, Family 17, little economic impact).

Technology-mediated interactions became the 'norm' or the default option, regardless of social, education or professional contexts. The transition to digital interaction both in social and business lives also sparked some concerns from some families. For instance, one father said:

Sometimes I wonder, maybe we are just lucky in Taiwan, that we had contained the pandemic well in the beginning. We (people in Taiwan) started out being super stressed and anxious, thus we protected ourselves very well... it was just a lucky hit. And the media was spreading the negative news like crazy, and this was so pervasive in any social media channels.... The situation in Taiwan is so different from the rest of the world, that maybe in the future we would then find out that we are being left behind because we did not make the transitions that other countries have made during the pandemic. Our challenge is in the future (father, Family 16, little economic impact).

Despite the challenges that came with the pandemic, many participants expressed gratitude for this opportunity the pandemic brought to slow down and 'reset' their life priorities. For instance, the father from Family 5 remarked:

> Many friends said that they choose to quiet down and rest during this (pandemic) time…. We talked about the power of being quiet. When we are noisy, we cannot hear what others are saying, and we miss a lot of subtle sounds. But when we are quiet, we can hear others' voice, we can hear the birds chirping, the wind blowing and the sound of the leaves. It requires us to quiet down. When we are quiet, our senses become more sensitive and refined. Then we will know better what we should do, and what are the most important things to do. Such is the power resulting from being quiet. This period is a time to prepare for a big change or huge challenge (father, Family 5, little economic impact).

Discussion

Our findings demonstrated the first tenet of what Thomeer et al. (2020) suggested, that the risks of specific COVID-19 outcomes and other health problems would be unevenly distributed across families. The families who had experienced a high economic impact from the pandemic, such as those whose income and job security were shaken, or those who worked in professions that might expose them to higher risk, might experience higher levels of stress as a result. Therefore, the risks different families were exposed to and experienced were not the same. As families are a key social factor shaping health outcomes and health disparities at the population level (for overview, see Umberson and Thomeer 2020), it is imperative to understand the impact of the COVID-19 pandemic at the family level to better devise policies to support them.

Thomeer et al.'s (2020) second tenet stated that the impact on the families' health during the COVID-19 pandemic is conditional on public policies (for example, school closure, unemployment benefits), organizational decisions (for example, limiting nursing home visitors, work furloughs) and concurrent events (for example, public protests, economic recession) (Berger and Carlson 2020). The importance of the context in specific countries to understanding the impacts of COVID-19 is precisely illustrated by the contributions to this book. Within the Taiwanese context, where there was never any form of lockdown during the period of our data collection, the impacts and discussions were mostly on employment sectors and how this had impacted the family economically.

Moreover, due to the previous experience of the SARS outbreak in 2003 (when a major hospital was contained, and all patients, visitors, and staff were quarantined within the building, causing elevated fear and anxiety in the general public), people in Taiwan showed a high level of alertness and endorsement to the pandemic-prevention measures that were swiftly set out by the government. All participants, regardless of the extent to which they had personally been affected by the pandemic, displayed a high level of approval and adherence to these pandemic control measures. Indeed, they not only demonstrated how much they adhered to the preventative measures but some of them even extended such pandemic prevention protocols at home (such as the families working in the medical profession).

The third tenet proposed by Thomeer et al. (2020) stated that many health inequalities driven by racism, sexism, classism, and other oppressive societal forces would be amplified during COVID-19, but the extent to which this is occurring is shaped by families and by the public policies, organizational decisions and concurrent events that also impact families and health. For our study, we focused on families with married heterosexual couples, so the most prevalent inequality factor between families was the family socio-economic status (SES). From our findings we could see a clear trend that the extent to which a family was affected by the pandemic was related to the level of their economic stability. Parents working in highly-skilled professions tended to have higher level of education, and higher income, and were thus less affected by the pandemic. These parents were most able to work from home and follow recommended pandemic prevention measures, thus avoiding risk of exposure to the virus. On the contrary, parents who worked in lower skill level jobs were more likely to be highly impacted by the pandemic, not only in terms of income and job security but also in their mental well-being, as these two are highly intertwined.

This also showed the limitation of our research in only recruiting families with one family structure – married heterosexual couples with children – as some preliminary data had indicated stark differences in the impact of COVID-19 on economic well-being based on family structure (for example, Bokun et al. 2020). Bokun and colleagues (2020) reported that 14.2 per cent of children living with single parents saw their parent lose their job in the early months of the pandemic, whereas only 6.4 per cent of children living with two parents had both parents become unemployed (Bokun et al. 2020). The two-parent structure also meant that parents could ostensibly share childcare responsibilities, especially for those with young children (Collins et al. 2020; Prickett et al. 2020).

Thus, the pandemic exacerbated the financial and economic well-being gap between single and married-couple parents, and the health of single-parent families may have deteriorated because of loss of employer-based health insurance, food insecurity or housing. Because COVID-19 had increased immediate economic disparities across family structures, it is likely that we will continue to see widening health disparities as higher SES families recover more quickly from the recession that followed, and lower SES families are left behind. Health disparities continue to emerge from the pandemic, and it is critical for researchers and policymakers to pay attention to the multiple ways that families mattered during the progression of the pandemic.

Conclusion

On a superficial level, daily lives in Taiwan at the time of our study did not seem to be affected that much by the pandemic, except for aspects relating to the pandemic control measures (such as not being able to travel internationally and needing to wear face masks in public). In reality, family lives had been affected more than one might expect, given how well Taiwan seemed to be controlling the pandemic. Our findings showed that parents from certain employment sectors (such as those working in travel, hospitality and medical organizations) were significantly affected by the pandemic in terms of their economic stability or workload, which could strongly affect their psychological well-being. Fortunately, their domestic lives and childcare responsibilities did not seem to be affected much by the pandemic, except for the social aspects and reduced opportunities to visit grandparents in person.

Additionally, it was also apparent that digitization in social and professional lives as well as in education sectors was further facilitated by the pandemic. The pandemic facilitated digital-mediated interactions between family members such as intergenerational interactions between the core family members and grandparents. This could potentially blur the boundaries between home and professional lives, as family members worked from home or engaged in school activities from home. Such blending of family and professional lives could be challenging in trying to maintain a healthy work–life balance.

Moreover, we had seen the resilience and the cooperation in people in endorsing and following the pandemic prevention measures, some of them even taking extra precautionary steps to ensure their family and their customers stay safe. Finally, Taiwan had a unique trajectory in the global pandemic outbreak, and its success in containing the virus was heavily reliant on policies that strictly forbade international travel. This might in some way further segregate Taiwan from the rest of the world. How Taiwan could sustain the health and well-being of its inhabitants in a globalized world without being isolated from the global community will be a challenging balance as the pandemic and its aftermath continues.

Note

1   The 14-day quarantine measure was valid at the time this chapter was written and remained valid until 7 March 2022, after which it was reduced to 10 days (Taiwan Centers for Disease Control 2022a). The quarantine period was further reduced to 3 days after 15 June 2022 (Taiwan Centers for Disease Control 2022b).

References

Barron, L. (2020) 'Coronavirus lessons from Singapore, Taiwan and Hong Kong'. *Time*, 13 March 2020. https://time.com/5802293/coronavirus-covid19-singapore-hong-kong-taiwan/ (accessed 13 February 2023).

Berger, L. M. and Carlson, M. J. (2020) 'Family policy and complex contemporary families: A decade in review and implications for the next decade of research and policy practice'. *Journal of Marriage and Family*, 82 (1), 478–507. https://doi.org/10.1111/jomf.12650.

Bokun, A., Himmelstern, J., Jeong, W., Meier, A., Musick, K. and Warren, R. (2020) 'The unequal impact of COVID-19 on children's economic vulnerability'. *The Society Pages*, 28 July 2020. https://thesocietypages.org/ccf/2020/07/28/the-unequal-impact-of-covid-19-on-childrens-economic-vulnerability/ (accessed 13 February 2023).

Chang, M.-H., Huang, F. and Chen, C. (2020) 'Taiwan to bar entry of foreign nationals to combat COVID-19 (update)'. *Central News Agency*, 18 March 2020. https://focustaiwan.tw/society/202003180007 (accessed 13 February 2023).

Chen, K.-T., Twu, S.-J., Chang, H-L., Wu, Y.-C., Chen, C.-T., Lin, T.-H., Olsen, S. J., Dowell, S. F., Su, I.-J. and Taiwan SARS ResponseTeam (2005) 'SARS in Taiwan: An overview and lessons learned'. *International Journal of Infectious Diseases*, 9 (2), 77–85. https://doi.org/10.1016/j.ijid.2004.04.015.

Collins, C., Landivar, L. C., Ruppanner, L. and Scarborough, W. J. (2020) 'COVID-19 and the gender gap in work hours'. *Gender, Work & Organization*, 28 (Supplement 1), 101–12. https://doi.org/10.1111/gwao.12506.

Davidson, H. (2021) 'Taiwan hits zero COVID cases for first time since outbreak in May'. *The Guardian*, 25 August 2021. https://www.theguardian.com/world/2021/aug/25/taiwan-zero-covid-cases-outbreak-vaccine-test-trace (accessed 13 February 2023).

Directorate General of the Budget and Accounting (2019) 'Statistics on the number of Chinese people working overseas in 2018' (in Chinese). News Release. https://www.dgbas.gov.tw/public/Attachment/91217104242H1AK10HM.pdf (accessed 13 February 2023).

Executive Yuan (2021) *Gender Statistics of the Gender Equality Committee Executive Yuan* (in Chinese). Government of Taiwan. https://www.gender.ey.gov.tw/gecdb/Stat_Statistics_Query.aspx?sn=MwEtyBleRxJh%24lZApHWboQ%40%40&statsn=iGJRpsNX45yniGDj!w1ueQ%40%40&d=&n=135918.

Gardner, L. (2020) 'Update January 31: Modeling the spreading risk of 2019-nCoV'. *Johns Hopkins University Center for Systems Science and Engineering*, 31 January 2020. https://systems.jhu.edu/research/public-health/ncov-model-2.

Kalekin-Fishman, D. (2013) 'Sociology of everyday life'. *Current Sociology*, 61 (5–6), 714–32. https://doi.org/10.1177/0011392113482112.

Our World in Data (2021–) 'Taiwan: Coronavirus Pandemic Country Profile' (live data). https://ourworldindata.org/coronavirus/country/taiwan.

Pan, T. and Yeh, J. (2019) 'Number of Taiwanese working in China hits 10-year low'. *Taiwan News*, 18 December 2019. https://www.taiwannews.com.tw/en/news/3839550 (accessed 13 February 2023).

Prickett, K. C., Fletcher, M. and Chapple, S. (2020) 'The parenting myth revealed by lockdown'. Victoria University of Wellington, 6 July 2020. https://www.wgtn.ac.nz/news/2020/07/the-parenting-myth-revealed-by-lockdown (accessed 13 February 2023).

Reuters (2020) 'Taiwan's "electronic fence" monitor for those quarantined raises privacy concerns'. *New York Post*, 20 March 2020. https://nypost.com/2020/03/20/taiwans-electronic-fence-monitor-for-those-quarantined-raises-privacy-concerns/ (accessed 13 February 2023).

Taiwan Centers for Disease Control (2021) 'Corona Virus Disease 2019 (COVID-19)' https://www.cdc.gov.tw/en/Disease/SubIndex/ (accessed 13 February 2023).

Taiwan Centers for Disease Control (2022a) 'Mandatory quarantine for arrivals to be shortened to 10 days beginning March 7'. Press release, 24 February 2022. https://www.cdc.gov.tw/En/Bulletin/Detail/xPj4hm0pClVP5EJv9TOjlQ?typeid=158 (accessed 13 February 2023).

Taiwan Centers for Disease Control (2022b) 'Starting June 15, Taiwan to gradually ease border controls, shorten quarantine period, and control number of arrivals'. Press release, 11 June 2022. https://www.cdc.gov.tw/En/Bulletin/Detail/rYB7LWBxxycgJznNucXoiw?typeid=158 (accessed 13 February 2023).

Thomeer, M. B., Yahirun, J. and Colón-López, A. (2020) 'How families matter for health inequality during the COVID-19 pandemic'. *Journal of Family Theory & Review*, 12 (4), 448–63. https://doi.org/10.1111/jftr.12398.

Umberson, D. and Thomeer, M. B. (2020) 'Family matters: Research on family ties and health, 2010–2020'. *Journal of Marriage and Family*, 82 (1), 404–19. https://doi.org/10.1111/jomf.12640.

Wang, S. and Lin, K. (2020) 'Foreign visitors to Taiwan up 7% in 2019'. *Focus Taiwan*, 6 January 2020. https://focustaiwan.tw/society/202001060014 (accessed 13 February 2023).

World Health Organization (2020) 'Pneumonia of unknown cause – China'. *Disease Outbreak News*, 5 January 2020. https://www.who.int/csr/don/05-january-2020-pneumonia-of-unkown-cause-china/en/ (accessed 13 February 2023).

Yi, C. C., Pan, E. L., Chang, Y. H. and Chan, C. W. (2006) 'Grandparents, adolescents, and parents: Intergenerational relations of Taiwanese youth'. *Journal of Family Issues*, 27 (8), 1042–67.

Zennie, M. and Tsai, G. (2021) 'How a false sense of security, and a little secret tea, broke down Taiwan's COVID-19 defenses'. *Time*, 21 May 2021. https://time.com/6050316/taiwan-covid-19-outbreak-tea/ (accessed 13 February 2023).

10
United Kingdom: inclusions and exclusions in personal life during the COVID-19 pandemic

Katherine Twamley, Humera Iqbal, Charlotte Faircloth and Nicola Carroll

Introduction

This chapter draws on data from 38 families with children (73 individuals in total) across the United Kingdom (UK), from a range of geographic, socio-economic and ethnic backgrounds, collected between May 2020 and June 2021.[1] Our aim in this chapter is to discuss how participants responded to the shifting national guidelines around social distancing during the COVID-19 pandemic, and the impact of these on everyday family and intimate life. We focus on how understandings of risk and perceived appropriate responses to risk provoked processes of inclusion and exclusion of intimate and non-intimate others. Our findings indicate that, for many, the home became a 'safe' location, where rules around social distancing were agreed and maintained. Those from outside of the home, in particular strangers 'in society', were considered with more suspicion and circumspection. We link these findings with research around risk and individualization, and consider their implication for participants' overall responses to the pandemic, as well as transformations to family and intimate life.

UK country context

The UK is an example of a 'late liberal' welfare state (Povinelli 2011), with a neoliberal economic approach combined with historical state welfare

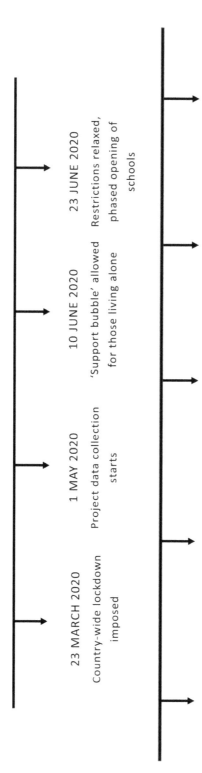

Figure 10.1 Timeline of COVID-19 in the UK. Source: authors.

provision, such as a universal public healthcare system. The COVID-19 pandemic occurred after a period of large cuts in funding for health and social care after years of 'austerity' policies from consecutive Conservative-led governments. Woods and Skeggs (2020) argue that this is part of an overall neoliberal political agenda of state withdrawal from health and social care, eschewing structural interventions and encouraging individuals and/or privately funded organizations to take up a greater role in the delivery of health and care. As we describe, the pandemic provoked a vast *increase* in state intervention in the health and everyday practices of individuals via social distancing measures implemented by the state. But in line with the overall (neo)liberal approach, personal responsibility was foregrounded in these social distancing guidelines, with notable implications for wider social relations (see Figure 10.2).

Figure 10.2 UK government public health poster, April 2020. Source: contains public sector information licensed under the Open Government Licence v3.0.

Moreover, while police were given powers to enforce the lockdown, individuals were encouraged to report observed infractions of their neighbours[2]. In some instances this led to public 'pandemic shaming' (Nabity-Grover et al. 2020; Reicher et al. 2021) of those deemed inappropriately following guidance.

The first of three national lockdowns began on the 23 March 2020. Although the four nations of the UK (England, Scotland, Wales and Northern Ireland) set their own policies in relation to public health responses, there was mostly convergence. In the first lockdown all schools and childcare settings were closed, except to the children of workers in essential services. A 'stay-at-home order' was introduced, with a ban on all non-essential travel and contact with people from outside one's household. Those with COVID-like symptoms were told to self-isolate at home. Figure 10.1 on p. 224 shows the timeline of COVID-19 spread and government response measures in the UK.

Such an approach revealed a number of assumptions on the part of policymakers around the composition and safety of households. It assumed that families live together under one roof when in fact it is not uncommon for couples to live in independent households (Duncan et al. 2014) or for children to live separately from a parent (DWP 2021). In some households several families, generations and/or individuals may share a home or other communal spaces, making self-isolating and shielding measures almost impossible to realize (Bambra et al. 2020; Burns 2021). The measures also appeared to assume that parents would be able to look after children while continuing to participate in paid work, particularly challenging for single parent families. Moreover, as pointed out by numerous domestic abuse charities, home is not experienced as a safe space for all. Indeed, during the first lockdown research using Google Trends showed a large increase in domestic-abuse-related internet searches during the first months of the pandemic (Anderberg 2020). In response to calls from activists and family organizations, in late April 2020 the government announced that isolation instructions did not apply to those who were experiencing domestic abuse (UK Home Office 2020). Then on 13 June 2020 'bubbles' were introduced to enable those who lived alone to create support bubbles with other households, with a gradual expansion over the ensuing months for families across multiple households (Department of Health and Social Care 2020).

A steady reopening of schools and childcare providers started in June 2020, with a full opening in September. A second lockdown was initiated in November 2020 for one month in parts of the UK, but with schools and childcare facilities remaining open. Restrictions mostly centred around leisure facilities. The third lockdown occurred in

January 2021 for three months. Once again schools were closed to all but the children of 'key workers', though nurseries remained open in recognition of the specific difficulties experienced by parents of young children in combining paid work and care, and the definition of 'key worker' expanded to allow more parents to send their children to school. In reality, many childcare institutions had to close either temporarily or permanently due to frequent infections among staff and children (Bonetti et al. 2021). Throughout the pandemic handwashing and keeping a physical distance of two metres from others were emphasized. In July 2020 mandatory mask-wearing was introduced. Measures were dropped and reinstated with the onset of new variants, though never reaching a fourth lockdown. At the time of writing (May 2022) there are no further restrictions or social distancing measures in place.

Other support for families focused on financial assistance for and through business institutions via wage subsidies and tax holidays. A Coronavirus Job Retention Scheme – "Furlough" – provided employers with a means to cover 80 per cent of employees' salaries while they were unable to work. As argued by Richardson et al. (2021) this relied on a 'trickle-down' to families via businesses and other employer institutions. They identify two potential issues with this approach: First, it focuses on individuals attached to the formal labour market, and second, it introduces a greater probability of procedural errors by outsourcing its management to individual employers. Fraud, error and implementation gaps were quickly identified by the National Audit Office (2020, 50). There is also evidence that women were more likely to be offered and to request furlough, further entrenching gendered work inequalities (Andrew et al. 2020). Those who were not eligible for employment or business-related support had recourse to 'Universal Credit' (UC), except those with limited residency rights.[3] Overall numbers of claimants almost doubled between April and June 2020 (Department for Work and Pensions 2020). Universal credit allowance was increased temporarily by £20 a week. However, even before the pandemic, payments had not been sufficient to cover basic living costs (Patrick and Simpson 2020; Taylor 2021), and the increase of £20 was felt by many to still fall short of meeting needs (Power et al. 2021; Pybus et al. 2021).

Studies around infection rates, deaths and illness in the UK have shown that economic deprivation is strongly associated with rates of COVID-19, and that minority ethnic individuals are two to three times more likely to die from COVID-19, irrespective of age and geographical region (Aldridge et al. 2020). The links between income, ethnicity and health are well established (Benzeval et al. 2014; Marmot et al. 2020; Nazroo 2003). Disparities arise from a combination of differences in access to, and use of, health services, as well as material and structural inequalities (poverty, housing, pollution and working conditions). In terms of mental health, while data from the national quarterly survey 'Personal Well-being in the UK', released by the Office for National Statistics (ONS), suggested that personal well-being declined overall in April to June 2020 compared with the same period in 2019 (ONS 2021), being on a low income was found to be a risk factor for anxiety and depression at the start of the first lockdown (Fancourt et al. 2020). Parents living with young children and women generally reported higher levels of stress (Shum et al. 2020; Pierce et al. 2020). This is likely to be a consequence of the greatly increased domestic and childcare work which was provoked once childcare institutions were shut. A time-use study published by the Institute of Fiscal Studies (IFS) found that in the first UK national lockdown, parents were doing childcare during nine hours of the day, and housework during three (Andrew et al. 2020). We have written elsewhere about the mechanisms which lead to such differing experiences of the pandemic (Twamley et al. 2023).

The rollout of the COVID-19 vaccine which started in early 2021 was initially fast, but was slow to vaccinate children. At the time of writing numbers of daily infections are still high, and over 177,000 people have died of COVID-19 in the UK to date.[4] Comparatively, we have experienced one of the highest numbers of deaths per capita compared to other countries, though the reasons for this are not yet fully understood.

Theoretical framework

Our focus in this chapter is on how everyday life shifted for families with children in response to Government COVID-related guidelines and a 'viruscene' rife with risk (Lupton 2021). We draw on a family practices perspective (Morgan 2013, 1996) that shifts the focus from family as household or institution onto the 'doing' of family in everyday life. This allows a dynamic and responsive consideration of how individuals create, maintain and/or disrupt a sense or meaning of family. In tandem, we take a relational approach, attending to the practices that are negotiated across and between connected individuals that inform life in lockdown. Relationality is integral to family studies (Smart 2011; Twamley et al. 2021) and is pertinent in the study of an infectious disease, where public health measures rely on a collective response.

How people understand and respond to risks is informed by the mechanisms and rhetoric of policy (De Graaff and Bröer 2019). As with

Bröer et al. (2021) we assume that health policies construct a specific understanding and experience of risk (Hajer 2003), as well as the responsibilities of individuals to respond to this risk (Lupton and Willis 2021). Ulrich Beck's (1992) work around the relationship between risk and individualism is relevant here. Writing in the 1990s, Beck argued that individuals are required to continuously engage in reflexive decision-making and take personal responsibility for mitigation of risks arising from globalization, industrialization and environmental crises in Western European societies characterized by uncertainty, financial insecurity, erosion of state welfare and threats to health. He posited that such processes would lead to the dissolution of family as a core institution of social life, as well as the waning of trust in political and scientific bodies. However, although families were predicted to be more volatile – with adults moving in and out of couple relationships – he and Beck-Gernsheim also argued that the parent–child relationship was taking on a heightened significance as a relationship which is comparatively durable and permanent (Beck and Beck-Gernsheim 2002). With our empirical focus on the interplay between a pandemic rife with risk and the everyday lives of families, we are attuned to the possibilities of a (further) entrenchment of these tendencies in contemporary British life.

Data collection and sample

We recruited 38 families with children living in the UK through a short recruitment survey distributed via social media and outreach organizations. We purposively sampled participants for maximum diversity. In terms of income, 11 families in our sample reported an annual household income of over £90,000 (henceforth 'high income'); 14 reported between £30,000 and £90,000 ('middle income'); and 13 less than £30,000 ('low income').[5] Everyone in the family aged 12 and upwards was invited to participate in the study, but parents were also asked to reflect on children's experiences. A total of 73 individuals participated: 13 young people, 8 grandparents, and 52 parents. Of the parents, 35 were mothers, and 7 of these were single mothers. A high proportion of the adult sample had a university education (71 per cent).

Most participants (52) completed multimodal diaries between May 2020 and 2021, with a final family-level online interview in May/June 2021. In addition, 11 participants completed an individual interview in June 2020. For the multimodal diaries we used the Indeemo data collection application (https://indeemo.com/), uploading a mixture of text, video and photos. Approximately 900 photographs with captions, 452 videos, and 903 text posts were uploaded by participants, with the most intensive activity occurring in the initial four months. But 22 participants took part via interviews only – one in June 2020 and a family-level interview in June 2021.[6] Lower-income participants were more likely to choose to participate via video or telephone interviews only, in part due to reduced access to smart devices. The different types of data (images, interviews and diary entries) were transcribed and analysed using thematic analysis techniques (Braun and Clarke 2006) using the software NVIVO. We used matrix tabulations for comparisons across groups.

Ethical approval was granted by the UCL IOE university ethics board. The multiple methods described were initiated as part of an effort to give our participants greater flexibility in how they participated. We were mindful in designing our study of the potential anxiety and stress which participants were likely to be experiencing, and respondents were regularly reminded that they could skip questions and activities, or indeed drop out completely (see Faircloth et al. 2021 for more details). All data collection occurred remotely. Participants were given a pseudonym – the same (plant) name for those from the same family.

Findings

In this section we outline how families in our study responded to the social distancing measures, and to what degree they reported changes over time. We then reflect on how such responses shaped everyday family life.

How did participants understand and respond to social distancing measures?

In general, participants in the UK welcomed the introduction of lockdown in March 2020 as a necessary precaution. A few participants felt that the first lockdown started too late and had already started to socially distance themselves by, for example, working from home or taking their children early out of school. Having children at home while (mostly) also trying to engage in paid work was a struggle for many, which was eased for those on furlough.

However, the necessity of following stringent guidelines in the first lockdown, as well as the overall shock and 'newness' of the experience, appeared to forge a resolve and commitment to follow rules appropriately amongst our participants, as reflected by one participant here:

> I find social distancing measures easy to follow. It's a lot of common sense and thinking of yourself and others around you. We haven't been away many places since the whole lockdown so we don't have much issues with it. It's quite rural where we live (father, Fig family, low income, white Irish; interview, June 2020).

Those on low incomes reported more stress and anxiety, due to having to leave the house more often. These families were unable to afford a weekly shop and had little space in their homes and often no garden in which to play or exercise, as one mother describes:

> There's myself and three little ones, eleven, ten and six. We basically live in a tall tower block in one bed and these times are challenging because nobody's got any space to themselves, there's no privacy. I fear that if any one of us got the virus, then there's no place to isolate. So it's been challenging, it's been very difficult in that sense and it's just trying to keep the kids occupied as well, with no technology and the school's being shut and whatever (mother, Mallow family, low income, British Bangladeshi; interview, June 2020).

Nonetheless, all participants at one time or another needed to leave their homes, and this was experienced as the most stressful and challenging point in their daily lives. A key issue was the difficulty of negotiating spaces with people from outside their household:

> The closest we come to breaking the rules is when we walk down a street with people. I find it easy enough to walk around people, but my sister uses a wheelchair and when people approach, they rarely get out of her way until the very last second and they are well within two metres (daughter, Bacopa family, middle income, white Irish; diary, July 2020).

> We find others less … concerned, or adherent to the guidelines, and sometimes we have to ask people to give us space (father, Begonia family, middle income; diary, May 2020).

> I found the shopping at supermarkets very stressful when other people didn't seem to understand social distancing and it was more stressful because the majority who didn't seemed to be the most vulnerable groups (mother, Damson family, low income, white Irish; diary, June 2020).

As we go on to discuss in more detail, the idea that some people were properly following the guidelines and others were not, was a common theme.

It was clear that not all participants perceived the risk of the pandemic in the same way. A small minority were sceptical of the overall UK (and global) approach, comparing the COVID virus to the common flu. For example, the Lavender family mother (low income, white English), a single mother and grandmother, expressed scepticism about the gravity of the virus, suggesting that reports of the numbers of deaths were exaggerated. As perhaps a corollary to this, she also found that the rules were too strict, and she continued to see her grandchildren, including indoors, for the whole period of the study, saying 'no government can ever tell me I can't have my grandkids in my home' (diary, July 2020). Overall, a lack of trust in governmental institutions or science provoked less regard for social distancing guidelines. Others clearly were confident in the soundness of scientific evidence around the virus, but simply felt or expressed less risk, and therefore were more prone to breaking guidance. For some participants, however, distrust in the government's approach actually resulted in the taking up of *stricter* measures, by for example following rules from other countries or as recommended by scientific publications, as we will discuss further.

Several participants appeared to experience the pandemic as very risky, including but not exclusively those who were more exposed to the virus (via their work, for example) or vulnerable to the virus due to their health status (such as diabetes or asthma) or ethnicity. The Ilama family, for example, reported rarely leaving their house in the first lockdown even for the daily exercise allowed. The 13-year-old daughter talked about her anxieties around her father leaving the house for work:

> Yeah because my dad is the main going out — apparently for males the risk is more, and then if you like a black ethnic minority, and if you like — I mean my dad's not that elderly – he's like 47. So. Yes. Still we are telling him you should be really safe. Make sure you wear a mask and gloves and everything. And he's like 'yeah, yeah I do, I do' (daughter, Ilama family, low income, British Bangladeshi; interview, June 2020).

Later lockdowns were reported as more difficult for a number of reasons. Many participants began to tire of restrictions or became despondent about their hopes for a more 'normal' life. The second and third lockdowns also took place in winter, meaning shorter days and colder weather and therefore fewer opportunities to meet people out of doors. This participant's response was typical:

> We all said that January was rubbish anyway but even more rubbish because of the pandemic. And nearly everybody said you had this novelty at the beginning of the pandemic during lockdown when you were having Zoom quizzes and catching up with people you wouldn't normally catch up with. But then by the time lockdown two and lockdown three came, you'd had enough of it (mother, Jasmine family, middle income, British mixed ethnicity; interview, June 2021).

We also noticed that participants reported more 'bending' of social-distancing rules – either themselves or observing that others around them were getting more relaxed in later lockdowns:

> Everyone kind of dodged each other in the early days, you would see them coming and they would also dodge and you dodge them, they're not like that anymore (mother, Juniper family, low income, black British; interview, June 2020).

> Last lockdown I limited my trips out, I'm so cross that I didn't bother this time. I went shopping regularly, whenever I wanted often just for one or two items (mother, Croton family, high income, white Welsh; diary, November 2020).

The mother from the Croton family, like some other participants, had reported 'losing faith' in government guidelines, which from their perspective had little logic. Others reported ignoring or loosening their approach to guidelines after the Chief Advisor to the Prime Minister (Dominic Cummings) was found to have broken COVID-19 social-distancing rules, but was not punished for doing so.[7] These accounts demonstrate the link between political trust and individual behaviour, though they may also be seen as means of accounting for or defending behaviour which was officially against the rules. As explained before, in the early part of the pandemic those with high levels of trust in science but low trust in politicians, followed more stringent measures (see also the Pakistan and USA chapters in this volume). Here we see a gradual deterioration of trust in politicians from some participants, coupled with a decreasing sense of risk, as participants relax in tandem with a general (but not complete) easing of social distancing measures. Similar findings were uncovered in the Netherlands, where Bröer et al. (2021) argued that the gradual easing and later reinstating of restrictions heralded different uncertainties, such as about the usefulness and effectiveness of various measures. As the risk of catching or dying from the virus felt more remote, risk and uncertainty shifted to the management of the response.

Participants still portrayed themselves as 'sufficiently' following the guidelines however, citing common sense or other pressing reasons which justified the bending or breaking of rules, as seen here:

> Um, so I think there were two occasions where we met up with three friends who don't have children, three adult friends, and I think our rationale for that was um … I think it was to do with mental health that we would be as careful as we could but we needed to do that to sort of keep going (father, Clover family, high income, white English; interview, June 2020).

> I have bent the rules for childcare and for company. Once I had five Zoom meetings back-to-back and we weren't supposed to see anyone yet but I called my mum to ask if she could look after [son] outside in the garden for a few hours as he'd had a meltdown the day before. The other time I broke it was with my friend [name]. I met her in the park and we had some cans of gin. Then I went back to hers and stayed in her spare room, we hugged each other a lot (mother, Damson family, low income, white Irish; diary, September 2020).

> We went for a picnic and there are few people and it's nearby, but we don't break the rules like other people do, we are careful (mother, Allium family, high income, white English; diary, June 2020).

In this last quote, the mother from the Allium family reports that 'we don't break the rules like other people', though picnicking at that time in the pandemic was against the rules. Here, we suppose, she is referring to a sense that although she is breaking the rules, she does so responsibly and with an awareness of the risks. This was a common theme, as we will discuss further.

Impact on family life: inclusions and exclusions

Common to all participants in our study, including those who were more sceptical of and resistant to measures, was the shrinking of social worlds during the pandemic. Participants were largely confined to socializing with those they lived with in their homes. Transnational or migrant families suffered the longest periods of separation, though intimacies were sometimes fortified through media technologies which previously had been used less often. Many parents reflected on the grandparental support which they missed, while children and young people missed their grandparents' company (and vice versa). For parents, the loss of informal and formal support mechanisms brought huge increases in care and domestic work. Some parents also had to juggle their paid employment with care work or to deal with the fallout of a sudden loss of income. Those on 'furlough' were most able to deal with the competing demands, but these were rarely extended beyond the first lockdown. Many key workers continued to send their children to school, but still were having to deal with shorter school days as wraparound school childcare was no longer functioning, in addition to sometimes very demanding work contexts. In most of the households, mothers reported taking on more of the additional childcare and domestic work (see Twamley et al. 2023).

Despite these at times very stressful situations, participants reported a new or heightened appreciation for their families and the household unit was often presented as united in responding together to the pandemic situation. For example:

> We haven't had any disagreements within our family regarding the roadmap. We are all clear on what we need to do and how to do it (father, Echinacea family, middle income, white English; diary, May 2020).

> Overall I'd say lockdown has definitely put a focus on my family relationships which is actually really nice and has been really good for my mental well-being and general happiness actually ☺ (daughter, Daffodil family, middle income, white English; diary, May 2020).

Disagreements within families and friend circles did arise, but more usually with those from outside the immediate household. Typically, disagreements with non-household members revolved around differing understandings of or attitudes to social distancing guidelines. Here, one mother discusses what happened when her mother-in-law called over to drop something off to her house:

> I was really angry when my mother-in-law came and then insisted on using the lavatory. I will not be allowing her to pop over again

> because if this ... I feel like it is so easy to get bullied into things and it becomes harder to insist on following rules (mother, Croton family, high income, white Welsh; diary, June 2020).

Likewise, another mother (Gardenia family, middle income, British Indian) said she stopped speaking with her sister, who had entered their mother's house during lockdown.

Judgements around appropriate responses to the pandemic could become highly moralistic at times. In these examples, others were criticized for not sufficiently adhering to the rules, but sometimes people were characterized as too risk averse. In the following diary extract the Kalmia family mother discusses being labelled as a 'coward':

> My brother said that when he goes shopping [this was before compulsory face masks] you see those 'coronavirus cowards' with masks on and trying to cower away from you if you get too close to them. Which is basically exactly how I am. Just because I thought that was what you were supposed to do – wear a mask inside and try to keep one or two metres away. But he said, with contempt, that those are the poor people who are so scared of getting coronavirus and he feels sorry for them ... I don't understand why it's so contemptible to so many people (mother, Kalmia family, high income, white English; diary, August 2020).

However, two months previously the same participant had reported the opposite experience, of feeling judged for not being careful enough:

> The last time I went to the shop, which is months ago now, I went to a local one a couple of villages over that I hadn't been to before and they were doing one in and one out, and I didn't realize and I tried to go in and this man waiting outside was so horrible to me. He just looked at me like I was scum of the earth and I was feeling judged and like he was thinking that I wasn't from round here and how dare I come here and ignore the rules. And then one of the things I'd come to [buy] was marshmallows and I had to ask an assistant if they had any and then I felt like he was looking at me like you've come over to our village shop in the middle of lockdown to buy marshmallows. And I basically haven't been to the shops since because it just felt so horrible (mother, Kalmia family; diary, June 2020).

In part, the differences in experiences reflect changes over time – in that, people were more relaxed as the pandemic went on. However, what was also clear from our participants, was that there were 'correct' and reasonable ways to break lockdown – visiting family or friends for 'mental health' reasons was fine but going out to a shop to buy marshmallows was not. Two issues emerged as particularly problematic – children's attendance at school or nursery, and vaccinations. The former arose since attendance at school for children under 5 is optional in the UK, and during COVID lockdowns key workers were able to send their children to school if they were unable to care for them at home. Here two participants discuss their experiences:

> It seems parents are not really getting the spirit of this national crisis, instead doing all they can to qualify for a place for their child at school. Staff safety is not a consideration for some parents (mother, Daffodil family, middle income, white English; diary, January 2021).

> We claimed key worker status in June last year so didn't send the kids in during the first lockdown. This time we sent them in from the start. Couldn't contemplate doing otherwise. So that's better. Guilt – But the guilt is horrific ... I feel ashamed when colleagues ask me how home schooling is going. When I tell them the kids are in school, they sometimes get annoyed. It's not in the spirit of the lockdown. Other friends have made it clear I'm being selfish (mother, Kalmia family, high income, white English; diary, December 2020).

What seems to be at issue here is the perception that some people were having an easier time than others. For example, while justifying meeting up with parents in a park which was outside the rules at the time, the mother from the Ursinia family (middle income, white English) told us: 'Also I am cross while we are all trying to social distance there are lots of people protesting and not distancing.' Her irritation at how she perceives others are *not* following social distancing guidelines, prompts her to also break the rules, as if their breaking of rules nullifies her own observance.

The rollout of the vaccine provoked another whole round of discussions and consultations for participants and was sometimes experienced as a divisive issue. Differences in attitudes to vaccination and social distancing measures reflected differing understandings of personal responsibility, individual autonomy and the role of the nation state, as well as trust in government agencies and scientific bodies (as discussed in relation to vaccines more generally in Estep and Greenberg 2020). This can be seen in the following accounts:

> I'm not enthusiastic about it [the vaccine], partly I feel because I've had COVID and I feel like I'd rather get other strains and allow my body to learn from it. I feel like I'm in a position to allow for that, I'm a healthy person. But if these passports come in then I'll have to have it (father, Iris family, high income, British Indian; interview, June 2021).

> Interviewer: Do you mind telling me a bit more about what your hesitancy [to get the vaccine] is about?
> Participant: I'm unsure about health risks and maybe not enough research (mother, Juniper family, low income, black British; interview, June 2021).

> Interviewer: And what about the vaccine? Have you received it? Do you intend to receive it or your thoughts on that?
> Participant: Yeah, I received it very early and I don't know if I posted [in the diary] about this because I have wrongly been on the clinically vulnerable list all the way through the pandemic … But I also in the end just felt the logic, you know, the vaccine is about collective protection and so someone in their 40s, actually, she's at the school gates every day, having had it. So I sort of reconciled with myself to it, and I've had both vaccines (mother, Begonia family, middle income, white English; interview, June 2021).

Some participants were surrounded by family and friends who were of the same opinion, either for or against the vaccine. Others reported their difficulties in dealing with differing opinions. The mother and father of the Fig family, who were both hesitant to take the vaccine, ultimately avoided telling others that they were not intending to take it. Some participants reported cutting social ties with those who had differing opinions on vaccination.

The result of such alignments and misalignments was that participants began to *include* those who they considered to be acting appropriately, by for example inviting them to meet in parks, online or sometimes inside their homes, and *exclude* others that they did not. In the main, the exclusions were about unnamed 'others', as seen in the accounts provided. Since the home was often characterized as a 'safe' space, in which members agreed upon and followed social distancing to a similar degree, this both consolidated intra-household relationships, but weakened relationships with those from outside. For example, the father of the Echinacea family (middle income, white English) told us he would invite his sister and her family to their home, saying 'I don't worry about this as we all know how to still social distance'. Excluding others could also sometimes help forge relationships, as participants felt closer to some people by constructing themselves as similar. For example, here a mother discusses meeting in a park with some friends and their children:

> We were in the park with some of my oldest son's friends and their mothers. We didn't allow our children to enter the play area as there were too many people, children with parents, grandparents, and none of the adults were keeping the social distance and they weren't wearing masks. Luckily, all of us agreed that the behaviour of the adults in the playing area was not right and all of us agreed that this is not normal. We felt uncomfortable with the behaviour of the others and we moved to a remote area where we could sit relaxed keeping the social distance and the children could play with their bikes (mother, Heather family, low income, Romanian; diary, August 2020).

The collective discomfort with others' behaviour, is contrasted nicely here with the 'relaxing' that the mother of the Heather family could achieve with those of similar attitudes.

At the other end of the scale, Begonia mother tells us that she cut off contact with other friends, realizing that they could not be trusted to appropriately socialize in a socially distant way:

> So for example I have a very good friend who is far more relaxed about all this than I am, and effectively disregards the social distancing advice, she is always seeing her sister and kids, and her mother. Then she asked for her daughter to see my daughter and I said fine if they are socially distancing. Then my daughter later told me that she did nothing about that, and in fact when she [saw] I was nearby, she told my daughter 'quick, your mother is on her way move further apart'. And that is really insidious, and I am worried about that, and about the future, it's an issue of trust. I now feel I cannot let my daughter see her children, and they are best buddies (mother, Begonia family, middle income, white English; diary, June 2020).

Meanwhile, the mother of the Magnolia family told us about her frustrations with a friend who was 'too' risk averse and her inability to meet up with her during the pandemic. We can see that participants aligned themselves then with others who they felt had similar approaches to managing risk, and sometimes cut off relationships with others, highlighting the fluidity of personal communities (Spencer and Pahl 2018) during this time. The shrinking of social worlds helped participants feel safe (less exposed to the virus) while also reassuring themselves that while they were bending some rules, fewer people were being put at risk. The implications here are that social cohesion is impacted – trust is given to only few others, while most others are looked upon with circumspection.

Discussion

On 23 March 2020 the UK government issued a stay-at-home mandate to all individuals, unless involved in essential services. These measures had huge repercussions for how we live our lives. First, families were largely confined to their homes for long periods of time. Some of our participants reported intra-household tensions which they attributed to increased confined presence (see also Risi et al. 2021) but the overwhelming narrative was of appreciation and understanding amongst household members. These findings are uncovered in other studies from the UK, which suggest that overall people reported positive experiences of being confined with their families during lockdown (Cooper et al. 2021; Levita et al. 2021). Such narratives were perhaps part of a coping strategy whereby individuals actively worked to attain a sense of shared trust and safety, a solace inside the home from the dangers constructed as outside its walls. We are aware, however, that our study methods and sampling may have precluded families with histories or experiences of abuse from participating. Their experiences would be very different, and indeed as mentioned previously, it appears that domestic abuse increased during lockdown in the UK (Anderberg 2020).

However, we also argue that the particular approach of the UK government reinforced the construction of the home as the site of safety and refuge for individuals and families, and outside the home, and importantly outside 'others', as risky. As outlined, personal responsibility was foregrounded in social distancing guidelines: Government officials often emphasized the role of individuals in making appropriate 'choices' in responding to various public health measures as key to combatting the pandemic (Williams 2021; Orgad and Hegde 2022). Such an approach can encourage victim blaming, whereby those infected with COVID-19 are characterized as responsible for their own infection and illness (Reicher et al. 2021). Perhaps more problematically, key government ministers often did not even follow their own guidance – flouting mask-wearing in public spaces, for example – while defending their behaviour on the basis of their familiarity with one another, thus reinforcing the perception that known others are somehow less risky than others (Reicher et al. 2021).

Research from previous pandemics has shown how blame and stigma may arise as individuals attempt to find a 'cause' for the pandemic (Lee et al. 2005). Although not explicitly reported in our study, analysis of crime statistics demonstrated an increase in racist attacks against people of Chinese origin in the initial months of the pandemic in London, indicating some blame attributed, at least initially, to Chinese citizens (Gray and Hansen 2020). In drawing on the work of Mary Douglas, we can understand how such processes arise. Douglas (1966) focuses attention on the role of risk in the shaping of conceptual boundaries, such as between 'self' or 'other'. She describes how contamination and purity are culturally constructed through boundary work. Individuals, families, communities and social institutions will take steps to maintain these boundaries both practically and symbolically in efforts to offset and manage such risks. According to Douglas, the allocation of responsibility for hazard events is a 'normal strategy for protecting a particular set of values belonging to a particular way of life ... shared confidence and shared fears, are part of the dialogue on how best to organize social relations' (Douglas and Wildavsky 1983, 8). That is, as our participants were working out how to respond to and understand the risks posed by COVID-19, they allocated responsibility for continued risks of the virus to 'others' who were 'breaking rules'. A sense of safety and agreed behaviour coalesces around those who believe they are responding correctly. Meanwhile those who transgress the new norms, are stigmatized as 'contaminating' (Douglas 1966, 113). In our study, people in supermarkets or those encountered on the streets were often characterized as insufficiently adherent to social distancing rules, even when participants sometimes broke these same rules themselves. Such processes of inclusion and exclusion demonstrated how trust was selectively given to (some) known others. The government had stipulated that this remains within the household, but over the course of the study we saw participants widen their 'circle of trust' beyond their homes. Unknown others continued to be typified as deviant rule breakers.

In parallel, we saw an increasing number of participants (though by no means all) lose trust in government officials and policies around social distancing. Ulrich Beck posited in 'Risk Society' (1992) that trust in science and government institutions was falling, since these very institutions were implicated in and were seemingly unable to attenuate the risks produced. We saw a more complex picture. A small number of participants had low levels of trust in science and government institutions, others had high levels of trust in both, many others had low levels of trust in government, but high trust in science and scientists. These findings are perhaps not surprising, given a high proportion of university-educated participants in our sample and that, presumably, participants with trust in science are more likely to take part in research. Moreover, the pandemic hit after a turbulent time in UK politics, with the UK having left the European Union ('Brexit') and after years of austerity policies – both of which were deeply divisive – therefore affecting political trust (Jennings 2021). In our study, those with trust in science but low trust in government were most likely to be the strictest in their attention to social distancing guidance, often surpassing official UK social distancing policy. These were also the participants who felt most vulnerable to the virus, or who thought that the UK government did not have their interests at heart (that is, were prioritizing the economy over the health of vulnerable individuals).

Social trust and political trust are commonly seen as linked (Rönnerstrand 2013) – that is, a fall in one leads to a fall in the other. Perhaps due to the individualized approach taken in the UK, or the very nature of a contagious virus, we saw low levels of social trust throughout the pandemic. This concurs with survey research around social cohesion in the UK. Borkowska and Laurence (2021) found that, contrary to the optimistic outlook of media and political narratives, levels of neighbourhood cohesion declined in the early months of the pandemic, including behavioural dimensions, such as talking to neighbours (not unexpected given social distancing requirements, as the authors note), but also perceptual dimensions, with a decline in neighbourly trust. More vulnerable groups (including economically disadvantaged communities, some minority ethnic groups and people with pre-existing health conditions) experienced a greater decline in perceived community cohesion, in some cases resulting in widening social inequalities and the withdrawal of resources and support (Borkowska and Laurence 2021). Particularly problematic in our study was a sense that some people were having a better time than others – we gave examples where some families were perceived to unfairly take up school places or who broke rules for 'trivial' reasons. The poorest families were also those who took the greatest financial hit, while wealthier families accumulated more wealth (Bourquin et al. 2020). As Lamarche (2020) has highlighted, in implementing measures to reduce the spread of COVID-19, collective needs have had to be balanced with individual needs. For social distancing and other preventive measures to be effective, the majority of the population must comply, which inevitably constrains individual liberties; if people feel their needs are 'consistently overlooked', they lose trust in individuals and institutions. This appeared to be happening with some individuals in our study.

Conclusion

Our findings show that boundaries around household members, which were in almost all cases understood as family as well, solidified over the course of the pandemic in the UK. Spending more time together created added tension in some cases, but also intimacy – a feeling of closeness and a greater depth of knowing one another. The risks posed by the virus also solidified the boundaries around the household, leading to a circumspection and exclusion of outside others. Family members and friends who were understood to have similar understandings of the risks the COVID-19 virus poses were also welcomed into the virtual and sometimes literal space of the household. According to Mary Douglas (1966), a focal point of blame helps individuals to assign responsibility and establish a sense of order and security in their lives, which helps explain these processes of inclusion and exclusion.

Additionally, similar to what Ulrich Beck (1992) observed in Europe in the 1990s, we saw that participants were often mistrustful of government regulations and guidance, and tended to arrive at their own judgements on appropriate family practices in light of risk assessments. But trust in science and scientists remained strong amongst most of our participants, and family bonds have been strengthened, indicating the enduring importance of kin for our participants. We have shown how households have tended to 'turn in on themselves' and formed units with friends or extended family members outside the household, particularly grandparents, who share a similar stance on avoidance of risk or the preservation of personal freedoms. This suggests that Beck's thesis on individualization of risk might be drawn on in explaining a process, but one that is more familial in nature, whereby family members across generations responded to uncertainty through mutual decision-making on how to mitigate risk, which rules to follow and who to include and exclude. Participants in our study often widened their net to include some chosen others from their 'personal communities' (Spencer and Pahl 2018), while excluding others, most particularly unknown others. This suggests a certain level of fragility in relationships with friends and wider family, with a concomitant reinforcement of nuclear family bonds. While comfort and intimacy created and sustained amongst some family and friends is something to be celebrated, we worry that the attendant exclusions may lead to fragmentation and a reduction in social cohesion overall. There was an opportunity under COVID-19 for an 'intimate public' (Berlant 2008) to arise. Berlant describes this as an 'affective sense of identification among strangers that promises a certain experience of belonging' (2008, viii). It arises through a shared consumption of texts or a historical moment. Such a shared intimacy could consolidate social cohesion. Instead, we found that micro-intimacies were formed in pockets of trust and solidarity. We argue that the individualized and at times surveillance approach of the UK government contributed to these processes of inclusion and exclusion. It remains to be seen what the long-term impacts may be.

Notes

1. We would like to thank our study advisory group for the invaluable support and suggestions which they have given us over the course of the project. These are: Carol Homden, Coram; Carol Vincent, University College London; Ellena Tesfay, Government Equalities Office; Ellen Finlay, Children in Northern Ireland; Fiona McHardy, The Poverty Alliance; James Nazroo, University of Manchester; Stacey Warren, Family Action; Tracey Reynolds, University of Greenwich; Val Gillies, University of Westminster; and Wendy Luttrell, City University New York. The study was funded by the British Academy, CRF\103775.
2. See: https://www.police.uk/tua/tell-us-about/c19/v7/tell-us-about-a-possible-breach-of-coronavirus-covid-19-measures/.
3. £409.89 per month for single claimants aged 25+ (temporary increase of £20 per week).
4. UK deaths with COVID on death certificate: as per https://coronavirus.data.gov.uk/details/deaths (accessed 11 May 2022).
5. Average household income of a family of four (two parents and two children) in the UK is approximately £42,000. See: https://ifs.org.uk/tools_and_resources/where_do_you_fit_in (accessed 21 February 2023).
6. In some cases only one member of a family participated, meaning both the first and final interviews were individual interviews. Three families never completed a final interview – Bacopa, Katsure and Narcissus.
7. See: https://www.bbc.co.uk/news/uk-politics-52784290 and Fancourt, Steptoe and Wright (2020).

References

Aldridge, R., Lewer, D., Vittal Katikireddi, S., Mathur, R., Pathak, N., Burns, R., Fragaszy, E. B., Johnson, A. M., Devakumar, D., Abubakar, I. and Hayward, A. (2020) 'Black, Asian and Minority Ethnic groups in England are at increased risk of death from COVID-19: Indirect standardisation of NHS mortality data'. *Wellcome Open Research*, 5 (88). https://doi.org/doi: 10.12688/wellcomeopenres.15922.2.

Anderberg, D., Rainer, H. and Siudae, F. (2020) 'Quantifying domestic violence in times of crisis'. *CESifo Working Paper No. 8593*. Munich: CESifo. https://www.cesifo.org/en/publications/2020/working-paper/quantifying-domestic-violence-times-crisis (accessed 21 February 2023).

Andrew, A., Cattan, S., Costa Dias, M., Farquharson, C., Kraftman, L., Krutikova, S., Phimister, A. and Sevilla, A. (2020) 'The gendered division of paid and domestic work under lockdown'. *IZA Discussion Paper No. 13500*. Bonn: IZA Institute of Labor Economics.

Bambra, C., Riordan, R., Ford, J. and Matthews, F. (2020) 'The COVID-19 pandemic and health inequalities'. *Journal of Epidemiology and Community Health*, 74 (11), 964–8.

Beck, U. (1992) *Risk Society: Towards a new modernity*. London: Sage.

Beck, U. and Beck-Gernsheim, E. (2002) *The Normal Chaos of Love*. Hoboken: Wiley.

Benzeval, M., Bond, L., Campbell, M., Egan, M., Lorenc, T., Petticrew, M. and Popham, F. (2014) *How Does Money Influence Health?* York: Joseph Rowntree Foundation.

Berlant, L. (2008) *The Female Complaint*. Durham, NC: Duke University Press.

Bonetti, S., Ziolkowski, S. and Athan Broadberry, J. (2021) *The Covid-19 Pandemic and the Early Years Workforce: February 2021 – May 2021: Staffing decisions in an uncertain environment*. London: Education Policy Institute. https://epi.org.uk/wp-content/uploads/2021/07/EPI-NDNA-july2021-report.pdf (accessed 15 March 2023).

Borkowska, M. and Laurence, J. (2021) 'Coming together or coming apart? Changes in social cohesion during the COVID-19 pandemic in England'. *European Societies*, 23 (Supplement 1), S618–36.

Bourquin, P., Delestre, I., Joyce, R., Rasul, I. and Waters, T. (2020) 'The effects of coronavirus on household finances and financial distress'. *IFS Briefing Note BN298*. London: IFS.

Braun, V. and Clarke, V. (2006) 'Using thematic analysis in psychology'. *Qualitative Research in Psychology*, 3, 77–101.

Bröer, C., Veltkamp, G., Bouw, C., Vlaar, N., Borst, F. and Nolting, R. de S. (2021) 'From danger to uncertainty: Changing health care practices, everyday experiences, and temporalities in dealing with COVID-19 policies in the Netherlands'. *Qualitative Health Research*, 31 (9), 1751–63. https://doi.org/10.1177/10497323211005748.

Burns, N., Follis, L., Follis, K. and Morley, J. (2021) 'Moving target, moving parts – the multiple mobilities of the COVID-19 pandemic'. In Lupton, D. and Lupton, W. (eds) *The COVID-19 Crisis: Social perspectives*. London: Routledge, 27–39.

Cooper, K., Hards, E., Moltrecht, B., Reynolds, S., Shum, A., McElroy, E. and Loades, M. (2021) 'Loneliness, social relationships, and mental health in adolescents during the COVID-19 pandemic'. *Journal of Affective Disorders*, 289, 98–104. https://doi.org/10.1016/j.jad.2021.04.016.

De Graaff, M. B. and Bröer, C. (2019) 'Governance and risk in everyday life: Depoliticization and citizens' experiences of cell site deployment in the Netherlands and Southern California'. *Journal of Risk Research*, 22 (12), 1586–601.

Department for Work and Pensions (DWP) (2020) 'Official Statistics. Universal Credit Statistics, 29 April 2021 to 9 July 2020'. https://www.gov.uk/government/statistics/universal-credit-statistics-29-april-2013-to-9-july-2020/universal-credit-statistics-29-april-2013-to-9-july-2020#mainstories (accessed 21 February 2023).

Department for Work and Pensions (DWP) (2021) 'Official Statistics. Separated Families Statistics April 2014 – March 2020'. https://www.gov.uk/government/statistics/separated-families-statistics-april-2014-to-march-2020/separated-families-statistics-april-2014-to-march-2020 (accessed 21 February 2023).

Department of Health and Social Care (2020) 'Guidance: Making a support bubble with another household'. https://www.gov.uk/guidance/making-a-support-bubble-with-another-household (accessed 21 February 2023).

Douglas, M. (1966) *Purity and Danger: An analysis of concepts of taboo and pollution*. London: Routledge.

Douglas, M. and Wildavsky, A. A. (1983) *Risk and Culture*. Berkeley: University of California Press.

Duncan, S., Phillips, M., Carter, J., Roseneil, S. and Stoilova, M. (2014) 'Practices and perceptions of living apart together'. *Family Science*, 5 (1), 1–10.

Estep, K. and Greenberg, P. (2020) 'Opting out: Individualism and vaccine refusal in pockets of socioeconomic homogeneity'. *American Sociological Review*, 85 (6), 957–91.

Faircloth, C., Twamley, K. and Iqbal, H. (2021) '"Er, not the best time": Methodological and ethical challenges of researching family life during a pandemic'. *Families, Relationships and Societies*, 11 (1), 39–43.

Fancourt, D., Steptoe, A. and Bu, F. (2020) 'Trajectories of depression and anxiety during enforced isolation due to COVID-19: Longitudinal analyses of 59,318 adults in the UK with and without diagnosed mental illness'. *Lancet Psychiatry*, 8 (2), 141–9.

Fancourt, D., Steptoe, A. and Wright, L. (2020) 'The Cummings effect: Politics, trust, and behaviours during the COVID-19 pandemic'. *Lancet*, 396, 464–5. https://doi.org/10.1016/S0140-6736(20)31690-1.

Gray, C. and Hansen, K. (2020) 'Did COVID-19 lead to an increase in hate crimes toward Chinese people in London?'. *Journal of Contemporary Criminal Justice*, 37 (4), 569–88.

Hajer, M. A. (2003) 'A frame in the fields: Policymaking and the reinvention of politics'. In Maarten, A. and Wagenaar, H. (eds) *Deliberative Policy Analysis: Understanding governance in the network society*. Cambridge: Cambridge University Press, 88–112.

Jennings, W. (2021) 'Political trust post-Brexit'. *UK in a Changing Europe*. https://ukandeu.ac.uk/brexit-and-political-trust/ (accessed 21 February 2023).

Lamarche, V. (2020) 'Socially connected and COVID-19 prepared: The influence of sociorelational safety on perceived importance of COVID-19 precautions and trust in Government Responses'. *Social Psychological Bulletin*, 15 (4), 1–25. https://doi.org/10.32872/spb.4409.

Lee, S., Chan, L. Y. Y. and Chau, A. (2005) 'The experience of SARS-related stigma at Amoy Gardens'. *Social Science & Medicine*, 61 (9), 2038–46.

Levita, L., Gibson Miller, J., Hartman, T. K., Murphy, J., Shevlin, M., McBride, O., McKay, R., Mason, L., Martinez, A. P. and Stocks, T. V. A. (2021) 'Report 1: Impact of COVID-19 on young people aged 13–24 in the UK-preliminary findings'. https://psyarxiv.com/uq4rn/.

Lupton, D. (2021) 'Revisiting Risk Theory in the COVID-19 world'. *SPSC Lecture Series*, University of Birmingham.

Lupton, D. and Willis, K. (2021) 'COVID society: Introduction'. In Lupton, D. and Willis, K. (eds) *The COVID-19 crisis: Social perspectives*. London: Routledge, 3–13.

Marmot, M., Allen, J., Boyce, T., Goldblatt, P. and Morrison, J. (2020) *Health Equity in England: The Marmot Review 10 years on*. London: UCL Institute of Health Equity. health.org.uk/publications/reports/the-marmot-review-10-years-on (accessed 9 February 2023).

Morgan, D. (2013) *Rethinking Family Practices*. Berlin: Springer.

Morgan, D. H. J. (1996) *Family Connections: An introduction to family studies*. Cambridge: Polity.

Nabity-Grover, T., Cheung, C. M. K. and Thatcher, J. B. (2020) 'Inside out and outside in: How the COVID-19 pandemic affects self-disclosure on social media'. *International Journal of Information Management*, 55, 102188.

Nazroo, J. Y. (2003) 'The structuring of ethnic inequalities in health: Economic position, racial discrimination, and racism'. *American Journal of Public Health*, 93 (2), 277–84. https://doi.org/10.2105/ajph.93.2.277.

Office for National Statistics (ONS) (2021) 'Personal well-being in the UK, quarterly: April 2011 to September 2020'. ONS. https://www.ons.gov.uk/peoplepopulationandcommunity/wellbeing/bulletins/personalwellbeingintheukquarterly/april2011toseptember2021 (accessed 21 February 2023).

Orgad, S. and Hegde, R. S. (2022) 'Crisis-ready responsible selves: National productions of the pandemic'. *International Journal of Cultural Studies*, 25 (3–4), 287–308.

Patrick, R. and Simpson, M. (2020) 'Universal Credit could be a lifeline in Northern Ireland, but it must be designed with people who use it'. Report. York: Joseph Rowntree Foundation. https://www.jrf.org.uk/report/universal-credit-could-be-lifeline-northern-ireland-it-must-be-designed-people-who-use-it (accessed 21 February 2023).

Pierce, M., Hope, H., Ford, T., Hatch, S., Hotopf, M., John, A., Kontopantelis, E., Webb, R., Wessely, S., McManus, S. and Abel, K. M. (2020) 'Mental health before and during the COVID-19 pandemic: A longitudinal probability sample survey of the UK population'. *The Lancet Psychiatry*, 7 (10), 883–92. https://doi.org/10.1016/S2215-0366(20)30308-4.

Povinelli, E. A. (2011) *Economies of Abandonment: Social belonging and endurance in late liberalism*. Durham, NC: Duke University Press.

Power, M., Pybus, K. J., Pickett, K. E. and Doherty, B. (2021) '"The reality is that on Universal Credit I cannot provide the recommended amount of fresh fruit and vegetables per day for my children": Moving from a behavioural to a systemic understanding of food practices'. *Emerald Open Research*, 3, 3.

Pybus, K., Wickham, S., Page, G., Power, M., Barr, B. and Patrick, R. (2021) '"How do I make something out of nothing?": Universal Credit, precarity & mental health'. *COVID Realities Blog*, 6 May 2021. https://covidrealities.org/learnings/write-ups/universal-credit-precarity-and-mental-health (accessed 24 February 20203).

Reicher, S., Michie, S. and Phoenix, A. (2021) 'After restriction: Why the public can only fulfill its responsibilities if the government fulfills theirs'. *The BMJ Opinion*, 29 June. https://blogs.bmj.com/bmj/2021/06/29/after-restriction-why-the-public-can-only-fulfill-its-responsibilities-if-the-government-fulfills-theirs/?utm_campaign=shareaholic&utm_medium=twitter&utm_source=socialnetwork (accessed 24 February 2023).

Risi, E., Pronzato, R. and di Fraia, G. (2021) 'Everything is inside the home: The boundaries of home confinement during the Italian lockdown'. *European Societies*, 23 (Supplement 1), S464–77. https://doi.org/10.1080/14616696.2020.1828977.

Rönnerstrand, B. (2013) 'Social capital and immunisation against the 2009 A(H1N1) pandemic in Sweden'. *Scandinavian Journal of Public Health*, 41 (8), 853–59. https://doi.org/10.1177/1403494813494975.

Shum, A., Skripkauskaite, S., Pearcey, S., Raw, J., Waite, P. and Creswell, C. (2020) *Report 07: Changes in parents' mental health symptoms and stressors from April to December 2020*. London: Co-SPACE study, UCL.

Smart, C. (2011) 'Relationality and socio-cultural theories of family life'. In Jallinoja, R. and Widmer, E. (eds) *Families and Kinship in Contemporary Europe*. Basingstoke: Palgrave Macmillan, 13–29.

Spencer, L. and Pahl, R. (2018) *Rethinking Friendship*. Princeton, NJ: Princeton University Press.

Taylor, R. (2021) 'COVID-19: Impact on child poverty and on young people's education, health and wellbeing'. *In Focus* (blog), House of Lords Library, 10 June 2021. https://lordslibrary.parliament.uk/covid-19-impact-on-child-poverty-and-on-young-peoples-education-health-and-wellbeing/.

Twamley, K., Doucet, A. and Schmidt, E. (2021) 'Introduction to Special Issue: Relationality in family and intimate practices'. *Families, Relationships and Societies*, 10 (1), 3–10. http://doi.org/10.1332/204674321X16111601166128.

Twamley, K., Faircloth, C. and Iqbal, H. (2023) 'Covid labour: Making a liveable life under lockdown'. *The Sociological Review*, 71 (1), 85–104.

UK Home Office (2020) *Home Office Preparedness for COVID-19 (coronavirus): Domestic abuse and risks of harm: Government response to the Committee's Second Report*. https://publications.parliament.uk/pa/cm5801/cmselect/cmhaff/661/66102.htm#footnote-003.

Wood, H. and Skeggs, B. (2020) 'Clap for carers? From care gratitude to care justice'. *European Journal of Culture Studies*, 23 (4), 641–7.

11
United States of America: polarization, politicization and positionality in COVID-19 policies and family practices

Marjorie Faulstich Orellana,
Sophia L. Ángeles and Lu Liu

Introduction

Given the tremendous geographical, racial/ethnic and social diversity of the United States, there is no single, representative 'US story' about the COVID-19 pandemic. One of the challenges that we faced in this study was to mobilize a set of participants who could speak to the vast diversity of experiences in this country, shaped by geographical, political, and social locations.[1] We worked hard to include voices of those who were least likely to be heard in public debates and other forums, and managed to recruit a sample that was varied in terms of household/family[2] composition, work/position in local economies and other indicators of social class, as well as race/ethnicity, immigration status and geographical location. Our goal was to seek both commonalities and variances in their experiences with the pandemic, and to consider these patterns in relation to those identified in other countries represented in this volume. We wanted to see what was particularly 'American' about how the pandemic played out in the United States.

Looking across our participants' experiences, over the months in which they self-reported on their lives to us (May 2020 through February 2021), the main thing that struck us was the shared experience of *confusion* that families expressed in the face of widely varying and rapidly shifting

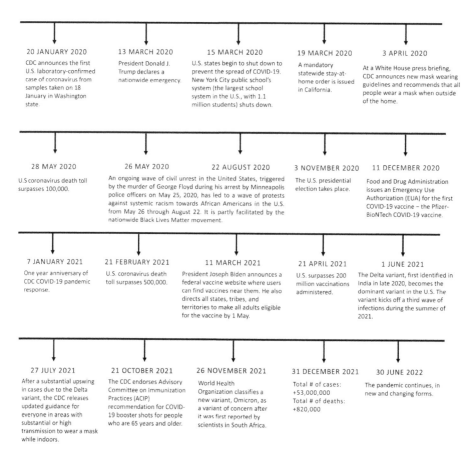

Figure 11.1 Timeline of COVID-19 in the United States. Source: authors.

local, state and federal policy contexts, set within a changing socio-political context, with increasingly overt expressions of racism, xenophobia and political polarization. In this chapter we look across families/households to show how participants made sense of these policies: how they got information about the pandemic and used this information to establish their own household-level policies. We look at how the choices they made – for pandemic-induced changes that they had control over (for example, social distancing) as well as those they did not (for example, school closures) – shaped or reshaped household divisions of labour.

Country context

The first coronavirus case in the United States was identified in late January 2020, during the presidency of Donald Trump (AJMC Staff

2021). Our study began in May 2020 and continued through February 2021, just after the inauguration of Joseph Biden as president, and just as the vaccine roll-out was beginning. Our description of the country context is concentrated on the pre-vaccine phase of the pandemic during this time of transition in the federal government. We briefly summarize changing policies during this time, the impact of the pandemic in terms of health and economic well-being, and differential impacts by race/ethnicity and gender, based on large-scale studies available to date, before turning to a qualitative analysis of the experiences of participants in our study. At the time of writing and revising this chapter (September 2021 through May 2022), and final editing (November 2022), the pandemic continued to unfold, with new variants of the virus emerging. The impact of the pandemic had been felt in new and different ways, shaped in part by the availability of vaccines. However, ongoing changes are beyond the scope of this chapter, in which we focus on the first year of the pandemic. Figure 11.1 on the previous page shows the timeline of COVID-19 spread and government response measures in the United States.

In the spring of 2020, when we began our study, federal guidelines regarding such things as mask-wearing, social distancing and 'stay-at-home' orders changed rapidly, and were implemented in different and uneven ways across the 50 states, 5 territories, and federal district (Washington, DC) that comprise the nation (*USA Today* 2021). Counties, cities, workplaces, schools and other institutions also took up these guidelines in different ways. These policies were often hotly debated and contested. Controversies were especially marked by the lines of the two main political parties (Republican and Democrat) (Gadarian et al. 2021; Kaiser Family Foundation 2021; Law 2020), but were shaped by many factors that defy simple categorization, as we discuss in this chapter.

The economic impact of the pandemic had also been uneven (Handwerker et al. 2020). Most affected were low-wage workers from leisure, hospitality and other service sectors (Bowman Williams 2020; Kochhar and Bennett 2021). Immigrants and black, brown or indigenous workers who make up the majority of this workforce experienced high levels of unemployment (Bowman Williams 2020; Kochhar and Bennett 2021). The United States is quite geographically diverse, and the economic effects of the pandemic were felt differently in rural and urban areas. More women than men (and more black women than white) were negatively impacted by labour market changes, both because of their location in the labour market and because the need to care for children during school closures was largely taken up by women, prompting many to leave the labour force (Bowman Williams 2020; Karageorge 2020; Kashen et al. 2020; Kochhar and Bennett 2021; Stefania and Kim 2021).

Federal and state governments attempted to ameliorate economic distress. On 18 March 2020, the United States Congress passed the Coronavirus Aid, Relief, and Economic Security (CARES) Act (US Department of Treasury n.d.b). This was followed in January 2021 by the Consolidated Appropriations Act. These measures provided economic relief for families and workers, small businesses, state and local governments, and American industries (US Department of Treasury n.d.a). However, large numbers of tax-paying workers who do not have legal status (that is, 'undocumented' immigrants, mostly from Mexico and Central America), as well as those attending college and those listed as 'dependents' by their parents (Huguelet 2020; National Immigration Forum 2020) were not eligible for economic relief. Each round of disbursement had varying eligibility requirements for both individuals and families. In spite of these inequities, 11.7 million people that received federal aid moved out of poverty during that year (US Census Bureau 2021).

As of September 2021 (when we first drafted this chapter), a total of 40,870,648 infections had been reported in the United States, with 656,318 deaths.[3] African Americans, Hispanic/Latino,[4] American Indian/ Alaska Native, Native Hawaiian/Other Pacific Islander and people identifying as 'multiple races' were over-represented among these COVID-19 cases and deaths, compared to their representation in the overall population. Hispanic/Latino(s) overall were more likely to be infected by COVID-19; African Americans were more likely to die from the disease. These racialized health disparities were likely due to the location of these populations in the labour force (disproportionately serving in 'essential' jobs where they had greater exposure to the virus), differential access to healthcare, and accumulated/historical social factors making these populations more vulnerable to death. We note parallels with the United Kingdom (see Chapter 10 in this volume) – a similarly racially/ethnically diverse society with long-standing disparities forged under colonialism.

The introduction of vaccines complicated the overall picture in terms of who was most vulnerable to hospitalization and death. Vaccines were introduced in the United States in January 2021 and were rolled out on a priority basis, going first to the elderly and those working in essential jobs. As of September 2021, 53.8 per cent of the total population were fully vaccinated and 63.1 per cent partially so. Among the fully vaccinated population, 63 per cent were over 12 years of age and 82.5 per cent were over 65. At that point, the vast majority of COVID-19 cases, hospitalizations and deaths were in those not fully vaccinated (Scobie et al. 2021). Vaccination rates varied across localities, with areas referred to as 'red' (that is, where over half of votes in recent political elections had gone to

Republicans) having significantly lower vaccination rates, and areas referred to as 'blue' (where voters tended to endorse Democrats) with much higher ones. There were also variations by race/ethnicity in terms of who opted to be vaccinated, likely due to distrust of medical authorities and/or access to medical information.

The pandemic has played out against a backdrop of rising xenophobia and ongoing historical tensions due to structural racism in the United States, as well as a growing income gap and political polarization. In 2020, an increase in anti-Asian hate crimes, including verbal and physical assault, was reported across the United States (Center for the Study of Hate and Extremism 2021). In June 2020, major cities saw massive protests about the murder of black people at the hands of police (Buchanan et al. 2020). On 6 January 2021, the US Congress was set to certify Democrat Joe Biden as winner of the 2020 presidential election when the country witnessed pro-Trump supporters storm the US Capitol building, apparently incited by President Trump (*New York Times* 2021; Tan et al. 2021).

Our study captured participants' perceptions about these unfolding circumstances between May of 2020 and February of 2021. We engaged a critical ethnographic approach to understand the family and household-level practices that were adopted by participants during this time, as influenced by the larger city, state and federal policy contexts that we have briefly sketched here.

Theoretical framework

Taking a sociocultural perspective on policy as practice (Levinson and Sutton 2001; McCarty 2011), our aim was to attend not only to official and unofficial governmental and other institutional acts but also to 'the historical and cultural events and processes that have influenced, and continue to influence, societal attitudes and practices' (Ricento 2000, 209). We examined how city, state and federal policies (for example, 'shelter-in-place' and 'stay-at-home' orders), were perceived not only as official texts and declarations but also viewed, interpreted and enacted in 'an ongoing process of normative cultural production' (Levinson and Sutton 2001, 1). Our examination included attention to the socio-political context that we described previously, and to how power was exercised, both implicitly and explicitly, in COVID-19-related policymaking. We considered how these policies were interpreted and negotiated within different households in diverse community contexts and then evidenced in everyday routine household activities as well as stated beliefs. To explore these issues, we asked how participants gathered information about the pandemic, how they understood policy guidelines around COVID-19, and what they thought about them. We further considered how participants' views changed during the first year of the pandemic in relation to the shifting socio-political context and changing practices (for example, closing and opening of schools). We examined how participants took up public policy guidelines and formed household-level policies to inform their own practices, and how they managed with policies that were imposed upon them. How did this shape their everyday family lives, and household divisions of labour?

Closely related to this sociocultural framework on policy as practice, we utilize sociocultural perspectives on learning to consider how participants *learned* the take-up of new practices, and how this learning was shaped by the social and cultural contexts in which they lived and moved. While much research framed by sociocultural learning theory looks at the learning that happens in particular social/physical contexts, such as classrooms, community centres or homes, often through ethnographic research in those spaces (see García-Sánchez and Orellana 2019 for a compendium of studies of everyday learning set in distinct cultural and social contexts), we considered virtual spaces as part of these social contexts. The pandemic, after all, did not take place in singular institutional, cultural or geopolitical spaces; it happened everywhere, worldwide. And just as the virus was not contained by borders, information *about* the virus moved freely, if unevenly and in patterned ways, through the internet. We looked at where and how families learned about the virus and mitigation strategies/policies, based on what they told us. We considered how their ideas related to larger circulating discourses and ideologies that were evident in public media.

Data collection and sample

For this ethnographically oriented study, we[5] invited participants and their families/households to keep 'coronavirus diaries' in a form of their choosing: voice-recorded, written, and/or using visual images such as photos. Our approach was informed by other diary-based studies and photo-elicitation techniques (for example, Alaszewski 2006; Bartlett and Milligan 2015; Luttrell 2020; Orellana 1999; 2017). We refer to our approach as 'ethnographically oriented' because while we were not able to engage in direct, participatory observations, we brought the sensibilities of ethnography to our work, intent on eliciting insiders' views of their own lives and experiences. Participants, who were located in different geographical regions across the country, also provided windows into the impact of the pandemic in their communities.

Recruitment

We began with a broad selection criterion for sampling: any households with children under 18 years old. Drawing on geographically – and culturally-diverse – personal connections in our recruitment efforts, we sought people of widely varying backgrounds: by race/ethnicity, national origins, immigration status, social class, occupation, language, age and geographical location. As a loose indicator of social class, we sought balance across three groups, on the assumption that these would be impacted in different ways by the pandemic: (1) those working in 'essential jobs'; (2) those working at home while juggling the care of children; and (3) those who had lost work due to the pandemic. We recruited immigrants and those with transnational ties (to China, Guatemala, Italy, Korea, Mexico, Peru and Vietnam); native-born and 'mixed-status' families; people working in the informal economy, in 'essential jobs' (health, education and food service), and as artists, teachers, businessmen and more. Participants lived in different regions within 10 states, including farming communities, big cities and small towns. Children were enrolled in different grades and kinds of schools. Household composition varied (two-parent, single-parent and multi-generational households, with children of different ages). People wrote/spoke their diaries in their preferred language, in Spanish, English, Chinese or Vietnamese, and we translated the prompts into those languages (ourselves, and with the assistance of a Vietnamese interpreter). We recruited a total of 35 families, 30 of whom continued for at least four months. All participants are referred to by pseudonyms, which were chosen by the participants.

The diaries

Participants were initially emailed two prompts weekly (via a private email account). Two families were contacted by phone in lieu of email and responded in audio-recorded conversations rather than written or spoken 'diaries'. (We did this to increase the diversity of our sample by ensuring that we were not just reaching people who were well-oriented to and had time for diary-writing.) We reassured participants that there were no 'right' ways to respond: we wanted to hear their experiences, and if the prompts did not feel helpful, they could write about anything on their mind.

We later recruited a second round of families, adjusting the prompts to reflect the ongoing pandemic situation along with other unfolding circumstances (for example, Black Lives Matter protests and the presidential elections). As participants completed the initial set of prompts and we saw that the pandemic was far from over, we invited families to continue by writing once a month; in total, 15 families elected to do so.

It is important to underscore that participants made choices about what to share, or not, with us, and how to tell those stories; their reports should not be taken as the sum total of these families' experience. Nor should they be generalized to the entire 'US pandemic experience'. The diaries *do,* however, offer insights into how a diverse cross-section of US households experienced this unprecedented time.

Data analysis

We worked with our data in multiple ways, first by importing diary datasets to a web-based qualitative software programme (Dedoose, available at dedoose.com) and establishing a collaborative coding process shared by the three authors, beginning with descriptive, emotion and values codes (Saldaña 2016) to identify key themes. We wrote open-ended analytical memos and crafted family portraits as we read through the diaries over time, and engaged in close narrative analyses in order to hear not just what participants said but how they said it, and what that suggested that was not made explicit. We also listened for things that were not said, recognizing that the diaries involved a particular kind of presentation of self and of family. For this chapter we focus on what participants told us about how they accessed and made sense of news and policy information on COVID-19-related measures, their reported decision-making processes about compliance to mandates, and what they indicated about how this shaped their daily lives. In other work we have looked in more detail at how families managed online learning for children (Liu et al. under review) and what they learned during, in and from the lock-down period of the pandemic (Orellana et al. 2022).

Our analytical procedures were recorded in reflective memos and transcribed recordings of our weekly Zoom team meetings, recounting the decisions we made each step of the way (Seidman 2019). We used 'mindful' ethnographic methods (García-Sánchez and Orellana 2019) to challenge our own assumptions and perspectives, looking for things we had not anticipated, and identifying patterns, while also actively seeking disconfirming evidence, and using it to challenge, deepen and complexify our findings. We were also attentive to our positionality, and to how our lived experiences and identities shaped both what and how we heard our participants' words; see Orellana et al. (2022) for elaboration on our team approach to seeing and hearing from diverse perspectives. We invited participants to review and respond to preliminary findings, as a form of 'member checking' (Merriam and Tisdell 2016) to ensure that we were accurately and respectfully representing perspectives and experiences.

Main themes and findings

How do participants understand and respond to social distancing measures? Political polarization and confusion

An important story that emerges in the US context is that of confusion about policies and practices. Virtually all adult participants in our project named confusion they felt, and saw around them, about public guidelines and protocol for safety and protection from the virus. Many commented that mask-wearing, social distancing and compliance with shelter-in-place[6] mandates had become highly politicized and polarized.

Indeed, at the time, news reports in the United States were filled with stories of fights breaking out in public spaces around mask-wearing. To a large degree, the polarization seemed centred across political lines, marked by the nation's two main political parties (Republican and Democratic) (Gadarian et al. 2021; Kaiser Family Foundation 2021; Law 2020). Democrats generally invoked public health officials' reasoning that the only way to stop the spread of the virus was for the public to follow the policy guidelines issued by the Centers for Disease Control and Prevention (CDC), while Republicans called for individual choice on these matters (Lerer 2021). 'Anti-maskers', as they came to be called, largely identified as Republicans and/or Trump supporters. They protested government imposition over their individual rights and freedom – values that generally aligned with Republican party values. In contrast, many vocal supporters of mask-wearing named ideological commitments to a larger social contract: to limit the spread of the disease and to protect other people (as well as the wearer).

Political polarization, complicated by conflicting and shifting guidelines by public health officials, contributed to confusion. Distrust of government, pharmaceutical companies and news agencies factored into resistance to the mandates.[7] Some people's distrust was based on personal histories of experiences – as in African Americans who were aware of the ways medical research has harmed their community, for example in the infamous Tuskegee experiments in which African American men who participated in a medical study were left untreated for syphilis and deceived about the nature of the study (Freimuth et al. 2001). Others distrusted based on the profit motive they saw undergirding pharmaceutical companies. Some were advocates for 'natural' approaches to building immunities. While on the surface there was polarization – with people either agreeing or resistant to government mandates – the *reasons* for people taking a particular stance on the issues varied.

Despite the confusing messages, most participants in our study claimed that they were compliant with local and federal guidelines on mask-wearing, social distancing, and 'stay-at-home orders', whether or not these were officially mandated in their locale. (These 'orders' were expressed differently in different cities and states and were virtually impossible to enforce.) They told us about rules they established for themselves, and volunteered exceptions they made to their own rules. Kathy Parker, an African American woman living in the state of Tennessee, for example, told us: 'During the stay-at-home phase of the pandemic I left only to get groceries, go walking and to doctor appointments.' As Kathy's words suggest, participants recognized that their own behaviours shifted as the context changed, with most alluding to the fact that they loosened the early prohibitions they had placed on their own movement, and/or viewed others around them relaxing their guard.

While no one in our sample expressed overt scepticism about the government's agenda, one hinted at it. Iosefa Tua, a health worker from California who identifies as Pacific Islander and who was employed at a private hospital in a wealthy area, wrote:

> Since the pandemic first started, I definitely felt a change of how I felt about the whole situation we are in. I do believe that there is a bigger agenda being pushed behind this virus and all media outlets are making it bigger than what it is … the inconsistency of the COVID-19 reports plus the lack of information, makes me question a lot. I don't have the sense of fear I once had at the start of all this, just a lot of confusion.

It was not clear from his diary exactly *who* Iosefa saw as pushing a 'bigger agenda', but it is important to note that he attributed his suspicion to the confusion he felt from public reports. Iosefa's wife, Rachel, echoed her husband's distrust and further named the confusion, writing separately in her own diary:

> I also don't feel like we can trust all these statistics/numbers that they're coming out with regarding the virus. I don't know what to believe – the numbers are different every day. The rules are different every day. It's annoying.

Reflecting on her husband's experiences at the hospital, she added:

> In the beginning, my husband was asked to take one day a week off because his hours were cut – because the hospital was slow – can you imagine, the hospital being slow in the midst of a pandemic? Crazy what the media tells you things to scare you versus what is actually going on.[8]

Iosefa and Rachel's case suggests how the confusion that people felt about 'all these statistics' could translate into larger public distrust. Like families in the UK, some of our participants distinguished between science experts, politicians and the news media, trusting scientists, but distrusting politicians and the media. But for others, distrust in media and politicians seemed to *foster* distrust in science. (Ironically, some might argue that people who bought into the stories of distrust were in fact *trusting* the media sources that fuelled their distrust.)

Families' united fronts

For the most part, families in our project seemed united in their beliefs about pandemic safety and in their responses to policy guidelines (as similarly found by Twamley et al. in the UK, see Chapter 10). In the example we have presented, Iosefa and Rachel each expressed scepticism about governmental guidelines. They presented their views separately, but in a way that suggests they had jointly 'analysed' the social world – drawing their conclusions based on Iosefa's work experiences in contrast with the numbers being reported in the press. Others, like Shelby Raja, who worked in the public health field in the Central Valley of California, seemed to speak for her family by using the first-person plural pronoun 'we', as she reflected on what she saw as surprising in the public actions of other people:

> The thing we've found most surprising is people's blatant refusal to accept/abide by the recommendations of the CDC, WHO [World Health Organization], and local Public Health Department.

Presumably, Shelby's comment about people's 'blatant refusal' to follow government guidelines is based on her observations of people out in public without masks, though she does not make this explicit. Her diary note suggests that this is something that she and her husband have discussed and commented on together.

Maria Johnson, who was the primary caregiver to two young children in the state of Nevada, also spoke about her family experiences as a collective, in a collection of statements written out almost like a poem, line by line. (We preserve the structure Maria chose for this diary entry here.)

> Our lives have remained the same.
> We don't go out as a family to public areas like stores. We do go to parks when it is safe to do so for hikes and walking around.
> People are now wearing masks a lot indoors but not much outdoors. We went to Lake Tahoe this weekend and stopped by a beach. No one was wearing masks but everyone was a safe distance from each other.
> Not everyone maintains a safe distance of 6 ft when I go to store.
> People walk by you without respecting the social distancing.

Like Shelby, Maria expressed concern about the behaviour of others in public spaces, while she focused her collective 'we' on what her family did to keep safe from contracting the virus.

A few diaries *hinted* at differences in household members' interpretations of policy guidelines, or their translation into practice. For example, 15-year-old River Albertson, who lived in the state of Ohio with her parents and three sisters,[9] differentiated her individual decision to go out to stores and restaurants a few times, while reporting on her *family's* policy of avoiding such spaces:

> Stores and restaurants have started to open up. I've gone out a couple of times, but my family is still trying to avoid going to restaurants and eating there. About half of the people are wearing masks, including myself. People are also trying to maintain 6 feet of distance. I'm happy that the economy is opening, but as it is opening cases are still rising. We still have to be very careful about what we do and where we go.

Olivia Lorca, mother of two preschool boys in the state of Washington, reported on her children's debates about what was safe to do during the pandemic:

Ringo seems to think that if things are open, they're safe. We passed by a restaurant the other day and saw people inside. Rolly said that we wouldn't be going, because it's still not that safe. Ringo said we could go. There are people there. He had the same response about the zoo (a month ago they only opened up the outside and had it go in one direction, but now everything is open as normal). Rolly and Ringo have debates about what's safe... Ringo and Rolly give socially distant hugs, which I have now sometimes adopted.

River's example suggests that family members may have made somewhat different choices when they had the ability to do so – as Rolly and Ringo really did not, given their young age. The Lorca example gives insights into explicit negotiation among family members (including very young ones) as they tried to work out their own feelings about risk and safety. But even when there were slight differences, families seemed to present a mostly united front, as revealed in River's use of the first-person plural, '**We** still have to be very careful about what **we** do and where **we** go' (emphasis added).

The united front that participants presented to us in their diaries seemed largely shaped *in contrast* with the behaviour of others, outside the household, who enacted different practices or were non-compliant with policy guidelines. We see this in Maria Johnson's statement about 'people' who 'walk by you without respecting the social distancing' in outdoor spaces. This is also evident in Shelby Raja's complaint about 'people's blatant refusal' to accept policy mandates. Similarly, Pedro Llosa (whose family migrated to the California Central Valley from Peru), used the passive voice to name 'the situation that has been created around the mask', by nameless/faceless 'people' (original in Spanish):

> The situation that has been created around the mask is very frustrating, although it is true that it is one of the ways to prevent the virus, it has been so politicized that the [mere fact of wearing a mask] marks people as being from one political party or the other.

River's father, Sven Albertson, wrote in his diary about attacks from 'both sides', while pointing out the irony of framing this as a question of individual freedom, which he noted that a nameless 'they' seemed to do:

> I respect the right of others to decide whether to wear a mask or not. I don't feel threatened by those who don't, but also don't appreciate when people attack others who do, or attack those businesses/

employees that require people to wear masks. The reason/excuse is that 'I am protecting my freedom' seems a bit misplaced in these instances. They also have the 'freedom' to choose to shop or not, at places where masks are required.

Some families contrasted the United States with other countries. Inga Buttermiller, a white doctoral student who lived with her son and domestic partner (a healthcare worker) in Southern California, imagined how the rest of the world saw the United States:

> I'm sure other countries around the world are laughing at us. We are a bungling country with a bungling president. What a joke. People are fighting over their right to not wear a mask in Costco. That's just nuts ... I wonder if this is the beginning of our collapse as a nation.

With this statement Inga set up another kind of 'us' and 'them' – contrasting 'we' in the United States with 'other countries', while simultaneously referring to 'people' who fight at Costco (not particular people, not people she names or seems to know).

The Chinese transnational families in our sample were particularly disturbed to see that there were no coherent national policies and health measures for combating the pandemic, and they compared their experiences here with reports from home. Helen Wong, a recent immigrant from China who worked as a screenwriter and lived with her husband and 13-year-old son in the state of North Carolina told us (original in Chinese):

> Through the epidemic, I began to think, why the United States, which has always been a modern country with a relatively advanced system, needs to be strengthened and improved in its response and organizational capabilities in the face of natural disasters? Why do all the parties in the United States still have their own goals in the face of disasters and cannot put the people's interests first to achieve unity?

Here, Helen referred to 'the people' as *all* of the people of the United States, and contrasted their welfare with 'all of the (political) parties' who had 'their' own goals.

The confusion that participants experienced is perhaps not surprising, given divergent policies at the local, state and federal levels, wide variation in how particular schools, workplaces and other institutions took up public policy guidelines (or established their own), changes in guidelines and policies over time, divergent models by public officials, and vastly different kinds of reports in different news outlets.

River's mother, Thea Albertson, described her view of the national situation, suggesting how President Trump could have unified the country:

> I feel that by allowing each Governor of the states to make their own laws regarding COVID also made it much more difficult to manage this pandemic in the USA. By people crossing county lines and making masks mandatory here in one county, but not another and then in this state, but not that one, only made zero sense. I feel President Trump could have sent an executive order to all of the States Governors and made masks mandatory for the entire country and a quarantine from the beginning to curb this virus from the start. Then we all would be under the same mandatory laws in governing in attempting to kill this off. There's just no other way that people will follow one rule here and there and whatever. Keeping it the same and strict for all in the beginning would seem most effective to all!

Thea seemed to suggest that President Trump should have helped to unify the metaphorical household of the nation. Arguably, not only did President Trump *not* send a unified message, but he actively *encouraged* state governors to decide for themselves (Baker and Shear 2020), modelled resistant behaviour (Victor et al. 2020) and in other ways provoked division (Spetalnick et al. 2021).

Impacts on family life: a complex calculus of decision-making

In the face of this confusing public policy climate, families engaged in a complex calculus of decision-making about domestic work that took them outside the home, such as food shopping, because these were the spaces in which they would be expected to comply with mask-wearing and social distancing mandates, and also the places where they would be most likely to be exposed to the virus. This was especially true at the start of the pandemic, because there was a great deal of confusion about the risk of contracting the virus while shopping in supermarkets. Families seemed to base their decisions about who would do the necessary household tasks that put them more at risk of contracting the virus on their interpretations of safety guidelines and their assessment of individual vulnerability. They told us about changes they made either in order to protect the most vulnerable, or appointing 'designated shoppers' based on availability and willingness to assume risk. Olivia Lorca noted that 'it was recommended that only one person in the household go out to stores, etc.'. Her husband Bob became the shopper because 'he enjoys shopping and errands more than I do'. She added that he was also less fearful about the risk of contracting the virus than she was.

Inga Buttermiller, who became the designated shopper because her partner was a healthcare worker who was therefore both more exposed to and more vulnerable to the virus, shared how she worked with her own calculus of risk in the timing of grocery shopping: 'As the numbers increase, I want to reduce our risk and that means shopping for more items so I can do it less frequently.' She wasn't sure what was 'the "right" thing to do', and her comfort level 'changed on a day-to-day basis', for reasons she herself couldn't figure out. She explained her general interpretation of the mandates that were in place in her city: 'I interpret the mask order as, "wear a mask when in public when you cannot socially distance"'.

For the most part, the safety-based policies that families established, especially in the early days of the pandemic, were centred around activities outside the home. For some, however, there were decisions to make in the movement in and out of homes. As a single parent and a healthcare worker who continued working outside the home, and as a person with some health concerns for herself, Sam Buzz (who identified as Latina, living in a working-class community in California), for example, was very worried about bringing the virus home, especially given the early uncertainty about how the virus spread. Sam established strict personal policy guidelines for herself that involved washing her clothes immediately upon arrival at home, then taking a shower before hugging her sons.

To guide this household-level policy formation, Sam attended to divergent sources of information. She seemed to make her own policy decisions based on what she saw promoted and modelled in her workplace, community and social circles, with Facebook as an important source of information. She was influenced by what was circulating on social media at the time, and we saw the uneven take-up of those circulating discourses in both her beliefs and her daily life practices, as expressed in her diary entries.

In early entries she detailed the care she took with items brought into the home, but a month later reported on changes to this practice:

> My co-worker showed me a video she saw on Facebook on how to properly handle groceries and other items brought from the outside

into your home, like cleaning packages with Clorox wipes, unpackaging bread. I followed a different version of that for a while but the process got tiring so I don't do that anymore. I've gotten comfortable too, I think.

Over time Sam acknowledged further relaxing her vigilance, based on what she observed in her community and at work. She saw few people wearing masks and commented: 'People don't really socially distance. We don't at work. We have to socially distance the residents, but we never do. My co-workers and I don't socially distance either.' This points to the fact that the take-up of policy into practice is often based on what people see other people *do* – not what they say. Sam's commentaries illuminate our point that circulating news and information was confusing, politicized and polarized, and that people were left to sift through it themselves, within their own social networks. It also suggests why close family were likely the greatest influencers of individuals' decisions, because they saw and heard from them the most, and they identified with them more than they did with the nameless, faceless 'people' they saw on the street.

The changes we have described thus far in household divisions of labour seemed to have been shaped by families' understandings of the risks and dangers of contracting the virus, and were centred on things over which they had some degree of choice or control. They could decide when or how often to go out to stores, and who should do such errands. These changes to household divisions of labour were also presumably rather small.

But what about the bigger changes to daily life that was forced upon families due to the closure of schools, and of many workplaces? The 'lockdown' periods of the pandemic meant that families found themselves sharing their home in new ways, as living rooms were turned into classrooms, and parents and children negotiated for both physical space and access to computers and the internet. Children no longer went out the door to school, where they would be educated, baby-sat and, in many cases, fed. Now parents were expected to supervise children's schooling at home, ensure their access to Zoom classrooms, prepare their meals, and provide for their other daily life needs.[10]

This imposed a whole series of *de facto* policy changes in households, which families had to negotiate and then establish their own household level policies and practices. Effectively, the social contract between homes and schools changed overnight, and parents were thrust into the position of being teachers, tutors, disciplinarians, taskmasters, technology brokers, health/safety monitors, food service providers and emotional caretakers for their children in dramatically changed ways. This caused considerable stress for many parents, especially for those who were also managing their own work at home.

Interestingly, the construction of these household-level policies about the new labour involved in supervising children's schoolwork and the other additional household work that resulted from children spending their days at home (for example, preparing lunch, managing their emotional states during this precarious time, and filling their free time as well) for the most part, did *not* seem to have been negotiated using the same kinds of decision-making calculi we described previously. Instead, families seemed mostly to fall back on traditional gender assumptions that childcare/supervision was women's work. Families may or may not have made conscious decisions in this regard, but across our sample, women disproportionately took up the supervision of children's schoolwork at home, as well as the worries associated with it. (They also disproportionately took up the work of reporting on that work, in our diaries.) They had a great deal to say about the stress of managing the extra work, and the *distress* they experienced as they found their responsibilities and relationships with their children altered in ways they hadn't bargained for. For example, Maria, living in Southern California with her husband, her parents and three children, shared with us (original in Spanish):

> I am not, I was not born to work as a teacher. This is what I say to you, and I have had to work as a teacher (laughs) and at the same time as a kind of psychologist.

Maria made no mention of her husband participating in the work of teacher and emotional support person for the children. She did not seem to assume that he should help out, or make any mention of a decision-making process about who should do this work; she seemed to assume the work was hers. This had been true before the pandemic as well, but the pandemic increased the workload and added new dimensions. Maria lived with her parents as well as her husband and three children, and thus had the support of extended family – a fact that helped them both weather the financial impact of the pandemic and manage the extra work. Maria and her father both lost work due to the closure of their jobs in a floral shop, and Maria's husband continued to work. And who took up the extra work at home? This seemed to fall to Maria and her mother, who helped with the additional cooking now required to feed the children breakfast and lunch, which they previously ate at school.

Sam Buzz similarly described in great detail how she supervised schooling for her two elementary-school-aged boys, as well as preparing their meals, and guided them on music and yoga – also while managing her outside work as a home health aide. She explained changes in the division of labour that she had established with the children's father: 'Before the pandemic began, their father would take them Friday nights, all day Saturday, and Sundays. Since the pandemic began, we decided the boys would not leave my home, so that is why their dad comes here to assist them with distance learning and to visit them.'

At the same time, like Maria, Sam was able to benefit from living in a multigenerational household. Sam notes that her parents took up some of the extra domestic work. This included her father, who was retired (while her mother continued to work outside the home, also in the health field). She explained:

> I'd like to add that since my mom and I work, my dad has taken over the house duties. He sweeps, every other day, mops on the days he doesn't sweep and cleans the two bathrooms every day. However, my mom does the laundry every evening. And I dust the living room sometimes since that is where my kids spend most of their time. When I don't work, I cook. When I work, my dad cooks. When I work (Thursday, Friday, Saturday, Sunday), my dad takes care of the kids but David (the kids' dad) comes over those days too so he helps too. I take over when I get home. When I don't work, I take care of the kids.

Sam seems to suggest, with her use of the word 'however', that her father's contributions were somewhat minimal, but she also suggests that the whole family, including her ex-husband, to some degree shared in the new work that was thrust upon them during the stay-home and school-closure period. In general, we found that families like that of Sam Buzz, who lived in multigenerational households, were able to adapt to the changing conditions with less stress than the two-parent households in our study. As Sam added, 'Blessed teamwork allows us to balance work and family life.' But even in these households it seems that women did more than their share.

At the other extreme, mothers with professional jobs whose work moved into homes during the pandemic, and who lived in nuclear households, expressed the most stress. Most of these dual-career couples had moved toward egalitarian parenting practices before the pandemic, but now experienced marked shifts away from egalitarianism. Inga, a graduate student whose husband worked as a hospital nurse, had a great deal to say about these changes. We quote her at length:

> After I gave birth to Fred, it shifted from less fun and freedom for mommy and the same fun and freedom for daddy. Covid exacerbated … the inequality. The funny thing is, I like to think of myself as a feisty, independent female. I am a partner, not a 'wife'. I never married Colonel, because I didn't want to be a wife and I thought opting for domestic partnership would help even the playing field. But here I am, sitting at home today while Colonel is out on a long mountain bike ride in the mountains. He left around nine and said he'd be back at three or so. I'm simultaneously working on my dissertation and listening to a conference with one headphone, feeding Fred, making sure he does his reading, and reminding him to get dressed before noon today… I don't think Colonel's world has changed one bit since COVID… Because I work from home, all of the home duties fall on my shoulders. I can be working on my computer and Fred will sit there and talk, talk, talk to me and I'm like, 'dude, does it not look like I'm working?'. When he's on the computer in the morning, it's like he forgets that Fred is around and hungry, so I have to make Fred's egg and toast. Before, I used to enjoy working from home because it was a treat. Now, I'd love to go back to my office on campus because that 'looks' like work. I will be afforded the same privileges as Colonel – for example, I can dump my dishes in the sink when I get home from work after my long day and let them sit there for a while. When working from home, god forbid there are clothes that need to be washed or a sink that needs to be cleaned because I'm home all day and of course there's time to do housework… I demand equality in my relationships and here I am, getting shit on by Covid and god-damned-antiquated-gender-roles that I fought SO HARD TO AVOID. I can explain my situation until I'm blue in the face but to Colonel, Inga-at-home-working = Inga at home.

In this and other diary entries, Inga expressed strong feelings about how the pandemic had reshaped her life. She always worked herself around to an expression of gratitude for the good things she had in her life, and acceptance of others. But it was very clear that she felt the unfairness of the impact of the pandemic, especially for people in her position: women living in nuclear families who were also mothers, and trying to launch professional careers during this time. Inga only had her partner to rely on, and she did not feel he had picked up the slack in the ways that she had.

Discussion and concluding reflections

When we drafted this chapter, in September 2021, confusion about the origins of the pandemic, its course of transmission, and ways of countering it, had far from subsided. New controversies had emerged around the efficacy, necessity and value of vaccines. Policies around indoor and outdoor mask-wearing, public gatherings and other safety protocols were continuing to change as well, and to vary across institutional, local, state and national contexts. Social media continued to promulgate confusion, and different news sources amplified distinct messages.

As we revised the draft chapter over the course of 2022, the pandemic was undergoing further phases, with the emergence of new variants and further roll-out of vaccines. Controversies about these things continued. The vaccine was generally available to people over the age of five, but only slightly more than 50 per cent of the US population had been vaccinated. Some had opted out of the vaccine due to medical concerns or age limitations. However, the majority were resistant based on politics, distrust of authorities and other ideological stances.

In this chapter, our aim is not to offer readers a unified, singular illustration of the US pandemic experience. Nor do we want to reinforce a *simple* story of political polarization. Instead, we have tried to illuminate how participants in our study sifted through a confusing, politicized and seemingly polarized policy context to make decisions for themselves. Simultaneously, we show how social positioning in terms of race/ethnicity, gender, social class and other differentiating factors really mattered – even as these played out differently in different household contexts, and in different arenas, as families made new, informal policies about divisions of labour for household tasks both inside and outside the home.

We examined these issues by describing the larger socio-political context and looking across the families in our project to see the sense-making processes that were revealed in their journals. We were guided by our conceptual framework, which draws attention to how public policies are enacted in and through quotidian activities in households and communities. We looked at how families appropriated government mandates and guidelines to determine for themselves their own family-level policies. We also contemplated what families *learned* through these experiences.

We found that individuals and families made decisions about when, where and how to follow policy mandates based on a complex calculus that included their assessment of risks/benefits, what they saw others doing, their own preferences, interests, values, and commitments, their own pre-existing domestic divisions of labour, what was possible in the face of institutional constraints (for example, school closures). The confusion of information, lack of resources and modelling of diverse responses in neighbourhoods, workplaces, shops, on television and in social media meant that families had to establish their own policies. And they had to determine their own exceptions to those policies, and justify them for themselves based on their needs and available resources (including human resources), as 'policy is kind of normative decision-making, and such decision-making comprises as integral part of everyday life' (Levinson and Sutton 2001, 3). This aligns with what others in this book (see especially Chapter 3 on Chile; Chapter 10 on the UK) reveal about the pressures on individuals (or family/household units) to manage their own calculus of risk in times of increasing precarity.

And what did families learn about public policy from this history-changing event? We fear that the main take-home lesson for many families was one of distrust (as was also shown to be the case in the chapters on Chile, Russia, South Africa and UK in this volume). This included distrust of authority figures in general, with some distrusting both public health leaders and politicians; and others just the latter, and of the news media, with some trusting certain sources but not others, and some trying to sift through conflicting messages. There was little shared agreement as to why we should either trust or distrust particular sources.

This is important to consider as people around the world will likely face more, similar and distinct challenges in this increasingly precarious time, with mounting social pressures forged by ecological changes, global economic restructuring and unresolved, long-standing social conflicts that fuelled the Black Lives Matters protests in the United States and other places as well as the class-based protests witnessed in Chile (see Chapter 3). How can we ensure that all people have access to accurate information about rapidly changing circumstances, from sources they trust, in order to make informed decisions for themselves? How can we educate our citizenry to be flexible, nimble and reflective as new information is acquired, recognizing the importance of adapting as we go? And what would it take to be able to collectively forge consensus in order to act responsibly for the social good?

Even while sounding this cautionary note, we want to underscore that the pandemic prompted most people to engage with policy issues and considerations of public health in unprecedented ways. Families in our project gathered information from multiple sources in order to establish their own household-level policies as they adjusted to life under dramatically altered circumstances. Participants researched how to mitigate the spread of the virus, how to protect themselves and their families, and they adopted new practices for health and well-being, as we detail elsewhere (Orellana et al. 2022). They were compelled to do this largely because of the confusion they encountered in policy messages in the public sphere. While we are concerned by this neo-liberal shift of state responsibilities onto individuals, we also see possibility here, in that individuals had opportunities to engage more critically with policy issues than ever before.

Intersectional understandings

Finally, we want to point to how *positionalities* mattered in terms of the impact of the pandemic on family lives, how it was experienced and understood, and what was learned from it. Social positions shaped the impact of the pandemic in many ways, including and especially in terms of health consequences, economic impacts and socio-emotional stress. The effects were uneven, often magnifying pre-existing inequities and sometimes introducing new ones. We also found a few surprises: things we might not have anticipated, in terms of what either aggravated or mitigated the effects of the pandemic. We thus want to help move conversations from a *generalized* sense of the inequities of the pandemic, to a more nuanced understanding of *how* race/ethnicity, class, gender and other social positions mattered in different ways, across various domains, and for distinct reasons. As we outlined in the introduction to this chapter, social positions shaped who was exposed to the virus, who got sick from it and who died. Social, cultural and racial/ethnic affiliations likely also mattered in terms of the information people had access to, and the sources they trusted. There is a long history of distrust of the medical world in black and Latinx communities in the United States, due to racist abuses of medical authority in the past. The economic impact was also uneven, with already-vulnerable sectors of the population made even more so. Those who lost work due to the pandemic suffered economically, though some found compensation through unemployment benefits and stimulus packages. Legal status mattered in terms of who was eligible for the stimuli.

We look in-depth at who took up the new work that was created in homes and communities, as schools moved into homes and families gathered at home for extended periods of time. Our data indicate that this was strongly shaped by gender, through a seeming 'default' to traditional gendered divisions of labour or a 're-traditionalization' of gendered norms. This resonates with Lupton's (2022) observations about how social crises like those introduced by the pandemic can bring to the surface tacit beliefs and reveal well-established ones that have been hidden from view. (See Chapter 12 in this volume for more discussion on this point.)

But even here, the story of 'who took up the new work' is complicated when one looks across different arenas. For tasks outside the home, families did not seem to operate with assumptions about the gendered nature of such work; instead, they made decisions about who should do this work based on an assessment of personal risk. But in domestic labour, and care of children, a re-traditionalization of gender norms was more evident, as women seemingly took up the work of cooking, cleaning, supervising children and guiding their school work. Perhaps 'errands' is not a kind of labour that is viewed as strongly gendered, while 'childcare' and 'cleaning' is. At the same time, the shifts that were demanded, and made, looked different across different households. Women in multi-generational households perhaps fared a bit better than those in nuclear families, because they were able to share everyday work.

In all of these ways, the pandemic exacerbated existing inequities, provoked new ones and occasionally brought some surprising *improvements* to people's lives. What we discussed here is the *already and always* intermingled inequalities of race/ethnicity, social class and gender (among other social categories). This is not a story that can be reduced to just one of these axes of difference. Though our data could never fully represent the story of the pandemic in the United States, we hope our analyses help to illuminate the *intersectional* nature of the pandemic's impact, as well as the complexities of the decisions people made as they enacted 'policy as practice' in their households.

Notes

1 We thank Amanda Quezada, Joanna Mendoza, Ann Phoenix, Ngoc Tran, Demontea Thompson, and the International Consortium and the families who shared their words with us. The research reported in this chapter was made possible by grants from the Social Science Research Council, the Bedari Kindness Institute at UCLA, and the Spencer Foundation (#202100032).

2 By 'family' we mean anyone who considers themselves family and who opted to participate, whether or not they lived in the same household. By 'household' we mean everyone living

under the same roof, whether or not they identified as 'family'. We challenge the assumption of heteronormative 'intact' nuclear families that the term 'family' invokes (Enciso 2016), and that problematically frames so much of public policy, as noted by Twamley et al. (Chapter 12). To avoid this normative model, we opt to use the terms family/household interchangeably. All household members over the age of 12 were invited to participate, as well as extended family members who lived nearby. Our aim was to have multiple participants from each household/family who wrote separate diary responses, lending insight into how differently positioned people experienced similar things. In other work, we explore just who took up this task (mostly mothers) and consider different vantage points of household/family members.

3   All data were cited from the Center for Disease Control and Prevention (CDC) at https://www.cdc.gov/.
4   We use the ethnic categories named in the data sources we cite. In this section we use Hispanic/Latino, the term used by the CDC, whereas in the rest of this chapter, we opt for the term Latinx to refer to people who live in the United States and have ancestral origins in Latin America.
5   Our team involves three researchers. Marjorie Faulstich Orellana, the principal investigator (PI) of the study, is a white, middle-aged professor and native English speaker who has worked in Spanish–English bilingual settings for 25 years, including as a bilingual classroom teacher, activist in the Central American Solidarity movement, and coordinator of an after-school programme serving a diverse group of children of immigrants living in Central Los Angeles. At the time of data collection, Sophia L. Ángeles was a doctoral candidate, native speaker of Spanish, daughter of Mexican immigrants, who grew up in California and studied in both the Northeast and Southeast US. Lu Liu is a postdoctoral researcher, a native speaker of Mandarin Chinese who has lived and studied in the US for 10 years with research focused on qualitative/ethnographic methodology, language policy and practice, and children and families.
6   Terms used for these policies (or 'orders,' 'mandates' or 'guidelines') varied across localities, as they do across countries as well. (See other chapters in this book.) The terms themselves bear consideration. For example, some localities advised people to 'shelter-at-home' while others referred to these as 'stay-at-home orders' or 'lockdowns'.
7   See Stewart (2020).
8   We wondered if Iosefa's hospital was slow because it was a private hospital, not one serving the general public. Other participants in our study who worked in the health field, like the Rajas, were distressed that more people did not defer to the expertise of public health officials.
9   River's father was a CEO of a company; her mother did not work outside the home. The family identified as white. They had recently moved to Ohio before the pandemic. All six family members wrote diaries for our project.
10 At some points in time, and in some contexts, families had choices about whether or not to send their children to school. In these cases, they seemed to calculate a risk-to-benefit ratio, based on the particular needs they saw for their children. Jeff Rogers, who lived with his wife Jessie and two elementary-school children in Georgia, explained (using the collective 'we' to express the family's position, and their feelings):

> Our daughter attends school in person, but our son is still at home learning virtually. He struggles a little but we feel better keeping him at home because both he and my wife have asthma. Our daughter is in special ed classes and needs to attend in person to get the most of her education, (she) needs that small class size attention. As long as it's done safely, which it appears to be at our local schools, we are not as worried about it but we still are a bit wary.

But in most cases, families did not have choices on the matter, because classrooms were moved 'online'.

References

AJMC Staff (2021) 'A timeline of COVID-19 developments in 2020'. *AJMC*, 1 January. https://www.ajmc.com/view/a-timeline-of-covid19-developments-in-2020 (accessed 25 February 2023).

Alaszewski, A. (2006) *Using Diaries for Social Research*. London: Sage.

Baker, P. and Shear, M. D. (2020) 'Trump says states can start reopening while acknowledging the decision is theirs'. *New York Times*, 16 April 2020. https://www.nytimes.com/2020/04/16/us/politics/coronavirus-trump-guidelines.html (accessed 25 February 2023).

Bartlett, R. and Milligan, C. (2015) *What is Diary Method?* London: Bloomsbury Academic.

Bowman Williams, J. (2020) 'COVID-19 widens disparities for workers of Color'. *ABA Journal of Labour & Employment Law,* 35 (1), 33–9. https://www.americanbar.org/content/dam/aba/publications/aba_journal_of_labor_employment_law/v35/number-1/covid-19-widens.pdf (accessed 25 February 2023).

Buchanan, L., Bui, Q. and Patel, J. K. (2020) 'Black Lives Matter may be the largest movement in U.S. history'. *New York Times,* 3 July 2020. https://www.nytimes.com/interactive/2020/07/03/us/george-floyd-protests-crowd-size.html (accessed 25 February 2023).

Center for the Study of Hate and Extremism (2021) *Report to the Nation: Anti-Asian Prejudice & Hate Crime. New 2020–21 first quarter comparison data.* https://www.csusb.edu/sites/default/files/Report%20to%20the%20Nation%20-%20Anti-Asian%20Hate%202020%20Final%20Draft%20-%20As%20of%20Apr%2030%202021%206%20PM%20corrected.pdf (accessed 25 February 2023).

Enciso, P., Edmiston, B., Volz, A., Lee, B. and Sivashankar, N. (2016) '"I'm trying to save some lives here!" Critical dramatic inquiry in the aftermath of Hurricane Katrina'. *English Teaching: Practice & Critique,* 15 (3), 333–54.

Freimuth, V. S., Quinn, S. C., Thomas, S. B., Cole, G., Zook, E. and Duncan, T. (2001) 'African Americans' views on research and the Tuskegee Syphilis Study'. *Social Science & Medicine,* 52 (5), 797–808.

Gadarian, S. K., Goodman, S. W. and Pepinsky, T. B. (2021) 'Partisanship, health behavior, and policy attitudes in the early stages of the COVID-19 pandemic'. *PLoS ONE* 16 (4), e0249596. https://doi.org/10.1371/journal.pone.0249596.

García-Sánchez, I. and Orellana, M. F. (eds) (2019) *Language and Social Processes in Communities and Schools: Learning from students from non-dominant cultural groups.* London: Routledge.

Handwerker, E. W., Meyer, P. B., Piacentini, J., Schultz, M. and Sveikauskas, L. (2020) 'Employment recovery in the wake of the COVID-19 pandemic'. *Monthly Labor Review, US Bureau of Labor Statistics,* December 2020. https://www.bls.gov/opub/mlr/2020/article/employment-recovery.htm (accessed 24 February 2023).

Huguelet, A. (2020) 'Updated FAQ: Here's what you need to know about the stimulus checks'. *USA Today,* 1 April 2020. https://www.usatoday.com/story/news/local/ozarks/2020/04/01/stimulus-checks-faq-heres-what-you-need-know/5103405002/ (accessed 24 February 2023).

Kaiser Family Foundation (2021) 'KFF COVID-19 vaccine monitor'. https://www.kff.org/coronavirus-covid-19/dashboard/kff-covid-19-vaccine-monitor-dashboard/ (accessed 24 February 2023).

Karageorge, E. X. (2020) 'COVID-19 recession is tougher on women'. *Monthly Labor Review, US Bureau Of Labor Statistics,* September 2020. https://www.bls.gov/opub/mlr/2020/beyond-bls/pdf/covid-19-recession-is-tougher-on-women.pdf (accessed 24 February 2023).

Kashen, J., Glynn, S. J. and Novello, A. (2020) *How COVID-19 Sent Women's Workforce Progress Backward.* Washington, DC: Center for American Progress. https://www.americanprogress.org/article/covid-19-sent-womens-workforce-progress-backward/.

Kochhar, R. and Bennett, J. (2021) 'U.S. labor market inches back from the COVID-19 shock, but recovery is far from complete'. *Pew Research Center,* 14 April 2021. https://www.pewresearch.org/fact-tank/2021/04/14/u-s-labor-market-inches-back-from-the-covid-19-shock-but-recovery-is-far-from-complete/ (accessed 24 February 2023).

Law, T. (2020) 'Democrats and Republicans aren't watching the same pandemic'. *Time,* 9 October 2020. https://time.com/5898231/republicans-democrats-coronavirus-news/ (accessed 24 February 2023).

Lerer, L. (2021) 'How Republican vaccine opposition got to this point'. *New York Times,* 17 July 2021. https://www.nytimes.com/2021/07/17/us/politics/coronavirus-vaccines-republicans.html (accessed 24 February 2023).

Levinson, B. A. and Sutton, M. (2001) 'Introduction: Policy as/in practice – A sociocultural approach to the study of educational policy'. In Sutton, M. and Levinson, B. A. (eds) *Policy as Practice: Toward a comparative sociocultural analysis of educational policy.* New York: Ablex Publishing, 1–22.

Liu, L., Ángeles, S. L., Orellana, M. F. and Phoenix, A. (under review) '"I wasn't born to work as a teacher…and as a sort of psychologist at the same time": A narrative analysis of three mothers' experiences with homeschooling during the COVID-19 pandemic'. Submitted to *Gender, Work, and Organization.*

Lupton, D. (2022) *COVID Societies: Theorising the coronavirus crisis*. London: Routledge.
Luttrell, W. (2020) *Children Framing Childhoods: Working-class kids' visions of care*. Bristol: Policy Press.
McCarty, T. L. (2011) 'Introducing ethnography and language policy'. In McCarty, T. L. (ed.) *Ethnography and Language Policy*. London: Routledge, 1–28.
Merriam, S. B. and Tisdell, E. J. (2016) *Qualitative Research: A guide to design and implementation* (4th ed.). San Francisco: Jossey-Bass.
National Immigration Forum (2020) 'Fact sheet: Mixed status families and COVID-19 economic relief'. *National Immigration Forum*, 12 August 2020. https://immigrationforum.org/article/mixed-status-families-and-covid-19-economic-relief/ (accessed 24 February 2023).
New York Times (2021) 'Mob attack, incited by Trump, delays election certification'. *New York Times*, 6 January 2021. https://www.nytimes.com/live/2021/01/06/us/electoral-vote (accessed 24 February 2023).
Orellano, M. F. (1999) 'Space and place in an urban landscape: Learning from children's views of their social worlds'. *Visual Sociology*, 14, 73–89. https://doi.org/10.1080/14725869908583803.
Orellana, M. F. (2017) 'Solidarity, transculturality, educational anthropology, and (the modest goal of) transforming the world'. *Anthropology & Education Quarterly*, 48, 210–20. https://doi.org/10.1111/aeq.12207.
Orellana, M. F. (2019) *Mindful Ethnography: Mind, heart and activity for transformative social research*. London: Routledge.
Orellana, M. F., Liu, L. and Ángeles, S. L. (2022) '"Re-inventing ourselves" and re-imagining education: Everyday learning and life lessons from the COVID-19 pandemic'. *Harvard Educational Review*, 92 (3), 413–36. https://doi.org/10.17763/1943-5045-92.3.413.
Ricento, T. (2000) 'Historical and theoretical perspectives in language policy and planning'. *Journal of Sociolinguistics*, 4 (2), 196–213. https://doi.org/10.1111/1467-9481.00111.
Saldaña, J. (2016) *The Coding Manual for Qualitative Researchers* (3rd ed.). London: Sage.
Scobie, H. M., Johnson, A. G., Suthar, A. B., Severson, R., Alden, N. B., Balter, S., Bertolino, D., Blythe, D., Brady, S., Cadwell, B., Cheng, I., Davidson, S., Delgadillo, J., Devinney, K., Duchin, J., Duwell, M., Fisher, R., Fleischauer, A., Grant, A., Griffin, J., Haddix, M., Hand, J., Hanson, M., Hawkins, E., Herlihy, R. K., Hicks, L., Holtzman, C., Hoskins, M., Hyun, J., Kaur, R., Kay, M., Kidrowski, H., Kim, C., Komatsu, K., Kugeler, K., Lewis, M., Lyons, B. C., Lyons, S., Lynfield, R., McCaffrey, K., McMullen, C., Milroy, L., Meyer, S., Nolen, L., Patel, M. R., Pogosjans, S., Reese, H. E., Saupe, A., Sell, J., Sokol, T., Sosin, D., Stanislawski, E., Stevens, K., Vest, H., White, K., Wilson, E., MacNeil, A., Ritchey, M. D. and Silk, B. J. 'Monitoring Incidence of COVID-19 cases, hospitalizations, and deaths, by vaccination status: 13 U.S. Jurisdictions, April 4–July 17, 2021'. *Morbidity and Mortality Weekly Report (MMWR)*, 70, 1284–90. http://dx.doi.org/10.15585/mmwr.mm7037e1.
Spetalnick, M., Shalal, A., Mason, J. and Holland, S. (2021) 'Analysis: Trump's legacy: A more divided America, a more unsettled world'. *Reuters*, 19 January 2021. https://www.reuters.com/article/usa-trump-legacy-analysis-int/analysis-trumps-legacy-a-more-divided-america-a-more-unsettled-world-idUSKBN29P0EX (accessed 24 February 2023).
Stefania, A. and Kim, J. (2021) 'Effects of the COVID-19 recession on the US labor market: Occupation, family, and gender'. *Journal of Economic Perspectives*, 35 (3), 3–24. https://www.aeaweb.org/articles?id=10.1257/jep.35.3.3.
Stewart, E. (2020) 'Anti-maskers explain themselves: "If I'm going to get Covid and die from it, then so be it"'. *VOX*, 7 August 2020. https://www.vox.com/the-goods/2020/8/7/21357400/anti-mask-protest-rallies-donald-trump-covid-19 (accessed 24 February 2023).
Tan, S., Shin, Y. and Rindler, D. (2021) 'How one of America's ugliest days unraveled inside and outside the Capitol'. *Washington Post*, 9 January 2021. https://www.washingtonpost.com/nation/interactive/2021/capitol-insurrection-visual-timeline/ (accessed 24 February 2023).
US Census Bureau (2021) 'Income, poverty and health insurance coverage in the United States: 2020'. 14 September 2021. Press Release Number CB21-151. https://www.census.gov/newsroom/press-releases/2021/income-poverty-health-insurance-coverage.html (accessed 24 February 2023).
US Department of the Treasury (n.d.a) 'Covid-19 Economic Relief'. https://home.treasury.gov/policy-issues/coronavirus (accessed 24 February 2023).
US Department of the Treasury (n.d.b) 'Economic impact payments'. https://home.treasury.gov/policy-issues/coronavirus/assistance-for-american-families-and-workers/economic-impact-payments (accessed 24 February 2023).

USA Today (2021) 'COVID-19 restrictions: Map of COVID-19 case trends and restrictions'. *USA Today*, 17 September 2021. https://www.usatoday.com/storytelling/coronavirus-reopening-america-map/ (accessed 23 February 2023).

Victor, D., Serviss, L. and Paybarah, A. (2020) 'In his own words, Trump on the coronavirus and masks'. *New York Times*, 2 October 2020. https://www.nytimes.com/2020/10/02/us/politics/donald-trump-masks.html (accessed 24 February 2023).

12
Family life in a time of crisis: trust, risk, labour and love

Charlotte Faircloth, Katherine Twamley and Humera Iqbal

During the turmoil of April 2020 – when we were frantically pulling this project together and firing off emails to potential international collaborators, funders and ethics committees alike – we had no idea that over two years later (the time of writing this chapter) we would still be living in a time of COVID-19. Back then we thought, naively, that we would conduct fieldwork with our participants in an intense but short-lived period of lockdown (in the UK at least) whilst 'the virus' raged. The plan was to have the remainder of the year to reflect on that period, when things were 'back to normal'. How wrong we were.

Things are still not, and perhaps will never be, 'back' to normal. Beyond the continuing presence of the COVID-19 virus, like previous major new or recurring infectious disease outbreaks, COVID-19 has been accompanied by significant sociocultural and political disruptions, and therefore transformations (Lupton 2022). Such crises call into question our very ways of viewing and understanding the world – a novelty from which there is no 'going back'. At the same time, our capacity to live in this transformed world is affected by factors that are all too familiar: long-running forms of social discrimination and inequality, which are themselves exposed and further entrenched. As Scambler (2020, 140) argues, the pandemic has functioned as a 'breaching experiment' which can provide us, as social scientists, with 'rare insights into the day-to-day practices, or artful accomplishment, of ordered living'. Medical historians, sociologists, anthropologists and cultural geographers have all shown that social, cultural and political responses to the emergence of deadly pathogens typically bring to the surface hidden and unacknowledged beliefs, as well as revealing more well-established ones (Lupton 2022). In this final chapter, we bring together some of the contributions of the project – both in terms of the project design, and the substantive cross-cutting themes in the chapters. We hope this will be elucidating for other scholars who are attempting to capture the impact of COVID-19 on families and communities around the world, as well as the impact of other crises and future pandemics. This moment in time helps us, as social researchers, to uncover the 'hidden and unacknowledged beliefs' around (for example) the role of the state in everyday life; personal familial and community responsibility in responding to a pandemic; managing risk; the very social discrimination and various forms of inequalities which are exposed through our analysis of how the pandemic has been experienced, as well as how it was differently responded to by differently positioned families. As such, it is our assertion that the common threads we pull out here have implications far beyond those of 'the pandemic'. Indeed, they inform our understandings of family life in periods of upheaval more broadly defined – whether that is caused by a pandemic, climate change, social conflict or otherwise.

There are also certain things that we do not do here, however. It is not our place, as qualitative researchers working with small samples of participants, to make far-reaching generalizations around (for example) the success of various national policy approaches to the management of the pandemic and mortality rates (just as it would not be our place to reflect on policies around climate change or in periods of war). Instead, locating our findings at what the *impact* of these measures were on family practices, we contextualize the 'success' of the different approaches to managing the virus with a deeper kind of knowledge: examining how well they meshed with local conceptions of selfhood, social relations and social institutions (Beck 1992).

We make some remarks around the general project design and its disciplinary and methodological orientation, before moving to some of the theoretical insights the contributions speak to, and that a perspective spanning 10 countries allows. We close by outlining some issues relevant to both policy and practice.

A global perspective

As a microscopic organism, the novel b-coronavirus SARS-CoV-2 certainly travelled, but as it did so, 'the virus' acquired a global significance as a concept in private lives as well as public discourses – what Lupton (2021) refers to as the 'viruscene'. The response by various agencies in trying to manage its spread, and the reception of these measures, however, was very much localized. Indeed, this depended to a great extent on local conceptualizations of the role of the state, the family and personal responsibility. Our intention with designing the project as an internationally comparative one was precisely to expose any differences in these conceptualizations. The opportunity to examine a global phenomenon with international colleagues beyond the borders of our own nation states demonstrated that different approaches and experiences were possible (see Chapter 1 for further discussion on this). This worked in an iterative way, of course: in our monthly team meetings, we discussed themes identified in our respective studies, meaning that we could carry out further investigations across the sites into points of convergence as well as difference. We realized that it was imperative to think about why these intersections might matter, not only now but also in the future.

Evidently, measures to prevent the spread of the virus – such as 'locking down' people in their homes – were met by families differently, both within and across the places we investigated. Sometimes with appreciation and adoption (being welcomed and readily embraced by participants); other times with adaptation, resistance or outright rejection (with participants bending the rules, or breaking them entirely). But the reasons behind these reactions were always contextual – due to a combination of both intra-familial factors (such as gender and generation) as well as inter-familial ones (such as class and ethnicity). These dynamics have been explored in the individual chapters. But what this book as a whole *also* offers is a more macro-level comparison, of family life set within broader socio-political regimes.

To give an example of the benefits of a global, comparative approach to understanding the implications of locking down families with children, we see how this had a different hue in societies where (for example) multigenerational living is the norm compared to those where it is not. This is because this 'norm' had a determining impact on families as they went about navigating issues around work and care. During school closures, and before 'bubble' legislation was brought in, in the UK,[1] we saw some families form new multigenerational households (or bend the rules around social distancing to form their own 'proto-bubbles' with non-resident grandparents). This provided all members with company and parents with some support with childcare, enabling them to continue with their paid work more easily. This was quite different to the experiences of families in our study from Pakistan, where multi-generational households were often the norm and therefore no reorganization of the family was required.

However, even if there was no reorganization of the family *form*, the *content* of the relationships within them was changed. Indeed, one might assume that the closure of schools was more readily absorbed by an extended family network. But this was not necessarily without problems: the account from our contributors in Pakistan indicates that this arrangement hugely exacerbated a gendered inequality in the division of care work and therefore had an impact on women's labour market participation (revealed by our more 'relational' approach to be something of a double-edged sword, in that some participants also welcomed this chance for increased family 'bonding'). This exacerbation of the gendered division of care work during lockdown was one of the loudest 'echoes' observed across the country case studies, notably in Argentina, Singapore and South Africa, where the authors called attention to this axis of inequality in particular, to which we return shortly.

Nevertheless, in saying this, one of the challenges of setting up an international project is to remain mindful of the importance of decolonizing research practice. As such, we wanted to make explicit what categorical assumptions are made in Euro-American ideas about families (and therefore selfhood or social relationships) to make sure we were not reading them in too readily to the various contexts in the study (seeing 'gender inequality' in a context where culturally relativist approach reveals something different; for example, see Strathern 1990). As such, we did not want the contexts to be seen as 'test sites' for theory derived from the Western European intellectual tradition, but to actually theorize from everyday lives – particularly everyday lives in the Global South, as in the chapters from Argentina, Chile, Pakistan, Singapore and South Africa here (see Balagopalan 2019 for more on this decolonizing endeavour[2]).

As we discussed in the introductory chapter (Chapter 1), whilst the editors initially drew on their own familiar Euro-American canon of literature in designing the study, this was taken as a starting point for reflection, contestation and discussion. As Rabello de Castro (2019) argues, this does not mean reading outwards from a taken-for-granted centre to periphery. Instead, it requires a reappraisal of knowledge 'assumed to be valid everywhere' (Rabello de Castro 2019, 9). This means a consideration of how various sites, practices and social relations are connected, fractured and differentially affected by global processes (Katz 2001; Mezzadra and Neilson 2013). To this extent, in setting up the project, we were acutely aware that 'the family' cannot be considered a taken-for-granted category, as a wealth of anthropological research around kinship and relatedness can attest (see for example Carsten 2013), even, or perhaps particularly, when policymakers in supranational organizations assume a correlation between 'household' and 'family'.[3] Narrowing down our frame of reference was one of the reasons we focused explicitly on families with children, although we remained attuned to the fact that the presence of these children did not necessarily indicate congruence with heteronormative ideals of the nuclear family mapped neatly onto a 'household'.

An interdisciplinary perspective

In part, these concerns about conceptual assumptions arise from our disciplinary orientations. As researchers, the initial project team in the UK included a sociologist, a social psychologist and an anthropologist. As we included more international collaborators this grew to incorporate scholars of education (in Russia), childhood studies (United States), and public administration (Argentina) amongst others. Projects are often talked about as 'inter' rather than 'multi' disciplinary, but in this case, and as the chapters attest, there was genuine interdisciplinary dialogue as we all tried to tackle similar research questions around the impact of COVID-19 with our respective disciplinary concepts and tool kits. This is reflected in the findings: We see talk of 'positionality' in the chapter from our US colleagues, an anthropological concept useful to explain the experience of confusion reported by individual participants in understanding government guidance, 'precarity' in Chile, a more sociological concept which emphasizes the structuring effect of class to the experience of lockdown, or 'resilience' in Taiwan, a psychological term which points to that discipline's interest in observing well-being within families. Yet the shared focus around the effect of COVID-19 on families with children means that these chapters can be read in a complementary way, coming at similar issues from different angles. (A shared theoretical heritage clearly helps, of course, and it is no coincidence that some of the work around risk and risk consciousness, which has had such an impact across so many disciplines, provided the contours for our investigations here, a point we return to shortly.)

But more than that, our own particular areas of interest within and across families proved to be complementary: our specialist areas included couple relationships and intimacy, childhood and youth perspectives and parenting and adult–child relations. Hearing the voices of participants from these groups, particularly young people, felt to us to be critical not only in terms of the substantive insights it generates but also in terms of documenting a monumental generational event from a variety of angles.

Methodological innovation

Much of the research that has so far been published on the impact of the pandemic and related public health measures is based on large-scale surveys. This examines the effect on mental health and well-being and considers differential effects on particular social groups, for example by age, gender and/or pre-existing vulnerabilities. There is little qualitative research that has been published so far (beyond analyses of an open-ended question in some surveys), and very little research has examined the impact on families. (Notable exceptions to this include the Leeds-based British Families in Lockdown,[4] the Oxford-based Co-SPACE study[5] and the Viral Loads volume, [see Manderson et al. 2021]). None to our knowledge have either the global scope of our project nor the rich, interconnected and deep qualitative knowledge around the role of kin relations in mediating behaviour during a pandemic that our research has generated.

We do not repeat our methodological orientation here, save to point out that it was informed by our various disciplinary orientations as well as our geographical locations. However, doing any sort of research in a pandemic requires some methodological acrobatics, particularly if that research might usually have been conducted face-to-face (arguably a hallmark of research into families and intimate relationships). For those of us who normally rely on deep 'hanging out' (or long-term 'participant observation', see Rosaldo 1994; Clifford 1997) in which the body is itself an embodied research instrument, the online interface presented challenges. Any sort of social happenstance is restricted, rapport is less easily developed and – perhaps crucially for those of us with a focus on inequalities – the availability of appropriate technological resources on the part of our participants is a prerequisite. As such, there were various methods through which we as researchers attempted to bridge that gap – whether through online or telephone interviews, diaries, a digital ethnographic app or more mixed methods (in the Taiwanese case). All of us in our own ways were attempting to get at that rich 'in-between' space between national directives and the practices of everyday life, perhaps most elegantly demonstrated by the US team here and the 'close up case' of one of their participants, based on journal entries. In Chapter 11, on the United States, the authors offer the account of one participant from a racially marginalized group (Sam Buzz, identifying as Latina, a single mother of two children in a multigenerational household) who demonstrates the confusion articulated by many of the US study participants in a particularly eloquent way. The vignette fleshes out how participants, to quote Chapter 11's authors, 'sifted through a confusing, politicized, and seemingly polarized policy context' to make decisions for themselves. In the absence of in-person interaction, the depth of this account, articulated within a relational context, is particularly striking.

These methodological (and therefore ethical) decisions around research also had a very different tone in each of these different locations – incentives for participants were considered essential in Chile, for example, but unethical in Sweden. Meanwhile, the use of the ethnography app Indeemo (as used in the UK) in Singapore would have been challenging when trying to work with the lower income, migrant worker population, many of whom had limited access to phones, Wi-Fi or knowledge of English (one of two languages the app is available in). Our international framework reminded us of the at once local and global repercussions of COVID-19, and how each must be accounted for as we attempted to manage an international comparative project (see Faircloth et al. 2022 for more on this).

Having a clearly defined set of shared research questions certainly helped in bridging differences in methodological approaches; as did a shared theoretical heritage which we could all 'speak back' to, and to which we turn here.

A theoretical contribution

Thinking with family: theorizing 'everyday life' and 'risk'

When we were designing the project, it was clear that theories of family practices (Morgan 1996; 2011), relationality and personal life (Smart 2007) as well as social capital and health (for example, Nazroo 2003; Marmot 2020) would be key to our research design, and therefore our findings (see Chapter 1). The chapters here certainly demonstrate how differing circumstances shape people's responses to – and ability to respond to – nationally mandated COVID-19 public safety measures.

However, in examining these links between micro-practices and wider social change, many of the contributors to this volume drew on another body of scholarship which we summarize briefly here – the sociology of everyday life (notably the UK, Chile, Taiwan and Singapore). As our Singaporean colleagues write, the sociology of everyday life takes the everyday, ordinary, taken-for-granted world we live in as an object of scrutiny (de Certeau 1984). This theoretical perspective asks questions about how society and a sense of social order are possible, how individual practices and thought processes contribute to the perpetuation of society, what implicit rules govern patterns of social interaction, how social interaction can proceed unproblematically (see Sinha et al., Chapter 6). As Neal and Murji (2015, 812) put it, 'Everyday life can be thought of as providing the sites and moments of translation and adaption. It is the landscape in which the social gets to be made – and unmade.'

Our focus here has specifically been on how everyday life has shifted for families with children in response to government COVID-19-related guidelines and a 'viruscene' rife with risk (Lupton 2021). As such, work on risk has also been key to our contributions. Comparing the current context to that in which Ulrich Beck (1992) wrote 'Risk Society', Lupton (2021) posits that such processes observed by Beck may be further heightened during the COVID-19 pandemic. Writing in the 1990s, Beck argued that industrialization and globalization increased the scale and potential for catastrophic events. The heightened awareness of such risks framed social life, shaping ideas of selfhood, social relations and social institutions. In particular, he argued that faith in 'experts' and science was eroded while social institutions were no longer trusted to keep people safe. This sense of insecurity and lack of trust heightened individuals' sense of personal responsibility in responding to and mitigating risks. 'Risk Society' is part of an overall thesis of the individualization of (Western European) society, in which individuals are thought to increasingly focus on their own personal needs and desires in making decisions about their lives. Again, we remained mindful that this was not a phenomenon that had uniform purchase or indeed effects in a cross-cultural context. At the same time, we recognized that it is one that has globalizing tendencies and was therefore a useful starting point for discussion (Rosen and Faircloth 2021).

According to Beck, family and other traditional structural formations, like gender and class, are of declining relevance (Beck and Beck-Gernsheim 2002). In fact, Beck argues that the ubiquitous nature and scale of risks in contemporary society mean that all social groups are equally vulnerable to risk in the contemporary era and that class is therefore a 'zombie category' in social research (Beck and Beck-Gernsheim 2001). Indeed, Beck's claim that risks are 'democratic' (Beck 1992, 36), or equally distributed across population groups, foreshadows the sorts of statements made by policymakers that 'COVID does not discriminate'.[6] Such assertions have been widely and repeatedly refuted since, as discussed in Chapter 1, studies have continued to show the unequal distribution of COVID-19 morbidity and mortality across different groups and different regions.

In the chapters here it is clear that class, gender and other socio-demographic categories remain of enduring relevance in shaping the experiences of individuals at times of great risk (as argued in Mythen 2007). Each of the contributions is therefore highly attuned to socio-demographic issues such as gender, generation, ethnicity or class which 'echo' through the chapters in all too familiar ways. For example, during the most intense period of the pandemic, it was shown in several of our country case studies that traditional gendered identities were magnified by lockdown conditions – this was particularly the case in Singapore, Argentina and Pakistan in this volume, while in Chile and Taiwan, class was the structuring factor highlighted by the authors that had a greater impact on families' abilities to thrive. Ethnicity appeared less frequently as a category of analysis in the chapters, but is discussed by the US authors in particular as a key axis of stratification.

Of course, scholars have long argued that Beck has overstated the individualist tendencies of people in contemporary life (for example, Twamley et al. 2021), and in centring our analysis at the level of *family practices* we implicitly critique the notion that this institution has declined in importance for contemporary lives. Studies from the sociology of families continue to highlight the importance of intimate others in people's decision-making. Certainly, our studies also show that participants *negotiated* with intimate others in how to respond appropriately to public health measures. This was even the case when, as contended by Beck (1992), responsibility was felt as located within individuals and less with governmental or other social institutions (as mentioned explicitly by participants in the UK, for example, in the context of declining trust in government). Throughout, we see the pervasive presence and influence of others in the narratives of participants, reflecting that their decision-making was relational, connected and embedded.

Bev Skeggs (2004) argues that processes of individualization associated with 'Risk Society' may in fact *exacerbate* inequalities, since social attainment may be attributed to personal efficacy in responding to events, rather than structural inequalities (again, this is something made particularly apparent in the Chilean case study, where a neoliberal ethic reinforces ideas of personal responsibility and therefore exacerbates inequalities for those with less access to resources). However, in the global context we are reminded yet again about the dangers of translation: being 'poor' in Sweden is not the same as being 'poor' in Pakistan. As such, the work of Pierre Bourdieu (1986) is helpful in exploring how responses to, and experiences of, the pandemic are shaped by the various forms of (relative) *capital* available to participants – and was fundamental to our thinking in establishing the project (see also discussion on Nazroo's (2003) work on social and ethnic health inequalities in Chapter 1). For example, families may be able to make use of economic capitals (access to savings, secure income and housing, space, etc.), social capital (networks who can provide help, advice and support), and cultural capital (using their own learning for 'home-schooling' their children, knowledge and confidence in navigating health services and so on).

To some extent then, the chapters collected together in this book offer a global perspective on the issue of pandemic management and its impact on individuals, families and communities; at the same time that they 'speak back' to the categorical assumptions made in this theoretical tradition and offer new ways of conceptualizing social relations and social change.

Family lives and political economy

Place, and history, matter, then. As we noted in the introduction, COVID-19 brought to the fore both the connectedness and the isolation of nations: on the one hand highlighting the seemingly boundaryless spread of an infectious disease, on the other, confirming ever more firmly nationalized hierarchies in access to global resources, as well as the hard edges of nation-states when borders were closed (discussed in Chapter 1). As such, these chapters show the benefit of taking an internationally comparative, or rather, global, approach to a subject like COVID-19 which arrives at a particular time in a particular place within Global North/South politics. A 'global approach' as we see it, examines how both international and national processes impact on events. For example, the origins of the virus in China impacted on how the virus was seen as (at least initially) the fault of Chinese citizens and/or those of Chinese descent (as discussed in the chapters from the United States and the UK here). Later mutations had similar effects, with borders closing specifically against citizens of particular countries, with repercussions for transnational families. Then the development and circulation of vaccines, as discussed in Chapter 1, brought into sharp relief how global inequalities shape everyday lives. At the time of writing, the Russian invasion of Ukraine rages on. At present it is unclear what the effect of this on the geopolitical landscape will be.

This point is palpable in the contribution from South Africa: COVID-19 arrived in a context irrevocably shaken by Apartheid and the HIV and AIDS epidemic (Haffejee et al., Chapter 7). This affected family and household patterns such that there is a large proportion of female-headed and multigenerational family systems, as well as child-headed households – chiming with some (but not all) of our previous comments about multigenerational families. Another example might be Chile – again, a location where there had been a series of crises before that of the COVID-19 pandemic. As the authors of the chapter on Chile put it: 'it is difficult to find a pre-pandemic life in which public and private stability, predictability and social security was the norm' (Vergara del Solar et al., Chapter 3).

This cannot be separated from wider issues of political economy, of course. In the contribution from our Chilean collaborators we see, for example, how the virus arrived in a context where 'neoliberalism' as a guiding political and economic principle is well established. This inevitably affected risk management in relation to viral transmission and how measures around social distancing were enacted: the assignment to individuals and families of responsibility for social problems is part of a long-running trend. The national effort to counter the virus was poorly coordinated and, in a context where the accumulation of economic capital is prioritized, there was little top-down intervention in the activities of large companies or expectation that they would protect workers; rather, there was an assumption that a number of lives would have to be 'sacrificed', particularly from those in poorer sectors.

Putting aside this all-too-brutal valuation of human life momentarily, the chapter on Chile (Chapter 3) makes clear that an ethic of neo-liberalization is not only in terms of political or economic policy, but also in terms of *subjectivation*. There was a perception by participants that authorities do not (perhaps even should not) provide sufficient security against the dangers of the virus, and therefore that the onus was on the individual (or individual family) to take such precautions from the bottom up. As such, compliance with measures around social distancing were not based on trust of authorities, but rather, on *distrust* of them, such that people had to 'care for themselves'. This was most clearly visible in Chile but the confusion around government guidance and a galvanizing of personal responsibility was also palpable in a range of settings, as we will discuss further.

Dis/trust

Indeed, this takes us to one of the most prominent themes within the chapters: trust. As Lamarche (2020) has highlighted, in implementing measures to reduce the spread of COVID-19, collective needs have had to be balanced with individual needs. For social distancing and other preventive measures to be effective, the majority of the population must comply, which inevitably constrains individual liberties; if people feel their needs are 'consistently overlooked', they lose trust in individuals and institutions, whereas if they feel their needs are being met, they are more likely to trust others and comply with restrictions. From a survey-based study, Lamarche found that when people felt safe and satisfied with their social relationships (that is, not too disconnected or over-connected), they were more likely to trust a government's handling of the COVID-19 crisis and more likely to comply with lockdowns and social distancing. People who felt their social safety was threatened, such as being dissatisfied with their personal relationships, were less supportive of COVID-19 restrictions and more likely to prioritize their individualistic interests; this was often in contexts where very survival was at stake. This of course has important policy implications for lockdowns as a measure to control COVID-19, as well as implications for loneliness, social relationships and well-being.

As predicted by Beck (1992), we see that distrust in certain institutions tends to give rise to an increased sense of personal responsibility in responding to risks (as demonstrated in the Chilean example). Returning to Lupton's remarks in opening this concluding chapter, however, we note that differences in attitudes to social distancing measures reflected differing understandings of personal responsibility, individual autonomy and the role of the nation state, *as well as* trust in government agencies and scientific bodies. Distrust in government to effectively manage the pandemic was particularly apparent in our study in Pakistan (where contradictory messaging between central and provincial governments led to confusion), Argentina (where participants reported 'information fatigue') and the UK (where the 'Dominic Cummings affair'[7] reduced trust in the government). Several of the country case studies, like the US, highlighted highly politicized contexts as one of the reasons for confusion, as there was a sense that (mis)information was correlated along partisan lines. Similarly, in Russia, participants spoke about being sceptical of government-issued guidance, where pro-Russia messaging is common-place on state media platforms. (They also spoke of the fear of being fined, which was a large part of the reason for their compliance, a reality that too great a focus on 'trust' perhaps eclipses.)

By contrast, in our Singapore and Taiwan country case studies there was a relatively high level of trust and confidence in the government's approach: in general, participants were compliant with various measures (which avoided full lockdown in Taiwan, unlike the majority of the other settings profiled here), and grateful for the actions taken by the state to keep citizens safe. Again, history matters. In part, the trust in Taiwan was born of experience of SARS in 2003, leading to a public who were largely vigilant and cooperative with measures such as mask-wearing and quarantine. Within that broader compliance, class continued to play an important role in how various families weathered the impact of the pandemic, of course. Conversely, in the South African country case study, past failures to deal with crises (such as the HIV AIDS epidemic) laid the groundwork for a low level of trust in government initiatives to control the virus.

A high level of trust in government was found in the study from Sweden, a setting renowned for its social support for citizens. However, there was a much greater emphasis on individual responsibility in this context than might be expected: the government did not enforce public lockdowns or other social distancing measures; rather, they issued *recommendations*. This was not without complications, then. The vagueness of the guidelines actually caused much frustration for participants in terms of how best to protect themselves from risks associated with the virus: participants may have assessed that there was risk of catching the virus, but this might not have been shared by their employer or the government, who seemed more concerned with 'business as usual' or keeping schools open.

Social trust and political trust should thus very much be seen as linked (Rönnerstrand 2013) – a fall in one leads to a fall in the other. This concurs with survey research around social cohesion in the UK. Borkowska and Laurence (2021) found that, contrary to the optimistic outlook of media and political narratives, levels of neighbourhood cohesion declined in the early months of the pandemic, including behavioural dimensions, such as talking to neighbours (not unexpected given social distancing requirements, as the authors note), but also perceptual dimensions, such as a decline in neighbourly trust. As such, whilst it is hard to generalize across the country settings, it is notable that we saw *higher* levels of compliance with governmental guidance in settings where there was a high level of trust in the respective governments than we did in those where there was not.

'COVID labour'
We move now to think about some of the implications of this. Across the settings, those that had least trust in a government's response to the pandemic undertook more labour in uncovering and interpreting

'trustworthy' information and in consulting with others as they sought to appropriately protect themselves and others (this is discussed in the Pakistani and US cases in particular, where there was a lack of consensus over pandemic management; see also Twamley et al. 2023). By contrast, those with low levels of COVID-19 (and high trust in the government) experienced less labour in the day-to-day business of living through a pandemic (such as Taiwan). This takes us to a final point around risk – and particularly, the *work* of risk assessment: how different risks are assessed and compared such as, for example, the risk of infection and the risk of unemployment or low income. This constant 'risk assessment' was made painfully clear in many of the contributions here – and not only those in the Global South. Such weighty responsibility brings a considerable burden to participants, even as they deliberate over their sources of information and how to interpret varying advice and scientific interpretations, sometimes with very low levels of trust in official sources.

Although ideas of individual responsibility, and trust in the authorities, were apparent in many of the narratives, government guidelines were negotiated and re-interpreted over time as families negotiated these competing concerns. As such, one of the major themes to come out of work in the UK context has been around the work of risk assessment, or what we term 'COVID labour' (Twamley et al. 2023), a theme we saw mirrored in some of the chapters here. COVID labour might be understood as an intermediary domain between government guidelines and participants' efforts to negotiate this new and uncertain 'viruscene' (Lupton 2021). Again, this is strongly shaped by factors around gender, generation, class and ethnicity. Overall, the chapters here demonstrate how differing circumstances shape people's responses to – and *ability* to respond to – government mandated COVID-19 public safety measures. Such trade-offs were most notable where limited resources increased risk and vulnerability, as is made most clear in the contributions from Chile and South Africa. These disparities help to explain the divergences in COVID-19 and mental health outcomes across different groups (Banks and Xu 2020; Beynon and Vassilev 2021) and to identify the deficiencies of government mandates which assume everyone will be able to respond to public health measures in similar ways. The research then contributes to a greater understanding of both everyday life 'under lockdown' for families with children, and how 'liveable' lives (Back 2015) are made under times of great risk, inculcating further (but mitigating other kinds of) risk (Twamley at al. 2023).

Our findings can also help explain why those on lower incomes and individuals from minority ethnic groups are more likely to suffer from adverse COVID-19 health outcomes (Aldridge et al. 2020) and demonstrate how 'risks' are differentially experienced and distributed, contra Beck's expectations (1992). The analysis lays bare the inadequacies of stay-at-home measures which make too many assumptions about the kinds of resources which individuals can draw on in attending to social distancing guidelines – those living in homesteads in South Africa, or indeed in areas of 'dense' population in Taiwan and Singapore would have had a very different sense of space to those 'at home' in the UK, Sweden or the US where access to outdoor space was more likely (although, of course, within-country differences might be more pertinent in this example). This should be useful for policymakers as they consider the context in which 'compliance' to social distancing and other measures are negotiated.

Our findings might also point to some of the reasons behind poorer mental health outcomes amongst women, those on lower incomes and those from minority ethnic backgrounds (Banks and Xu 2020). Again, the chapters from Pakistan, Argentina, Russia and Singapore demonstrate the uneven divisions of care labour within families, and how these fell particularly on women. The heightened levels of 'COVID labour' which these individuals experience could be likened to a cognitive burden, akin to the 'mental load' uncovered in recent studies around the division of labour within families (Mackendrick 2014). Such labour can have significant psychological and behavioural consequences (Mullainathan and Shafir 2013; Vohs et al. 2008).

Indeed, studies have suggested that a sense of control is one of the most important components of a person's mental well-being. A loss or reduced feeling of control (or uncertainty) has been linked to stress, anxiety disorders, depression, fear, pessimism, hopelessness and helplessness and drug and alcohol addictions (Anderson 2019). Uncertainty can also have an impact on our physical health. Korte and colleagues observe:

> Health pandemics share certain features including being singular widespread traumatic events, often marked by waves, apparently indefinite to the public, and characterized by ambiguous endpoints. Uncertainty and health-related anxieties grow organically in the peri- and post-pandemic periods. People fear infection, ineffective prevention, inadequate intervention efforts, and uncontrolled viral spread (Korte et al. 2021, 645).

This is perhaps particularly hard when participants attempt to deliberate between equally unappealing and sometimes life-threatening options.

This suffering is likely exacerbated by processes of individualization and an emphasis on individual culpability in any failures of COVID-19 public health measures (Reicher et al. 2021); see in particular the examples of Russia and Chile here, as well as the accounts of participants from contexts where there were multiple competing sources of information such as the US or Pakistan.

As argued by Lupton (2021), individuals have long been pressed to manage their own risks through the rise of self-governance, but in 'COVID Society' such responsibilization is taken to new levels, and the chapters here point to the consequences. In all settings it was clear that risks of social isolation, in the sense of personal well-being, weighed heavily on the minds of participants, particularly as it related to intergenerational relations (within families) or wider community solidarities (notably peer relationships for children); again, this was a burden largely managed by women. In taking a longitudinal approach, we are also able to see hints of the 'psychological fallout' of the pandemic for many – through loss of a loved one, long COVID (when, for some, there are long-term effects from contracting COVID-19) or the extended uncertainty they faced.[8] As such, the project contributes to a greater understanding of how 'Risk Society' is manifested in the contemporary COVID-19 era (Lupton 2021) and how particular approaches to the pandemic shaped these processes.

Taking 'care' forward: risk and parenting

There is therefore a final area of academic scholarship that the chapters here contribute to, which emerged somewhat post hoc. Across the country settings, we chose explicitly to focus on families *with children living at home* during the pandemic. As we noted in the introduction, this was partly to examine the additional demands placed on parents during the height of social distancing restrictions which in most cases included a shutdown of regular childcare or educational settings. This saw parents in many countries attempting to carry out their paid work at the same time as educate and care for their children. If the pandemic did one thing, therefore, it was to make visible much of the normally invisible labour of social reproduction, and the often gendered, generational expectations that accompany it.

These findings inevitably contribute to theorizations of care, which, in its multiple variants, is one of the structuring axes of social and economic relations. As the authors from Argentina write: 'It refers to those activities that are indispensable for satisfying the basic needs of people's existence and reproduction. It implicates the provision of physical and symbolic elements that enable people to live in society' (De Santibañes and Marzonetto, Chapter 2). It includes self-care, direct care of other people (the interpersonal activity of care), the provision of the preconditions in which care takes place (cleaning the house, buying and preparing food) and care management (coordinating schedules, commuting to educational or care centres or supervising paid care work at home) (Rodríguez Enríquez and Pautassi 2014).

At the particular level of our analyses here (that is, families), the quality of life of individuals depends on care: both for those who receive it and for those who provide it, whether unpaid or paid, within the household or through services outside of it. The COVID-19 pandemic disrupted care relations as the boundaries of people's public and private lives were blurred. Since families began to work and learn from home and were forced to stay indoors, the pre-established care 'balances' were destabilized, giving rise not only to changes in daily dynamics but also to reflections about the course of life in the long-term.

But it also did more than this. As anthropologists have long noted (Goody 1982; Strathern 1993), in talking about these 'balances' there is an asymmetrical relationship between parents and children in that children require care and parents have a duty to provide it. During lockdown, this responsibility for dependents fell ever more squarely on 'primary carers', often with no external support, formal or informal. One of the insights we would like to take forward then, is around how care work intersects with some of our findings around risk.

The 'moral responsibility' of parenthood is an area ripe for an investigation of risk and care. Like Lupton, Murphy (1999), a sociologist, has argued that we live in an age where individuals are continually encouraged to minimize risk-taking behaviour. Following Mary Douglas (1966), she suggests, however, that actions that are considered risky for the health of *another person* have attained special significance: this weighs especially heavily on parents when the message is communicated that the child is *at risk* and it is the task of parents to protect them, however Herculean that task. This dovetails with a trend towards what has been called a more 'intensive' parenting culture, which rests on the notion that children are highly vulnerable and that parental actions have a determining influence on children's outcomes (Lee et al. 2014) – such that 'love' itself is cast as a solution to a more anxious parenting culture.

The drive to protect children 'at risk' and to increase the safety of children is clear in many of the accounts here, as is the fact that these messages are internalized more strongly by mothers than fathers. In the context of a global pandemic, mothers weighed up the 'risks' their children faced from infection but also those risks around the dangers of missing out on school or seeing extended family (see the examples of Sweden and Argentina here, where mothers were explicitly concerned with their children's lack of socializing outside the home and the impact of this on their well-being). We understand this as a fruitful area of research, and consider how these accounts take forward the development of theorizations of risk: if parents feel an inexorable demand to parent as a risk manager at the *best* of times, what effect does the worst of times have on how we think about questions of social reproduction, moving forward (see Faircloth et al., forthcoming)?

Taking things forward: recommendations

The main 'takeaway' from this book is probably rather a mundane one: the reception of measures around pandemic management was very much contextual, requiring 'deep conceptual knowledge' of a particular place at a particular time to properly grasp. But it was also patterned. Contra Beck's expectation, in highlighting the importance of *relationality* as a lens, we have documented an unprecedented period in history and presented highly textured, enmeshed accounts from families around the globe. This is particularly pertinent in the study of an infectious disease where to keep everyone safe relies on all members of the family or household to maintain the stipulated or recommended measures, and is particularly important as we think about what might be done to support people better should we face another pandemic. But the findings are pertinent to studies of family life in periods of crisis more widely, whatever their geopolitical cause.

Our studies demonstrate that even in a 'neoliberal' era, relationality has important implications for policymakers in that it draws attention to the added *labour* and fractures in relationships. The findings in several settings reflected the fact that families were confused or unclear about government guidelines, particularly as the pandemic continued – and that a lack of trust in politicians undermined this compliance (as seen in the contributions from Argentina, Chile, Pakistan, Russia, South Africa, the US and UK in particular and also in Sweden, for reasons discussed). *This indicates that guidance needs to be coherent and clearly communicated with senior figures 'leading by example' in their own behaviour.*

Secondly, the findings also show that moralistic and individualistic discourse around social distancing guidelines can create divisions amongst communities. *This means that public health and safety messages need to be communicated in a way that is non-judgemental and promotes collective responsibility.*

Thirdly, several of the contributions here call attention to the generation of young people who have been severely affected by the pandemic and the long-term effects this might have on their education and mental health. *This shows that investment in mental health should be a top priority to avoid long-term effects at a population level.*

Finally, the findings show that the most deprived families around the world faced the greatest financial hardship, stress and risk as existing inequalities were exacerbated during the pandemic (this was acutely clear in the contributions from the Global South, notably Chile and South Africa). *This means that financial support needs to be rapidly accessible particularly for lower income families with little social support, and those in poor housing conditions.*

However, as well as the familiar stratification of inequalities, there were some lighter findings in the contributions: The enjoyment that families gained from having more time together (mentioned in the UK, Argentina and Pakistan studies in particular), in the fostering of a sense of family connectedness and resilience (in the studies from South Africa and Taiwan) and even the transformative existential potential of the pandemic in terms of gender relations (in the study from Argentina, where in the context of shrinking networks of care women reported a reinvigorating of their sense of their mothering identities and a renewed sense of purpose).

More than that, then, the chapters collected in this book demonstrate the astounding *plasticity* and resilience of families. In both Russia and Chile the contributions speak in particular of incredible feats of agency: individuals did not remain static or passive in the face of events. Even in structural frameworks of great precarity they tried to lead their own lives and those of their families as far as possible. Further, like the Taiwanese case, our South African colleagues in particular pointed to the way that challenges of COVID-19 were mediated not only by family togetherness, but by *community* support through sharing resources and structural supports. We see across the settings a high level of pragmatism – in the act of constantly weighing up pluses and minuses of various actions families choose that break or bend the rules because they cannot trust higher agencies to have their well-being at heart. This means that there might be a complex kind of compliance going on; a performance of adherence to social distancing regulations that our more ethnographic investigations reveal to be more nuanced.

The COVID-19 crisis provides a unique lens on families and communities by de-familiarizing the familiar: There has been a devastating impact on both physical and mental health outcomes, which when read through the prism of the global economy can be understood to have exacerbated pre-existing inequalities both within and across countries, and within and across families. We hope that both our methodological as well as theoretical contributions will have resonances for others attempting to understand this phenomenon and other similar global upheavals better, at the same time that we recognize some of the gaps in our analysis (for example, those families who moved across nations and which our international perspective inevitably avoided; although the inclusion of migrant families in Sweden goes some way towards demonstrating how this lens might be better incorporated). Nevertheless, in drawing attention to the multiple meanings and practices of 'family' in complex societies, this work has demonstrated the need for a closer and more refined inquiry into a set of cultural practices and ideologies central to the emergence and maintenance of communities, societies and nations, particularly in times of crisis.

Notes

1. A 'bubble' is when two households can act as one. See Gov.uk. 2020 Guidance: *Making a Support Bubble with Another Household* (note, guidance now withdrawn, but still visible via this link: https://www.gov.uk/guidance/making-a-support-bubble-with-another-household, accessed 7 November 2022).
2. See https://worldpopulationreview.com/country-rankings/global-south-countries for the list of 'Global South' countries, taken from UN definitions (accessed 7 November 2022).
3. For example, the WHO assumes that those in the 'household' are relatives:

    Someone in my household tested positive for COVID-19 ... What should I do to keep myself and others in the household healthy?

    It's hard when someone close to you is unwell. Even though you may want to provide comfort and company to your ill relative, it is important to reduce the likelihood that you or other family members catch COVID-19. For people with mild or moderate symptoms, the best thing you can do is provide the care they need while also keeping a safe distance. (https://www.who.int/news-room/questions-and-answers/item/coronavirus-disease-covid-19-home-care-for-families-and-caregivers, accessed 7 November 2022).

4. https://www.leedstrinity.ac.uk/research/british-families-in-lockdown-study/ (accessed 7 November 2022).
5. http://cospaceoxford.org/ (accessed 7 November 2022).
6. As senior UK cabinet minister Michael Gove commented in March 2020 (see https://news.sky.com/video/coronavirus-virus-does-not-discriminate-gove-11964771, accessed 7 November 2022).
7. A close advisor to the UK prime minister was found to have been in breach of lockdown restrictions (see for example, https://www.bbc.co.uk/news/uk-52811168, accessed 7 November 2022).
8. The head of the American Psychological Association discusses how past traumas such as natural disasters and terrorist events can leave people dealing with psychological issues for years at https://www.apa.org/news/apa/2022/covid-psychological-fallout (accessed 7 November 2022).

References

Aldridge, R., Lewer, D., Vittal Katikireddi, S., Mathur, R., Pathak, N., Burns, R., Fragaszy, E. B., Johnson, A. M., Devakumar, D., Abubakar, I. and Hayward, A. (2020) 'Black, Asian and Minority Ethnic groups in England are at increased risk of death from COVID-19: Indirect standardisation of NHS mortality data'. *Wellcome Open Research*, 5 (88). https://doi.org/10.12688/wellcomeopenres.15922.2.

Back, L. (2015) 'Why everyday life matters: Class, community and making life livable'. *Sociology*, 49 (5), 820–36.

Balagopalan, S. (2019) 'Childhood, culture, history beyond "multiple childhoods"'. In Spyrou, S., Rosen, R. and Cook, D. T. (eds) *Reimagining Childhood Studies*. London: Bloomsbury Academic, 23–40.

Banks, J. and Xu, X. (2020) 'The mental health effects of the first two months of lockdown and social distancing during the Covid-19 pandemic in the UK'. *Fiscal Studies: The Journal of Applied Public Economics*, 4 (3). https://doi.org/10.1111/1475-5890.12239.

Beck, U. (1992) *Risk Society: Towards a new modernity*. London: Sage.

Beck, U. and Beck-Gernsheim, E. (2002) *Individualization: Institutionalized individualism and its social and political consequences*. London: Sage.

Beynon, B. and Vassilev, G. (2021) *ONS Personal and Economic Well-being in Great Britain: May 2021*. ONS Report. London: ONS.

Borkowska, M. and Laurence, J. (2021) 'Coming together or coming apart? Changes in social cohesion during the Covid-19 pandemic in England'. *European Societies*, 23 (Supplement 1), S618–36. https://doi.org/10.1080/14616696.2020.1833067.

Bourdieu, P. (1986) *Distinction: A social critique of the judgement of taste*. London: Routledge.

Carsten, J. (2013) 'What kinship does – and how'. *HAU: Journal of Ethnographic Theory*, 3 (20), 245–51.

Clifford, J. (1997) 'Spatial practices: Fieldwork, travel, and the disciplining of anthropology'. In Gupta, A. and Ferguson, J. (eds) *Anthropological Locations: Boundaries and grounds of a field science*. Berkeley: University of California Press, 185–222.

De Certeau, M. (1984) *The Practice of Everyday Life*. Berkeley: University of California Press.

Douglas, M. (1966) *Purity and Danger: An analysis of concepts of pollution and taboo*. London: Kegan Paul.

Faircloth, C., Twamley, K. and Iqbal, H. (2022) '"Er, not the best time": Methodological and ethical challenges of researching family life during a pandemic'. *Families, Relationships and Societies*, 11 (1), 39–43. https://doi.org/10.1332/204674320X16073443900591.

Faircloth, C., Twamley, K. and Iqbal, H. (forthcoming, 2024) '"Parenting" after Covid-19: When the quantity of "quality time" becomes untenable'. In Lee, E., Bristow, J., Faircloth, C. and Macvarish, J. (eds) *Parenting Culture Studies* (2nd ed.). Basingstoke: Palgrave MacMillan.

Goody, E. (1982) *Parenthood and Social Reproduction: Fostering and occupational roles in West Africa*. Cambridge: Cambridge University Press.

Katz, C. (2001) 'On the grounds of globalization: A topography for feminist political engagement'. *Signs: Journal of Women in Culture and Society*, 26 (4), 1213–34. https://doi.org/10.1086/495653.

Korte, C., Friedberg, R. D., Wilgenbusch, T., Paternostro, J. K., Brown, K., Kakolu, A., Tiller-Ormond, J., Baweja, R., Cassar, M., Barnowski, A., Movahedi, Y., Khol, K., Martinez, W., Trafalis, S. and Leykin, Y. (2021) 'Intolerance of uncertainty and health-related anxiety in youth amid the COVID-19 pandemic: Understanding and weathering the continuing storm'. *Journal of Clinical Psychology in Medical Settings*, 29, 645–53.

Lamarche, V. (2020) 'Socially connected and COVID-19 prepared: The influence of sociorelational safety on perceived importance of COVID-19 precautions and trust in Government responses'. *Social Psychological Bulletin*, 15 (4), 1–25. https://doi.org/10.32872/spb.4409.

Lee, E., Bristow, J., Faircloth, C. and Macvarish, J. (2014) *Parenting Culture Studies*. London: Palgrave Macmillan.

Lupton, D. (2021) 'Contextualising COVID-19: Sociocultural perspectives on contagion'. In Lupton, D. and Willis, K. (eds) *The COVID-19 Crisis: Social perspectives*. London: Routledge, 20–38.

Lupton, D. (2022) *Covid Societies: Theorising the coronavirus crisis*. London: Routledge.

Mackendrick, N. (2014) 'More work for Mother: Chemical body burdens as a maternal responsibility'. *Gender & Society*, 28 (5), 705–28.

Manderson, L., Burke, N. J. and Wahlberg, A. (eds). (2021) *Viral Loads: Anthropologies of urgency in the time of COVID-19: Embodying inequalities*. London: UCL Press.

Marmot, M., Allen, J., Boyce, T., Goldblatt, P. and Morrison, J. (2020) 'Health equity in England: The Marmot Review 10 Years on'. *The Health Foundation*, February 2020. https://www.health.org.uk/publications/reports/the-marmot-review-10-years-on (accessed 25 February 2023).

Mezzadra, S. and Neilson, B. (2013) *Border as Method, or, the Multiplication of Labor*. Durham, NC: Duke University Press.

Morgan, D. (1996) *Family Connections: An introduction to family studies*. Cambridge: Polity.

Morgan, D. (2011) *Rethinking Family Practices*. Basingstoke: Palgrave Macmillan.

Mullainathan, S. and Shafir, E. (2013) *Scarcity: Why having too little means so much*. New York: Times Books.

Murphy, E. (1999) '"Breast is best": Infant feeding decisions and maternal deviance'. *Sociology of Health and Illness*, 21 (2), 187–208.

Mythen, G. (2007) 'Reappraising the Risk Society thesis'. *Current Sociology*, 55 (6), 793–813.

Nazroo, J. Y. (2003) 'The structuring of ethnic inequalities in health: Economic position, racial discrimination, and racism'. *American Journal of Public Health*, 93 (2), 277–84.

Neal, S. and Murji, K. (2015) 'Sociologies of everyday life: Editors' introduction to the special issue'. *Sociology*, 49 (5), 811–19.

Rabello de Castro, L. (2019) 'Why global? Children and childhood from a decolonial perspective', *Childhood*, 27 (1), 48–62. https://doi.org/10.1177/0907568219885379.

Reicher, S., Michie, S. and Phoenix, A. (2021) 'After restriction: why the public can only fulfill its responsibilities if the government fulfills theirs'. *The BMJ Opinion* (blog), 29 June 2021. https://blogs.bmj.com/bmj/2021/06/29/after-restriction-why-the-public-can-only-fulfill-its-responsibilities-if-the-government-fulfills-theirs/?utm_campaign=shareaholic&utm_medium=twitter&utm_source=socialnetwork (accessed 25 February 2023).

Rodríguez Enríquez, C. and Pautassi, L. (2014) *La organización social del cuidado de niños y niñas: Elementos para la construcción de una agenda de cuidados en Argentina*. Buenos Aires: Interdisciplinary Center for the Study of Public Policies (Ciepp).

Rönnerstrand, B. (2013) 'Social capital and immunisation against the 2009 A(H1N1) pandemic in Sweden'. *Scandinavian Journal of Public Health*, 41 (8), 853–9. https://doi.org/10.1177/1403494813494975.

Rosaldo, R. (1994) Plenary Address, '*Anthropology and "the field"*' conference, Stanford University and UC Santa Cruz, 18–19 February 1994.

Rosen, R. and Faircloth, C. (2020) 'Adult–child relations in neoliberal times: Insights from a dialogue across childhood and parenting culture studies'. *Families, Relationships and Societies*, 9 (1), 7–22. https://doi.org/10.1332/204674319X15764492732806.

Scambler, G. (2020) 'Covid-19 as a "breaching experiment": Exposing the fractured society'. *Health Sociology Review*, 29 (2), 140–8.

Skeggs, B. (2004) 'Exchange, value and affect: Bourdieu and "the self"'. *The Sociological Review*, 52 (Supplement 2), 75–95. https://doi.org/10.1111/j.1467-954X.2005.00525.x.

Smart, C. (2007) *Personal Life: New directions in sociological thinking*. Cambridge: Polity.

Strathern, M. (1990) *The Gender of the Gift: Problems with women and problems with society in Melanesia*. Berkeley: University of California Press.

Strathern, M. (1993) *Reproducing the Future: Anthropology, kinship and the new reproductive technologies*. Manchester: Manchester University Press.

Twamley, K., Doucet, A. and Schmidt, E.-M. (eds) (2021) 'Special Issue: Relationality in family and intimate practices'. *Families, Relationships and Societies*, 10 (1). https://doi.org/10.1332/204674321X16111601166128.

Twamley, K., Faircloth, C. and Iqbal, H. (2023) 'Covid labour: Making a livable life under lockdown'. *The Sociological Review*, 71 (1), 85–104. https://doi.org/10.1177/00380261221138203.

Vohs, K. D., Baumeister, R. F., Schmeichel, B. J., Twenge, J. M., Nelson, N. M. and Tice, D. M. (2008) 'Making choices impairs subsequent self-control: A limited-resource account of decision making, self-regulation, and active initiative'. *Journal of Personality and Social Psychology*, 94 (5), 883–98.

Index

adolescents 28, 71, 87, 93, 178, 185, 192, 194
agency (agentic behaviour) 66, 97, 102, 114, 118, 180, 185, 295
AIDS epidemic 147, 149, 287, 289
anti-racism protests, *see* Black Lives Matter protests
anxiety
    and methodological reflections 230
    around infection 31, 88
    around shifting public health guidelines 34
    in children and young people 7, 35
    risk factors 7, 228, 231
    symptoms 7, 35, 62, 72, 89, 107, 141, 142, 218, 291
apartheid 147, 166, 287
Argentina 1, 13, 15, 16, 25–48, 280, 285, 288, 291, 292, 294, 295
attributing blame for the pandemic 8, 241, 243
austerity 12, 225, 242

Beck, Ulrich 12, 229, 242, 243, 278, 284–5, 288, 291, 294
bending lockdown rules 185, 233–4, 240, 279, 295
Biden, Joe 251, 253
Black Lives Matter protests 256, 270
blame, *see* attributing blame for the pandemic
boundaries
    and neoliberalism 55
    around conceptions of family 243
    between self and other 241
    collapse of work and home 8, 64, 135, 219, 293
borders and border controls 15, 25, 128, 202, 208–9, 286
Bourdieu, Pierre 55, 286
breaching experiment 277

care
    homes 176
    of self 30, 32, 84, 88–9, 92, 93, 293
care work
    children's participation in 85
    experiences 26, 29–30, 40, 43, 75, 92, 95, 136, 235, 293
    gendered differences 6, 25, 35, 45, 65, 71, 73, 75, 90, 91–2, 138, 280
    outsourcing 126, 136
changes to daily life 20, 26, 31, 39, 56, 62, 111, 151, 184, 189–90, 210, 265, 293
    minimal 210–11, 219

Chile 11, 12, 15, 16, 49–69, 270, 280, 283, 284, 285, 287, 288, 290, 292, 294, 295
circuit breaker
    implementation 17, 123, 127
    new routines during 143
    support for 134, 136
citizenship
    biological 61
    responsible 112
    and relationship to state 7, 80, 84, 199, 289
civic culture 91
class, *see* social class
compliance to public health guidance
    and civic responsibility 133–4, 145
    high levels of 133, 166
    impacted by structural constraints 158–9, 166, 289, 291
    low levels of 80, 148
    and political affiliations 20, 257
    and social capital 8–9
    state enforcing of 101, 166, 288
    and trust in government 58, 91, 158, 159, 287, 289, 294
concerns for children 34, 39, 72, 160, 161, 294
confusion about public health guidance 19, 34, 106–9, 249, 257–9, 262, 263, 265, 269–71, 283, 287, 288, 294
conspiracy theories 60, 91
COVID information sources
    evaluating between different 91, 102, 106–7, 109, 118, 179, 258, 264–5, 271, 288, 290
    government 80–1, 108
    media 20, 60, 81–4, 90, 108
    medical professionals 109, 253
    see also misinformation
COVID labour 289–92
COVID society 292
COVID-19 infections
    correlations 8, 54, 101, 227, 241
    following reports of 82
    stigma related to 91
COVID-19 Memorial Wall 1
COVID-19 pandemic confinement, *see* lockdown
COVID-19 pandemic lockdowns, *see* lockdown

crises beyond the pandemic
  economic 15, 37, 41, 50, 60, 84, 167, 209
  political 16, 51
Cummings, Dominic 233, 288

death and grief 31, 62, 63, 64, 88, 232, 292
decolonizing research practice 280
deprivation 8, 227
digital divide 150
digitization 216, 219
discrimination 8, 12, 277, 278; *see also* stigma
distrust
  of media sources 109, 257–8
  of other people 19, 61
  of scientists or science 253, 257–8, 259, 271
  of state authorities 50, 58, 60, 158, 232, 257–8, 269, 270, 287, 288
domestic abuse 226, 240
domestic help 84, 86, 126, 136; *see also* outsourcing care work

emotional labour 17, 73, 75, 85, 87–8, 91, 92, 93, 113
emotional work, *see* emotional labour
ethics approval procedures 13
ethnicity
  and experience of the pandemic 20, 144, 232, 242, 251, 269, 271, 272, 279, 285
  and health 8, 12, 227, 290–1
  and vaccination take-up 253
ethnography 129–30, 131, 255
  critical 253
  digital 76, 103, 104; *see also* indeemo
  micro 57
exercise, *see* physical activity

face masks 101, 102, 106, 109, 110, 111, 127, 133, 208, 219, 236
family, *see* household/family
family practices approach 9, 11–12, 228, 283, 285
family system 147, 153, 163, 166
financial difficulties 8, 160
Finch, Janet 10
Folbre, Nancy 75, 91
foreign domestic workers 136
friendship 11, 37, 42, 63, 101, 108, 109, 118, 140, 184, 189, 190, 194, 215, 237, 243–4
  children's 35, 87–8, 186–7, 191, 239
furlough 205, 227, 230, 235

gendered division of labour 30, 124, 129, 131, 134, 137–8, 144, 267, 291; *see also* care work
global north 4, 9, 156, 286
global perspective 278–81, 286
Global South 4, 9, 280, 290, 295
grandparents
  and digital communications 144, 219
  and relationship with grandchild 87, 88, 92, 189, 235
  care-giving 40, 93, 176, 179, 213, 235

gratitude 42, 60, 64, 66, 84, 216, 268

handwashing 156, 177, 189
health inequalities 9, 12, 204, 218, 286; *see also* ethnicity
healthcare
  access to 8, 9, 12, 30, 51, 56, 228, 252
  workers 8
HIV epidemic, *see* AIDS epidemic
home schooling 7, 16, 37, 98, 114, 118, 163, 191–2, 237, 272, 286
home working 100, 101, 124, 135, 136, 137, 139, 188, 218
household/family
  extended 10, 17, 71, 84, 87, 92, 114, 215, 243, 266, 280
  joint 71, 73, 89, 93
  nuclear 10, 126, 139, 244, 267, 268, 272, 273, 281
  post-separation / divorced 126, 141, 176
  single-parent 176, 218–19, 226
household-level policies 250, 254, 266, 271

ICo-FACT COVID 4
Indeemo 14, 57–8, 181, 229, 283
individualisation 19, 65, 223, 284, 285
  of risk 243, 292
informal economy 27, 28, 83, 255
interdisciplinary 5–6, 49, 281–2
intergenerational relations 7, 10, 31, 129, 179, 193, 194, 213, 292
intersectionality 126, 271–2
intimacy 6–7, 10, 11, 20, 243–4, 281
intimate public 244

job loss, *see* unemployment
joint families, *see* households/families

leisure
  and well-being 26, 31, 45–6
  difficulties in accessing 30, 35, 36, 43–4, 135, 178, 226
  gendered differences in access 25–6, 30
  new activities in 142–3
longitudinal research 12, 292
Lupton, Deborah 12, 180, 184, 190, 193, 228, 229, 272, 277–8, 279, 284, 288, 290, 292, 293

masculinity/masculine norms 18, 86, 92, 137
mask wearing, *see* face masks
Mason, Jennifer 10
mental health
  and children or young people 33, 34, 87, 178, 295
  challenges 161, 162, 174, 237
  risk factors 7, 54, 66, 142, 178, 179, 228, 290, 291
  triggers 7, 8, 87, 185, 195
  see also anxiety
methodological innovation 282–3; *see also* indeemo

migrants
  COVID infection vulnerability of 8, 15, 127, 177
  experiencing constraints to participate in research 283, 296
  family separation experienced by 235
  lack of access to government support 227, 252
misinformation 91, 131; *see also* conspiracy theories
moral discourse 30, 66, 236, 293, 294
morbidity and mortality rates 15, 54, 60, 285
Morgan, David 9, 11, 228, 283
mortality rate, *see* morbidity and mortality rates
multigenerational living, *see* households/families
multimodal diaries 14, 57, 148, 229; *see also* indeemo

National Vaccination Programme (Singapore) 128
Neal, Sarah 9, 11, 284
neoliberal
  model 51, 54
  policies 50, 65
neoliberalism 16, 287
neoliberalization 50, 54, 55, 65, 287
new routines 6, 38
non-compliance to public health guidance, *see* compliance to public health guidance
non-routine 103, 111, 118, 119
  categories 103
  labour 103, 104
  manual labour 104
  occupations 97, 109, 111, 116
  parents 116
  tasks 103, 107, 108, 109, 111, 112, 113, 117
  work 105, 108, 109, 111, 112
  workers 109, 111
nuclear families, *see* households/families

Omicron variant 126, 128
online class 3, 29, 54, 64, 65, 88, 90
online learning 90, 113, 116, 150, 160, 256
outdoor space, access to 7, 231
outsourcing care work 35, 37; *see also* domestic help

pandemic generation 3
pandemic shaming 226, 237
parentification 93
parenting culture studies 293
participant recruitment 12, 76, 130, 154, 182, 205, 229, 255
patriarchal 71, 126, 129
patrilineal 71
personal life 9, 10, 11, 180, 185, 190, 192, 193, 194, 223, 283
phenomenology 103
physical contact during pandemic 18, 177, 179, 191, 193, 194
policy as practice 19, 253, 254, 272
policy implications 288

political polarization 19, 250, 253, 257, 269
population density 124
positionality 249, 257, 271, 281
prayer 89, 215
precarity 6, 49 (neo-liberal), 50, 55, 56, 59, 64, 65, 66, 270, 281, 295
precarization 54
Preventative and Mandatory Social Distancing measure (DISPO) xi, 27, 33
Preventive and Mandatory Social Isolation (ASPO) xi, 25, 27, 47
public health emergency 80, 202
public health measures 5, 11, 16, 25, 26, 228, 240, 282, 285, 290, 292
public health messaging 77, 91, 225, 288

racialized health disparities 179, 252, 269
racism 8, 20, 204, 218, 250, 253
recommendations (public health)
  by the authors 294
  compliance with 58, 110, 111, 204
  criticism of 186, 193
  distrust of 118
  in place of restrictions 4, 15, 18, 173, 176, 289
  refusal to abide by 179, 259
refugee 181
relationality 9, 11, 228, 283, 294
research during a crisis 4–6, 294–6
resilience 134, 147–8, 153, 165, 193, 219, 295
responsibility 34, 66, 110
  communal 134, 166, 278, 295
  moral 293
  personal 55, 173, 193, 225, 229, 237, 279, 285–9
responsible citizenship, *see* citizenship
risk
  and parenthood 293
  assessment 161, 173, 180, 191, 243, 290
  awareness 190, 193
  individualisation of 229, 243
  juggling different kinds of 184–5, 193, 263
  theory 12, 180, 241, 284
routine and non-routine work 105, 108
Russia 97–121

Safe Entry 128
SARS 19, 127, 199–200
SARS-CoV-2 278
school closures 7, 64, 97, 100, 150, 160, 210, 251, 270, 279; *see also* home schooling
schoolwork during COVID-19 pandemic, *see* home schooling
self-care, *see* care
selfhood 278
sexism 204, 218
shelter in place order 253
Singapore 4, 11, 12, 13, 15, 17–18, 123–46, 280, 283, 284, 285, 288, 291
Skeggs, Bev 225, 285
smart lockdowns 73
Smart, Carol 10, 180, 190
social class 37, 269
social cohesion 242, 289
social connection 42

INDEX 301

social distancing 33, 58, 80, 106, 156, 230, 257, 263
social institutions 80, 241, 284
social media, *see* COVID information sources
social networks 9, 265
social outbreak 50, 65
social solidarity 21, 60, 244
social subjectivity 50
social welfare 60, 150
social-ecological theory 204
sociology of everyday life 9, 18, 204, 284
soup kitchens 60
South Africa 1, 2, 4, 15, 18, 147–71, 270, 280, 287, 289, 290, 291, 294, 295
Standard Operating Procedures 73
stay at home order 101, 106, 226, 253
strategy of 'safeguarding' 58
structural inequalities 8, 12, 123, 228, 285
subjectivation 54, 287
Sweden 2, 3, 4, 7, 13, 15, 18, 173–199, 283, 286, 289, 291, 294, 296

Taiwan 2, 4, 12, 13, 15, 19, 199–221, 281, 282, 284, 285, 288, 289, 290, 291, 295
teenager, *see* adolescents
telegram 106
theoretical heritage 281, 283
time use surveys 25, 30
Trump, Donald 250, 253, 257, 263
trust
 and family life 240
 and social cohesion 233, 242, 289
 and values 98
 in 'science' and scientific authorities 242–43

in state authorities 51, 90, 173, 185, 193, 242, 270, 285, 287
lack of trust 51, 91, 111, 179, 229, 242
see also COVID information sources; distrust
unemployment
 as a risk factor for ill-health 148, 162
 due to COVID-19 pandemic 16, 37, 53, 151, 161, 177, 271
 support 150, 271
 worries about 193, 209, 290
United Kingdom (UK) 2, 4, 7, 9, 11, 12, 15, 19, 223–47, 259, 270, 279, 285, 288, 290, 291, 294, 295
United States of America (US) 1, 2, 11, 13, 15, 19, 233, 249–75, 283, 286

vaccine
 access to 2, 9, 81, 151, 177, 251–2, 269, 286
 development 2, 98
 hesitancy 91, 237–8, 269
 take-up rates 2, 128, 177, 228
vignettes 131, 134, 283
vulnerability to COVID-19 infection 3, 112, 127, 134, 144, 188, 232, 242, 252, 263–4, 282, 284, 290

WhatsApp or Zoom for data collection 14, 77, 106, 124, 131–2, 154–5
World Health Organisation (WHO) 2, 15, 109, 111, 112, 200, 202, 259

Zoom classrooms, *see* online class
Zoom for socialising 88, 140, 142, 143, 144, 233

Milton Keynes UK
Ingram Content Group UK Ltd.
UKHW022036310823
427823UK00007B/238